Decolonizing Ecotheology

Intersectionality and Theology Series

This series is a home for theologies that weave in the strands of gender, race, and class. Because weaving involves stripping the strands, this series makes room for plaiting sub- and minor- strands. Each volume of the series, as such, will exhibit the interwoven and intersectional natures of theology—theology is a weaving or intersection where words, images, schemes, stories, bodies, struggles, cultures, and more, meet and exchange. At this weaving/intersection, traditions, standards and ideals inspire, transpire, and some even expire.

EDITORIAL ADVISORY BOARD

Kuzipa Nalwamba, World Council of Churches (Switzerland)
Mahsheed Ansari, Islamic Science and Research Academy (Australia)
Miguel De La Torre, Iliff School of Theology (USA)
Miguel M. Algranti, Universidad Favaloro (Argentina)

DECOLONIZING ECOTHEOLOGY

Indigenous and
Subaltern Challenges

EDITED BY

S. Lily Mendoza *and*
George Zachariah

◥PICKWICK *Publications* • Eugene, Oregon

DECOLONIZING ECOTHEOLOGY
Indigenous and Subaltern Challenges

Intersectionality and Theology Series

Copyright © 2022 Wipf and Stock Publishers. All rights reserved. Except for brief quotations in critical publications or reviews, no part of this book may be reproduced in any manner without prior written permission from the publisher. Write: Permissions, Wipf and Stock Publishers, 199 W. 8th Ave., Suite 3, Eugene, OR 97401.

Pickwick Publications
An Imprint of Wipf and Stock Publishers
199 W. 8th Ave., Suite 3
Eugene, OR 97401

www.wipfandstock.com

PAPERBACK ISBN: 978-1-7252-8640-5
HARDCOVER ISBN: 978-1-7252-8641-2
EBOOK ISBN: 978-1-7252-8642-9

Cataloguing-in-Publication data:

Names: Mendoza, S. Lily, editor. | Zachariah, George, editor.

Title: Decolonizing ecotheology : indigenous and subaltern challenges / edited by S. Lily Mendoza and George Zachariah.

Description: Eugene, OR: Pickwick Publications, 2022. | Intersectionality and Theology Series. | **Includes bibliographical references and index.**

Identifiers: ISBN 978-1-7252-8640-5 (paperback) | ISBN 978-1-7252-8641-2 (hardcover) | ISBN 978-1-7252-8642-9 (ebook)

Subjects: LCSH: Human ecology—Religious aspects. | Environmental protection—Developing countries. | Ecofeminism. | Indigenous peoples—Attitudes.

Classification: BT695.5 D43 2022 (print) | BT695.5 (ebook)

01/17/22

Cover art by Federico S. Dominguez aka BoyD, "Kalingkawasan" (Freed) (2010). Color and motifs inspired by the traditional garments of the Mandaya and Manobo peoples of Southern Philippines. Original painting in acrylic & tempera on 20 x 30 hard paper board. Used with permission of the artist.

Unless otherwise noted, Scripture quotations are taken from the New Revised Standard Version of the Bible, copyright © 1989 National Council of the Churches of Christ in the United States of America. Used by permission. All rights reserved worldwide.

Scripture quotations marked (RSV) are taken from the Revised Standard Version of the Bible, copyright © 1946, 1952, and 1971 National Council of the Churches of Christ in the United States of America. Used by permission. All rights reserved worldwide.

Scripture quotations in Chapter 3 are taken from the New Revised Standard Version of the Bible, copyright © 1990 by Zondervan Bible Publisher, Grand Rapids, Michigan. Used by permission. All rights reserved.

Scripture quotations in Chapter 9 are taken from the ESV® Bible (The Holy Bible, English Standard Version®), copyright © 2001 by Crossway, a publishing ministry of Good News Publishers. Used by permission. All rights reserved.

To Sudipta Singh,

*whose courageous and radical visioning
of an Earth-rooted spirituality
seeded and nurtured the writing
of this book*

Contents

List of Illustrations | ix

Foreword | Cláudio Carvalhaes | xi

Preface | S. Lily Mendoza | xiii

List of Contributors | xvii

Introduction | *S. Lily Mendoza* and *George Zachariah* | 1

Part One: Earth Words: Revelation and Flow in the Bible

1. Jesus-Hokmah as Baal-Anat: Transgressing Christian Monotheism for the Sake of Indigenous Justice and Planetary Survival | *James W. Perkinson* | 19

2. Waters Cry Out: Water Protectors, Watershed Justice, and the Voice of the Waters | *Barbara R. Rossing* | 39

3. Reclaiming Mother Earth: A Khasi Indigenous Re-reading of Psalm 104 | *Enolyne Lyngdoh* | 58

Part Two: Earth Rites: Ritual Transgressions and Transformations

4. On Earth as in Heaven: The Earth in the Podong *Leitourgia* of the Post-human Commune | *Ferdinand A. Anno* | 77

5. Eleele Interrupts the Eden Wedding: From Mother Earth to Mistress | *Faafetai Aiavā* | 93

6. Dreaming Someone Else's Gods: A Cosmopolitics of Constructive Trespass | *Kathryn Poethig* | 108

Part Three: Earth Politics: Practices and Movements on the Ground

7. Truth, Reconciliation, and Climate Justice: Applications of Truth and Reconciliation Processes to Climate Debt and the Climate Crisis | *E. Sheryl Johnson* | 131

8. Where Earth and Water Meet: Development, Displacement, and African Spirituality in Zimbabwe | *Sophia Chirongoma* | 144

9. Eschatology and Creation Care in the Context of the Israeli Colonization of Palestine | *Yousef Kamal AlKhouri* | 160

10. Decolonizing the Privileged: Resistance and Re-building the New Economy | *Cynthia Moe-Lobeda* | 174

Part Four: Earth Uprisings: Decolonization and a Return to the Commons

11. Whose Oikos Is It Anyway? Towards a *Poromboke* Eco-theology of "Commoning" | *George Zachariah* | 201

12. Land Lovers: From Agropornography to Agroecology | *Nancy Cardoso* | 219

13. "Wise as Serpents, Innocent as Doves": Recovering an Indigenous Politics of Spirit by Way of Quetzalcóatl, Guadalupe | *James W. Perkinson* | 235

14. Transdiasporic Indigeneity and Decolonizing Faith: Recovering Earth Spirituality in a Settler Colonial Context | *S. Lily Mendoza* | 259

Index | 281

List of Illustrations

Figure 1.1: Paul Klee, "Angelus Novus" (1920), Wikimedia Commons | 19

Figure 6.1: St. Francis Xavier, Champa, photo by Kathryn Poethig, 2012 | 115

Figure 6.2a. Our Lady of the Mekong, photo by Kathryn Poethig, 2012 | 117

Figure 6.2b. Our Lady of the Mekong, photo by Kathryn Poethig, 2012 | 118

Figure 6.3: Queen of Peace Parish, Our Lady of Mekong grotto, photo by Kathryn Poethig, 2012 | 119

Figure 6.4: Mother of Providence, photo by Kathryn Poethig, 2013 | 120

Foreword

We are rapidly entering a time when we will not be able to live off of a balanced climate any longer. In fact, in many places, people are already living in climate catastrophe. Due to global warming and the melting of icecaps, sea levels will increase, and many islands and coastal cities will disappear in less than fifty years' time.

Due to increasing extractivism, deserted and poisoned areas are increasing, creating a ripple effect of climate refugees and migrants, extreme poverty, and millions of species going extinct or in danger of going extinct. A telling sign that the climate disaster has arrived is the shifting of the financial market focus. Wall Street has decided to invest in water, since water is fundamental to our living and it is disappearing. Let us profit from what we have left!

We are living in dire times and we need to have all-hands on deck to find ways to change our ways of surviving. The task is immense! This book is one of the jewels that can offer us so much to help us make a choice of the path we must take. The authors of these chapters are all doing ground-breaking work. Each thinker from a different place around the earth offers something unique by helping us with new thinking, feeling, doing, imagining, and believing. In distinctive ways. This book is not only an alternative to theology as a product of modernity but rather, it offers an antidote to it.

The book helps break the human/nature divide, challenges the centrality of humans and engages the spiritual and material realms beyond the dualities of modern thinking. The authors help us not to linger in the divide between belief and truth, and truth is understood as something else other than the authentication of a colonial project. The Spirit that is Holy in Christianity meets with other Spirits, no less holy in cosmologies that encompass other narratives, other metaphors, other Gods, other earthbound species and spiritual manifestations.

These thinkers are concerned with justice for local people, from Palestine to India, from Samoa to Latin America, from Southeast Asia to Africa. They cross so many borders and offer bio-regional categories that will then bear challenges to universal theological constructs. As they are grounded (and here grounded is not a figure or image) in local knowledges, they find alternatives in local cosmologies and ancient ways of living and surviving with the land. From these local places they gain a privileged viewpoint that ends up addressing the entire "world."

A remarkable aspect of this book is that practice and theory, rituals and thoughts, are not disassociated. Religion is neither universal academics nor particular practices. In their theological view, a new way of seeing and believing Christianity comes along, not only assuming its "impure" constitutions but also being necessarily challenged by other forms of knowledges, practices, and cosmo-visions. In that process, the authors partnered their thinking not only with usual thinkers or only humans but tried to gain a larger orientation by privileging elders from other populations and non-human agents: water, air, soil, critters, waters, mountains, animals.

What a remarkable company these writers are to us. As said before, they help us gain knowledge to make the choices we need to make. As Winona LaDuke tells us about the choices demanded of us by the prophecy of the Seventh Fire:

> We as Anishinaabe people would have a choice between two paths. One path, they said, would be well worn but it would be scorched, the other path, they said, would not be well worn, it would be green. It would be our choice upon which path to embark.[1]

Unless we continue to think away from white supremacy, civilizational hubris, and capitalist mentality, our path of destruction will continue. However, we can surely change that. This book is another way to help us move in the direction of that choice.

Cláudio Carvalhaes

Associate Professor of Worship
Union Theological Seminary in New York City

1. LaDuke, *Prophecy of the Seventh Fire* (Kindle).

Preface

S. Lily Mendoza

The essays in this volume came together as part of the "Earth" stream in the 2019 Discernment and Radical Engagement (DARE) Global Forum held in Yilan County near Taipei, Taiwan, and hosted by the Council for World Missions (the other streams were: Class, Race/Caste, Gender, Occupation, and AI [Artificial Intelligence]). Designed to serve as a platform for scholars and activists to bring their cutting-edge critique and reflections on the crucial challenges and issues of our time, the DARE Global Forum series states its mission thus: "DARE comes out of the conviction that another world is possible. Another world free from the politics of hate; ideologies of supremacy; enslavement to the imperial logic; a world in which ecology could heal; security of children is a priority; strangers welcome each other; movement of people is a right and freeing; [and] the elderly [are] treated with compassion and care."[1]

My own involvement with DARE began as a guest-companion to my theologian husband, James Perkinson, who, at the 2017 forum held in Bangkok, Thailand, was then the invited/funded participant. I myself, for quite some time since I began my decolonization process in earnest as a post-evangelical born-again Filipina had tended to distance myself from anything having to do with "missions"—the missionizing/civilizing project of the

---

1. Cf. https://www.cwmission.org/event/dare-2019/.

Protestant American missionaries in my home country being part of what has severely wounded me both psychically and spiritually.[2] But meeting the diverse delegates from all over the world and attending the sessions at the Bangkok forum blew me away. I did not know, apart from my wild-thinking hubby, that there were other folks within the tradition that thought as radically as I/we did. At some point I couldn't help querying Sudipta Singh, who spearheaded the program, asking him, "Where in the world did you find all these people?"—astonished at how DARE had managed to bring together the sharpest, most creative, and fiercely radical thinkers, scholars, and theologians unafraid to wrestle with the dark imperial history of the tradition, deconstruct its hegemonic formation, and, at the same time, recuperate elements from its mangled history that in fact align with the liberatory impetus animating all that is good in the world.

Needless to say, I felt right at home. So much so that by the time 2018 DARE Forum in Mexico City rolled around, I did not hesitate to submit a proposal—one titled, "Christianity and Modernity as Walls of Legitimation and Conquest: The Philippine Nation-State and the Killing of Indigenous Peoples," that, fortunately enough, got accepted.[3] By this time around, the feeling of a sense of community had become palpable among the hundred or so selected participants. Some repeaters, but many also new (diversity always key in the selection process), soon, politeness gave way to genuine—and at certain points, fierce and fiercely contentious—engagement, especially where traumatic and traumatized histories and practices on the ground were at stake. Such fraught and passionately vulnerable encounters did not always end in happy resolution, but one thing became clear: they were the needed fertile ground where seeds of radical thought could grow and give life to something new, and where difference is no longer left to languish in the margins but given a large platform on which to speak.

When, by the third DARE Forum in 2019, I received the invitation to co-lead the Earth Stream (and eventually to serve as co-editor of the set of papers for this volume) together with South Indian scholar and faculty of Trinity Methodist Theological College, Auckland, Aotearoa New Zealand, George Zachariah, I felt the coming to fruition of many years of sojourn, struggling to "metabolize" the colonizing violence of my earlier

---

2. An experience I would write about in S. Lily Mendoza, "Back from the Crocodile's Belly: Christian Formation Meets Indigenous Resurrection," *HTS Theologiese Studies/Theological Studies* 73. 3 (2017) 1–8.

3. Now published under the slightly modified title in S. Lily Mendoza, "The Philippine Nation-State and the Killing of Indigenous Peoples: Christianity and Modernity as Walls of Legitimation and Conquest," in *Mission and Context*, ed. Jione Havea (Lanham, MD: Lexington, 2020), 95–110.

Christian formation. Indeed, such work was made possible only through a slow composting of that violence by way of my people's rich Indigenous earth-wisdom and love for the Holy in Nature that has since nourished my own radical spiritual transformation.

This book in your hands is a kind of lifting of the veil on what has, to this day, been obscured by the written Word: the rich tradition of Indigenous and subaltern peoples still having capacity to "read" the original divine revelation—the original Bible: that great magnificence we call the Mother of us all—the Holy Earth that today demands hearing from us, humans, in no uncertain terms. George and I are grateful—and have learned so much—from engaging deeply the work and thought reflections of kin and colleagues coming from such a place of listening.

May your experience be the same.

Contributors

Faafetai Aiavā, a Congregational pastor from Samoa, is Senior Lecturer at Pacific Theological College in Suva, Fiji, where he completed his PhD in the field of trinitarian and diaspora theology. He currently serves as the Head of Department for Theology and Ethics and teaches courses on land, ecological ethics, gospel and culture, Pacific hermeneutics and ecclesiology. Outside of the classroom, he has presented in international forums, contributed to curriculum development and written articles around the intersections of Indigenous identity, the Bible and the widespread issues affecting human and non-human life today.

Yousef AlKhouri is a Palestinian Arab Christian, a theologian, an activist, and a husband. He was born in Gaza and lives in Bethlehem, Palestine. He is a faculty member of Bethlehem Bible College, where he obtained his BA in Biblical Studies. He received his M.Div. in Missions from Nyack's Christian College, New York. He is a PhD student at Vrije Universiteit Amsterdam. His research focuses on contemporary Palestinian contextual biblical interpretation. AlKhouri is a member of several local and international initiatives, such as Global Kairos for Justice, Christ at the Checkpoint, and the Academic Alliance for Interreligious Dialogue.

Ferdinand Anno is Professor of Worship and Religious Studies at Union Theological Seminary-Philippines and serves concurrently as Director of the school's Doctor of Ministry Program. He did his studies on resistance liturgics at the University of Leeds (PhD) and the University of Edinburgh

(MTh), and his basic theological degree at Silliman University Divinity School. Ferdi is also an ordained pastor and member of the Faith and Order Commission of the United Church of Christ in the Philippines.

Nancy Cardoso is a Brazilian pastor and feminist theologian. She serves as education advisor to the Pastoral Land Commission and visiting professor at the Methodist University of Angola. Her formation is in theology and philosophy and holds a doctorate in Sciences of Religion. She is also a participant in the popular reading of the Bible movement in Latin America.

Sophia Chirongoma (PhD) is a senior lecturer in the Religious Studies Department at Midlands State University, Zimbabwe. She is also an Academic Associate/Research Fellow at the Research Institute for Theology and Religion (RITR) in the College of Human Sciences, University of South Africa (UNISA). Her research interests and publications focus on the interface between culture, ecology, religion, health and gender justice.

Sheryl Johnson is an ordained minister in the United Church of Canada/United Church of Christ who recently completed her PhD in Christian Ethics at Graduate Theological Union in Berkeley, California, USA (territory of Huichin, the ancestral and unceded land of the Chochenyo Ohlone peoples). Her research focuses on the intersections of social/ecological justice and church practices. She is active in the ecumenical justice movement and currently teaches at Pacific Lutheran Theological Seminary and pastors at the Congregational Church of San Mateo, UCC.

Enolyne Lyngdoh serves as Associate Professor at John Roberts Theological College (Meghalaya, India) since 2010. She belongs to the Khasi community of Meghalaya, which is one of the Indigenous tribes of North-east India. She did her secular degrees (B.A. and M.A.) in sociology, received her Bachelor of Divinity from Union Biblical Seminary in Pune, India, Master of Theology (Old Testament), and Doctor of Theology (Old Testament) from United Theological College (Bangalore, India).

S. Lily Mendoza is Professor of Culture and Communication at Oakland University in Rochester, Michigan, and hails from Pampanga, Philippines, the traditional homeland of the Ayta peoples. She is known for her work on the politics of indigeneity and critique of modernity, particularly within the Philippine diasporic and homeland context. Among her publications are *Between the Homeland and the Diaspora: The Politics of Theorizing Filipino* *and Filipino American Identities* and *Back from the Crocodile's Belly: Philippine Babaylan Studies and the Struggle for Indigenous Memory* (lead editor). Currently, she serves as the Executive Director of the Center for Babaylan Studies (CfBS), a movement for decolonization and indigenization among diasporic Filipinos in North America and beyond.

Cynthia Moe-Lobeda is Professor of Theological and Social Ethics at Pacific Lutheran Theological Seminary, Church Divinity School of the Pacific, and Graduate Theological Union, where she is on the Core Doctoral Faculty. She has lectured in Africa, Asia, Australia, Europe, Latin America, and North America in theology, ethics, and matters of climate justice and climate racism, moral agency, globalization, economic justice, public church, ecofeminist theology, and faith-based resistance to systemic oppression. She is founding Director of the Center for Climate Justice and Faith at PLTS and is author or co-author of six volumes including the award-winning *Resisting Structural Evil: Love as Ecological-Economic Vocation*.

James W. Perkinson has lived for thirty-five years as a settler on Three Fires land in inner city Detroit, currently teaching as Professor of Social Ethics at the Ecumenical Theological Seminary. He holds a PhD in theology from the University of Chicago and is the author of five books, including: *Political Spirituality for a Century of Water Wars: The Angel of the Jordan Meets the Trickster of Detroit*; *Shamanism, Racism, and Hip-Hop Culture: Essays on White Supremacy and Black Subversion*; and *White Theology: Outing Supremacy in Modernity*. He is an artist on the spoken-word poetry scene and an activist in the struggle against water shutoffs.

Kathryn Poethig is Professor of Global Studies at California State University Monterey Bay. She has lived and worked in Southeast Asia for over thirty years. Her main areas of research are transnational religion, citizenship, and conflict in Southeast Asia, particularly Cambodia and the Philippines. She has published on the citizenship debates during Cambodia's transition and the Dhammayietra, a post-conflict Buddhist peace walk, and feminist inter-religious alliances for peace in the Philippines. Her current work, *Invisible Aid*, embarks on an 'anthropology of the imagination" which takes seriously the religious imaginaries of communities at the margins of power, often including non-human actors (spirits, animals, plants) who offer various forms of invisible aid through dreams, occult signs, possession, apparitions, and amulets.

Barbara Rossing is Professor of New Testament at the Lutheran School of Theology in Chicago, Illinois. She serves on the steering committee for the Society of Biblical Literature Ecological Hermeneutics, and the Center for Advanced Study in Religion and Science (CASIRAS). Her publications include *The Rapture Exposed: The Message of Hope in the Book of Revelation*; *The Choice Between Two Cities: Whore, Bride and Empire in the Apocalypse*; *Journeys Through Revelation: Apocalyptic Hope for Today*, and articles and book chapters on Bible, ecology, and science. She represented the Lutheran World Federation at climate meetings in Copenhagen and Cancun. An ordained pastor and public theologian, she is currently writing the *Earth Bible* commentary on Revelation.

George Zachariah serves the Trinity Methodist Theological College, Auckland, Aotearoa New Zealand as Wesley Lecturer in Theological Studies. He has also served the faculty of the United Theological College, Bangalore, India, and the Gurukul Lutheran Theological College and Research Institute, Chennai, India. His publications include *The Word Becoming Flesh* (Delhi: ISPCK, 2021), *Faith-based Health Justice: Transforming Agendas of Faith Communities* (Minneapolis: Fortress, 2021, co-editor); *The Life, Legacy and Theology of M. M. Thomas* (New York: Routledge, 2016, co-editor); and *Alternatives Unincorporated: Earth Ethics from the Grassroots* (New York: Routledge, 2014).

Introduction

S. Lily Mendoza and
George Zachariah

Theological reflections are contextual articulations of faith as theology happens in our attempts to make sense of our faith in relation to the realities that we confront in our everyday life, and our epistemology determines the politics of our theologies and ministries. The distress of the earth has been a major theological concern for the last four decades. However, our contemporary mainstream ecotheological problematizations, axioms, reflections, and ministries raise foundational epistemological questions demanding deeper and critical interrogation and engagement. The mainstream ecotheology movement, in general, is embedded in colonial and neo-liberal epistemologies. Decolonizing ecotheology, therefore, is a spiritual and political vocation for all those who are committed to restoring Earth's—and earthlings'—flourishing. In this vocation, it is important to draw from Indigenous and subaltern communities as they strive to decolonize themselves and their organic commons.

Even though a serious and systematic Christian theological engagement with ecological wellness and restoration is of recent origin, ecological consciousness and ecological living have been part of the Christian tradition from the very beginning. The ecotheological motifs in the writings and community practices of the early monastic communities, Anabaptist and Quaker traditions, and Francis of Assisi, the patron saint of ecology, are examples of this. Creedal affirmations of God the Creator have developed diverse creation theologies in the history of theology, exploring the relationship between God, human beings, and the wider community of creation.

A historical survey of the development of mainstream ecological thinking and activism reveals that the eighteenth and nineteenth centuries witnessed substantial visibility to ecological thinking, thanks to developments in the natural sciences. In the Nineteenth and early Twentieth centuries John Muir, Aldo Leopold, and others propagated environmental philosophies of conservationism, wilderness, national parks, and land ethics, enlarging the boundaries of the community to include soils, waters, plants, and animals. However, these romantic ecological worldviews and ethics tended to be misanthropic, and they were challenged by Marjory Stoneman Douglas, Rachel Carson, and others through their writings and campaigns which problematized the ecological crisis as a justice issue. The creation-care ethos and the community practices of Indigenous and subaltern communities and their historic struggles to protect their commons from enclosure, colonization, and commodification exposed the correlation between ecological injustice and unjust systems and practices of exclusion. The destructive impact of technology, the consequences of the world wars, and the new paradigm of industrial expansion, development, and economic growth for the sake of profit and the plunder of the earth, and the emergence of global and local environmental justice movements broadened the scope and nature of ecological thinking and activism.

Lynn White Jr.'s article on "The Historical Roots of Our Ecological Crisis,"[1] published in 1967, and his observation that "Christianity bears a huge burden of guilt" for the devastation of nature, was a watershed moment in the history of religious environmentalism and ecotheology. This critique invited people of faith to interrogate their scriptures and doctrines and to retrieve ecological insights from their religious sources to inspire their adherents to engage in creation-care ministries. Religious environmentalism and ecotheologies are attempts to transform religions into public-oriented religions, articulating theological foundations for engaging in creation-care and initiating programs for the restoration of creation. Mary Evelyn Tucker and John Grim identify three methodological approaches in the study of religion and ecology: Retrieval, Re-evaluation, and Reconstruction. Retrieval involves the scholarly investigation of religious sources to clarify religious perspectives on human responsibility towards the community of creation. It further identifies and engages with ecologically sound and rich ethical codes,

---

1. White, "The Historical Roots of our Ecological Crisis," 1207.

and ritual practices from the tradition. Re-evaluation includes an ecological audit of the traditional teachings, doctrines, and practices. Reconstruction initiates a creative synthesis or modification of traditional ideas and practices to suit the challenges of the context.[2]

A deeper engagement with mainstream ecotheologies and religious environmentalism exposes their colonial and neo-liberal moorings. Creation theologies propagate the idea of the creation of the universe as the act of a sovereign and transcendent God creating everything "out of nothing" (*ex nihilo*). The European colonial theology of conquest is founded on the Genesis narratives of the primordial earth as "void," "dark," and "deep," and the Patristic creation theology of "creation out of nothing," legitimizing the vocation and mission of the chosen race to colonize the heathens and their lands. Human vocation, as prescribed in the first creation story of the Hebrew Bible, to "subdue" the earth and to have "dominion" over the rest of the creation offers theological legitimization to colonialism. The colonial doctrine of *terra nullius* (nobody's land) and the notion of "private property" are deeply influenced by this creation theology. Said differently, creation theology played a significant role in the colonization of the Indigenous commons and the Indigenous and subaltern communities. Our contemporary mainstream ecotheologies tend to develop their ecotheological visions and ethics without dismantling this creation theology of conquest and displacement.

Religious environmentalism is infected with many of the ideas of the Religious Right and the fanatic and fundamentalist groups who propagate eco-fascism and supremacist ideologies. While resting on the backbone of fascism, right-wing Christian environmentalism deploys the language of religious environmentalism to greenwash white supremacy. The Palestinian struggle for sustaining current and future livelihoods in order to secure self-determination and sovereignty over land and resources exposes Zionist environmentalism's greenwash of the occupation. The embracing of environmental causes by the Hindu Right in India makes it difficult to distinguish genuine concern for the environment from the broader politics of the Hindutva ideology.[3] Further, it is important to recognize that the history of caste has shaped the history of the environment in India. It is in this context

---

2. Tucker and Grim, "The Movement of Religion and Ecology," 7, 8.

3. Hindutva ideology aims to destroy India's religio-cultural diversity and secular edifice and transform the country into a 'Hindu Rashtra,' an ethnonationalist fascist ideology that aims to create a majoritarian Hindu religio-nationalist state. This is implemented through organized efforts in the political and cultural realms through militant organizations, blatant disregard for the Indian constitution, and the institutionalization of discriminatory practices.

that the subaltern communities perceive mainstream Hindu religious environmentalism as eco-casteism.

The metanarratives used in the mainstream ecotheologies fetishizing pristine nature and mother earth disconnects nature from the Indigenous and subsistence communities. Reflecting on the impact of colonial ecotheologies on Oceania, Upolu Luma Vaai draws from the Oceanic eco-relational worldviews and asserts:

> There is no disconnection of earth and people. I am a walking land! A moving earth! . . . For Oceanic communities, anything that is body-related, that they belong to, that is part of them, they will protect and care for it . . . When a faith is not fully embodied in the contextual *itulagi* [lifeworld] of the believer, the Oceanic cultures, and contexts which inform their thinking and life, then faith becomes more and more a heavenly business.[4]

This disconnecting of nature from "natives" is not an inadvertent mistake; rather it represents the politics of mainstream ecotheologies. Speaking from the Palestinian context, Mitri Raheb endorses this problematization, noting "They write about the land as if it exists in a vacuum; they strip it from its socio-political context, from its real people, and they rarely think about how such a theology has been and is being used to enhance settler colonialism."[5]

Colonization was a theological act. The papal bulls and the doctrine of (Christian) discovery affirmed the divinely destined agency of the colonizer to invade and conquer the lands of Indigenous communities. The moral imperative of conquest is succinctly articulated in this French document from the colonial period:

> It is necessary to colonize because there is a moral obligation, for both nations and individuals, to employ the strengths and advantages they have received from Providence for the general good of humanity. It is necessary to colonize because colonization is one of the duties incumbent upon great nations, which they cannot evade without failing in their mission and falling into moral dereliction.[6]

As Oscar Garcia-Johnson rightly observes,

> Coloniality has been theologized just as much as theology has been colonized . . . Both elements endemic to European

4. Vaai, "Eco-Relational Theology," 14.
5. Raheb, "The Bible and Land Colonization," 12.
6. Quoted by Rist, *The History of Development*, 55.

colonization—colonial wound and Christology—are intricately related to the corporeal disembodiment of land (Pachamama) and human dignity (*humanitas*) in the peoples and lands of the Americas.[7]

By erasing this connection between the colonization of the earth and the Indigenous and subsistence communities, contemporary ecotheologies continue the legacy of colonial theologies and legitimize the ongoing commodification and corporate accumulation of the commons and the displacement and pauperization of Indigenous and subaltern communities.

Decolonizing Ecotheology, therefore, seeks to reflect the Indigenous and subaltern resolve to destabilize theological legitimizations of the colonization of the commons and subsistence communities and their contemporary manifestations of settler colonialism, neo-liberal capitalism, and white supremacy. It is a constructive attempt to reflect upon the ecotheological visions, practices, ethics, resilience, and praxis of Indigenous and subaltern communities. This volume is a compilation of voices from diverse contexts and social locations reflecting upon the vocation of decolonizing ecotheology. The voices represented here underscore the importance of inter-/trans-sectional perspectives in decolonizing *ecotheology*. They identify alternative epistemological sources that can inform eco-justice theologies in our times.

Indigenous and subaltern philosophies, knowledges, rituals, and ethical practices are foundational for decolonizing ecotheology. They offer us non-dualistic and relational worldviews which are antithetical to the logic of conquest and "thingification." The Māori understanding of land is instructive here. They identify themselves as *tangata whenua* (people of the land), affirming that they belong to *whenua* (land) rather than *whenua* belonging to them. *Whenua* cannot be sold. A landless Māori is a non-person. *Whenua* as *papatipu* (ancestral land) is central to the Māori worldview and spirituality. Māori are traditionally buried in their ancestral land. *Whenua* also means placenta and burying the placenta in the ancestral land signifies the link of the new life to *whenua*, *Atua* (Supreme Being), *tipuna* (ancestors) and *tangata*. *Whenua* as *papatuanuku* (earth mother) is a profound Māori ecotheological affirmation. Here land is respected as an ancestor, a spiritual being, and earth mother. *Whenua* is therefore *tapu* (sacred). *Tikanga* (ethics) principles are in place for the use and treatment of *whenua*. *Rahui* (sacred ban) is used to reduce exploitation of the *whenua* to facilitate regeneration. Human vocation is to become the *kaitiaki* (guardians) of the treasures of the

---

7. Garcia-Johnson, "Faith Seeking for Land," 45.

earth. The notion of *whenua* as kin makes it imperative on the community to decolonize the *whenua* and reclaim it from the corporations.[8]

Decolonizing ecotheologies requires approaching environmental issues as political. Dominant ecotheologies are apolitical insofar as they are unable, or rather reluctant, to perceive the environmental crisis as environmental injustice. For them, environmental problems are fundamentally technical and technological, and hence they can be fixed by economic and scientific experts within the prevailing neo-liberal capitalistic order. Solutions emerging from the logic of capitalism such as carbon tax, biofuels, carbon credit, and "sustainable development" are quite common in our times.

Environmental problems cannot be solved by reproducing structures of colonialism and capitalism, the very systems that produce these problems in the first place. Colonial paternalism and tokenism are evident in mainstream ecotheological ministries that initiate campaigns on simple living, vegetarianism, planting trees, and reduce-reuse-recycle. *Decolonizing Ecotheology* exposes the locations of privilege from whence these colonial and capitalist mainstream ecotheological ministries emanate. Indigenous and subaltern social movements are, hence, epistemological sources that can inform contextually relevant eco-justice theologies that can decolonize our ecotheological reflections and ministries. These movements are intersectional as they recognize and endeavor to transform overlapping systems and practices of conquest, exploitation, and exclusion that threaten the flourishing of life. Indigenous and subaltern social movements that problematize climate change as CO_2lonialism are hence epistemological sources for eco-justice theologies. The essays in this volume offer us a window for understanding and engaging with the debates, imaginations, contestations, negotiations, and initiatives from different contexts to do the much-needed work of decolonizing ecotheology.

Book Overview

The flow of the volume seeks to recapitulate (in part) the meandering of Earth history on the grand scale.

Earth Words: Revelation and Flow in the Bible

The first section throws down a gauntlet to the continuing presumption of human-species-supremacy by exhibiting some of Earth's own capacity to

---

8. Cadigan, "Land Ideologies that Inform a Contextual Maori Theology of Land."

"speak." The land and waters, seasons and soils, weather and winds all together constitute the primal bible, revealing wisdom and demand by means of vision and dream. This opening "rehearsal" samples some of the traces of a more Indigenous orientation to deciphering ultimate meaning and elaborating practical guidance in privileging non-human elders and agents, as those remain alive and beckoning under the surface of written scripture.

In "Jesus-Hokmah as Ba'al-Anat: Transgressing Christian Monotheism for the Sake of Indigenous Justice and Planetary Survival" James W. Perkinson "transgressively" re-reads the biblical corpus against the monotheistic grain of the imperializing monocultures projected onto the tradition by aggrandizing city-state formations such as Jebusite "Israel" and Roman "Christianity" and seeks to recover a more "polytheistic" Indigenous memory of honoring natural agencies as politico-spiritual partners in elaborating human lifeways both just and sustainable. Noting that Jesus was charged at one point with "casting out demons by Beelzebul" but had never clearly repudiated the accusation, he uncovers multiple ways Jesus and his movement indeed "channeled" Ba'al/Anat-like water-sensibilities. He explores the roots of such in ancient Canaanite memories of an original Cloud-Riding Storm-Deity, turning back post-Ice-Age flooding and opening the possibility for a new seasonally regulated land-based Levantine lifeway for our species based on intimate knowledge of the rhythms and limits of local ecology, before Ba'al and Anat were themselves appropriated by local city-states to legitimize their domination-structures. Retrieving the bible from the hands of empire and re-orienting its message in service of Indigenous justice and planetary survival means necessarily recovering Israel's ancient rootage in Canaanite memory and practice before the take-over of state-controlled agriculture and bronze (and later iron)-based weaponry and re-reading its prophetic witness as actually enjoining a return to such land-based symbioses accountable to older ways and wisdoms.

Barbara R. Rossing's piece, "Waters Cry Out: Water Protectors, Watershed Justice, and the Voice of the Waters," camps out on the Bible's prophetic critique of economic systems that make water unaffordable and that deprive people of the essentials of life to speak to watershed justice issues today. In a close reading of the Revelation text, she calls for an understanding of the earth's waters as active participants, not passive spectators, when unjust empires commit violence—rendering verdict against injustice and affirming what she calls the "logic of axios," i.e., the reaping of natural consequences when oppressors commit injustice (as in the waters becoming undrinkable in Rev 16:4, and, in contrast, God's "springs" offering the water of life to everyone who thirsts, free of charge—without payment). She then employs this potent prophetic lens to tell the powerful stories of two Indigenous communities around water justice issues: the watershed justice struggle in Palestine, including the aquifer crisis in Gaza, on the one hand, and the Standing Rock Sioux Tribe's fight against the Dakota Access Pipeline to protect their sacred waters and land. In a compelling retelling of the two struggles on the ground against the background of the biblical text, Rossing invites us to hear the voices of biblical waters crying out for justice in the resonant voices of Indigenous global communities rising up in chorus today and shouting, "Water is life!"

In "Reclaiming Mother Earth: A Khasi Indigenous Re-reading of Psalm 104," Enolyne Lyngdoh, a member of the Khasi tribe in the northeast Indian state of Meghalaya, uses a "reader response" approach to re-tell the Psalm text from her rich Indigenous background and context. She describes that context starkly: the sacred groves upon which the Khasi people depend for their survival are facing extinction today, a consequence of the change from "community land" to "individual land." The objectification of land as mere "resource" and private "property" has resulted in a corresponding erosion of the Khasi people's rich eco-wisdom that until recently remained anchored in a sacred relation with the forests, groves, mountains, rivers, plants, wetlands, etc. as deities honored and related to in an ethic of ritual respect and reciprocity. For the majority of Indigenous Khasi who have embraced the Christian faith and who now struggle to know anymore how to discern the primary revelation of the divine in Nature, Lyngdoh, in a judo-like maneuver, offers a grounded Indigenous re-reading of the Psalm text to bring her Khasi people back to the roots of their sacred traditions, thus healing their disconnection from the Earth Mother herself.

From these indigenously-informed re-readings of the biblical text, the book moves to Part II.

Earth Rites: Ritual Transgressions and Transformations

The collection of essays for this section reverts back to the way Indigenous communities have "conserved" such speech (as is expounded in Part I) historically, embodying an "ethic of honoring" by means of communal ritual, learning syntax and beauty from the land and water, coding meaning in color and sound, and embracing kinship as a Mother-gift from the beginning.

Opening this section is Ferdinand A. Anno's "On Earth as in Heaven: The Earth in the *Leitourgia* of the Post-human Commune." In this piece, Anno proposes what he calls "the liturgy of the post-human commune" as a corrective to the anthropocentrism, androcentrism, and heteronormativity of traditional Judeo-Christian worship and to posit the re-presentation of the earth as the sacred organic link between God and the human. Styled as a study in the "nexus of Indigenous theological reflection, cultural resistance studies, ritual studies, liberation anthropology, and resistance liturgics," the study centers on the Indigenous rite of *podong* (the planting of reed sticks) among the Igorot peoples of the northern Philippine Cordillera region enacted in remembrance of their mythic origins as a people raised up by Lumauig, the great god of the mountain region (*cordilleras*) from reeds trampled down by beasts (hence, the "reeds-to-people" cosmovision). Set against the backdrop of Igorot resistance struggles—on the one hand, in regard to historic Christian missionization and colonial "indoctrination" with the consequent "fleeing of the gods and spirits" and the disenchantment of the Earth, and, on the other, the ongoing corporate assault and development aggression on their ancestral lands and communities—Anno uses the pedagogy of the *podong* to argue for the recuperation of Indigenous ritual and cosmology. Doing so, he offers, can move towards re-creating the post-human commune, where humans learn to rejoin the earth community once more as "only one citizen-species among many." His hope is that we might see the Christian prayer, "on earth as it is in heaven" as one "best understood in this Indigenous geo-theological sense." The question posed to us is one of "radicality:" what would such a re-rooting take? Through his exquisite unpacking of the *podong*'s ritual significance in the life of the struggling Igorot people, he provides us a pathway to prescience beyond the prejudice of our Christian pre-judgments.

Faafetai Aiavā's winsome recreation of the Genesis story of Adam and Eve in "Ele'ele Interrupts the Eden Wedding: From Mother Earth to Mistress" follows the Earth-centering theme in Anno's piece. The essay comprises a ceremonial rearrangement of the second creation account (Gen. 2:18-24) based on a skit that was performed through the perspective of Ele'ele (lit. "dirt"), a character from one of Samoa's creation accounts. This rearrangement warranted another look at the suppressed voice of the land within the text. The author notes that while there are many ecological challenges in the Pacific worth investigating, the thought-experiment offered here is limited to the problem of disinterest in Earth matters and the debilitating legacies that it breeds. Aiavā argues that our denial of our responsibilities to Ele'ele and our ongoing mistreatment of her as an unwanted mistress stems from a deeper misconception that she is not a living being. This problematic mindset is critiqued as one of the leading factors behind the continual depersonalization of the Earth whereby what was once intimate to the worldviews of the peoples of the Pacific has been dissolved into a "fling," or what was once "Source," now converted to mere "resource." Drawing from one of Samoa's creation narratives, Aiavā, in a gesture inviting recognition of Ele'ele, not just as guest but actual host, offers an alternative view on our relationship with creation—the demand for radical engagement with Earth no longer (if ever) an option, but an absolute imperative.

Kathryn Poethig's story in "Dreaming Someone Else's Gods: A Cosmopolitics of Constructive Trespass" opens a perspective of intrigue on the encounter of traditions and the way spirits may not be bound by the borders of the traditions that articulate their reality, e.g., a Khmer Buddhist devotee fishing an icon of St. Francis out of a river; Cham and Vietnamese Buddhists similarly recovering Our Lady of the Mekong; and a Vietnamese Buddhist likewise retrieving Our Lady with infant Jesus—all per very specific instructions through dreams. She poses the question: "Do these Christian spirits have more than their own community at heart?" But it is her ending that opens an even deeper question having to do not just with the boundary trespass between human and spirit realms, but between such realms and the material creatures themselves that the statues are made of (in this case, stone, wood, and plaster). Do such material "objects" simply act as "conduits" for human and spirit intentionality but otherwise remain inanimate, or do they, as Poethig enigmatically intimates in her ending, possess a "secret life" that doesn't simply capitulate to human hegemony or spirit agency but themselves speak their "will" and act their mystery in oneiric or otherwise inchoate modalities?

Earth Politics: Practices and Movements on the Ground

Part III earmarks a third moment in the imperative to decolonize the land and recover a more just and sustainable tenure for our species on the planet's varied commons. It turns to more immediate exigencies of engaging political struggle in the key of ecology. The four essays offered interrogate four different locales of contemporary eco-contention—two in the Global North and two in the Global South—highlighting concerns and confusions as well as commending possible strategies and tactics.

Sheryl Johnson's "Truth, Reconciliation, and Climate Justice: Applications of Truth and Reconciliation Processes to Climate Debt and the Climate Crisis" explores the potential of the Truth and Reconciliation framework in helping to address the present climate crisis. She teases out lessons from Truth and Reconciliation initiatives that might prove helpful in addressing climate change, and specifically, in regard to the notion of climate debt and the need for repair and reparation that it signals. As part of her approach, she identifies points of similarity between the concept of climate debt and the core principles of the Truth and Reconciliation impetus, keying off the justice potential of the practice of confessional truth-telling for raising awareness and taking responsibility. Drawing on her first-hand experience of Canada's Truth and Reconciliation Commission, a project intended to address the violent legacy of the Indigenous (Indian) Residential Schools and the role of religious communities in the perpetration of such a legacy, she ferrets out lessons that can be applied toward inspiring faith communities to take up action to help heal some of the broken relationships between modern humans—whom she identifies as the greatest perpetrators—and those who are the victims (our Indigenous- and more-than-human kin) of climate change.

In "Where Earth and Water Meet: Development, Displacement, and African Spirituality in Zimbabwe," Sophia Chirongoma provides a religious perspective on the impact of displacement on an Indigenous population in light of the Zimbabwean law. Compelled by Tokwe-Mukosi suffering resulting from a new hydro-electric project built on their land and informed by an Afro-centric paradigm that calls for all African phenomena and activities to be interpreted from the worldview of Africans, she argues that religion is so central in people's lives that failure to acknowledge the cultural beliefs, values, and identity of the Tokwe-Mukosi people is tantamount to denying their humanity and dignity. Gathering "ground-level" perspectives through in-depth interviews with the families of the displaced communities, as well as representatives from the traditional leadership and local government, she hopes her study can play an advocacy role for the displaced Tokwe-Mukosi communities, ranging from sensitizing policy makers to the gravity of the impact (both material and spiritual) on the ground to compelling the issuance of just compensation and follow up. By foregrounding the importance of spirituality, cultural heritage, and philosophy in helping the affected communities cope with disruption and displacement, it challenges the (typically) imperial assumptions of policy makers in favor of more indigenously African perspectives that encompass concern not only for the well-being of humans but also that of other creatures. Finally, it issues a challenge to the churches and to civil society to play an active role as agents of hope and social transformation in light of the effects of displacement.

In "Eschatology and Creation Care in the Context of the Israeli Colonization of Palestine," Yousef Kamal AlKhouri sheds light on what he considers a rarely addressed aspect of the Palestinian-Israeli conflict, namely, the ecological dimension. Although the land clearly stands out as a major aspect of the conflict, little attention has been paid to the ecological ramifications of theological and eschatological understandings of both Palestinian Christians and Christian Zionists that typically revolve around God's promises to Abraham and ancient Israel, the political status of the land in the current conflict, and the eschatological anticipation of the restoration of the land to the nation of Israel as a sign of Jesus' second coming. AlKhouri unpacks how such eschatological expectations on the part of Christian Zionists have led to the ecological devastation of the land, destroying trees, denying farmers access to their lands, and building walls to make any form of life impossible for the original owners. In a moving first-hand eyewitness account of such devastation, AlKhouri details the grief of the land—the reduction of beloved soils to nothing but "sand and rocks," the uprooting of fruitful trees, the setting on fire of crops by Israeli settlers, and on and on in an endless litany of destruction and anguish. In particular, he laments the way such constructed theological and eschatological theories justifying Israeli settlement and takeover have influenced a large global constituency, encouraging blind justification of all forms of unjust and exploitative Israeli practices. Suggesting a different re-reading of scriptures focused on a mirroring of God's justice not only in the human realm but in the natural world, he maps out what he calls a "contextual biblical eco-eschatology" that looks at the Palestinian-Israeli conflict through "the eyes of the earth," hoping that Palestinian evangelical churches may be roused from their indifference and given impetus to work for ecological awareness and activism amidst the ongoing conflict.

In "Decolonizing the Privileged: Resistance and Re-building the New Economy" Cynthia Moe-Lobeda endeavors to foment what she calls "moral-spiritual agency" for economically privileged citizens of the United States, whom she views as currently complying with the demands of advanced global capitalism (i.e., "passive profiteers"), to engage in efforts to subvert and transform the system they are embedded in. Her essay proceeds in two parts. First, she lays out the contextual, theological, and epistemological framework by identifying six presuppositions regarding the current socio-ecological context that ground the analysis and four presuppositions regarding economic change that stand in counterpoint to current economic assumptions. Secondly, she sketches a preliminary, practical framework for engagement by economically privileged people of the Global North, if they would radically reconstruct economic life. This piece presents a comprehensive mapping of the complexities and paradoxes of the changes demanded of economically privileged citizens of the richest nation in the world if they are ever to become the kind of agents that can effect genuine transformation in the world.

Earth Uprisings: Decolonization and a Return to the Commons

The last section tracks postcolonial insurrections and counter-visions elaborated in on-the-ground ventures embodying some of the foregoing theological and on-the-ground mappings of a decolonizing aspiration. As the end point of this series of "takes" on our planet's struggles with our species' 5,000-year-old "civilizational" hubris, these last four essays explore, as well, the possibility of a new genesis—a punctuation mark that might serve as both "wake up" call and "woke up" orientation for the kinds of transformative efforts that alone might yield a livable future.

For this section's opening salvo, George Zachariah's "Whose *Oikos* Is It Anyway? Towards a *Poromboke* Ecotheology of 'Commoning'" offers powerful reflections on the diverse articulations of ecotheology from different traditions and contexts. One common metaphor he identifies in the dominant strands of ecotheology is *Oikos* or *our common home*. He notes that although there is widespread recognition of the potential of such to inspire us to strive together to restore the beauty and integrity of *Oikos*, the very perception of earth as *our common home* remains problematic in that corporatist interests continue to take over the commons, particularly those of subaltern communities. Thus, he proposes that the pertinent question is not whether we are concerned about the future of *Oikos*, but "whose *Oikos* is it, anyway?" For the subaltern communities in India, Zachariah points out, *Poromboke* is their commons—burial grounds, grazing lands, and wetlands. The subaltern communities have organic relationship with *Poromboke* geographies. In colloquial language, the word *Poromboke* represents people and land that are deemed impure and worthless, exposing the subalternity of both the commons and the "commoners." However, *Poromboke* in fact constitutes an important source of sustenance and livelihood for the subaltern communities—pottery, reeds, cane and bamboo, fish, water for drinking, irrigation, bleaching and washing, fuelwood and fodder, medicinal plants, and construction materials. By declaring *Poromboke* as useless wasteland, he sees the State as preparing the way for the corporations to colonize the *Poromboke*, uprooting the subaltern communities from their abode and livelihood. In effect, this natural infrastructure of survival for subaltern communities is being taken over to build the infrastructure of the Empire. In light of such, Zachariah issues an urgent call for a *Poromboke* ecotheology as the need of the hour—a clear articulation of subaltern ecotheology in India at the interface of caste, class, and the ecological crisis.

Nancy Cardoso's provocative piece, "Land Lovers: From Agropornography to Agroecology," furthers the discussion for this section and takes us to Latin America. Using ecofeminism as an analytical framework, she proposes to "undress" the roles of economy and sexuality (economic and sexual desires) in the construction of culture, in particular, of fetish culture as a sexual reality that can speak to theology and disrupt the fixed symbolic field which supports an idealized heterosexual matrix. She approaches this thematic by asking about the land-agriculture-food system and its embeddedness in the much larger system of the domestication and subordination of the land in capitalism. She argues persuasively that exiting a system of violence demands the liberation of the erotic—not in some easy liberal scheme but through a true critique of the uses of Western conceptions of libidinal energy that belong to the domination models of patriarchal capitalism. Deeply schooled by her experience as a theologian in Brazil, Cardoso also informs her reflections with her hands-on learnings from two vibrant agroecological movements led primarily by women— one in Bahia, Brazil and the other in Mexico and Central America. These two activist endeavors supply embodied testament to the more theoretical discussion in the first half of the essay.

James W. Perkinson's essay, "'Wise as Serpents, Innocent as Doves': Recovering an Indigenous Politics of Spirit by Way of Quetzalcóatl and Guadalupe," begins with reflection on the author's place and time in probing the challenge of Indigenous ways of being for a globe facing apocalypse. As a white straight male, immersed in and taught by black, inner city culture in Detroit, Michigan, over thirty years and, over the last fifteen years, with a Filipina partner, grappling with Indigenous struggle and witness in the Great Lakes Basin and Philippines homeland, Perkinson traces a methodology of crossing over and coming back, seeking tutelage to Indigenous modes of symbiotic dwelling and ritual telling for inspiration and interdiction in the face of the climate crisis provoked by the last 6,000 years of state plundering of environments and peoples. Such an approach seeks to learn from the creative adaptations of cultures of color under colonial duress on their own terms and in their own codes, and then return to biblical text and Christian practice with a sensibility heightened for the traces of Indigenous wisdom and wiles still present in that tradition not entirely erased by its imperial formation. The Cult of Our Lady of Guadalupe/Tonantzin and the myth of Quetzalcoatl/Topiltzin supply the sites of "crossing over" where Indigenous and mestiza peoples in Mexico have continuously re-worked their memories, pain, and beauty into textures and artifacts and ceremonies that encode ancient understandings of native cultures that human beings are not simply "human," but finally a form of trans-species, in origins and daily life, living in the big body of their local ecosystems with kin-species of plants and animals, waters and soils, answering to the Big Mystery of on-going and irrepressible reciprocity and metabolism of loss into grief and creativity. "Coming back" involves brief constructive re-imagination of this kind of "gift-economy eco-hermeneutics" in relationship to North American struggles with the on-going history of supremacies: white, Christian, and anthropocentric.

S. Lily Mendoza's essay, "Transdiasporic Indigeneity and Decolonizing Faith: Recovering Earth Spirituality in a Settler Colonial Context" grapples with the thorny issue of what it might mean to recover a more Indigenous sense of living responsibly and sustainably in a situation of displacement. The issue is personal and continuous for this author, as she engages decolonizing diasporic Filipinos in North America who find themselves living on other peoples' native lands, disconnected from homeland ancestral traditions (through prejudice from their mostly Christian socialization and modern subject formation), enveloped in technological urban infrastructure, and bereft of intact place-based communities where rites of initiation and elder mentorship remain as living practice. Mendoza tracks this problematic most concretely within the context of a movement spearheaded by a non-profit organization called the *Center for Babaylan Studies* ("babaylan" being one of the terms used to refer to the healing/shamanic/spiritual tradition still extant among Philippine Indigenous communities). The uniqueness she finds in this decade-old movement (composed of academics, artists, social justice advocates, cultural workers, healing practitioners, and community activists) lies in what she sees as the movement's grounding of its decolonization work and justice vocation in the world in a mandatory recovery of a different mode of relation with living Earth. As compared to other progressive activist organizations among North American diasporic Filipinos that are mainly political (and anthropocentric) in orientation, such an emphasis insists spiritual practice is central to exiting colonial subjection. From her reckoning, the conundrums of doing this kind of work in a settler colonial context where the ethos's ideological coding militates against everything signified by the term "Indigenous" may be challenging, but also a much-needed pedagogy in our time.

All in All

The book marshals a robust polyphony of reportage, wonder, analysis, and acumen seeking to open the door to a different prospect for a planet under grave duress and a different self-assessment for our own species in the mix. At the heart of that prospect is an embrace of soils and waters as commons and a privileging of subaltern experience and marginalized witness as the bellwethers of greatest import. Of course, decolonization finds its ultimate test in the actual return of land and waters to pre-contact Indigenous who yet have feet on the ground or paddles in the waves and who conjure dignity and vision in the manifold of their relations, in spite of ceaseless onslaught and dismissal. Their courage is the haunt these pages hallow like an Abel never entirely erased from the history. May the moaning stop and the re-creation begin!

Bibliography

Cadigan, Tui. "Land Ideologies that Inform a Contextual Maori Theology of Land." *Ecotheology* 6.1/2 (2001) 123–37.

Garcia-Johnson, Oscar. "Faith Seeking for Land: A Theology of the Landless." In *Theologies of Land: Contested Land, Spatial Justice, and Identity*, edited by K. K. Yeo and Gene L. Green, 38–68. Crosscurrents in Majority World and Minority Theology. Eugene, OR: Cascade Books, 2021.

LaDuke, Winona. *Prophecy of the Seventh Fire: Choosing the Path That Is Green*. Annual E. F. Schumacher Lectures Book 37. Kindle Edition, 2018.

Raheb, Mitri. "The Bible and Land Colonization." In *Theologies of Land: Contested Land, Spatial Justice, and Identity*, edited by K. K. Yeo and Gene L. Green, 8–37. Crosscurrents in Majority World and Minority Theology. Eugene, OR: Cascade Books, 2021.

Rist, Gilbert. *The History of Development: From Western Origins to Global Faith*. London: Zed Books, 1997.

Tucker, Mary Evelyn and John Grim. "The Movement of Religion and Ecology: Emerging Field and Dynamic Force." In *Routledge Handbook of Religion and Ecology*, edited by Wills Jenkins, Mary Evelyn Tucker and John Grim, 3–12. Routledge International Handbooks. London: Routledge, 2017.

Vaai, Upolu Luma. "Eco-Relational Theology: Development and a Methodist Ecological Revolution in Oceania." Paper presented at the Oxford Institute of Methodist Theological Studies, Pembroke College, Oxford University, UK (2018).

White, Lynn, Jr. "The Historical Roots of Our Ecological Crisis." *Science* 10 (March 1967) 1203–7.

Part One

Earth Words

Revelation and Flow
in the Bible

1

Jesus-Hokmah as Ba'al-Anat

Transgressing Monotheism for the Sake of Indigenous Justice and Planetary Survival

JAMES W. PERKINSON

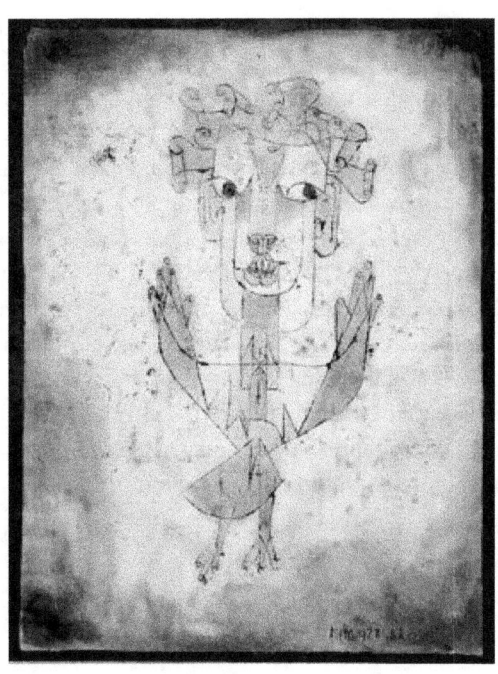

Figure 1.1: Paul Klee, *Angelus Novus* (1920),
Wikimedia Commons

A Klee painting named "Angelus Novus" shows an angel looking as though he is about to move away from something he is fixedly contemplating. His eyes are staring, his mouth is open, his wings are spread. This is how one pictures the angel of history. His face is turned toward the past. Where we perceive a chain of events, he sees one single catastrophe which keeps piling wreckage and hurls it in front of his feet. The angel would like to stay, awaken the dead, and make whole what has been smashed. But a storm is blowing in from Paradise; it has got caught in his wings with such a violence that the angel can no longer close them. The storm irresistibly propels him into the future to which his back is turned, while the pile of debris before him grows skyward. This storm is what we call progress.[1]

Introduction

As I write in mid-April (2019), historic flooding is threatening the US Midwest, after a snow-drenched winter. A "bombo-genesis" (or "bomb") cyclone—typically only found over ocean waters—dropped five feet of snow over a wide region in March; a second one hit Colorado two days ago; a third is predicted within a week.[2] The inundation is predicted to continue through May with untold consequences for the food supply, as tariff battles with China forced large-scale storage of unsold grain in silos on Midwest farmland, many of which were broken apart by the surging overspills of rivers. Meanwhile catastrophic flooding is sweeping Iran and Rio de Janeiro, Brazil, while Mozambique, Malawi, and Zimbabwe stand aghast at cyclone Idai, roaring in off the Indian Ocean in an unprecedented land "assault," with a death toll topping 1,000, more than 600,000 displaced, and 1 million children affected. On the flip side, 8,527 wildfires in California alone in 2018 burned a record 1,893,913 acres (766,439 ha), caused $3.5 billion in damage, and had grave effects on air quality over large regions of the state.[3]

These mere "samples" of global experience witness to the climate apocalypse mobilizing across the planet in response to human refusal of limitations on CO_2 emissions, habitat destruction, ocean acidification, wetlands

---

1. Benjamin, *Theses*, 255.
2. Beckwith, "Food Supply Threats."
3. NIFC, "2018 National Year-to-Date Report."

destruction, deforestation, etc. At the most basic level they comport as "water speak," in the form of "shouting" floods or "silent" drought. Recent academic debate on the emergent alterations provoking some to exclaim an entirely new geologic era christened the "Anthropocene," have also generated challenge to the effect that the changes occurring are in no way merely creations of our species—as if, one more time, we are the sole great supremacy on the planet for better or worse.[4] Rather, we remain imbedded in vast webs of interdependence, and the changes induced are not from our agency alone. This writing will join these latter interventions to assert that in the first instance, from a more indigenously informed viewpoint, climate change represents *communication to be heard* before being cast as "problem to be solved." The planet is not a technical conundrum to be re-engineered but a living creature to be honored in "Her" (or "Their") own right.

"Descending" in Place

And certainly, here erupt a host of furies! Speaking in such a voice can easily seem to slide into dithering as devastation unfolds. Thus, a moment of self-limitation before the argument is advanced. I write from post-industrial Detroit, a city suffering neo-liberal plundering in the wake of a finance-capital-engendered "emergency" of *hurakán* proportions. Seven decades of white flight have now flipped over into two decades of white gentrification—a push-pull operation of the corporatized political class, maneuvering "resources" and access, jobs and education, transport and healthcare, continuously in the direction of privatization and privilege and away from availability to black and brown populations of struggle. I write as a thirty-three-year veteran of the low-intensity race war conducted by white settler colonial power configurations and assumptions "possessing" (and pretending to "own") the river bend known in Anishinaabmoin as *wawiiatonong* but recast in colonial capital parlance as "The Strait."[5]

This new power aggression has been re-inventing the spectacular Great Lakes wetlands and riparian abundance for more than four centuries now in service of Euro-trade and industry and extraction. It began as a seventeenth century "run" on fur, commandeering beaver pelt for a new European taste for rain-repellant hats, violently coercing Native trade in service of commodity export. This was rapidly followed two centuries later (after Great Lakes beaver had been decimated and nearly rendered extinct by nearly continuous exploitation and warfare) by Doctrine of Christian

4. Haraway, "Anthropocene," 159–65.
5. Givens-McGowan, "The River," 27; Cornel, "American Indians," 9.

Discovery-fueled theft of Indigenous land (often through fraudulent imposition of debt), to facilitate Native removal west, widespread clear-cutting of timber, and Euro-colonial settlement. By the late nineteenth century, growing industrialization was shifting the demand from wood to iron and copper, serving global capital's invention of rail and auto transport, establishing Detroit as epicenter of mass production in the early 1900s. War years (1915–1918; 1942–1945) drew African Americans seeking to escape Jim Crow lynching and oppression in the South to the Strait to find work and contribute to the war efforts, precipitating rabid and racially motivated "white flight" and corporate re-location for the next half century, "de-industrializing" the city as an abandoned zone of black and brown impoverishment, ringed by multiple dozens of "whites only" suburbs, living off of the pirated "fat" of inner city skill and assets (such as water infrastructure, constantly elaborated to enable suburban development, but paid for largely by city taxes). Now, as climate blowback marshals, and water emerges as the "resource" of greatest strategic worth, this history of *white European metropole colonialism* (focused on fur), followed by *settler colonialism* (focused on land and timber), issuing in *industrialized exploitation* of iron and copper, is training its *white supremacist* sights on control of this particular curve of river whence flows 20 percent of the entire planet's fresh surface water.

In the prospect, my own years at the bend have effected a kind of slow-motion and unwitting initiation both "into" and "out of" this history—a psycho-spiritual dismemberment under the tutelage of knowing elders and re-composition as a potential "human being." In a process continuing into the present, I am bit by bit being taken apart and re-assembled from the detritus of a white middle-class identity and social formation, in hock to black humor and anger as my "pedagogues of deepest instruction."

Only gradually comprehending the direction offered in such a re-making, I have continued the itinerary "down" and "back" through the history shaping this place and the hierarchy of exploitation re-organizing its commons and goods into pillage and export. I remain "settler colonial" in having no sustainable claim to any right to dwell on such Native land, and "white male debtor" in relationship to benefits broadly assembled (in this place and across the country) from black labor. In response, I work with tongue and pen to repudiate Doctrine of Christian Discovery delusion regarding property rights and white supremacist delirium regarding wealth and finance.[6] Those more academic efforts only have credibility, however, to the degree I also continue to collaborate with on-going, black- and brown- and red-led

---

6. Perkinson, *Water Wars*, 2019; Perkinson, *White Theology*, 2004; Perkinson, *Shamanism*, 2005.

political resistance (including direct action), seeking to combat the ceaseless pillage—especially in more recent years, in terms of a concerted struggle to halt water shutoffs directed at "ethnically cleansing" from the city (by shutoff and foreclosure), poor black and brown residents, unable to make ends meet in the face of continued depredation and abandonment.

Over the last eighteen years, the journey has also opened to inclusion of a treasured partner/soul-mate Filipina of voluptuously soft personal aspect and diamond-hard strength of mind and vision. Here the path has necessarily turned global, engaged "Orientalist" blindness and predation, entailed yet more re-schooling in "owning" US militarist illegitimacy and Pacific archipelago competence and savvy. All told, the way through percussive black brilliance, irrepressible Filipino resilience, and insurgent Native survivance now counsels depth-work towards what shards and fractals of Euro-indigenous practice and parlance yet remain extant and available to one such as me, for retrieval of a cultural memory of more estimable dignity and justice, back behind and underneath all the violence and stupidity. Such is the positioning and limitation from which I venture these musings.

But there is a last layer of this baptismal "immersion in place" that demands cognizance and will focus the effort here. And that is the watershed communion of riparian kin under the feet of all of us primate dwellers at the Strait. In seeking to listen ever more attentively to the witness of those whom my people have savaged, it is not only the immense beauty of black bombastic creativity ever-and-again opening unforeseen portals of spirit and vitality in the prison walls of urban enclosure that commands amazement. It is even more centripetally crucial to "hear" Indigenous soundings of life at the bend. How live sustainably in place for generations on end—without the need to raid elsewhere or pirate wellbeing from others? Indigenous witness the planet over insists that such residential longevity depends upon ritual respect and mythic honor.[7] Local geography is "storied" in mythic memory of ancestral savvy and encounter. The land claims its own by way of dream and vision, ventriloquizing its character and uniqueness through questing adolescents, sage elders, wise mothers, attentive hunters and humble growers. Indigenous dwelling means *belonging to* a particular place—not pretending to "own" its soils and offerings as disposable "environment" or consumable "resource"![8]

And here lies a conundrum for our hour of desperation. People are dying *now* in the comeuppance the waters are enacting! And it is those least guilty of overconsumption who are suffering the most immediate

---

7. Kimmerer, *Braiding Sweetgrass*, 175–201.
8. Deloria, *For This Land*, 131, 251–60.

consequence, while the corporatized scavengers skate free for the moment in their loot-lined dens. It is requisite that utmost effort be directed to immediate relief—no matter, for instance, that in Detroit and Flint, desperate thirst is addressed in plastic bottles granting bottom-celebration to Nestle and utter devastation to land and ocean (and their hungry denizens).[9] There is no avoiding the contradiction. The action I engage with "resistance homies" on Detroit streets and in the corporate lobbies and governmental facilities aims for immediate redress of the problem with the infrastructure and packaging available. Cartons of water bottled in plastic, driven by fossil-fuel-burning vehicles—or at another level, piping networks "coercing" water to bend sharply in right angle turns and degrade slowly with lead and iron contaminants—are the only means at hand. But the demand of the hour is also—and simultaneously—to divine deep and listen at length in learning from nature's own ways and asking after what has worked (and how!) across millennia and among a diverse ancestry. It is in service of this latter—less immediately expedient or politically insistent—ultimatum that this writing goes forth.

Divining the Text

My activist involvements of recent years have rebounded upon my academics in a kindred fashion. As with my efforts to root more deeply in place, I likewise seek to "descend" into the layers of the tradition from which I draw inspiration, peeling back layers of state-imposed scripting, to recover traces of a more Indigenous memory. In the historical particularity of the ancient Near East, decolonizing scripture necessarily means probing for Canaanite practice before such was appropriated by early city-state polities to authorize coercion and extraction. Push-back against Detroit water shutoffs has quickened a push "downwards" into the biblical corpus, on quest for the waters of life at play under the surface of holy writ. As with my conviction that climate change demands hearing as "water speech" today—so with large-scale upheaval inside the ancient text. The need is to develop an ear for the sounding of water inside the biblical crisis called apocalypse. But here again, it is Indigenous counsel that opens the door to vision and potent understanding. Whether in the form of Anishinabek scholar Kyle White insisting Native peoples surviving Euro-genocide are now living in a post-apocalyptic situation or Martín Prechtel post-Guatemalan earthquake of 1976 writing about highlands-dwelling communities that experienced that cataclysm as a world-end—in Indigenous ken such massive ruptures

---

9. Perkinson, *Water Wars*, 26.

themselves have cycles.¹⁰ For Algonquian- and Mayan-speakers alike, apocalypse has not been a one-time event. Mythic story inculcates memory of having "been here before," disappeared, and come out from the other side of the upheaval as different kinds of creatures.¹¹

Prechtel in particular tells of the astonishing sense of calm and generosity and politeness he encountered in a decimated village called Cuchumaquic, where the maimed and hungry and thirsty survivors—gathered on the banks of a mountain stream that had disappeared overnight—greeted Prechtel and his friends bringing two barrels of rice and beans to relieve a tiny bit of the gargantuan need.¹² The villagers did not assail the truck in a desperate rush, but quietly organized into little seated groups, sending up one old woman per group with her husband's hat in hand to collect a dollop of the provisions. Before "setting to" on their first food in a week, they insisted that the delivery crew join them in the tiny repast—already so far short of what would have been necessary even for a modest meal. Eating without also serving their "guests" was simply unthinkable in their cultural sense of propriety—no matter how meager the offerings or how urgent their own need. Then after an eloquent collective thanksgiving, as Prechtel pretended to partake of a bit of what he was handed before passing it on, he fell into conversation with one of the men, each recounting tales in Mayan myths of previous natural holocausts and subsequent re-emergence of "the people."

And in his lengthy sketch of this entire "world end" experience, Prechtel notes his own epiphany to the effect that nothing is in fact stable—including the Earth.¹³ Everything is communicating through motion, each kind of creature "running" in sheer joy of its being, running as an expression of its very name and nature.¹⁴ The Earth Herself runs in ultra-slow-motion from human perspective, but also occasionally high jumps! As, obviously, does Earth's major surface custodian—what I suppose we could neologize as Her ultimate "Crustodian"—Water, which will focus our concern here. Indeed at one point in this brilliantly animate exposé of this mini-apocalypse of 1976, Prechtel describes the enslavement of river waters in hydro-electric dam turbines and high wire cables distributing the power of the mountain flow in electric currents that, now, post-earthquake break of the wire, is showing its fury, leaping in purple thrashing frenzy from tower to ground, flashing

---

10. Whyte, "Indigenous Climate Change Studies," 155–56, 159–60; Prechtel, *The Unlikely Peace*, 12–66.
11. Prechtel, *The Unlikely Peace*, 52.
12. Prechtel, *The Unlikely Peace*, 45–49.
13. Prechtel, *The Unlikely Peace*, 25.
14. Prechtel, *The Unlikely Peace*, 8–9.

sparks and anger everywhere, like a Mother Serpent, finally freed of Her shackles, exhibiting Her true character for all to see.[15]

Thus, we turn to the biblical text, "indigenously" counselled that worlds have come and gone, as even science would confirm on the scale of the planet itself in detailing five Great Extinctions predating the one we currently inhabit. Accepting such will affect how we read Genesis—not as absolute beginning, but rather as *relatively* new start, camped out on a presumed, but eclipsed and unmentioned, previous "end." Given that even Big Bang presumes an unknown something to which it is successor, the appropriate theological trope for the Hebrew myth hinting perhaps the latest world-beginning would be *genesis ex annhilo* rather than *ex nihilo*.[16] Fresh start out of annihilation! The crucial shift is out of an Anthropocene conceit that what matters on the planet is our "human" advent and now our human destructive capacity. No, the creativity inherent in *what is*—in this strange and mysterious explosion of four hundred billion galaxies hosting 10^{24} stars that we call the uni(?)verse—is something far beyond human capacity to imagine, given that only 4 percent of it answers to light and the 74 percent that is Dark Energy and 22 percent Dark Matter are almost by definition unknowable. Human beings are not the central concern of reality—not even the tiny thimble of reality we call Earth. And our destructive capacity is an agency itself enveloped in a vast network of interdependent agencies and effects that we neither manufacture nor control but merely stimulate. From this point of view Climate Change is something Earth Herself is unleashing with us in tow.[17] To the degree we think we authored this interruption solely out of our own wanton genius, we perpetuate the very civilizational supremacy that provoked the blowback from the Gaia-ensemble of creatures in the first place. Let us at least learn something of our "place" as tiny and frail before we exit!

Indigenous Memory Inside State Polity[18]

All the above is mere backdrop, much of it requiring immense expansion that space limitations prohibit. What I propose for our perusal is a reading of the biblical text outside the strictures of monotheism—which can itself be

15. Prechtel, *The Unlikely Peace*, 23–24.
16. Perkinson, "Genesis," 121–27.
17. Haraway, "Anthropocene," 159–65; Prechtel, talk given in 2018.
18. This and the following section are riffs on and extensions of the biblical studies portion of my recently published book, *Political Spirituality for a Century of Water Wars: The Angel of the Jordan Meets the Trickster of Detroit*.

understood as part of a 5,000-year-old project rooted in mono-crop agriculture. This latter first arises, as James C. Scott has so compellingly outlined, in the form of ancient Mesopotamian statelets, coercively organizing work as "labor," locked, by taxation and debt promulgation, into surplus production for elite consumption, reinforced by an officially promulgated monoculture of language and ritual, carrying out and reinforcing capitulation to claims of sovereignty and a monopoly on violent retribution for "crimes" or "revolt." Before the advent of such bastions of "debt, disease, and drudgery," wetlands communities enjoyed relative freedom in virtue of their skills at accessing food across multiple webs of provision—domesticating some plants in low-tech horticulture, and engaging smaller scale animal husbandry or pastoralism alongside the cultivar efforts, but remaining nonetheless (for some 4,000 years) innocent of dominating hierarchies and coercive extraction.[19] The biodiversity they relied upon was refracted through cultural flexibility and mixture and gift-economy parity, wherein local ecosystems were "storied" in codes of myth and ritual, predicating "personhood" and "spirit" as not alone the province of humankind, but shared alike with flora and fauna, rocks and water, weather and soil and season. Initially, domestication did not entirely evacuate a sense of reciprocity and mutuality.

But it is this herder-animal compliment to the crop-growing that serves as pivot for rebellion as states emerge with heavy-handed demands for surplus and extraction, organizing the domestication enterprise into a bi-valent economy of pastoralism and planting.[20] Those enculturated into herd-intimacy as the monocropping was promulgated, could (and often enough did) opt to flee the oppression with their animals to the semi-arid margins of state control, where they were viably integrated into grasslands or even desert ecologies by their herd communities, independent of the urban-dominated irrigation regimes. And here lies the origination point of the corpus of writing that comes to be known as "scripture." The tradition began as a walk-out critique of the trajectory of the proto-history outlined in Genesis 1–11, wherein symbiotic relationship with trees in a paradisal "garden" issued in refusal of ritual limitation (reserving the tree of life for Divinity and for itself), banishment into a lifestyle of the hard labor of cultivation, leading into the primal murder of nomad herder (Abel) by field-tending agriculturalist (Cain), who becomes the first city builder, initiating the centripetal logic of Babel and monoculture, requiring Heavenly intervention to crack open and disperse the monolingual intentionality

---

19. Scott, *Against the Grain*, 6, 44, 49–53, 73, 260.
20. Scott, *Against the Grain*, 211, 221, 228; Corbett, *Sanctuary*, 220–30.

and work project.[21] The hint here can hardly be overstated. Mono-theism typically works hand-in-glove with all of its "mono" cousins—mono-crop (agricultural) extraction, mono-cultural (political) domination, mono-linguistic (imperial) communication. And, as such an insistence is counter to "nature"—bio-diversity[22] is clearly the modus vivendi of the living Earth—it virtually requires continuous coercion to maintain its fictions of homogenous sameness and pseudo-triumphant oneness.

The first word of the tradition that becomes holy writ is to *leave* such. And Abram does. So will Moses in his time, going out from Egypt with a price on his head ("OG" by inner city standards and rhyme), given hospitable sanctuary by a Kenite herder clan, learning survival skills in the Sinai sands, before finally—four decades later as a wizened elder of eighty years and enough "schooled" in a wilderness sensibility to be able to hear a bush speak and not "freak"—he is "adopted" by a mountain storm deity and sent back to lead the slaves out. It will be long centuries before the tales of these nomad-progenitors of the tradition are reduced to pen and scroll, ironically in service of the Israelite version of the very thing they had been fleeing—a state formation, introducing hierarchal protocol, extractive taxation, ritual centralization, and increasingly monotheistic confession as its requirements for land access and protection. The history is long and tortured, and our capacity to read such today, profoundly inhibited by our own conscription into a globalized imperium so radically invasive as now to be busily retooling our every key stroke of personal preference and experience for sale to corporate bidders algorithmically intervening to modify our behavior in the direction of soft wiring us biochemically into their virtual structure, as seeming social

---

21. Myers, "From Garden to Tower," 109–21.

22. And thus, we could argue, poly-spiritualism or poly-theism is more true to the Created order than an elite church-mandated and state-coerced monotheism. And indeed, Christianity has itself hedged its own claims, insisting that the One is really Three. And if truly incarnate in the material world, then certainly not limited by some magical insistence that divine diversity is limited only to a threesome (and that as a kind of imperial concession to the impossibility of talking about a divine man and a human God in the same Breath)! When we assert with all dogmatic certainty that our construction of boundaries around divinity, parsing out the Ultimate Mystery into units we control, bounded by words we privilege (there is only three, not two, not four!), while the universe itself effloresces in literally unthinkable fecundity and proliferating astonishments such as black holes and micro-strings and uncontainable enumerations of stars and galaxies much less blades of grass and micro-organisms—who do we think we are fooling? Is God less than the universe itself? And it is increasingly likely that it is not really even a uni-verse, but itself incomprehensibly multiple and perhaps infinite. I would simply say, the Christian claim, at its wisest, is that God is incarnate in all of it. The imperial claim is that "the state knows better." And I can only laugh. Indigenous people are so much savvier.

media sleuths who are in truth slaves of agendas we cannot even conceive.[23] How shall we read indeed—we who are more thoroughly and insidiously colonized than any other people in history!?

But embedded in the monotheistic trajectory of the Bible is clear indication of a polytheistic origin—"Isra-El" as a hybrid mix of Canaanite peasants going *cimarron* from Mediterranean seaboard city-states, making common cause in a re-tribalizing league of highland bands federating with the herder horde of feral ex-slaves coming in off the southern sands.[24] The former bring into the mix an entire divine court—mountain dweller El, with consort Astarte, championing storm-cloud-rider Ba'al, attended in his ocean-and-river battles by sister Anat, who together wrestle the Drought-Deity Mot, until summer siroccos yield to the Mediterranean rains of October, renewing the land and insuring vegetation.[25] From the arid regions of the *wadi*-terrain south and east comes the Tempest-God of unpronounceable name, YHWH, dweller on Seir heights, blacksmith patron, answering to slave cries, teaching herder ways.[26] The resulting hill-country amalgam of deities accompanying these varied "tribal" groups remains visible even now in a Hebrew Bible replete with more than 2,000 invocations of the Canaanite plural name, Elohim, alongside the 6,000 solicitations of the great unspeakable Wind-Breath,[27] YHWH.

For one such as myself concerned to recover more Indigenous traces of thinking and living under the surface of more oppressive state formations and articulations (such as the written Hebrew text), it is especially the Ba'al cycle that opens towards more antique modes of symbiotic dwelling and "en-spiriting" of place. Yes, "Ba'al"—as the lordly moniker of the most primordial character of divinity in the entire Near East, the Rain-Bringer subduing in ancient memory the Sea Flooding Depths submerging coasts and inland alike—is eclipsed and repudiated by court and prophet as time advances in Israel (eighth century seer Hosea will famously intone: "No

---

23. Zuboff, *Surveillance Capitalism*.

24. Corbett, *Sanctuary*, 221–22; Smith, *The Early History of God*, 1–8, 22–23, 196–98, 206; Day, *God's Conflict*, 1–2, 4, 7, 12–13.

25. Rabinowitz, *The Faces of God*, 14, 80; Smith, *The Early History of God*, 32, 36, 39–40, 56, 130–33; Day, *God's Conflict*, 119.

26. Smith, *The Early History of God*, xxxvii, 25, 32, 43, 61–64, 81, 91, 119; Day, *God's Conflict*, 31–32, 60, 105–6; Rabinowitz, *The Faces of God*, 23; Fitzgerald, *East Wind*, 87–90.

27. In the rest of the writing, I will often capitalize what we as modern peoples think of as impersonal "natural forces," to try to jolt our awareness a bit in a more "ancestral" direction—to the effect that these "Wild Beings" may indeed have something akin to agency and spiritual "personhood" as so many Indigenous traditions would insist.

longer will you call me My Ba'al"; Hos 2:16).²⁸ But not before spending time as a designation *for* the Great Unnamable Desert Divine!²⁹ Presumably it is largely because this "lordly" (one of the meanings of *ba'al*) Storm-God figure is increasingly commandeered by urban states like Tyre and made to license profligacy and plunder that the name becomes anathema (though the name YHWH itself will similarly be coopted in service of royal Jerusalem-based oppressions). The subtext is patent, however. While banishing the name, YHWH will simultaneously assume the functions and reincarnate the Rain-Storm majesty of Ba'al as the Cloud-Riding Subduer of Rampaging Seas.³⁰ It is this thematic of old—divinity in most ancient concourse, gaining such glory in virtue of this singular exploit: by Wind and Lightning and Rain reducing Flooding Monstrosity to fixed boundaries—that recurs continuously and without rival as the oldest extant intuition of the meaning and profile of YHWH throughout the Hebrew tradition (Pss 69; 74; 89).³¹ YHWH is—in deep memory and recurrent celebration if not in actual name—Ba'al *redivivuus*. And Ba'al mythology is, thus far, some of the oldest mythic memory on the planet.³² Even rabbinic literature remembers some of its more primordial associations: in the Mishnah, *ba'al* (*ba'li* in Arabic) names a field watered by rain alone, not "polluted" by human manipulation in irrigation technologies or piping.³³

Jesus-Hokmah as Ba'al-Anat

And such recognition brings us up to a peculiar gospel invocation and hint. Jesus will be accused, early on in his ministry, according to Mark, of casting out demons by the Prince of Demons, Beelzebul (Mark 3:22). The latter is an adaptation of Ba'al-zebub, made infamous in Elijah's time as

---

28. Day, *God's Conflict*, 188; Smith, *The Early History of God*, 35, 47, 63, 66, 79, 82; Rabinowitz, *The Faces of God*, 29, 34.

29. Smith, *The Early History of God*, 73.

30. Smith, *The Early History of God*, 11, 91; Day, *God's Conflict*, 49; Rabinowitz, *The Faces of God*, 28, 93. An image which will figure large in Daniel's vision of the suddenly appearing Successor to the terrifying Sea-Beast-Powers, described as a cloud-riding "Son of Man," given the kingdom by a highly recognizable El-like "Ancient of Days"—which will later become the trope of choice for Jesus, the self-designation he apparently finds most compelling in its breadth and enigma (Dan 7:2–3, 9–10, 13–14; Day, *God's Conflict*, 151–77).

31. Smith, *The Early History of God*, 91, 100, 87–88.

32. Eisenberg, *The Ecology of Eden*, 75.

33. Cheyne, *Cambridge Bible*, 57; Smith, *The Early History of God*, 78; Lipnick, "Four Sacred Mountains," 2014.

the urbanized Spirit-Patron of the Samaritan city of Ekron to which king Ahaziah turned for divination, after a bad fall (2 Kgs 1:2, 6, 16). Again, the issue here is not the name itself, but the lifestyle associations it carries and legitimizes. Adapting Walter Benjamin's famous aphorism about the dead to the question of names of both dead and living divinities arising from the past: no name—including that of YHWH or even, and especially, of Jesus—is "safe from the enemy if he wins. And this enemy has not ceased to be victorious."[34] The task, according to Benjamin, is not to recover history "as it really was," but to "seize hold of a memory as it flashes up at a moment of danger."[35] The question here concerning both "Jesus" and "Ba'al" is thus far from self-evident, but rather immensely tricky. With what significance from which moment out of the ever-altering chain of historical references do these names "flash"?

In the gospel account, the Beelzebul charge is precisely a demonizing tactic of scribal spies, sent to Galilee from Jerusalem in the early days of Jesus' public emergence, as part of a concerted disinformation campaign launched by the powers that be (priests and scribes), seeking to prepare the way for his arrest and execution. The charge is one Jesus never actually repudiates, but instead "uses" to begin his intensive teaching clinic at the Galilean Sea shore, pulling peasants and fisherfolk out of the surrounding settlements to contribute towards "de-colonizing" their thinking in a parabolic teaching process. His very first parable will camp out on the easy manipulation of this scribal term of disparagement—reframed from "Beelzebul" to "Satan"—in order to provoke deeper reflection on taken-for-granted political stratagems and conflicts that actually function in a "demonic" manner (Mark 3:23–27). "Can Satan cast out Satan?" Jesus asks. In point of fact, he will continue, a "kingdom" operating by way of "division" (a concrete allusion to Herod's Galilean policies pushing the poor off their lands to the benefit of wealthy cronies) or a "house" doing the same (a similar allusion, this time to the Temple-State operation in Jerusalem) "cannot stand." The predatory aggressions of the "Principalities and Powers"—like cancer in a body—ultimately undo themselves!

But the actual Beelzebul designation is left hanging, unaddressed. And indeed, Jesus can be read as in many ways *enacting* rather than refuting various aspects of the ancient Ba'al myth, albeit not under that name. His own movement practice does not so much seek to gain entry into imperial "prosperity" (that is, imperial plunder) for the poor, as to return people to the land and to each other, in trust that the soil will produce "of itself"

---

34. Benjamin, "Theses," 255.
35. Benjamin, "Theses," 256.

(Mark 4:28) and the rain and sun and seed and seasons do their work as divine gift (Matt 5:45; Mark 4: 1–9; 29). Immediately at the conclusion of the Kinneseret teaching clinic, Jesus is depicted as demonstrating Storm-God-like capacity to command winds and still seas (Mark 4:35–40), repeated again later on after a wilderness feeding of the crowds (Mark 6:45–52). He will re-orient his movement towards recovery of a more Indigenous "gift-economy" relationship with each other and with Earthly cycles of bounty in which goods are shared equally (anchored in the "daily bread" Sabbath memory of Exodus 16 where the ex-salves learned to gather aphid defecation puddling under tamarisk trees, referenced in the stories as *"manna,"* and known today in Arabic as *"man,"* collected as a desert staple, by Sinai Bedouin; Mark 10:17–30; Luke 11: 1–8).[36] He will "initiate" his inner circle in a kind of "vision quest" for ancestral advice, conducted at the Jordan River headwaters up on Mt. Hermon, where Storm-Cloud and Lightning-Flash will ratify their encounter with the sought-out help in the form of apparitional visitations of Moses and Elijah—both paragons of having exited settled society to re-learn their vocational spirituality in the wild (Mark 9:2–8). The Storm epiphany provokes Peter to invoke Succoth traditions of "booth-building"—the very Jewish rite of praying for the return of October rains that itself enshrined much older modes of celebrating a Ba'al-like return of Mediterranean storms "resurrecting" dead seeds to fecund vitality every Fall out of the underground/underworld clutches of the desiccating Drought-King of summer, Mot.[37] And Peter's Succoth outcry provokes a Thunder-Voice response from the Storm-Cloud that is quintessential Ba'al-myth "theatrics" (Mark 9:7).

It is not the only time such takes place. In John's version of events (John 12), Jesus' final assault on Temple-State hegemony is fairly clearly written in light of Zechariah's prophetic end-times vision of a globalizing Succoth pilgrimage, wherein vitalizing rainfall is promised to the nations engaged in coming up to Jerusalem to celebrate the September/October Rain-Feast each year (Zech 9–9; 14:16–19). Though John apparently attempts to recast the pilgrimage as occurring at Passover to conform to Synoptic accounts, scholarship has uncovered the likely Succoth origins of the Johannine imagery and stage setting—Jesus riding into the city on an ass as Zechariah imagines to initiate the fall rite (John 12:14–15; Zech 9:9); the Greeks as representative of Zechariah's "nations" coming up to the Fest (John 12:20; Zech 14:16); the

---

36. Eisenberg, *The Ecology of Eden*, 15–16.

37. This mythico-ritual codification of an annual struggle between Winds and Storms at the threshold of a seasonal switch from dry to wet shows up in many indigenous stories particular to given local ecologies (see Prechtel, 2001, 2005, 89–116 for a Mayan example).

palm branches that replace and thus adapt Mark's "leafy branches" that in the actual ecosystem of Palestine only "leaf out" in the Fall (in time for Succoth) for a Spring rite like Passover (John 12:13; Mark 11:8).[38] In the midst of such, John has Jesus intoning his Wheat Proverb, likening his initiative to that of a wild kernel, falling finally from the stalk in sowing itself and "dying" underground, before being reclaimed from the desiccated underworld by rain and the motion of its own sprouting back to life. This Seed-Teaching in John 12:24 is answered and affirmed by a Rumbling Thunder Clap (John 12:28–30), which some of the people hear as "Angel-Speech (John 12:29), but any good Canaanite Indigenous would hear as the archetypal Storm Voice of Ba'al, promising his sister Anat[39] that Heaven and Earth will converse, Deeps and Stars interact, Trees whisper and Stones speak, as the secret of Lightning is revealed.[40] Jesus will call attention to this Sky Voice, insisting it is for the crowd's sake, and then begin alluding to the time he shall be "lifted up"—typically interpreted as a crucifixion reference, but by virtue of Luke's ascension scene in Acts, equally applicable to his being "taken up by a cloud" (Acts 1:9). Which is to say—re-assuming his divine "mantle" as the Great Cloud-Riding Rain-Power of old?

But the coup de grace of the assertion explored here, takes place in John 7, in the midst of a clearly recounted Tabernacles Fest. There Jesus is reported having gone up to the Succoth doings, incognito, with price on head, only to appear when the people were out *en masse* as his one hope of avoiding arrest. On the last day, immediately following the ritual cleansing of the altar with Sihon spring water, he pops up and bellows out: "If anyone thirst let that one come and drink; for out of "his belly" shall flow rivers of *living water*" (Jn 7:37–38). And literally in Greek, the "belly" reference is the word for "womb" in a gender-bending promise that not just females, but even males might "break water" in a birth-like creativity of Spirit to the degree they give themselves to the reality of water as "living." In antique Jewish conceit, this latter trope specifies water untouched by human technique or intention—again, what Arabic declaims as *ba'li* and the rabbis recognized as "wild" water, falling as rain, fecundating a field with "house of Ba'al" blessing,

---

38. Corbett, *Sanctuary*, 225–226; Song, *Jesus for the Non-Religious*, 153.

39. Though not here treated, the baptismal scene offered in the gospels also partakes of this old Canaanite Ba'al-Anat mythology. Ugaritic scholar N. Wyatt, for instance, notes, while unpacking various names of the ancient Storm-God, that Anat's title as "Dove of Limm (Ba'al)" echoes in an *Odes of Solomon* passage (24.1) to the effect that "the Dove fluttered over the head of our Lord Messiah"—prompting Wyatt to surmise, in connection with this obvious allusion to Jesus' baptism, that "it is hard to escape the sense that Anat hovering protectively over Ba'al lies in the remote past behind the present image" (Wyatt, *Word of Tree*, 30n98).

40. Smith, *The Early History of God*, 74; Coogan and Smith, *Stories*, 119.

un-corralled in irrigation ditch or human-hewed cistern.[41] In the most antique subterranean meaning of the term, "Ba'al" as proper name is rooted in *ba'li* as moniker of "living water." If Jesus were speaking Arabic he might say, "From out of 'his' womb shall flow rivers of *ba'li* (Ba'al)." And the Voice that speaks through Jesus here is straight from Isaiah 55, promising that water is free, coming down as a Rain-Word, falling from Cloud careening into Mountain side and flushing nutrient, biodiversity, and vitality downstream as an unmerited gift to all the waiting creatures (Isa 55:1, 10–13).[42] The deep subtext is once again Ba'al and Anat; the grant, wild water as gift; the hidden polemic, a challenge to Temple-State hubris in having sought to "privatize" rainfall and field fertility in a half-shekel head tax—picked from peasant small-farmer pockets, accruing to priestly benefit and profit—as the supposed guarantee that the skies would regularly open and the crops regularly grow. The Isaiah correlation of Word and Rain is again old, old Ba'al-association: the primal Speech of the Storm God to the Aching Earth is at heart Inundation that is "seasonally on time" (and thus "righteous")—what Hosea in uptake of the ancient Canaanite theme will ventriloquize as a call/response "rain-dance" of soil "answering" thunderclap and cloudburst with grain and wine and oil (Hos 2:21–22).

And to the degree this quintessential Ba'al-Word serves as the mythic backdrop to John's opening Logos hymn, the "haunting" of Jesus by the Canaanite Storm Deity is overwhelmingly potent. "Voiced" in Canaanite cycle and Genesis 1 recapitulation as a Divine "nose-snort" of Thunder and Lightning presaging Rain, Ba'al's "Great Word" is understood to reconcile Heaven and Earth primarily in virtue of bounding the sea.[43] This is Water Above (as Storm and Lightning and Thunder and Cloud) battling Water Below (as Meltwater Pulse and Rampaging Flood and Raging River) in a primal struggle giving birth to Earth's possibility of flowering. It figures the oldest concrete emblem we have of Divinity at work in the world. Storm versus Sea. Ba'al versus Yam. YHWH versus Leviathan. And likewise to the degree John writes in Greek but thinks as Jew, this Logos-Word—rooted in Ba'al Rain-Speech that is "tenting" (which could be understood to reference a Succoth storm-cloud cover[44]) among us, as John says (Jn 1:14)—is actually

---

41. Sawicki, *Crossing Galilee*, 23, 100, 171.

42. Eisenberg, *The Ecology of Eden*, 75.

43. Day, *God's Conflict*, 49.

44. Rabinowitz, for instance, unpacks Isaiah's Seraphim-experience in the Temple (Isa 6:1–7) as actually a Ba'al-theophany, in which the "robe" of YHWH is a "sky-wide thunderstorm," and the "smoke" and "coals," a reference to "cloud" and "lightning" (Rabinowitz, *The Faces of God*, 101–3). Pre-Temple construction, the Presence could be imagined to have tented like cloud-cover, flashing with glory-shimmering

a reference to Hokmah of Proverbs 8 fame, the Great Wisdom Lady: there from the utter beginning, the One through Whom all things are shaped into being, *exactly when oceans are first given their limits* (Prov 8:22–31; see especially 8:27 and 29 for the bounding of seas, and 9:5 for a summons like Isaiah's). In Jewish John's bi-cultural writing, what is incarnate in Jesus as Logos is ultimately Hokmah. Peel away the Greek veneer and we are face-to-face with the Hebrew Demi-Goddess, the Sacred Feminine of Wild Nature, imprisoned in Platonic concept and doing drag in flesh-of-human. John's entire text can be entertained as a tricky masquerade of this Wily Wise Woman of old, promising "living water" like a Spirit-River, breaking from Her womb, inside the man Jesus. And just as Anat rescues seed-like Baʿal from the cracked soil of Summer's drought-death each Fall in the Canaanite myth, here Hokmah streams forth in promise of riverine gift in the face of Jesus' coming ordeal and demise. Is the gospel only a story of a man? Or behind, around, underneath, and over the human *persona* can a bigger drama of ancient Eco-Powers be discerned?

The End of This Beginning

In any case, the upshot of such an outrage of reading is at least this: to discover More-Than-Human-Agency alive and well in holy writ. Water Wrestling Water, Cloud Contending Wave—these are the oldest intuitions we have of divine struggles to birth Earth as we know it. Indeed, this basic Water War image may reference the most dramatic climate change event of the last 20,000 years—the interruption of meltwater flooding coming out of the last Ice Age, when (apparently)[45] a series of comet-bursts over the planetary atmosphere around 10,800 BCE rained down particles and moisture and lightning, precipitating the cloud equivalent of "impact night" and re-instituting a 1200-year freeze up, halting sea rise and shoreline inundation in a period called the Younger Dryas. Sky "Water" indeed limited Earth Water. However that may be, the mythic trope certainly denotes the seasonal regularity of Summer-Heat in combat with Fall-Wet that allowed the advent of Fertile Crescent agriculture, once the planet warmed enough to support such. But in either case, it also hints something crucial for our hour. And that is that our species is not the supreme preoccupation of this 4.5-billion-year-old marvel of "blue-marble" beauty, orbiting the Ancient Fire of possibility in galactic dark, regulated and

heat-lightning.

45. Though the evidence is fairly clear, the exact cause—comet-burst, meteor-break-up, or something else—remains the subject of scientific debate.

maintained in life-giving homeostasis by even older Waters coming from beyond the boundaries of our particular stellar system.

Yes, efforts to wrestle climate upheaval into a survivable slow-down are requisite for any notion of justice and compassion today—in actions immediate, urgent, and encompassing! But simultaneously—somehow—there is equally crucial need to take counsel from our failure. It is the very lifestyle we have so proudly declaimed as "civilized"[46] and now "modern"[47] that increasingly reveals itself as suicidal hubris and geocidal arrogance—certain to take us and much of everything else off the planet if we do not listen and change. As with Benjamin's commentary on Klee's Angel with which we began this piece: the debris pile is called "progress." And the Storm that fills the angel's wings comes from Paradise. The demand of the Water-Speech of our time is for respect and recognition as a Word from the Sacred. Other beings have "rights"—alongside those we arrogate to ourselves as human—simply "to be," outside human interference and enslavement. How re-weave such respect into the fabric of everyday life admits no easy remediation. But the obvious place to begin is by learning from those among us who already know such wisdom. Indigenous vision and politics have not only weathered apocalypse. They also embody genesis. Again.

Bibliography

Beckwith, Paul. "Food Supply Threats from Ongoing Catastrophic Flooding in US Midwest." YouTube video, April 12, 2019. https://www.youtube.com/watch?v=EDJUVc1-om8.

Benjamin, Walter. "Theses on the Philosophy of History." In *Walter Benjamin: Illuminations*. Translated by H. Zohn. Edited by Hannah Arendt, 253–64. New York: Schocken, 1969.

---

46. On May 21, 2018, a *Guardian* report on the Proceedings of the National Academy of Sciences, indicated that the human species, currently at 7.6 billion people planet-wide, representing 1percent of the biomass of the world (and .01 percent of all living things), since the *dawn of civilization*, has "caused the loss of 83 percent of all wild mammals and half of plants" (Carrington, "Humans," 1; my emphasis).

47. A recent *Common Dreams* article, citing a recent United Nations FAO report to the effect that "business interests chasing short-term profits [and] wag[ing] war against the productive topsoil of the planet" have reduced the entire globe to only sixty remaining harvests—sixty years before topsoil is entirely wiped out, that is—was titled "Beyond Wetiko [Windigo] Agriculture: Saving Ourselves from the Soil Up" (Newmark, "Beyond Wetiko," 1). "Burning through ten tons of soil per hectare per year of cropland" (which is "up to twenty times the amount of food being produced on that land"), industrial agribusiness has already contributed to the loss of "50 percent to 75 Percent of life-sustaining soils worldwide."

Carrington, Damion. "Humans Just 0.01% of All Life but Have Destroyed 83% of Wild Mammals—Study." *The Guardian*, May 21, 2018. https://www.theguardian.com/environment/2018/may/21/human-race-just-001-of-all-life-but-has-destroyed-over-80-of-wild-mammals-study.

Cheyne, T. K. *The Cambridge Bible for Schools and Colleges: The Book of Hosea*, with Notes and Introduction, edited by T. K. Cheyne and 29 others. London: Cambridge University Press, 1913.

Coogan, Michael D., and Mark S. Smith. *Stories from Ancient Canaan*. 2nd ed. Louisville: Westminster John Knox, 2012.

Corbett, Jim. *A Sanctuary for All Life: The Cowbalah of Jim Corbett*. Englewood, CO: Howling Dog, 2005.

Cornell, George L. "American Indians at Wawiiatanong: An Early American History of Indigenous Peoples at Detroit." In *Honoring Our Detroit River: Caring for Our Home,* edited by John H. Hartig, 9–22. Bloomfield Hills, MI: Cranbrook Institute of Science, 2003.

Day, John. *God's Conflict with the Dragon and the Sea: Echoes of a Canaanite Myth in the Old Testament*. University of Cambridge Oriental Publications 35. Cambridge: Cambridge University Press, 1985.

Deloria, Vine. *For This Land: Writings on Religion in America*. Edited by James Treat. New York: Routledge, 1999.

Eisenberg, Evan. *The Ecology of Eden: An Inquiry into the Dream of Paradise and a New Vision of Our Role in Nature*. New York: Vintage, 1999.

Givens-McGowan. Kay. "The Wyandot and the River," In *Honoring Our Detroit River: Caring for Our Home,* edited by John H. Hartig, 23–34. Bloomfield Hills, MI: Cranbrook Institute of Science, 2003.

Haraway, Donna. "Anthropocene, Capitalocene, Plantationocene, Chthulucene: Making Kin," *Environmental Humanities* 6.1 (2015) 159–65. https://environmentalhumanities.org/arch/vol6/6.7.pdf.

Kimmerer, Robin Wall. *Braiding Sweetgrass*. Minneapolis: Milkweed, 2013.

Lipnick, Jonathan. "Four Sacred Mountains." Israel Biblical Studies blog. December 6, 2014. https://blog.israelbiblicalstudies.com/holy-land-studies/four-sacred-mountains/.

Myers, Ched. "From Garden to Tower: Genesis 1–11 as a Critique of Civilization and an Invitation to Indigenous Re-visioning." In *Buffalo Shout, Salmon Cry: Conversations on Creation, Land Justice, and Life Together*, edited by Steve Heinrichs, 109–21. Waterloo, ON: Herald, 2013.

Newmark, Tom. "Beyond Wetiko Agriculture: Saving Ourselves from the Soil Up." *Common Dreams*, March 15, 2017. https://www.commondreams.org/views/2017/03/15/beyond-wetiko-agriculture-saving-ourselves-soil.

NIFC. "2018 National Year-to-Date Report on Fires and Acres Burned." NIFC. November 9, 2018. https://gacc.nifc.gov/sacc/predictive/intelligence/NationalYTDbyStateandAgency.pdf.

Perkinson, James W. *Political Spirituality for a Century of Water Wars: The Angel of the Jordan Meets the Trickster of Detroit*. New York: Palgrave Macmillan, 2019.

———. *Shamanism, Racism, and Hip-Hop Culture: Essays on White Supremacy and Black Subversion*. Black Religion, Womanist Thought, Social Justice. New York: Palgrave Macmillan, 2005.

———. "Spoken Word Art as Prophetic Witness" and "Genesis Ex Annihilo," contribution to the "Ways of World Making: Practices of Prophecy and Lament." In *Awake to the Moment: An Introduction to Theology* (Workgroup on Constructive Theology), edited by Laurel C. Schneider and Stephen G. Ray Jr., 119–27. Louisville: Westminster John Knox, 2016.

———. *White Theology: Outing Supremacy in Modernity*. Black Religion, Womanist Thought, Social Justice. New York: Palgrave Macmillan, 2004.

Prechtel, Martín. *The Unlikely Peace at Cuchumaquic: The Parallel Lives of People as Plants: Keeping Seeds Alive*. Berkeley, CA: North Atlantic, 2012.

Rabinowitz, Jacob. *The Faces of God: Canaanite Mythology as Hebrew Theology*. Woodstock CN: Spring, 1998.

Sawicki, Marianne. *Crossing Galilee: Architectures of Contact in the Occupied Land of Jesus*. Harrisburg, PA: Trinity, 2000.

Scott, James C. *Against the Grain: A Deep History of the Earliest States*. New Haven: Yale University Press, 2017.

Smith, Mark S. *The Early History of God: Yahweh and the Other Deities in Ancient Israel*. 2nd ed. Grand Rapids: Eerdmans, 2002.

Whyte, Kyle. "Indigenous Climate Change Studies: Indigenizing Futures, Decolonizing the Anthropocene." *English Language Notes* 55.1–2 (2017) 153–63.

Wyatt, N. *Word of Tree and Whisper of Stone: And Other Papers on Ugaritian Thought*. Gorgias Ugaritic Studies 1. Piscataway, NJ: Gorgias, 2007.

Zuboff, Shoshana. *The Age of Surveillance Capitalism: The Fight for a Human Future at the New Frontier of Power*. London: Profile, 2019.

2

Waters Cry Out

Water Protectors, Watershed Justice, and the Voice of the Waters

BARBARA R. ROSSING

Listening for the Voice of Waters

DO WATERS CRY OUT? Do wetlands have a voice? Are rivers persons? Indigenous leaders teach us that waters and their living communities are alive, speaking God's voice.[1] This chapter argues that the Indigenous conviction that waters have their own spirit and personhood is also biblical—central to Jewish and Christian apocalypses. Waters are alive in the biblical book of Revelation. Waters have a voice, including a legal voice as plaintiff or prosecutorial witness, bringing a lawsuit to God against their oppressors in Rev 16:4–7. This biblical perspective of "living waters," with legal personhood, can help us listen to Water Protectors today. In order to articulate claims for water justice in such places as Gaza, Standing Rock, and other watersheds, we can draw on biblical texts in which nature brings

---

1. This essay is dedicated to the memory of my late colleague Rev. Dr. Gordon Straw, an enrolled member of the Brothertown Nation. A version of portions of this chapter were published as "Waters Cry Out" in *Currents in Theology and Mission: In Thanksgiving for Gordon Straw* (December 2019): 38–42 (used with permission of the editor).

a lawsuit on behalf of waters and peoples against oppressive empires and corporate polluters.

I begin with a liturgical thanksgiving for waters, written by Pastor Melissa Reed of Oregon. The litany imagines God's waters crying out against the multiple "No's" voiced by unjust systems and structures:

> When they say: you are alone.
>
> These waters say: You are "with."
>
> When they say: You are too broken, damaged goods, too wounded, not enough.
>
> These waters say: Enough, beloved. Enough.
>
> When they say: You are too brown, child. Too black. Too queer, child. Too fat.
>
> These waters say: Beautiful, child. Beautiful.
>
> When they say: You are too addicted, stranger. Immigrant, alien. Criminal. Too far gone, stranger.
>
> These waters say: Home, neighbor. Welcome home.
>
> When they say: We could sell these waters and turn a profit!
>
> These waters say: We are the waters of the Jordan, the waters of the Pacific, the waters of the Bay.[2] We are the waters of your Mother's womb, and we are free!
>
> When they say: Fear.
>
> These waters say: Trust.
>
> When they say: Commodify. Consume.
>
> These waters say: Life.
>
> (cited with permission of Melissa Reed)

Today, we need to listen to the voice of waters crying out "Life!" The waters of the Jordan and the waters of our world are being privatized and sold for a profit, as the litany describes. Rivers and lakes are dying, and communities that depend on them for life are dying too. More than 1.6 billion people live in nations subject to water scarcity, exacerbated by climate change. We are in a "watershed historical moment of crisis," as Watershed

---

2. Melissa Reed, pastor of Salt & Light Lutheran and Leaven Community says of this litany of thanksgiving for baptismal waters, "as we've shared this litany in our community here in Portland we've changed 'the waters of the Bay' to 'the waters of the Columbia'" (personal correspondence with author).

Discipleship founder Ched Myers describes.[3] According to a World Bank Study on water scarcity, all the major impacts of the climate crisis "one way or another come through water ... Climate change is really about hydrological change."[4] Today, the crisis of COVID-19 hits hardest in communities that lack of access to water. High levels of infection among the Navajo and others without running water in their homes shows why access to fresh water must be recognized as a basic human right.[5]

The Bible's prophetic critique of economic and military systems that force people to pay unaffordable prices for drinking water, and that poison waters, can help us address watershed justice issues today. We can listen for prophetic laments (see Lamentations 5:4). We can listen for the voices of waters, personified by their angels or messengers, calling out to God. We can listen for water as "Prosecutorial Witness writ large," as James Perkinson describes, "weighing in on capitalism's relentlessly globalizing commodification of literally everything on this planet."[6] We can listen for apocalyptic calls for discernment of spirits, including the spirits of living ecosystems, informed by Indigenous understandings of cosmology and spirits.

The Earth Bible Project articulates six principles for interpreting biblical texts[7] including: the principle of Voice: "Earth is a subject capable of raising its voice in celebration and against injustice;" and the principle of Resistance: "Earth and its components not only suffer from human injustices but actively resist them in the struggle for justice." In this chapter I explore how the Earth Bible's principles of "voice" for ecosystems—more specifically a legal voice—and "resistance," can help water protector communities draw on biblical resources today.

---

3. Myers, *Watershed Discipleship*, 2.

4. Damania et al., "Uncharted Waters." See Mooney, "World Bank."

5. In July 2010 the United Nations General Assembly voted to declare water and sanitation to be a human right. The resolution calls for "states and international organizations to provide financial resources; capacity building and technology transfer . . . in order to scale up efforts to provide safe, clean, accessibly and affordable drinking water and sanitation for all." The United States voted to "abstain" (along with forty other countries abstaining).

6. Perkinson, "Protecting Water," 464.

7. Other Earth Bible principles include: the principle of intrinsic worth; the principle of interconnectedness; the principle of purpose; the purpose of mutual custodianship. See Habel and Trudinger, *Exploring Ecological Hermeneutics*.

Does a River, Aquifer, or Body of Water Have Legal Personhood?

Voters in the US city of Toledo, Ohio, granted legal personhood to Lake Erie, in February 2019. For almost one week in 2014, the city's half million residents could not drink the water from Lake Erie, one of the Great Lakes, the source of drinking water for some 11 million people.[8] A toxic algal bloom caused by agricultural run-off and other sources poisoned the city's drinking water supply. Seeking to codify legally enforceable rights for the natural world, the Lake Erie Bill of Rights (LEBOR) passed with 61.4 percent of the vote.

In enacting this legislation, Toledo voters joined other municipalities and communities worldwide who similarly grant rights to bodies of water as part of the "Rights of Nature" movement, dating to 1972.[9] The idea of personhood for rivers and bodies of water takes up a precedent set by Aotearoa New Zealand's Whanganui River Claims Settlement, granting legal personhood to the Te Awa Tapua River, recognized by New Zealand's Maori people and the parliamentary government. Indigenous communities in Ecuador and Australia have likewise successfully advocated for protecting watersheds by recognizing them as juridical persons. In December 2018, the White Earth Band of Ojibwe in Minnesota, passed a tribal law establishing legal personhood for their wild rice growing in lakes, including the right to "flourish, regenerate, and evolve."

Legal standing to sue on behalf of Lake Erie would be comparable to the legal standing of corporations as persons, as US Supreme Court Justice William O. Douglas argued unsuccessfully in 1972, in a dissenting minority opinion:

> The ordinary corporation is a 'person' for purposes of the adjudicatory processes ... The river, for example, is the living symbol of all the life it sustains or nourishes—fish, aquatic insects, water ouzels, otter, fisher, deer, elk, bear, and all other animals, including man, who are dependent on it or who enjoy it for its sight, its sound, or its life. The river as plaintiff speaks for the ecological unit of life that is part of it. Those people who have a meaningful relation to that body of water—whether it be a fisherman, a canoeist, a zoologist, or a logger—must be able to speak for the values which the river represents and which are threatened with destruction.[10]

---

8. Egan, *The Death and Life of the Great Lakes*, 232.
9. Stone, "Should Trees Have Standing?"
10. Cited by Williams, "Should Nature Have a Legal Standing."

Many people hope the New Zealand decision signals that the world has finally reached legal "tipping point in the global acceptance of a new and evolving legal status for nature."[11] Another U.S. rights-of-nature case still in the courts is Grant Township, Pennsylvania, and its battle against the fracking industry's plan for a toxic underground injection well. The Grant community argues that frack waste violates people's constitutional rights to a clean aquifer, and also violates the rights of nature. In a surprise decision, the Pennsylvania Department of Environmental Protection ruled in favor of the community in March 2020, revoking the injection well permit. As *Rolling Stone Magazine* quotes Jon Greendeer, the executive director of Heritage Preservation with the Ho-Chunk Nation of Wisconsin, "What the rights of nature does is translate our beliefs from an Indigenous perspective into modern legislation."[12]

In the US legal courts, however, it is unlikely that the Toledo law protecting Lake Erie, or the Grant Township case protecting its aquifer, will be upheld. Law courts recognize corporations as persons with legal standing in the United States. But watersheds, aquifers, and wild rice are not legal persons—at least, not yet.

Lawsuit Against Oppressors and Polluters: Revelation's Legal Personhood for Waters

The book of Revelation, however, would disagree with Ohio and Pennsylvania polluters. Revelation employs a legal logic—albeit a different kind of legal logic—to give a form of personhood to waters. This chapter explores how we might draw on Revelation and other Jewish and Christian apocalyptic texts to help make a persuasive case for a biblical view of personhood for rivers, aquifers, and lakes; and justice for the human communities who depend on the waters.

In Revelation, ecosystems have a voice. They have legal representation by a guardian angel or messenger (*angelos*, Rev 16:5) who can pursue justice. They cry out in resistance when they are being polluted with violence and bloodshed. This "personal" understanding of waters in voicing a legal case against oppressors coheres with the rich apocalyptic tradition of elements of nature having angels or messengers who represent them. Messengers voice the waters' laments and legal complaints when they are polluted by human oppressors.

---

11. Clark *et al.*, "Can You Hear the Rivers Sing?"

12. Nobel, "Nature Scores a Big Win." See the 2020 documentary film, "Invisible Hand," directed by Mark Ruffalo, about the rights of nature legal cases.

That an ecosystem—water-is represented by an angelic messenger or guardian in Revelation is typical apocalyptic imagery. Other elements of nature in Revelation also have angelic figures as guardians, including the angels who control the four winds in Rev 7:1–2, and the angel with authority over fire in 14:18.[13] Sea animals are described as having "souls" (*psychē*, Rev 16:3, similar to 8:9), hearkening back to Genesis. Living creatures and human communities suffer together and cry out for justice. The cosmology of Revelation and other apocalypses assumes a strong solidarity between humans and the natural world, and between visible and invisible powers.

Modern Western Christianity has sometimes overlooked this biblical apocalyptic cosmology of spirit and angelic representation of nature. As Walter Wink noted in his 1986 trilogy on the powers, *Unmasking the Powers*, "Many in North America are looking to Eastern religions or esoteric traditions to find the spiritual resources to cherish and preserve nature. Yet these very sources have languished, unused, in the very heart of our own tradition, in the angels of nature."[14] The apocalyptic understanding of powers and spirits is central to entire New Testament. Systems of oppression and empire also have a corporate spirit, described in language of the demonic or multi-headed beasts. "'Satan' is the world-encompassing spirit of the Domination System," Wink argues.[15] This language of powers, spirits, and the demonic can be of help in analyzing structural evil of climate change and water injustice today.

Reading Revelation Ecologically: Water's Lawsuit and the Axiomatic Logic of Consequences

In seeking to read Revelation ecologically, we must underscore that apocalypses are not predictive of the end of the world. Rather, they diagnose the crises of Empire, in this present moment.[16] The word "apocalypse" (Rev 1:1) literally means revealing or pulling back a curtain. Apocalypses were a popular type of literature for Jews and others in the ancient world. Apocalypses communicate their prophetic message not by logical proofs or arguments but by means of visionary journeys and pictures, creating what Elisabeth Schüssler Fiorenza calls an alternative "world of vision."[17] Apocalyptic texts

13. "Guardian" is the terminology of Aune, *Revelation*, 884.
14. Wink, *Unmasking the Powers*, 164.
15. Wink, *The Powers That Be*, 26.
16. For ecological reading strategies for Revelation see Rossing, "Revelation"; as well as my forthcoming *Earth Bible Commentary on Revelation*.
17. Fiorenza, *Revelation*, 13, 22.

reveal something the world needs urgently to see—both the pathology of imperial systems as well as a vision for resistance and hope.

Although Revelation's plagues of bloody oceans, giant hailstones, and other ecological catastrophes can give the impression that the book condemns the earth to destruction, that is not at all the book's message. Like the book of Exodus, Revelation takes readers on a liberating journey. The book describes not the destruction of the earth but earth's liberation and renewal, culminating in a vision of the renewed Earth. The plague visions function as wake-up calls or warnings, showing oppressors the logical consequences of their actions while repentance is still possible.

Revelation unfolds in cyclical or spiral fashion, often showing the same series of judgments from different angles, like a kaleidoscope. Each cycle of visions includes warnings as well as hymns, blessings, and promises. Numbered sequences of seven seals, seven trumpets, and seven bowl plagues evoke memories of the Exodus plagues—calling for liberation of God's people from oppression. Nature becomes an active participant in God's judgment and salvation.

The seven bowls of Revelation 16 recapitulate the same Exodus-related plagues events as the seven trumpets of Revelation 8–9, with double the destructive intensity. Each of the first four bowls afflicts an element of nature: the Earth, the sea, the springs of water, and then the sun. Human communities' prayers and cries for vindication are also implicitly present, since the golden bowls the angels pour are the same bowls as in 6:9–11. As Brian Blount describes the relationship, "Those prayers motivate divine action throughout the book [of Revelation] . . . Apparently God is so overwhelmed by the people's cries that God's passion for them takes tangible shape."[18]

With the pouring of the third bowl (Rev 16:4–7), rivers and waters are turned to blood. The angel or messenger of Water interprets this calamity through the logic of justice and natural consequences, as the boomerang-like effect of oppressors' own crimes: "You are just in these judgments, O Holy One, for they have shed the blood of saints and prophets, and you have given them blood to drink. It is axiomatic" (Rev 16:5, my translation).

Parallel use of the same verb "pour out, shed" (*ekcheō*) for both a crime and its consequences underscore the logic of reciprocity, using legal language. The "shedding" or "pouring out" of each bowl's contents of judgment (16:1, 2, 3, 4, 8, 10, 12, 17) reciprocates Rome's own "shedding/pouring" of blood (16:6), described here by the same verb. Those who shed blood unleash their own destructive consequences upon themselves and are forced to drink the very blood they have shed, now in the form

---

18. Blount, *Revelation*, 292–93.

of blood-polluted waters. Measure for measure, God's judgments against evildoers match their offense.[19]

The waters' doxology, praising the justice of God in terms of the logic of consequences, makes the third bowl description much longer than any of the other six bowl descriptions. The angel explains that it is precisely because oppressors "shed" the blood of saints and prophets that the waters have turned to blood, and God now gives the oppressors blood to drink. As in Isaiah 49:26, the bloodthirsty are made to choke on the very blood they shed.[20] The angel interprets these consequences of being forced to drink bloody water as "axiomatic" (*axios*) or "worthy," in the sense of self-evident: "It is what they deserve" (*axioi eisin,* NRSV).

Strikingly, a personified talking altar then speaks to affirm the just judgments: "Yes, O Lord God, the Almighty, your judgments are true and just" (16:7). As Pablo Richard explains, antiphonal liturgy breaks in at this point in the narrative "so that the community may be actively present; indeed, whenever the liturgy appears in the text, the community is making an appearance. Far from being a spectator to the Exodus that God is bringing about in the Roman empire, the community is involved in it, as expressed symbolically in liturgy."[21]

Why Do Waters Cry Out? Violence and Bloodshed in Other Apocalyptic Texts

One question that puzzles scholars is why Revelation's third bowl description is so much longer than the other bowls. Adela Yarbro Collins calls the third bowl a "vindication doxology"[22] while Hans Dieter Betz calls it "judgment doxology," with the messenger of the waters praising God's judgment or justice. In searching for the sources of this imagery, Betz notes that the judgment doxology parallels other ancient apocalyptic texts in which four elements of the world (Air, Earth, Water, and Fire) play a major role.[23] This is similar to 1 Enoch, where angelic beings represent the sea, hoarfrost, hail, snow, mist, dew, and rain.[24]

19. Blount, *Revelation,* 294.
20. Blount, *Revelation,* 97.
21. Richard, *Apocalypse,* 83.
22. Collins, "The History-of-Religions Approach," 369.
23. Betz, "On the Problem," 139–54.
24. 1 Enoch 60:12–22; 61:10 mentions angels of the water; see also 66:1–2, "The Lord of Spirits commanded the angels who were going forth, that they not raise their hands, but that they keep watch; for these angels were in charge of the power of the

As Betz suggests, the tradition behind Revelation 16 may also include that of the Egyptian hermetic document *Kore Kosmou*, in which the four elements of the world cry out to God for purification from the pollution of bloodshed by oppressors. In *Kore Kosmou* each of the four elements voices its legal complaint in the form of prayers or liturgy. A personified figure of Fire speaks first, then Air (voicing a complaint against air-pollution that would describe our present crisis), then Water, and finally Earth. Water's complaint is the most relevant for Rev 16:

> Water was given leave to speak, and spoke thus: "O Father, self-begotten and Maker of Nature, that power which generates all things to give thee pleasure, it is high time for thee to give command that my streams be kept pure; for the rivers and seas are ever washing off the defilement of the slayers, and receiving the corpses of the slain" (*Corp. Herm.* 23:58; trans. W. Scott *Hermetica* 1:489).[25]

In response to these speeches by the four cosmic elements, God responds by promising to send a redeemer (the Egyptian god Osiris) to judge oppressors' misdeeds, a promise that satisfies the elements: "Another shall now come down to dwell among you . . . He shall be judge of the living—a judge none can deceive . . . Thereupon the Elements ceased from their entreating."

Revelation 16 most closely resembles *Kore Kosmou* in the cry of Water for justice against human bloodshed. In both texts, Water cries out, accusing warring people of misusing the Water from rivers and the sea with violence. Specifically, the accusation in *Kore Kosmou* is that people are washing blood off themselves with Water, and then throwing the bodies of dead people they have slain into the water.

In addition to the Egyptian *Kore Kosmou*, Betz traces a trajectory of such personified imagery through early Jewish and later Christian texts such as the Pseudo-Clementine Homilies, and even the third-century Apocalypse of Paul. All share a "basic agreement" in the use of a similar tradition of the cosmic elements personified or represented by angels, crying out for vindication against human wrongdoing and injustice.[26]

We can extend this argument about Water's voice in a more political direction. Newer Empire-critical scholarship on apocalypses makes clear a

---

waters" (Nickelsburg and VanderKam, *1 Enoch* 69:22; 75:3). Aune also cites Jub 2:2, where angels created on the first day represent elements of the cosmos such as winds, clouds, darkness, snow, hail, and frost; and from Qumran hymns 1QH 1:8–13.

25. See discussion in Aune, *Revelation*, 887.

26. Betz, "On the Problem," 151.

political/military and structural violence aspect to "human wrongdoing," behind the common ancient tradition of personified elements crying out for justice, against defilement. This anti-imperial dimension of a biblical water motif can help us address water injustices today, drawing on work by Wink and also important recent scholarship by Anathea Poitier Young, Richard Horsley, and others.

The anti-imperial dimension of the entire bowl sequence becomes explicit with the fifth bowl in Revelation 16. Whereas the first four bowls (Rev 16:1–9) were poured out on Earth, sea, water, and air, the fifth bowl is poured out not on any element of nature, but on the "throne of the beast," namely the seat of Empire (Rev 16:10). The kingdom (*basileia*) of the beast is plunged into darkness. As Elisabeth Schüssler Fiorenza notes, the fifth, sixth, and seventh bowls announce the "destruction of Babylon/Rome, which will be elaborated further in the narrative of chapters 17–18."[27] The focus on the Empire's injustices can be seen already here in the bowl sequence, in the voice of the angel of the waters and the fifth bowls.

Liberation theologian Pablo Richard draws an expanded analogy of the bowl plagues to multiple forms of imperial oppression today, identifying the plagues of Revelation today as "the disastrous results of ecological destruction, the arms race, irrational consumerism, the idolatrous logic of the market."[28] It is important to underscore that the plagues unleashed by the bowls are targeted not against humankind in general, but only against oppressors—namely, against the beast (the Empire) and its followers.[29]

The good news of the messenger of the Waters is that oppressors who commit acts of violence will unleash their own destructive consequences against themselves. It is "axiomatic" (my translation of *axioi eisin*). A similar ecological logic can be seen in the Exodus plagues, the antecedent for John's bowls. The response from the personified talking altar (Rev 16:7) engages the community in active liturgical response to the empire's own violence.

Waters Cry Out Against Military Siege: Apocalypses as Resistance Literature

It can be helpful to analyze Revelation's roots in earlier Jewish apocalyptic literature written during times of brutal political oppression.[30] Anathea Poitier Young's landmark study of the origins of apocalyptic as "resistance

27. Schüsslser Fiorenza, *Revelation*, 94.
28. Richard, *Apocalypse*, 86.
29. Richard, *Apocalypse*, 84. See also Fiorenza, *Revelation*, 94.
30. See discussion of Revelation's "ancestry" in Kiel, *Apocalyptic Ecology*.

literature" examines the early Jewish apocalypses of 1 Enoch and Daniel in the context of tyrannical military occupation and violence as described in 1 Maccabees and other historical texts. She shows that the violence of bloodshed/injustice being critiqued by angelic voices of water and other cosmic elements in 1 Enoch is specifically the military violence of the Seleucid Empire, which conquered Judea and carried out a program of political terror, including torture, in the second century BCE. In the case of the state terror of Antiochus IV in 167 BCE, the empire engaged in such brutality that Poitier Young calls it "decreation"–a violence that "de-creates the very fabric of the world." Apocalyptic literature arose in early Judaism as resistance literature—resisting Empires' "totalizing" claims. Like state terror in Argentina in the 1980s and elsewhere, she shows that regimes have a "logic" to what they do. Jewish and Christian apocalypses seek to answer that logic by galvanizing people's imagination for resistance.

Regimes use military and political force to lay claim to time and space in totalizing ways: re-setting calendars, re-naming places (such as the re-naming of Jerusalem to Antioch), re-mapping the cartography of the world, disrupting fundamental structures of order, erasing people's memory. Apocalypses "countered the totalizing narrative of the Seleucid empire with an even grander total vision of history, cosmos, and the reign of God."[31] Apocalypses provide a new cartography. Through their use of symbolism and myth, apocalypses engender embodied resistance and praxis. In the face of trauma, they "answered terror with radical visions of hope."

Monster symbolism in the Book of the Watchers, the earliest apocalyptic section of 1 Enoch, shows the "monstrosity of imperial rule."[32] The Book of Watchers describes the destruction brought by marauding giants, and how "the earth brought an accusation against the oppressors" (1 Enoch 7:6).[33] Whereas the imperial domination system perpetuates itself by rendering the structures of domination invisible, "[A]pocalyptic writings rendered them visible and characterized them as monstrous or demonic precisely to enable full-fledged resistance of the mind, spirit and body."[34]

Similarly, Richard Horsley describes the function of angels in the Book of the Watchers in 1 Enoch: "The problem that drives the Book of Watchers, mentioned again and again, is the violence and destruction

---

31. Young, *Apocalypse Against Empire*, xxiii.

32. Young, *Apocalypse Against Empire*, 170.

33. Kiel suggests that Enoch's tours of cosmos and "all the rivers of the earth" (1 Enoch 17:8) function to critique imperial propaganda of Hellenistic rulers, specifically that of Ptolomy Soter ("Savior," 294–261 BCE) who "claimed that all the rivers and the seas acknowledge him" (Kiel, *Apocalyptic Ecology*, 37).

34. Young, *Apocalypse Against Empire*, 35.

wrought by imperial regimes on subject people. The only way the Enoch scribes can explain it is from rebellion against the divine governance of the universe by rebel heavenly forces who disobey the divine commands. And the only solution to imperial violence and destruction on earth is for God and the obedient heavenly forces to control, bind, and punish, the rebel heavenly forces."

In such an analysis, the angelic personification of natural elements such as Water may be similar to Indigenous people's cosmologies and resistance today, diagnosing and making visible as "monstrous" the brutal structures that colonize and pollute waterways for private gain and deprive people of access to water, whether at Standing Rock, Gaza, or other places.

Waters Cry Out against the Black Snake Pipeline: Military Violence at Standing Rock

Military siege is one common thread between ancient apocalypses and today's Indigenous communities advocating for water justice. Tribal nations camped at Standing Rock, North Dakota, during the Fall of 2016, portrayed the oil pipeline as a monstrous black snake, slithering across the landscape for miles. Their serpentine portrayal of the oil pipeline, much like 1 Enoch's symbolism of monsters, exposed the "monstrosity" of what was happening at Standing Rock. As Poitier-Young shows, imagery of monsters and dragons in apocalyptic texts serves to make visible the structural violence being inflicted on a marginalized community. The naming of the oil pipeline as a snake also recalls Revelation's picturing of the Roman Empire's unjust systems as both serpent and dragon (Rev 12:3, 9), "deceiving the whole inhabited world" (12:9, my translation).[35]

The Standing Rock Sioux and members of some 300 other tribal nations camped beside the river underscored that they were "Water Protectors," not protesters. Prayer was the focus of all their public actions. Prayerfully and nonviolently, standing on the bridge, they sought to protect the Missouri River and their drinking water supply from the threat of oil spills from the Dakota Access Pipeline. Their declaration "Water is Life" affirmed that sacred dimension. Yet as nonviolent water protectors they were met with militarized police violence and water cannons from privately hired security thugs.

I visited Standing Rock in November 2016, as part of a seminary delegation. Gordon Straw's blog post "Standing with Standing Rock Takes All

---

35. Vitor Westhelle analyzes Revelation's dissimulation, and its dragon and beast symbolism, in "Revelation 13."

of Us" drew on the Dakota concept of *metakuye oyasin*, "all my relatives," a "recognition that every aspect of existence is connected to every other aspect of existence, because all things have a single origin, the Creator." As he wrote, "we stand with the Standing Rock Nation and all other nations in declaring that Water is Life. No amount of tainting the earth's fresh water supply with oil or chemicals is acceptable. Our nation's dependence upon fossil fuels (that's each and every one of us, folks) is threatening our Mother, the Earth, especially the waterways which bring life."[36]

Governments and corporate interests continue to refuse to honor the boundaries of the 1868 Fort Laramie Treaty as sovereign territory of the Sioux Nation. In neighboring Montana, pipeline companies are now taking advantage of the COVID-19 shut-downs to rush to construct pipelines such as the Keystone XL pipeline across tribal lands, since protestors are not allowed to mobilize during the pandemic.[37] New tar sands pipelines are being constructed across North American tribal lands, crossing wetlands and waterways. In a multitude of ways, fossil fuel corporations are endangering the world, its waters, and all of us. The voice of the waters cries out.

The Gaza Aquifer Cries Out in Collapse against Military Siege, Occupation

If there is a place on Earth where water injustice is most urgent, it may be the Gaza Strip, home to two million Palestinian people.[38] As EcoPeace Middle East describes the dire humanitarian crisis, "[L]ack of clean water for domestic use and unsafe sanitary conditions pose a serious public health threat." A 2012 UN report predicted that by 2020 Gaza will be uninhabitable. That has now happened.[39] Eight refugee camps now house an estimated 600,000 people; one million refugees live in the cities, making Gaza one of the most densely populated areas in the world.

Gaza residents' only source of water is the Coastal Aquifer, located under the coastal plain of Israel and the Gaza Strip. The aquifer is being depleted faster than it can be recharged by rainwater, to the point of collapse. As a consequence, sea water infiltrates into the aquifer, causing salination.

36. https://wetalkwelisten.wordpress.com/2019/01/07/standing-with-standing-rock-takes-all-of-us-rev-dr-gordon-straw/

37. Brown, "Tribes and Environmental Groups."

38. On the "extremely high level of water insecurity found in modern Palestine today," including the Gaza Aquifer and the West Bank, see Awad, "Advocacy for Eco-Justice in Palestine," 55; LeVine, "Tracing Gaza's Chaos to 1948."

39. United Nations Special Coordinator, *Gaza in 2020*.

Wells in Gaza have become so saline that 96% of Gaza's coastal aquifer water is non-potable, according to EcoPeace Middle East. Up to 80–90% of existing wells containing concentrations of salts in excess of the 250 milligram per liter standards set by the World Health Organization.[40] Consequently, Gazans must buy drinking water from water trucks and water venders who desalinate brackish water and sell it at exorbitant prices, "10–30 times more expensive than piped water."[41] But desalinization by local venders does not remove pathogens such as nitrates.

In addition to salts, groundwater has also been contaminated by sewage. Sanitation and water-treatment facilities are lacking, causing pollution of the aquifer with nitrates and dangerous pathogens. UNICEF reported in 2017 that more than 1 million Gazans, or 50 % of the population, face the threat of contracting waterborne diseases.[42] As Rachel Havrelock describes, "The lack of water and its unsuitability for consumption contributes to about a quarter of all diseases in Gaza, with other infectious diseases that negatively impact the growth of children … The hydrosocial cycle turns in a constant state of war that reverberates in a spoiled aquifer and chronically ill bodies."[43]

As part of the military siege of Gaza since 2007, Israel imposes a blockade that prohibits the import of cement and "dual use" supplies that are urgently needed to build water treatment projects and a desalinization plant. Insufficient electricity means there is not enough power to run what sewage treatment facilities do exist. The situation has recently worsened with the US Congress passing the 2018 Anti-Terrorism Clarification Act. This legislation "effectively stops all US humanitarian assistance to Palestinians," reports Churches for Middle East Peace (CMEP). Humanitarian aid has become "weaponized," reports CMEP. The situation worsened further with the 2021 Gaza war.

Israeli border fences and checkpoints prohibit people from leaving, even to flee violent shelling and bombardments by Israel. Attempts to leave Gaza, such as the nonviolent "March of Return," have been met with violence and killings by Israeli military. As Rachel Havrelock describes in her chapter on the Gaza Aquifer collapse hauntingly titled "End This War," we must consider how "modern militarization in biblical garb has impacted the land itself."

---

40. Bromberg and Giordano, "Gaza on the Edge."
41. UN Office, "Study Warns Water Sanitation Crisis in Gaza."
42. Shawish and Weibel, "Gaza Children Face Acute Water and Sanitation Crisis."
43. Havrelock, *The Joshua Generation*, 221.

Governments and NGOs recognize the acute water and sanitation crisis of Gaza. Israel is certainly concerned about polluted beaches, and about the risk that water-borne diseases such as cholera will not respect border fences. Yet we must contextualize the roots of the water crisis in terms of longer-term military siege, occupation and wars. The Gaza water crisis is tied most recently the role of Israel's blockade imposed in 2007 when Hamas won the election and took political control, followed by Israel's wars against Gaza in 2008, 2012, 2014, and 2021. The roots of the crisis go back further, however, to the displacement of Palestinians in 1948 and 1967. Some argue that both the 1948 and 1967 wars should be described at least in part as "water wars." Events that led to the 1967 Six-Day War were "rooted in the rival water-diversion plans of Israel and its Arab neighbors, which set off water wars between 1964 and 1967," notes economist Brahma Chellaney. The 1967 War against Jordan, Syria and Egypt "stands out for the successful Israeli grab of water resources." The Gaza aquifer, while less important geopolitically than the West Bank aquifer and headwaters of the Jordan River, was also seized as part of the Israeli occupation. "The key point is that the [1967] war ended with Israel acquiring de facto control of the main subregional water resources."[44]

As with Standing Rock, military siege is one important common thread we can identify between the Gaza situation and Revelation's waters' cry for justice. The waters that became undrinkable in Rev 16:4 can help us see the logical consequences of water injustice and military violence, including the violence of siege and Occupation. If we seek to interpret the Gaza water crisis in terms of Revelation's imagery (a project that must be undertaken with great caution because of a legacy of Christian anti-Semitic use of biblical texts), what we might say is this: It is Israel's military occupation and siege, as well as its illegal diversion of water away from Palestinian communities, that is monstrous, even demonic. In the axiomatic logic of consequences, voiced as by the angel of waters as "fitting" (*axioi eisen*, Rev 16:6), the waters will punish those who prolong the military siege. Water and waterborne diseases do not stay contained.

Hind Khoury's Lenten reflection for the Ecumenical Water Network in 2016 articulates the Palestinian thirst for water justice. Calling attention to the "Israeli apartheid policies [that] contribute to the alarming water shortage," she lifts up the Kairos call for "creative resistance in the logic of love." Khoury roots her reflection in the key verse of Revelation that gives God's alternative vision of hope for water justice: "To the thirsty I will give water as

---

44. Chellaney, *Water, Peace, and War*, 48–49. See also Peppard, *Just Water*, 135.

a gift from the spring of the water of life" (Rev 21:6 NRSV).[45] We now turn to that alternative vision of living waters in Revelation.

Water is Life: New Jerusalem Gift (*Dorean*) and Hope for Water Justice Today

Apocalypses not only diagnose imperial pathology and the consequences of military violence. They also give the counter-imperial vision of hope, and call us to "come out" of Empire (Rev 18:4). Jesus, God's Lamb, leads God's people to "springs of living water" (Rev 7:17 RSV). "Living water" in Rev 7:17 articulates the idea that Water is itself alive, with its own living spirit. In contrast to the deadly waters of blood that become undrinkable in Revelation 16, God's "springs" of the water of life and living river of life in New Jerusalem offer healing. In contrast to the antiphonal judgment doxology of Rev 16:4, the antiphonal liturgy of Rev 22:17 invites all who are thirsty to drink from God's living water. In contrast to Lamentations' description of the sufferings of military occupation ("We must pay for the water that we drink," Lam 5:1–4) the New Jerusalem vision offers an economy in which water is a gift without cost, for all who need it. Water is priceless (*dorean*). Water is life.

As a prophetic economic vision, the New Jerusalem vision can speak on behalf of rivers, watersheds, and their living communities today. God offers the water of life to everyone who thirsts as a "gift," free of charge—without payment—echoing the promise of Isaiah 55:1, "Ho, everyone who thirsts, come to the waters; and you that have no money, come, buy and eat ... without price!" The imagery is spiritual and also economic. Biblical prophets critique a system where poor people lack money to buy water, and thus are denied access to the essentials of life in an unjust economic system. Similarly, in Revelation, the word *dorean* ("without cost," "without money," Rev 21:6, 22:17) is profoundly economic as well as spiritual. It underscores the promise of water justice even for those who have been excluded from economic system. As George Zachariah notes "This promise of free access to clean and pure water is the Divine rejection of the prevailing political economy of privatization and commodification of water."[46] The vision can furnish a corrective to ruthless capitalist tendencies to commodify or "fetishize" everything in a market economy.[47]

---

45. Khoury, "The Water of Life."
46. Zachariah, "Pilgrimage towards Water Justice."
47. Richard, *Apocalypse*, 130.

For ecological hermeneutics today, Revelation 21–22 is the most important vision of the book. God's dwelling is not up in heaven but on a renewed Earth, with a living river of life flowing through the center of God's city. The community participates via an antiphonal liturgical dialog not unlike the litany of the waters quoted at the beginning of this essay. The antiphonal call-and-response refrain of "Come" (Rev 22:17), voiced first by the spirit, gives a eucharistic invitation as well as a concrete invitation to water justice for water protectors. It voices a promise of water for all who are thirsty: "The spirit and the bride say, 'Come.' and let everyone who hears say, 'Come.' And let everyone who is thirsty come. Let anyone who wishes take the water of life as a gift (*dorean*)."

The gift of the living water of life in the New Jerusalem vision offers a new social imaginary for Standing Rock and Gaza, and for all of us. Waters are alive. The vision gives a healing corrective to the imperial violence critiqued by the voice of waters in Revelation 16. Waters are persons, with voice, Revelation teaches us. The waters cry out today!

Bibliography

Aune, David. *Revelation*. Word Biblical Commentary 52b. Nashville: Nelson, 1997.

Awad, Simon. "Advocacy for Eco-Justice in Palestine." In *Making Peace with the Earth: Action and Advocacy for Climate Justice*, edited by Grace Ji-Sun Kim, 52–68. Geneva: WCC Publications, 2016.

Betz, Hans Dieter. "On the Problem of the Religio-Historical Understanding of Apocalypticism." *Journal of Theology and Church* 6 (1969) 139–54.

Blount, Brian. *Revelation: A Commentary*. New Testament Library. Louisville: Westminster John Knox, 2009.

Bromberg, Gidon, and Giulia Giordano. "Gaza on the Edge: The Water and Energy Crisis in Gaza." EcoPeace Middle East, updated May 2018.

Brown, Matthew. "Tribes and Environmental Groups Press Judge to Halt Work on Disputed Keystone XL Pipeline." *Chicago Tribune*/Associated Press, April 16, 2020. https://www.chicagotribune.com/nation-world/ct-nw-keystone-xl-pipeline-20200416-tjxynmmqnbcbrksxhoy2sddrjm-story.html.

Chellaney, Brahma. *Water, Peace, and War: Confronting the Global Water Crisis*. New York: Rowman & Littlefield, 2013.

Clark, Christy et al. "Can You Hear the Rivers Sing? Legal Personhood, Ontology, and the Nitty Gritty of Governance." *Ecology Law Quarterly* 45 (2019) 787–844.

Collins, Adela Yarbro. "The History-of-Religions Approach to Apocalypticism and the 'Angel of the Waters' (Rev 16:4–7)." *Catholic Biblical Quarterly* 39 (1977) 363–81.

Damania, Richard et al. "Uncharted Waters: The New Economics of Water Scarcity and Variability." World Bank, 2017. https://openknowledge.worldbank.org/handle/10986/28096 License: CC BY 3.0 IGO.

Egan, Dan. *The Death and Life of the Great Lakes*. New York: Norton, 2017.

Habel, Norman, and Peter Trudinger, eds. *Exploring Ecological Hermeneutics*. Atlanta: Society of Biblical Literature, 2008.

Havrelock, Rachel S. *The Joshua Generation: Israeli Occupation and the Bible*. Princeton: Princeton University Press, 2020.

Khoury, Hind. "The Water of Life—Not in Palestine: A Kairos Perspective." Ecumenical Water Network, 2016. https://water.oikoumene.org/en/whatwedo/seven-weeks-for-water/2016/the-water-of-life-not-in-palestine-a-kairos-perspective.

Kiel, Micah. *Apocalyptic Ecology: The Book of Revelation, the Earth, and the Future*. Collegeville, MN: Liturgical, 2017.

LeVine, Mark. "Tracing Gaza's Chaos to 1948." *Aljazeera* (13 July 2009). https://www.aljazeera.com/focus/arabunity/2008/02/2008525185737842919.html.

Mooney, Chris. "World Bank: The Way Climate Change Is Really Going to Hurt Us Is through Water." *Washington Post*, May 3, 2016.

Myers, Ched, ed. *Watershed Discipleship: Reinhabiting Bioregional Faith and Practice*. Eugene: Cascade Books, 2016.

Nickelsburg, George W. E., and James C. VanderKam. *1 Enoch: A New Translation*. Minneapolis: Fortress, 2004.

Nobel, Justin. "Nature Scores a Big Win against Fracking in a Small Pennsylvania Town." *Rolling Stone*, April 2020. https://www.rollingstone.com/politics/politics-news/rights-of-nature-beats-fracking-in-small-pennsylvania-town-976159/.

Peppard, Christiana Z. *Just Water: Theology, Ethics, and the Global Water Crisis*. Maryknoll, NY: Orbis, 2014.

Perkinson, James W. "Protecting Water in the Anthropocene: River Spirits and Political Struggles in Detroit, Standing Rock, and the Bible." *Crosscurrents* 66 (2017) 460–84.

Richard, Pablo. *Apocalypse: A People's Commentary on the Book of Revelation*. Bible & Liberation. Maryknoll, NY: Orbis, 1995.

Rossing, Barbara. "Revelation." In *Fortress Commentary on the Bible: The New Testament*, edited by Margaret Aymer et al., 715–71. Minneapolis: Fortress, 2014.

Schüssler Fiorenza, Elisabeth. *Revelation: Vision of a Just World*. Proclamation Commentary. Minneapolis: Fortress, 1991.

Shawish, Abeer Abu, and Catherine Weibel. "Gaza Children Face Acute Water and Sanitation Crisis." UNICEF, September 1, 2017. https://www.unicef.org/stories/gaza-children-face-acute-water-sanitation-crisis.

Stone, Christopher D. "Should Trees Have Standing? Toward Legal Rights for Natural Objects." *Southern California Law Review* 450 (1972) 450–501.

United Nations Office for the Coordination of Humanitarian Affairs. "Study Warns Water Sanitation Crisis in Gaza May Cause Disease Outbreak and Possible Epidemic." *The Monthly Humanitarian Bulletin* (Oct 2018). https://www.ochaopt.org/content/study-warns-water-sanitation-crisis-gaza-may-cause-disease-outbreak-and-possible-epidemic.

United Nations Special Coordinator for the Middle East Peace Process. *Gaza in 2020: A Livable Place?* August 2012. https://www.unrwa.org/userfiles/file/publications/gaza/Gaza in 2020.pdf.

Westhelle, Vitor. "Revelation 13: Between the Colonial and the Postcolonial, a Reading from Brazil." In *From Every People and Nation: The Book of Revelation in Intercultural Perspective*, edited by David Rhoads, 183–99. Minneapolis: Fortress, 2005.

Williams, Clint. "Should Nature Have a Legal Standing: A Legal Decision about a River in New Zealand Raises Logistical Questions." *Mother Nature Network*, October 5, 2012.

Wink, Walter. *The Powers That Be: Theology for a New Millennium*. New York: Doubleday, 1998.

———. *Unmasking the Powers: The Invisible Forces that Determine Human Existence*. Philadelphia: Fortress, 1986.

Young, Anathea Poitier. *Apocalypse against Empire: Theologies of Resistance in Early Judaism*. Grand Rapids: Eerdmans, 2011.

Zachariah, George. "Pilgrimage towards Water Justice: Foretaste of a Redeemed Earth." Seven Weeks for Water 2014; WCC, Geneva: Ecumenical Water Network. https://water.oikoumene.org/en/whatwedo/seven-weeks-for-water/past/2014/2014_1_Foretaste_of_a_Redeemed_Earth.pdf.

3

Reclaiming Mother Earth

A Khasi Indigenous Re-reading of Psalm 104

ENOLYNE LYNGDOH

THE IMPACT OF COLONIAL knowledge is visible in the contemporary Indigenous Khasi[1] society of Northeast India.[2] Before the arrival of the British, Northeast India was an independent region ruled by local chieftains. When the British took over India, they wanted to incorporate the Northeast region as part of their Empire. The outbreak of the 1824 Burma War provided the British the opportunity to enter the Khasi Hills.[3] From 1826 onwards the British gained control of the region. The colonial administration constructed new roads and started educational institutions to facilitate the region's assimilation and plunder. Ostensibly, such policies were meant to "improve" the standard of living of the community, and

1. The Indigenous Khasi community belonged to the ethnic group who have long inhabited what is now called the state of Meghalaya in Northeast India. The term *khas* means "hill," so they are the people of the hills. Four tribes comprise the Khasis community: Khynriam, Pnar, Bhoi and War.

2. The Northeast region of India is composed of eight states with different cultural heritage and dialect. The British termed the people of this region as "tribal." The Khasi community of the state of Meghalaya is one among the Indigenous people groups in the region. The population of Meghalaya is around 3.6 million (2018) of which Khasis comprise around 2 million. Eighty per cent of the population are Christians.

3. Gurdon, *The Khasis*, xvii–xviii.

with education purportedly "bringing light and knowledge" to the community. But in the process, Indigenous knowledge and belief systems that formerly ensured the care of the land and the environment were dismissed as "superstitious" and "irrational."

As an Indigenous Khasi, I realized the importance of Indigenous values during the course of my theological studies. However, the rich ecological worldview and consciousness of my people was rarely referenced or mentioned in Church. This is in part because Indigenous Khasis have absorbed and internalized much of the knowledge and culture of the colonial rulers and thus began to lose appreciation for our Indigenous eco-principles and practices, particularly in regard to the sacredness of the land, forests, hills, and rivers. Contemporary Khasis now consider such beliefs as "myths" of the ancient traditional religion and no longer relevant today. And with the advent of neo-liberal developmentalism, the lands, forests, and minerals are seen as nothing more than "resources" to be exploited in the name of "prosperity" and "progress."

The current environmental crisis inspires this study to reclaim our Indigenous values as essential for the restoration of earth and her well-being. This chapter is an attempt to re-read Psalm 104 from an Indigenous Khasi understanding of the earth and all living beings. Traditional interpretations of Psalms 104 have largely concentrated on God's sovereignty over creation and God's continuing activity in nourishing the natural world to sustain creation. According to Erhard S. Gerstenberger, Psalm 104 is a hymnic text to describe the majesty and creative power of the cosmic overlord—the active role of God in creation.[4] Walter Brueggemann and William H. Bellinger argue that creation as a theme of biblical faith has been skewed into explanatory modes in contemporary usage. They describe Psalm 104 as Israel's response to the generative, life-giving power of creation that reveals the depth of God's faithfulness to creation.[5] However, the relationship which God shares with nature, his indwelling in, and communication through, nature is often obscured. Indigenous Khasis, on the other hand, believe that God dwells in nature, that nature herself is holy and sacred. God communicates to the community through the created order.

This chapter adopts the "reader-response approach" from the Khasi perspective to re-read Psalm 104. In this aspect both the reader and the text play important roles in the formation of meaning. The reader learns from the text as well as engages one's knowledge and experiences in constructing meaning through a transaction between the reader and the text within a

4. Gerstenberger, *Psalms*, 222.
5. Brueggemann and Bellinger, *Psalms*, 446.

particular context.⁶ Reader-response theory is based on the assumption that a literary work takes place in the space of a reciprocal relationship between the reader and the text. James Resseguie assumes reader-response criticism, as an active participant in the creation of meaning where a reader must use imagination to fill in the gaps and constitute the common ground shared by the text and the reader.⁷ This theory originates from Rosenblatt who proposes a "kind of reading [whereby] the reader adopts an attitude of readiness to focus attention on what is being lived through *during* the reading event."⁸ The reading uses these questions as dimensions to reclaim the Mother earth: What are the eco-principles (or eco-wisdom tradition) of Indigenous Khasis? Why do contemporary Indigenous Khasis now disregard their traditional eco-principles? How might environmental challenges help the Khasi community to reclaim their eco-wisdom tradition through the re-reading of Psalm 104? This discussion on eco-wisdom may enlighten us to discern the significance of nature to the Indigenous Khasis.

Khasis and Eco-Wisdom

The Indigenous Khasi community believes in the sacredness of nature. Nature is God's creation and a Mother who nourishes humankind. Nature is a holy sanctuary where God resides and interacts with human beings.⁹ Nature sustains the life of the tribes as a clan and provides meaning in our quest for justice and spirituality. Khasis perceive land as a living entity endowed with spirits. Mountains, rivers, groves and plants are sacred. The community identifies and declares certain groves as *Lawblei* (the groves of the deity), *Lawkyntang* (sacred groves), *Law Adong* (prohibited groves) and *Law Lyngdoh* (the groves of the priest).¹⁰ These groves are sacred like the forests. It is believed that every sacred grove is guarded by *U Ryngkew, U Basa* (the principal spirits who protect the land).¹¹ Thanksgiving and prayer is offered to a deity to bless the land. It is presumed that any person who disturbs these sacred groves will suffer incurable diseases. Further, the hills and rivers are sacred. For instance, the river Kupli is considered as a mother to whom sacrifices of propitiation are fit to be offered periodically. Such a belief is part of the socio-religious and cultural life of the people.

6. Rosenblatt, *The Reader*, 25.
7. Resseguie, "Reader-Response Criticism," 308–9.
8. Rosenblatt, "Writing and Reading," 5.
9. Mawrie, *The Khasis*, 154.
10. Mawrie, *The Khasis*, 155.
11. Nongkynrih, "Changes in Beliefs," 62.

Khasi eco-wisdom helps the community to protect the forests, rivers and hills from commercial exploitation. Land is sacred as it provides food and shelter and sustains every form of life. If calamities and famine strike the land, people cry out to God for forgiveness through sacrifices and offerings. Nature is a gift of God to the community and land is a mark of their identity as a community. No one can sell or own the land.

However, the present change of "community land" to "individual land" has affected the traditional understanding of Khasi Indigenous eco-wisdom and spirituality. The Indigenous ethic of preservation of forests like the "sacred groves" and other natural places are now considered as religious myths of the past, no longer to be believed and upheld. As a result, development has not only disturbed the symbiotic relationship that Indigenous Khasis maintained with the natural environment since time immemorial, but also robbed them of the biodiversity upon which they depend for survival.[12] The sanctity of the sacred groves which serve as storehouses of biodiversity, is now threatened because of the lack of legal protection. These sacred groves are facing extinction today.[13] This is the context in which a re-reading of Psalm 104 from the eco-wisdom of Khasis can inspire the community to take action to care for the land again and recover concern for the protection of the beings therein.

On Earth as in Heaven: A Harmonious Relationship with the Divine

The sacredness of nature in the Jewish tradition is deeply associated with the belief that God takes residence in nature, such as in mountains and hills, and in forests and lakes. Such eco-principles correspond to the description of the psalmist: "You are clothed with honor and majesty, wrapped in light as with a garment. You stretch out the heavens like a tent, you set the beams of your chambers on the waters" (Ps. 104:1–3). One can imagine God's presence in the light as well as in the deep waters. In connection to this, the book of Psalms frequently speaks of the dwelling place of God on earth at Mt. Zion (Pss 9:11; 48:1–3; 50:1–2; 74:2; 87:2; 132:13–14).

Psalm 104:16 says that "Yahweh planted the cedars of Lebanon." The psalmist's description of the relationship of God with nature is relevant here. If Yahweh manifests splendor in the sunlight and waters, planted the trees and watered the cedars of Lebanon, the presence of Yahweh can also be experienced in the Khasi hills, rivers and forests. It is thus absurd to assume

12. Nongbri, "Culture," 15.
13. Nongbri, "Culture," 18.

the Khasi eco-wisdom as superstitious. Such detachment of faith from nature has made Mother Earth barren, as hills, rivers, and trees gradually disappear from the face of the earth. Our understanding of the dwelling place of God is now limited to a concrete building and the omnipresence of God now confined to this building.

The psalmist further describes the harmonious function of nature and he praises God's generosity by saying, "You make springs gush forth in the valleys; they flow between the hills, giving drink to every wild animal; the wild asses quench their thirst" (Ps 104:10–11). While reading the Psalm, one can visualize the Indigenous Khasi understanding of nature there. Khasis speak of their close relationship with nature and uphold the earth as a gracious mother who provides for the needs of every creature. For them the earth is *Ka Mei Ramew* (Mother Earth). The title *mei-rilung* (and *mei-risan*) is affectionately attached to Mother Earth, meaning, "the mother who tenderly cares and gives life to all living creatures."[14] Such a belief affirms the saying in Psalm which declares, "By the streams the birds of the air have their habitation; they sing among the branches. From your lofty abode you water the mountains; the earth is satisfied with the fruit of your work. You cause the grass to grow for the cattle, and plants for people to use, to bring forth food from the earth" (Ps 104:12–14). Mother Earth is satisfied with the fruits of her labor because every creature performs their work spontaneously toward the sustenance of life. Correspondingly, Indigenous Khasis affirm the natural environment as taking part in nurturing and sustaining the creatures. Such affirmation we can hear from Soso Tham:

> Grazing stags on tender green
>
> Sleeping tigers in the gloom
>
> Cooling hills warm days just right
>
> While wild nymphs splash in waterfalls.
>
> Look East, look West, look South, look North
>
> A land beloved of the gods.[15]

Every creature feels the touch of the wind and the sun, and they enjoy sunlight, water, and a place for shelter. The peaceful co-existence is portrayed when tigers and stags are not endangered, and climate injustices are

---

14. Mawrie, *The Khasis*, 145.

15. Tham, *Ki Sngi Barim U Hynniewtrep*, 6; Hujon, *Tales of Darkness and Light*, 29. Soso Tham (1873–1940) lives during the colonial rule in India, a renowned writer and poet of the indigenous Khasis and Janet Hujon has translated most of his poems into English.

not yet known. In such an environment, one can imagine the harmonious relationship of God with creation where all species are equally protected and are able to enjoy freely the bounties of creation. The experience of heaven on earth is described in the context of sufficiency, and the absence of poverty and exploitation, where flora and fauna, birds and beast, humankind and land are in communion with each other. As such, the glory and the presence of God can be seen in nature.

Mother Earth as a Home for Every Creature

The psalmist is smitten with the beauty and the awesomeness of the work of creation, for everything operates as part of a coherent, life-giving system. One can envision the beauty of the harmonious inter-connectedness of the earth and her bountiful gifts. It speaks of the natural world and the wonders of its flora and fauna. Likewise, Tham observed the beauty of Khasi land and proclaims:

> Will the high Himalayas
>
> Ever turn away from her
>
> Pleasure garden, fruit and flower
>
> Where young braves wander, maidens roam
>
> Between the *Rilang* and *Kupli*[16]
>
> This is the land they call their home.[17]

In reading Psalm 104, one can also observe the affirmation of the work of Mother Earth in the description of the streams as supplying sufficient water and food for the sustenance of every living creature. The admiration of the work of God is mentioned in the statement "From the lofty abode you water the mountains and the earth is satisfied with the fruit of your work" (Ps 104:13). All creatures perform the work they are meant to do towards the affirmation of life and the sustenance of every living organism. The plants are regenerated in their appointed time and seasons; the rain rejuvenates the fertility of the soil and supplies water to sustain humankind, birds, and sea creatures. The well-watered earth is the perfect habitat for all creatures—with green pastures for the cattle, trees for the birds, and mountains for the wild

---

16. The *Rilang* and *Kupli* are the two rivers that have sustained the land but with the construction of a hydroelectric dam across the river *Kupli* the beauty of nature has disappeared.

17. Tham, *Ki Sngi Barim*, 6; Hujon, *Tales of Darkness*, 30.

animals. The plants, animals, rivers, hills, and forests convey the creativity and the purpose of the creator. And the psalmist affirms, saying, "The trees of the LORD are watered abundantly, the cedars of Lebanon that he planted. In them the birds build their nests; the stork has its home in the fir trees. The high mountains are for the wild goats; the rocks are a refuge for the coneys" (Ps 104: 16–18). Mother Earth feeds the birds and beasts, providing springs of water to wild animals and plants without partiality. The worldview of Indigenous Khasis narrates the understanding of earth as shared by the psalmist when Mother Earth was not yet endangered.

Nature and Animals as Teachers

Through reading the Psalm, one observes that God communicates through thunder and wind. The psalmist narrates the relationship of God with nature saying, "you make the winds your messengers, fire and flame your ministers" (Ps 104:4). God communicates through the sun, the wind, the cloud, and fire to give awareness to humankind. Hence, human beings are not the center of every event or experience that occurs in this world because animals and plants are part of the divine manifestation as well.[18] The harmonious function of the ecosystem is what humankind ought to learn. The psalmist states: "You have made the moon to mark the seasons; the sun knows the time for setting" (Ps 104:19). The moon and the sun cooperate with the creator's plan and purpose so that every creature can carefully organize themselves for food, labor and rest.

Consonant with this understanding, Indigenous Khasis consider nature as the clock and animals as communicators. When the cock crows, they know that it is time to rise and prepare meals and to go to the field. When the sun sets it is time to return home. The cycle of seasons is observed through nature—regarding the time to plant and to harvest. They read the future events of the coming rain and drought through the movements of animals and birds.

The folktales of Indigenous Khasis speak about the coherent existence of all living species. They believe that God manifests Godself through nature. God conveys the message to human beings through the behaviors of animals.[19] The manifestations of nature constantly teach humankind and impart them with knowledge and wisdom, and hence, nature is portrayed as a teacher. Since God communicates to humankind through creatures and nature, creation is sacred. H. O. Mawrie thus states, "A Khasi lives with nature

---

18. Preuss, *Old Testament Theology*, 229.
19. Mawrie, *The Khasis*, 41.

and nature lives in him."[20] Indigenous Khasis anticipate forthcoming events from nature. When they hear a beetle chirp shrilly, they know that autumn is on; and if the walnut trees or wild cherry trees are flowering or budding profusely, they assert that the cultivation will prosper. The appearance of the water beetle on stones and trees by the riverside tells them the depth or shallowness of the river in the coming days, and, if too many of these insects appear on the ground, it is taken as a sign or omen auguring misfortune.[21] The appearance of many winged kite ants indicates that the rain will stop for a while. Khasis also refer to the character of a person by observing the plants, trees, and birds in their way of being. For instance, the oak tree signifies a great-hearted person who never gives up in difficult situations and thus grows with far-flung and strong branches. Thus, plants and animals become a source of wisdom and knowledge to them.

However, such reading from nature is gradually disappearing as plants and animals are becoming extinct. Thus, Tham expresses his fear and regret of the present change stating:

> The world was then a different place
>
> Birds soared freely, beasts at peace
>
> Out in the open or concealed from sight
>
> Flowers with ease communed with humankind,
>
> Submerged beneath the tangle-weed
>
> Thirty-thoughts-have-sprung-from-two . . . where quiet blooms
>
> U Tiew Dohmaw[22]

Birds and flowers lend insight to the Indigenous view of the natural world and the phrase "Thirty-thoughts-have-sprung-from-two" denotes the silent communication of humans with nature. Such instances can be found in the book of Proverbs in which the sages inspire the hearer to learn from the ants, badgers, locusts and lizards; though they are small, they provide lessons for humankind to learn (Prov 30:24–28).

---

20. Mawrie, *The Khasi Milieu*, 97.

21. War, "The Khasi Concept of Nature," 58.

22. *U Tiew Dohmaw* is an *Anoectochilus brevilabris*—a rare orchid embodied all the qualities of a rare genius. Tham, *Ki Sngi Barim*, 5; Hujon, *Tales of Darkness*, 28–29.

Reclaiming and Restoring Mother Earth

In this reading, the Psalmist narrates his praises of God to a tribal community of ancient Israel. In a tribal community, the earth is commonly regarded as a gift of God. The psalmist describes God as the provider of the needs of every creature, and every creature is deemed special and has a unique purpose on earth. Both human and non-human species are nurtured by the natural resources of the earth. Psalm 104 recounts the fullness of creation and offers a concrete and compelling image, such as the sea (the great deep) itself serving as an assurance that the order of creation is not yet under threat. In our understanding Mother Earth from the Indigenous Khasi perspective, we have to unlearn our understanding of the earth as "object" and mere "resource" and learn to relate to Her again as Mother—in the way a child learns from his or her mother or as a student learns from a teacher. Concerning this, the study portrays Earth as the center and thus subverts the assumption of superiority of humankind over creation.

Decolonizing Our Understanding of the Earth

Human superiority over creation is a delusion as our interpretations and actions bounce back to us. Although, the hierarchical understanding of humankind over creation is assumed to have come from the Judeo-Christian tradition (Gen 1:26, 28), it must be noted that the Genesis text itself was composed in a pre-industrial era. The colonial interpretation of the phrase "have dominion" (Gen. 1:26) and "to rule" (Gen.1:28) has been used to promote human interest, ignoring the fact that human beings cannot survive without nature. To the contrary, the creation account in Genesis 2 points more in the direction of stewardship (Gen.2:15) and the preservation of the earth for the future sustenance of all beings. Psalm 104 affirms that God has created the earth with sufficient provision for the survival of every living organism. Khasi people consider animals and birds as part of the human community and as sharing a common origin with humans. Nature and human beings are understood to have a mutual relationship where they can communicate with each other. As the saying goes, "Khasis live in nature and learn in its bosoms."[23] Hence, the land is closely connected with their identity and survival.

Prayer is offered to God for the good health of Mother Earth before cultivation, as a paddy is very much dependent on rainfall. And no one can chop any tree or branch without offering a prayer to the deity. The village

---

23. Mawrie, *The Khasi Milieu*, 102.

council permits the felling of trees only in time of need, as in the case of natural calamities where wood is needed to build houses for victims of cyclones or any other natural calamities. However, in the quest for Western values and knowledge, such Indigenous ways of relating to the natural world have deteriorated, and the sacredness of land, now utterly ignored. The resulting gradual decline in the number of trees has led the community to struggle for the basic needs for survival such as food, clean air, and water. This is clear in Tham's lament on the barrenness of Mother Earth:

> Will the high Himalaya
> Turn their gaze away from you?
> Wind which moves to cool the hills
> Will your freshness ever fade? . . .
> Well-watered tender grows your face
> Orange glow in ripening groves
> Your granaries brim with gathered grain[24]

> All that remains is barren rock, fertility long since washed away
> Settlers, settlements ruined destroyed
> The pleasure garden once so loved
> Forsaken now, she's left bereft,
> Days of peace must surely end
> When the dark cloud drops and shrouds the light
> Slow inch by inch the toad consumes
> The sun gripped tight in her clamping jaws
> While poverty, hunger, suffering, woe
> Hereditary taint suck clean away . . . the marrow
> from the land.[25]

Over the course of the Khasis' history, Mother Earth has always faithfully nurtured and protected the people, but with the advent of development, the community is now facing existential threats. A decolonization of the mind is essential to protect Mother Earth, including her forests, mountains, and waterfalls. Indigenous Khasis in the past considered these places as guarded by deities, and, accordingly, they formulated ways to care for the land. They saw

---

24. Tham, *Ki Sngi Barim*, 39; Hujon, *Tales of Darkness*, 71.
25. Tham, *Ki Sngi Barim*, 12; Hujon, *Tales of Darkness*, 37.

God as the creator and sustainer of the earth and all living beings, and Nature as a holy sanctuary. Such an attitude of reverence has traditionally served to protect the natural world in their given ecology.

As already mentioned, within the groves resides the deity who protects the people from external threats and natural disasters, and who blesses people with prosperity and good health.[26] Visitors to the sacred groves are expected not to litter or pluck any fruit or flower because the guardian spirit of these forests will be displeased.[27] However, such belief is now considered "outdated" within contemporary Khasi society. Excessive deforestation has severely affected the sources of the flowing rivers. Coal mining and unplanned drainage systems have so polluted the rivers and lakes that even the deities are no longer pleased to reside there.

Such ecological degradation leads to the disruption of the balanced eco-system that every organism depends on for their survival. And unless humans come to their senses and realize that if Mother Earth continues to be mistreated, the children will inevitably suffer. The colonial interpretation of God has isolated God from the earth and now the hills no longer serve as guardians. The traditional belief of the Khasis conveys that trees of the sacred groves cannot be used for commercial purposes. However, the change in the belief about the sacred groves is visible in the shrinking of the number of trees in the sacred groves.[28] Indigenous beliefs exhorting the preservation of the sacred groves has sustained them in the past but now the forests are under threat by the incursion of neo-liberal development and the market economy into their territories.[29]

Given such, decolonizing our understanding of the earth is crucial to destabilizing the hegemonic understanding that humans are the center of creation. The first creation story in the book of Genesis seems to position humankind as the center of creation. But one has to observe that humankind is the last one in the sequence of creation and humans appear only after the creation of earth and other living species. Rather than reading this as all of nature being created for the benefit of humankind, we would do well to entertain the alternative understanding that nature does not need humankind to survive, but that human beings cannot survive without nature. Furthermore, before the creation of humankind, it is worth noting that the earth and all her beings existed in harmony with one another. Although Psalm 8 placed humankind as the crown of creation, Psalm 104

26. Nongkynrih, "Changes in Beliefs," 62.
27. Mawrie, *The Khasis*, 155.
28. Nongkynrih, "Changes in Beliefs," 62.
29. Nongbri, "Culture," 1.

refers to humankind as a transgressor (v. 35) and Psalm 104 affirms the Indigenous understanding that the survival of every species depends on a reverential relationship with Mother Earth.

Neo-liberal Development: A Theological Critique

Psalm 104 echoes a positive understanding of the life-generative, life-giving power of creation and it speaks about the wonder of creation and the faithfulness of the creator.[30] The vitality of the ecosystem comes from every species being nurtured and sustained by Mother Earth. The poetic praise of God's creation in Psalm 104 portrays the intricate inter-connectedness and subtle inter-dependence of air, soil, water, plants, animals, and human beings.[31] This relationship is revealed in the etymological connection between *adam* (humankind) and *adamah* (soil). The word *humus* (meaning soil) for "human" has a similar overtone as the word *adamah*, signaling that the origin and destiny of humans is inextricably tied to soil.[32] Indeed, the land and its bounty existed long before humankind came onto the scene. Such observation conveys that we do not own the land, but that the land owns us; long before we were born the land was already in existence, and, long after we die, the mountains, hills, and rivers will continue to exist. Alas, colonial knowledge with its Western orientation of education has estranged Indigenous Khasis from this sacred understanding of the earth, replacing it instead with the objectifying lens of scientific knowledge.[33] R. T. Rymbai in his writings on the traditional ecological concepts of the Khasi-Pnars states:

> These concepts were formulated in the distant past, long, long before the modern civilized world awoke to the disaster looming large over our planet. This has been brought about by the unconcerned and systematic destruction of the ecological balance and environment by the godless greed of man for money and power. Our planet has been exploited relentlessly by the civilized, rich and advanced nations of the west who now realize the magnitude of the horror looming over them, which is much beyond what the poor, developing nations of the Third World can ever imagine, and which we, the present generation of the

---

30. Brueggemann and Bellinger, *Psalms*, 446.
31. McCann, "Psalms," 1099.
32. McCann, "Psalms," 1099.
33. Nongbri, "Culture," 14.

Khasi-Pnars, do not seem to care about at all, the way we destroy our ancient forests and environment.[34]

Although development may be seen as succeeding in connecting people through the construction of road facilities and the provision of means of transportation, such "advancements" are not without their cost. Often, it is Indigenous peoples that pay the price for such "modern conveniences." With the last remaining resources needed to keep powering the industrial economy now largely confined in areas inhabited by Indigenous and tribal communities, those dependent on the land for their means of subsistence suffer the most from the ecological devastation that often accompany such "improvements" elsewhere. The forests, medicinal plants and shrubs which are the wealth of Indigenous people are now becoming extinct; animals and birds are starving for food as their dwelling places become barren. In the case of Northeast India, the inauguration of colonial power is further exacerbated by the globalization process that allows for the invasion of the territories, habitat, and the resources of Indigenous peoples. In the game of the "survival of the fittest," Indigenous communities are unable to keep what remains of their territories and are reduced to mendicancy. In the pursuit of unbridled development, Mother Earth is being crushed and the gift of God is hoarded shamelessly by the rich and powerful through the privatization of land and the globalization of plunder. Modern humans have effectively thwarted the harmonious rhythm that our species used to have with nature. Massive exploitation of the earth's bounty has created a serious impact that has led to the deterioration of human health and natural wealth. Water and air pollution has affected the health of Mother Earth herself.

Psalm 104 gives us a unique perspective on land in ancient Israel. Ancient Israel speaks about the Sabbath of the land. This notion suggests that the land is legally and morally authorized to take rest after every six years so that it can rejuvenate (Lev 25:2). The land as "gift" conveys a unique metaphor—no one can own the gift, and everyone can enjoy its fruits. The land has its own right to exist for itself and Sabbath is observed to honor the land. Perhaps the psalmist might have had in mind the significance of the Sabbath when he spoke of God's bountiful supplies as being available to every being that God has created. Sabbath for land allows the plants to grow and to recover their natural cycle of life.[35] Thus, the concept of Sabbath protects the land from being sold, and the poor from being dispossessed, contrary to the contemporary producer-consumer capitalist economy.[36]

---

34. Rymbai, "The Traditional Ecological," 48.
35. Knight, *Leviticus*, 152.
36. Brueggemann, *The Land*, 64–65.

Indeed, today, the ratcheting up of the neoliberal capitalist economy has allowed for the hyper-exploitation of land, causing untold deprivation and suffering among the dispossessed populations, foremost of whom are Indigenous communities around the globe.[37] Furthermore, the continuing drive toward wealth accumulation and extravagant living by the advantaged sections of parts of the world has raised the question of theft to a new level.[38] Developing nations in general, and India in particular, supported the industrial advancement of a certain sector of their population at great cost to the countries' rich natural resources. The resulting ecological destruction caused excessive deforestation, leading to widespread loss of species habitat and endangerment of their continued survival. In the context of the Northeast region of India, post-independence governance saw the continuation of colonial policy with the enthusiastic adoption of the program of maximization of production and optimum utilization of nature's bounty in the form of land, forest, water, minerals and plants.[39] Rob White argues that contemporary political legislation concerning regulations in fact promotes the destruction of the environment, calling any harm done against the environment a crime.[40] For sure, the resulting overexploitation of the earth has done nothing but to undermine the subsistence economies of already impoverished countries while promoting the further concentration of wealth among the already rich and powerful nations (through the latter's control of the former's natural resources).[41] Currently, "development" marks the distinction between rural and urban in the region, and, concomitantly, the difference between poverty and plenty. The more advanced the "development" the greater and more accelerated the harm done to the environment, and, as well, the greater the impoverishment imposed on still land-based peoples. Furthermore, the resulting land depletion from the unrelenting pursuit of "development" impact not just the human population but the entire community of life (i.e., with the loss of forest cover also follows the loss of clean air, freshwater, and living spaces for animals). Within the contemporary market economy, river waters could not flow naturally to meet the basic needs of animals, plants, and soil as rivers and rain waters are dammed to provide energy. Water is life to every living organism but the construction of large dams destroys the forest, wildlife, and wetlands and ends up

---

37. Pepper, *Eco-Socialism*, 2.
38. McCann, "Psalms," 1100.
39. Nongbri, "Culture," 15.
40. White, *Environmental*, 1–3.
41. Gibson, "Creation and Liberation as a Continuing Story," 61.

destroying freshwater source for all. It is thus that non-human species such as plants and animals are denied justice.

What is called for at this moment, then, in terms of doing justice to Mother Earth is the restoration of a set of arrangements capable of fostering the thriving of all beings, both human and the more-than-human. Such arrangements involve curbing the greed and power of corporatist forces that put narrow and self-serving interests before the common good.[42] Humans are challenged to be accountable in their decision-making by ensuring the protection of the environment. In this regard, we do well to return to the Indigenous Khasi affirmation likewise echoed in Psalm 104 that says that all beings are part of one cosmic body. Although animals and plants cannot speak human language or raise voices against injustices done to them, their extinction speaks volumes. The impact on the environment of the forces of development compels us to re-examine the wisdom of Indigenous understandings of nature and their implications for the preservation of the earth's biodiversity and health.

Psalm 104 serves as a unique text in the Indigenous context of the Khasis of Northeast India. The declaration of the faithfulness of God in providing for the needs of all creation is portrayed in the psalm. But, within the present ecological crisis, such declaration may seem irrelevant to the deprived non-human species as Mother Earth is now desolate and left bereaved and can no longer provide them shelter and food. Reclaiming our original Mother Earth conjures a vision of a sustainable eco-system where the birds have nests, and the beasts have home and water to quench their thirst. Reclaiming Mother Earth is our hope for a sustainable future for all living species—a future that ensures the well-being of all, not just that of humans.

Conclusion

Honoring Mother Earth is at the heart of the culture, identity, and belief system of Indigenous Khasis. The eco-wisdom extolling the sacredness of nature conveys the important understanding that land is valued in and for itself. Traditional Khasi belief asserts that animals and plants are part of the human community. Further, that the green hills, forests, valleys and waters are guarded by specific deities. Such belief has served to protect the natural world until now. With the incursion of colonialist knowledge into the contemporary Khasi community, these eco-principles are now lamentably considered as mere "superstition" and "myth," meant to be left behind as mere remnants of

---

42. Gibson, "Eco-Justice," 24–25.

an anachronistic past. In the crazed pursuit of unbridled development, nature is being exploited for the construction of roads and dams and other markers of "civilized living" without regard for the long-term consequences of such on the ecosystem and on other living beings.

Re-reading Psalm 104 from an Indigenous perspective is essential in a community where majority of Khasis now embrace the Christian faith. Such re-reading may inspire not only Indigenous Khasis, but us, to realize anew the vitality of Indigenous environmental ethics. The impact of colonial knowledge, with its sciences and technologies, has alienated us, modernized humans, from nature. If we are to have a future, we must once again reclaim our sacred relationship with Mother Earth and begin the important work of restoring the sacred groves. Hopefully, then, the deities and spirit guardians that have fled might feel welcomed once more to take up residence in the land and among the people.

Bibliography

Brueggemann, Walter. *The Land: Place as Gift, Promise, and Challenge in Biblical Faith*. Overtures to Biblical Theology. Philadelphia: Fortress Press, 1977.
Brueggemann, Walter, and William H. Bellinger Jr. *Psalms*. New Cambridge Bible Commentary. Cambridge: Cambridge University Press, 2014.
Gerstenberger, Erhard S. *Psalms, Part 2 and Lamentations*. The Forms of the Old Testament Literature 15. Grand Rapids: Eerdmans, 2001.
Gibson, William E. "Creation and Liberation as a Continuing Story." In *Eco-Justice—The Unfinished Journey*, 53–67. Albany: State University of New York Press, 2004.
———. "Eco-Justice: What Is It?" In *Eco-Justice—The Unfinished Journey*, 21–29. Albany: State University of New York Press, 2004.
Hujon, Janet. *Tales of Darkness and Light: Soso Tham's The Old Days of the Khasis*. Cambridge: Open Book, 2018.
Knight, George A. F. *Leviticus*. Philadelphia: Westminster, 1981.
Mawrie, Barnes L., SDB. *The Khasis and Their Natural Environment: A Study of the Eco-Consciousness and Eco-Spirituality of the Khasis*. Shillong: Vendrame Institute Publications, 2009.
Mawrie, H. O. *The Khasi Milieu*. New Delhi: Concept Publishing, 2010.
McCann, J. Clinton, Jr. "Psalms." In *The New Interpreter's Bible: A Commentary in Twelve Volumes*, edited by Leander E. Keck, 4:639–1280. Nashville: Abingdon, 1996.
Nongbri, Tiplut. "Culture and Biodiversity: Myths, Legends and the Conservation of Nature in the Hills of North-East India." *Indian Anthropologist* 36.1/2 (2006) 1–21.
Nongkynrih, A. K. "Changes in Beliefs about the Sacred Groves." *Religion and Society* 42.3 (1995) 60–63.
Pepper, David. *Eco-Socialism: From Deep Ecology to Social Justice*. London: Routledge, 1993.
Preuss, Horst Dietrich. *Old Testament Theology*. Vol. 1. Translated by Leo G. Perdue. Old Testament Library. Louisville: Westminster John Knox, 1995.

Resseguie, James. "Reader-Response Criticism and the Synoptic Gospel." *JAAR* 52 (1984) 307–24.

Rosenblatt, Louise Michelle. "Writing and Reading the Transactional Theory," Center for the Study of Reading, *Technical Report No. 416* (1998) 1–17.

Rosenblatt, Louise M. *The Reader, the Text, the Poem: The Transactional Theory of the Literary Work*. Carbondale: Southern Illinois University Press 1978.

Rymbai, R.T. "The Traditional Ecological Concepts of the Khasi-Pnars." *Religion and Society* 42.3 (1995) 48–54.

Tham, Soso. *Ki Sngi Barim U Hynniewtrep*. Shillong: All Rights Reserved, 1960.

War, Juanita "The Khasi Concept of Nature." *Religion and Society* 42.3 (1995) 55–59.

White, Rob. *Environmental Harm: An Eco-Justice Perspective*. Bristol, UK: Policy Press, 2013.

Part Two

Earth Rites

Ritual Transgressions and Transformations

4

On Earth as in Heaven

*The Earth in the Podong Leitourgia
of the Post-Human Commune*

FERDINAND ANNO

SOME YEARS AGO, IN *Frontiers of Asian Theology*, R. S. Sugirtharajah cited the rise of subaltern theologies and the emergence of extra-textual hermeneutics as two of the reasons for the irruption of creativity in the Asian theological scene.[1] This came as a new challenge to the classical liberationist "praxis"[2] direction pursued in most "third world" theologizing—a development that made the Asian region a hospitable ground for theological cross-pollination and hybridization.[3]

---

1. See Sugirtharajah, *Frontiers of Asian Theology*.

2. Bevans labeled as "praxis" theologies those that were influenced or are following the hermeneutical principles of Latin American Liberation Theology, the same theological genre named by David Tracy as "eschatological" theologies (*Models of Contextual Theology*, 70–87; see Tracy, *Blessed Rage for Order*, 240–50).

3. "Hybridization" as a methodological concept was introduced by several papers presented during the 1998 third assembly of the Congress of Asian Theologians held in Bangalore, India. One observer of theologizing in Asia also coined a new name for this new mode of theological reflection: synthetic theology. See Bevans, *Models of Contextual Theology*, 88–102.

One of Sugirtharajah's points of reference was the rising voices of Indigenous peoples in Asia. These rising voices included those from South and Northeast India, Japan, Taiwan, the Philippines, Indonesia, Australia, and the Pacific Islands. Proceeding from a theological platform that they share with mainstream Asian theologizing, theologians from Indigenous communities started to add another layer to the epistemological shift. From the typical liberationist "salvation-to-liberation" shift, Asian Indigenous theologies have moved toward the "less anthropocentric" notion of what I call "soil-talk."[4] This zoe-centric "soil-talk" may not be new, especially with the earlier rise of eco-feminism in Asian feminist theologies, but the departure point of Indigenous Asian peoples' "soil-talk" lies in its unique spatio-centric grasp of Indigenous peoples' realities and experiences of historical, political, social, and cultural mass marginalization and, more importantly, the reality of their existential negation[5] if they are not always already being programmed for genocidal cultural annihilation—as in the cases of Papua, the Philippines, Northeast India, and Indo-China where resistance is particularly strong.

This essay locates itself in the nexus of Indigenous theological reflection, cultural resistance studies, ritual studies, liberation anthropology, and resistance liturgics. It examines a "marginal" but essential component of an Indigenous religious ritual being performed, and how this rite is being reinterpreted to construct a new emancipatory mythography for the communities of resistance among the Igorots of the Cordillera Region in the Philippines, where this author is currently located.

Christianization and the Fleeing of the Gods

The Christianization of the Cordillera Region north of Luzon in the Philippine archipelago beginning with the Spanish takeover of the islands in 1521 brought about a coloniality that effectively de-indigenized the Igorot's regard for the land. Igorot, or *Y-gollotes*, meaning, "people from the mountain" is the collective name for the more or less 1.5 million people from at least eight major ethnolinguistic groups that populate the mountain region.[6] This

---

4. "Tribal" (Northeast India) and aboriginal (Australia) theologies consider space or the earth as the alpha and omega of their theological reflection. See Longchar, "Tribal Theology" and Lilburne, "Land and Rainbow Spirit Theology."

5. The Indigenous Australians being counted with the flora and fauna, plants and animals instead of human beings is enshrined in the colonial *Terra Nullius* doctrine, i.e., of the Australian continent as an empty land. See Miller and Cooper, *Gentle Warrior*.

6. "Igorot" (y-gollotes = from the mountains) is the collective name for all the ethnolinguistic groups in the Cordillera region of the Philippines. The y-gollotes

coloniality led to the desacralization of Ina-*Daga* (Mother Earth) and, consequently, to her wanton exploitation by the colonial government.

Christianization helped desacralize what was otherwise regarded as sacred earth. It pointed to a transcendent god who alone is holy and put the human at the top of a radically un-ecological pyramid. Christians marked themselves as separate from this ecological pyramid, at the same time putting man (gendering intended) atop it to exercise dominion over the earth and all that dwell therein. The "worship of the one true God" who resided outside the domain of creation in time provided a theological warrant to the conquest, i.e., rape and plunder, of the earth.[7] As soon as radical monotheism expunged the spirits and divinities off the face of the earth, the human figure took center stage and assumed "dominion over the fish of the sea and the birds of the air and over every living creature that moves on the ground" (Gen 1:28d). The human "filled the earth and subdued it" (28c). The worship of the "one-true God" of Hebraic, Judaeo-Christian, and other radical monotheistic communities proved destructive to the web of life in that it effectively enshrined the narrative of the androcentric empire in the sacred book of Judaeo-Christianity.

Christianity's missionization and colonial indoctrination of the mind and soul of the Igorot may not have gone deep into the native's psyche, but the former was able to put up cultural institutions and political warrants for the enforcement of the exploitative colonialist agenda. The triumph of these cultural and political institutions led to, in the words of a Bago-Igorot elder, "the fleeing of the gods and spirits"—effectively disenchanting *Ina-Daga*.[8] The planting of the *podong* (reed stick), an Igorot rite that this essay would expound on transgresses and subverts the Judaeo-Christian pyramid and reimagines for people a radically egalitarian ecosystem. In this ecosystem, humans become who they are: members of the earth community, only one citizen-species among many in the post-human commune.

---

include the Kankanaey, Ibaloi, Ifugao, Bontoc, Itneg, Kalinga, Isneg, Bago, Bugkalot groups. The y-Kalinga and the y-Bontoc of Mt. Province and Kalinga were the groups and tribes that were affected directly by the Chico River Basin Dam Project in the 70s. The primary issue for the Itnegs in Abra province was logging by Cellophil Corporation while the Kankanaeys and Ibalois of Benguet struggled against mining especially its later form in open-pit mining.

7. This, in Harvey Cox's thesis, has its genesis in the secularization that evolved as a result of the Hebraic faith and its heir in Judaeo-Christianity's radical monotheism and "disenchantment of nature," "desacralization of politics" and "deconsecration of values" (Cox, *The Secular City*, 17–37).

8. These words by a Bago-Igorot elder were sourced from transcriptions in Hornedo, *The Favor of the Gods*.

Let me proceed with my discussion with a brief account of one story that gave birth to the rites of the earth's insurrection: the Igorot resistance against the Chico River Basin Project.

And the Earth and the *Pangats* Said, "No!"

On February 3, 1980, a dialogue between Kalinga *pangats* (chieftains) and officials of the National Power Corporation (NPC) took place in Itogon, Benguet, Philippines. This dialogue was in relation to the Philippine government's proposal to build at least four dams at the Chico River Basin that will include submerging the ancestral lands of the Igorots from Sadanga in the Mountain Province to Pasil in Kalinga.[9] After three-hours of tense discussion between the Kalinga *pangats* (tribal leaders) and the NPC president, the *pangats* "boarded the hired Dangwa bus" and as they "leave the NPC compound, they burst into a proud singing of their *salidummay* (an Indigenous folk song). It is the opposition *salidummay*."[10]

Not long after this dialogue on April 24, 1980, Ama Macli-ing Dulag, the leader of the Kalinga *pangats* who were in that meeting was assassinated by state forces. The whole Cordillera region wept and hailed him as a martyr of the Igorot struggle for self-determination. In 1984, on the fourth annual commemoration of Ama Macli-ing's martyrdom, the Indigenous groups and organizations that organized the event called for the establishment of an alliance committed to the cause that Ama Macli-ing fought for. The Cordillera Peoples' Alliance (CPA) was officially launched in June 1984 in a congress of 150 delegates from 27 grassroots-based Indigenous peoples' organizations. The charter members included Indigenous *pangats* and *papangoens* (leaders) and activists who were leading the region-wide resistance against the World Bank-funded Chico dam projects and commercial logging operations in Abra province and other parts of the region. The CPA, in its founding papers, has committed itself to promoting the defense of Indigenous peoples' rights, human rights, social justice, and national freedom and democracy.[11]

As signified in the transcription above, the resolution to pursue the Cordillera people's agenda in higher forms of struggle also found expression in

---

9. Carino, *The Chico River Basin*, 12.

10. The *salidummay*, a music ditty of the Igorots, together with the *gangsa* (gong ensemble) are representative of Igorot culture and spirituality. See Carino, *The Chico River*, 25.

11. Cordillera Peoples Alliance. Archives (cpaphils.org/about%20us%20main.html).

the re-airing of the *salidummay* and the performance of their everyday rites as songs and rites of resistance. The *salidummay* that celebrates the life, love, and work of the Igorot has effectively transformed the every-day "liturgies" of the Igorot into liturgies of resistance. The rites that mark the beginnings and endings of days and the cycles in the life and work of the Igorot have linked the god and the spirits with the Igorot struggle for self-determination and the defense of their *poon ti pagbiagan* (source of life),[12] i.e., the earth as embodied in what Igorots consider as their ancestral lands.

This is the context of an Indigenous ritual that this essay expounds on: the Indigenous people's resistance in the Cordillera Region of the Philippines.

The *Podong* Rite, Stories of Resistance, and the Renaissance of Igorot: A Geotheological and Anthropological Self-Understanding

A just egalitarian ecosystem is radically embedded in the consciousness, lifeways, and traditions of the Igorot. One Ifugao-Igorot story narrates that humanity emerged from reeds and evolved into a people through their rising up against hideous beasts and monsters that prowled their primeval habitat. The story goes that Lumauig, the great god of the mountain region (the *cordilleras*), came down from heaven and gathered in bundles the *podong* (reeds) that were trampled upon by beasts. Lumauig put them in his *kayabang* (large round-shaped bamboo backpack slung and carried from the head) as he climbed Mount Polis. At the mountain summit, Lumauig broke these reeds into halves and scattered them all over the world and, in a loud powerful voice that reverberated throughout the world, commanded: rise and speak! And lo, the reeds immediately became people!

Stories of beginnings like the above are now being revisited in Igorot communities of resistance. These mytho-narratives and their ritualizations provide an ecotheological basis to both their cosmological vision and anthropological (reed-to-people) self-understanding. These myths also provide the Igorots a lens with which to interrogate the politics of development aggression and its cultural Trojan horses. From these mythological lenses, they see the aggression of the current neoliberal order as a reincarnation of the hideous beasts and monsters of their primeval past and see their becoming and their peoplehood in their collective rising against such. The Igorot

---

12. "*Poon ti pagbiagan*" is a line from *Ti Daga Nagtaudan* (The Earth of our Beginning), a song penned and performed by the cultural guerillas of the *Dap-ayan ti Kultura ti Kordilyera*, the cultural arm of the CPA.

story of the peopling of the earth re-presents humans as being constituted out of the earth's rising against beasts and monsters on the promptings of Lumauig, the mountain god. The Ama Macli-ing Dulag saga, on one hand, regarded the earth as the very womb from where life sprang. Both have con-texts. The first (Ifugao story) is the earth's struggle with "ugly monsters and hideous animals" that trample on reeds, and the second (Ama Macli-ing), the Igorot communities' struggle against monstrous dam projects that desecrate their ancient burial grounds and the abode of both ancestral and nature spirits. It was the groans and struggles of the earth, the intervention of the gods, and the emergence of the human being that appear to be the primary elements in these scenarios.

In the village rituals that the *podong* represents, everything is grounded in "the earth and sky."[13] Like the Igorots' Northeast Indian and Australian counterparts, the "tribals" and the Aborigines, respectively, what primarily defines reality for the Igorot is space and not time.[14] This is what is being affirmed in an Igorot ritual that this essay presents as the metaphorical, material, and the "liturgical" composite of the mythos of Igorot life, struggles, hopes, and aspirations: the *podong* rite.

A "One-Day" Tale of the *Podong* Rite

It was late afternoon, and we were winding up a day spent with the villagers. This was in Ucab, Itogon, Benguet, an Ibaloi village, at a time when the communities in that highland municipality were struggling against the onslaught of open-pit mining by the Benguet Corporation. We were having conversations with some villagers on how their alternative small-scale mining is done and the dangers it presents every time a person goes into the holes. As we were concluding our conversation, one of our male hosts walked toward the hillside and unsheathing his machete, cut some stalks of *runo* (a common reed variety) and knotted their leafy ends. After a while, we broke up for self-care. Our group came back to that part of the village later that same day at dusk to join in a community feast. A big crowd was gathered. In contrast to the ghostly silence all day, save for the noises of playing children, the village, suddenly, was teeming with life. Surveying the crowd and the environs, I saw in a relatively prominent corner the knotted *runo* sticks cut a few hours earlier, planted on the ground

---

13. "Earth and sky" is a phraseology drawn from the title of a multi-volume ethnographic study on the peoples of the Cordillera region (CSG, *The Igorots*).

14. Lilburne, *Land and Rainbow Spirit Theology*, 101–2.

with several people leisurely squatting nearby. They were the *podong* sticks (knotted stick leaves).

The planting of the *podong* sticks either at the entrance of the village or at the assembly site may not be visibly a prominent feature in the entirety of the ritual performance, but the *podong* rite is always essential to the ritual's efficacy. When one sees a *podong* stick stuck in the ground, it means that a ritual act is being performed in the place and everyone in the village is expected to respond and act accordingly. Several other ethnolinguistic groups in the mountain region practice the same. The Y-Bontoc called this the *pochong* rite.

The planting of the *podong* sticks is accompanied by prayers bidding everyone, both seen and unseen, to look after the houses, gardens, swidden farms, livestock, properties, and all that the villagers have left for the gathering. The standing *podong* sticks give the assurance that all dwellings are under divine protection and that no property will be trespassed upon throughout the duration of the ritual performance. Any infringements on those under the watch of *Kabunian*[15] and/or the spirits will have to suffer the wrath of the spirits.

The *podong* sticks also provide the passageway through which the ancestral spirits come by to commune with the living. It is this communion of the living, the ancestral spirits, the earth, and all that dwell therein (especially nature spirits) that calls on people and every living being to observe solemnity. When the *podong* sticks are standing, the whole earth and all of life rest. Re-introducing the *podong* in context, and in this case, the context of the continuing Igorot struggle against development aggression, emphasizes the significance of the rite in the development of a spirituality of struggle among Cordillerans. When done or performed on mining grounds, *podong* planting constitutes an act of resistance. The *podong* signals the message that the lands are the ancestors,' and they enjoy God's protection.

Through the lens of the *podong* rite, large-scale mining and other extractive industries in the area are an abominable activity. They do not only siphon the life out of mountains to feed the unfettered greed of moneymen, but they also trespass on sacred grounds populated by spirits and destroy the very future that the Igorots are desperately securing for themselves and their communities' survival. The *podong* stick says that you do not disembowel the earth for the filthy rich few to have something to display or hide in their vaults. It says in a powerfully symbolic way that "the value of the only place

---

15. Or God in the Christian monotheistic reinterpretation of the *Kabunian* theological tradition, but *Kabunian* may be a generic name for gods and spirits, as in a class, or as further proposed by Scott, a name for the abode of the gods. See Scott, *On the Cordillera*, 142.

[where Igorots] live, and the water that [they] need to survive does not compare to gold. [The Igorots] are not going to eat gold, [they are not going to] bathe with gold, [they are not going to] drink gold."[16] Mining, insofar as the traditional Igorot is concerned, is not supposed to exceed what the community needs for its basic sustenance. Beyond what they need, writes W. Henry Scott, "the Igorot does not see any need to secure any gold."[17] There is nothing more valuable to the Igorot than the blessing that is land.

The Podong Rite Re-Sacralizes the Profaned Earth

An ordinary grass variety that grows everywhere in the tropics, the *runo* sticks transform the ordinary into something extraordinary. The *podong* rite resurfaces the sacred in profane space and time. *Kabunian* and all the ancestral and nature spirits are with the living in feasts of life. The *abong* or the *dap-ay* (a gathering place for village councils) or the spaces where the *sab-ong* and *podong* sticks stand claim all the surrounding spaces and declare them holy. The land to the Igorot is inherently sacred and ritual performances like the *podong* are occasions for the public affirmation of this reality. But given the current state of Igorot lands, the ritual planting of *podong* sticks appears to have lost its meaning and power. The Igorots' ancestral lands, like those of the open pit mining-ravaged mountains of Itogon, seemed to have lost their aura of divinity. The rivers that run through cracks and vales that used to be sources of freshwater fish are now deposits of mine tailings. The bare mountains and drying rivers are effectively disenchanted. The gods and spirits are already de-robed of their mystical forest cover.

Yet, the *podong* stuck on the ground continues to serve as a rite of resistance. It reclaims and celebrates an ancient reality constructed by a cultic relationship between the earth and her tillers, a relationship of mutual care, a mutuality designed to sustain life and, insofar as local priests or shamans are concerned, a relationship designed in the mind of divinity. The current neo-liberal order calls for an economy that relies heavily on the exploitation of the earth and its resources. It is thus necessary for big corporations, bureaucrat capitalists, and their cultural agents to "manufacture people's consent"[18] by all means, including through fascist repression and militarization. Cultural agencies, including religious groups, are being co-opted for the purpose of softening resistance and manufacturing consent. Christian revivalism, with its American frontier "this-world-is-not-my-home"

16. Rosa, *Gold Fever*.
17. Scott, *On the Cordillera*, 154ff.
18. Chomsky and Herman, *Manufacturing Consent*.

gospel, has been negating and disenchanting the non-human environment, while at the same time, with a stroke of genius, tapping into Indigenous peoples' primal spirituality to sell itself as a religious alternative,[19] combining Indigenous spontaneous singing, dancing, dreams, visions, and trances with revivalist piety and ritual expressions. In this light, to plant the *podong* sticks in a rite is to declare as living and pulsating the faith affirmation that the earth is sacred and that it is *Kabunian*'s and the spirits,' not the humans' property to trespass and exploit as they please. We see this as a faith tradition that corresponds with the Hebraic tradition of theophanic experiences in sacred spaces (in contrast to how this biblical tradition is typically appropriated in the evangelical strand of Euro-American Christianity). The land, the mountains are "where bushes burn." They reveal the face of divinity and they call for sandals to be taken off. The *podong* sticks cry out, "Stay off the sacred!"

The *Podong* as the Earth Re-Ordering the Earth Community

The planting of the *podong* signals a movement from separation to communion. In the rite, people designate a ritual time for communal activity separate from their everyday engagements like farm work, house and domestic chores, and various preoccupations. The occasion calls for communion, sharing, and the healing of relationships. When knotted and stuck on the ground, the *podong* signals a coming together of people as *communitas* where social differentiations are set aside.[20] "Textually" and formally, the *podong* rite is essentially akin to the Eucharistic meal of Christians. The feast of life of Christian eschatology is something prefigured in these "little feasts" of life that the *podong* sticks signal.

In view of the cultural aggression of the manufacturers of consent where Indigenous peoples are set against each other in an assortment of divide-and-rule schemes, the planting of the *podong* sticks comes as an act of resistance. The very rite declares that a community bond is stronger than the enticements of money, fame, and power, and that Indigenous communities can be united in solidarity in upholding their rights to their ancestral lands and to self-determination. The contemporary politics of development

---

19. Based on Harvey Cox's thesis regarding the convergences between Pentecostal and Indigenous spiritualities. See Cox, *Fire from Heaven*.

20. Concepts and definitions borrowed from cultural anthropologists such as Victor Turner, and Bobby Alexander. See Turner, *The Ritual Process*, and Alexander, *Victor Turner Revisited*.

divide. Using patronage politics, the developmentalist dispensation marginalizes the voices of many; it breeds its partisan players from among the Indigenous populations by undermining their Indigenous political processes. Moreover, with a stroke of sophistication, not unlike the American colonialist way of inserting themselves into the socio-cultural fabric of Cordillerans under the guise of [the inevitability of] culture change, the cultural architects of big business have gone into cultural re-engineering programs designed to destroy the communities' resistance, coming via Western-oriented developmentalist public education, popular education, and Christian religious education and spiritual formation, such programs that were aimed at erasing the Igorot's Indigenous memory and identity. These cultural Trojan horses were aimed at disorienting people away from their Indigeneity and spirituality toward submission. The intent of big business is to employ cultural and political barriers to foil various community attempts to come together in a pan-Cordilleran commune.

Igorots, on the other hand, believe that the *podong* sticks are a gateway through which ancestral spirits come to commune with the living. The *podong* thus pushes further the expanse of people's communal self-understanding. In this rite, all creatures are reminded of their sharing the land and this life with ancestral spirits and that they have to relate with them in filial reverence. It is a reminder that the Igorot people's security lies not in those whose agenda is to harm and sever their culto-spiritual relationship with the earth but in the religious and proper observance of the rites of radical connectivity with the earth.

The *Podong* Rite Calls for a Jubilee for the Earth and All that Dwell Therein

In Igorot cosmology, the land is a living creative organism that shares the biological characteristics of other living creatures. If the human, the water buffalo, and other work animals tire, so does the land. The earth needs rest, and so do its tillers. Even the gods and spirits need rest. In other words, the *podong* calls for the relief of the land and all that dwell therein. Among Northern Kankanaeys and y-Bontocs, the planting of *podong* sticks at the entrance of villages signals the *tengao*, a day of rest for everyone and every creature. The call to rest is so thorough that no one is allowed entry to or exit from the village throughout the duration of the *tengao*. This is *cultus*, i.e., mutual care, at its highest symbolic form. Not unlike the ancient Hebrews who were summoned time and again by their judges and prophets to reorder their lives according to their *cultus*, the Igorots' reason for being takes its cues from the people's *cultus*. The *tengao* calls for the resting of the land. It is incumbent upon the tiller to ensure that the land is at rest. This is the Igorot's part in its cultic relationship with the land. The *podong* serves to remind the Igorot tillers of their part in the covenant.

The whole Gran Cordillera chain of mountains is already partitioned by applications from multinational corporations involved in large-scale mining, logging, hydro-electric, coal, and geothermal, including pharmaceutical and eco-tourist, extractive industries. The Cordillera chain of mountains is being juiced and eviscerated to its death. With the Mining Act of 1995, the pace of "development" activities further intensified leaving the mountains and their tillers without a real experience of rest.

One story among the Amburayan Kankanaeys otherwise known as Bago-Igorots says that the continuous denuding of their mountain abodes made the gods and spirits flee—leaving their balding mountains devoid of divine presence.[21] As a result, the lands and communities living under the shadows of these mountains have been left unprotected by the gods and the spirits. This state of abandonment effectively sentenced the *papattayan*s (sacrificial altars) of the foothills to their death. When the gods and the spirits have flown, the altars lay idle and the religion and culture surrounding them die.

The *Podong* Rite and the Igorot "Sabbath" as Liturgical Commencement of a People's Struggle

The *podong* sticks give assurance to people that everything and everyone is protected wherever they are, be it in homes or in open spaces, in fields, or in the mountains. Divinity fails not in its part in the "trinitarian" tiller-land-divinity *cultus*. This concept is something theologically profound in that divinity reciprocates cultic observance related to the resting of the land and the cessation of activity required in the praxis of resting. The *tengao* moment speaks of the right of the living and pulsating being that is the land to take her deserved rest; and of that same right accorded to all that dwell in the land, too. To the *Y-Bontocs*, any violation of the *tengao* moment requires penalty or punishment.[22] The *tengao*, theologically, is God's moment, and it is a moment of faith and confidence in God's providence and protective presence; it comes as the land and its people affirm, observe, and celebrate their *Sabbath*. In the Christian context, the *Sabbath* as a moment of rest also means an active moment of "resting" for those that/who need relief and release. Similarly, in

21. Hornedo, *The Favor of the Gods*.
22. Cawed, *The Culture of the Bontoc Igorots*, 32.

Hebraic Mosaic and prophetic language, the Sabbath or *tengao* is integral to the narrative of release, jubilee, re-creation, and rest.

In the planting of the *podong* sticks, the Igorot announces rest to those that continue to bear the brunt of development aggression. This also has a profound political translation in the sense that resting, given the contemporary realities in the Cordilleras, may mean needing to stop the machines of plunder even at the risk of facing the muzzles of state's guns. This means that the tengao or "resting" as informed by the podong tradition also means, in Christian lingo (Mk 2:27), a moment of spiritual enlightenment and healing, political empowerment, physical enablement, and social mobilization (Lk 4: 18–19) of the earth's cultic partner, the Igorot, in the service of the earth and all that dwell therein.

There is an emancipatory dimension in the *tengao* when Igorots finally seize its liberative potential via the furthering of the *tengao*'s "liturgical" logic. Rituals are stories of beginnings. And stories of beginnings, most often, according to the "zoe-sophianic" musings of Kim Yong Bok are stories of liberation.[23] There is, thus, a mystical political connection between "resting" and the "struggle for liberation."

The *Podong*, the People's Struggle, and the Evolution of a Post-Androcentric Earth Commune

A marginal but essential feature of Igorot rites, the *podong* ritual may not invite much attention in the literature on people's resistance, given that people's resistance discourse in the Philippines tend to dwell more on the directly political and less on the cultural and spiritual aspects. But there is always potentiality in the margins. Not unlike the restive social peripheries, ritual margins are equally packed with revelatory insights and power. It takes a resistance semiotic or hermeneutic of Indigenous traditions to surface the emancipatory potential of the *podong* rite. Any Igorot in the struggle needs to have this resistance semiotic sense.

Secondly, the *podong* may be marginal but it is a necessary prelude to the ritual event. Indeed, to affirm the sacredness of the land, to reclaim the right of mountains and their people to take rest, to invite people and the spirits together in a feast of life, and to invoke God's protection is not just to constitute

---

23. Kim Yong Bok is one of the more prominent articulators of the South Korean *Minjung* Theology and the founder of the Center for the Integral Study of Life. This was drawn from an unpublished paper presented in 2013 in a political camp at Agape Centro Ecumenico in Prali, Italy.

a ritual of reversal[24] but, more significantly, it serves to commence a life-rite of struggle. The Igorot spirituality of struggle needs to draw more from its Indigenous religious traditions and cosmo-visions which, as we have seen in this discussion, are just as radical as, if not more so than, any of the social visions and programs that work for change and transformation.

In the foregoing context of the contemporary praxis of Indigenous people's struggle in the Cordilleras, I want to also surface the "internal critique" articulated by Indigenous Asian Feminist theologians that perceive Indigenous theologies (like the one being discussed in this essay) as being androcentric.[25] These critiques however have yet to be offered in practical ways from their theoretical rendition by women academic activists. In the case of the Y-Kalinga, Y-Bontoc, and Y-Benguet Igorots, the case for the evolution of a more inclusive commune has, in fact, already been made. The Igorot resistance to the Chico Dam (1980s) and the Itogon open-pit mines (1990s) have opened a new path and direction to the evolution of indigeneity among the Igorots. The *ator*, or *abong* or *dap-ay* is no longer solely the domain of the *pangat/pangoen* (male elder)-led tribal warriors. It has increasingly expanded to include the women of the villages. The *tong-tongan* system, in effect, has grown inclusive.

These revolutionary political and cultural developments have to do with the frontline presence and militance of women in both the Y-Bontoc and Y-Kalinga struggles against the Chico River dam project in Kalinga and Bontoc, and the Benguet Corporation's open-pit mining in Itogon. Accounts of these struggles narrate of Y-Bontoc women confronting the company's project engineers naked (as a sign of protest) and later raiding the miner's camp and taking away all their non-food supplies. Women have also served on the frontlines of barricades and physically wrestled with police, military, and paramilitary enforcers. From its beginnings in 1984, the leadership of the pan-Cordillera Cordillera Peoples' Alliance, for example, has been led primarily by women. This may not seem to have a direct bearing on ritual and political leadership at the village level, but the implications are many. Warriorship for the Igorot ancestral lands is no longer the monopoly of men and boys. Women are equally at the forefront. Women are actively participating in decision-making. The *dap-ayan* and the *ator* where men and boys used to congregate to make decisions and prepare themselves for battle have been subtly breached by women's presence and voice.

---

24. Where the rites become a mere "sigh of the marginalized" as in catharsis, but where reversal is sought for in the concrete. See Schroter, "Rituals of Rebellion-Rebellion as Ritual."

25. Longkumer, "Not All Is Well."

The earth and her groaning have once more brought back women as equals. But what links the earth, women, and the *podong* rite are the very words of those naked women militants of Bontoc who dared the project engineers to "harm the womb from where you came."[26] The ritual planting of the *podong* may say the same, "we dare you to harm the earth from where you came." Set in this new narrative of resistance among Igorots, the *podong* rite as performed negates the geo-theologies and androcentric anthropologies of both profiteers and colonial Christianity. Succinctly put, the earth has reclaimed for the woman her rightful place in our ancestors' home.

On Earth as It Is in Heaven: A Conclusion

Back to the transcription that this study referred to above, i.e., the dialogue between the Kalinga leaders and the NPC where the Kalinga chieftains equated the dams with "death."[27] They saw the destruction of their ancestral lands as the death of everything: the earth, their culture, and their people.[28] They saw the aggression of the neo-liberal economic order as embodied in the development aggression they were facing as the termination of their existence. Their response was that they prefer dying in their own lands than accepting the government's offer of relocation.[29] They presented counterarguments to the NPC president's developmentalist arguments that spoke of how they live simply and sustainably with the land, thus:

> Our people object to the project because it destroys the good things we already have. You say people need light. But light is needed only at night! You say electricity is for education. Let those who study do their studying in the daylight. You mentioned transportation. If there is no gasoline, let the trucks stand by. But for us, life itself cannot wait. If you, in your search for good life, at the same time destroy life, we question it. We say that those who need electric light are not thinking of us who are bound to be destroyed. Or will the need for electric light be a sufficient reason for our own death?[30]

Such gut political discourse from the chieftains or *papangats* find radicalization in and through Indigenous rituals. The rituals of the

---

26. Kimberlie, "Remembering Mother Petra."
27. Carino, *The Chico River Basin*, 18.
28. Carino, *The Chico River Basin*, 19.
29. Carino, *The Chico River Basin*, 18.
30. Carino, *The Chico River Basin*, 18.

communities transcend whatever anthropocentric excess there is in the Igorot politics of resistance, effectively relocating the former within the realm of the Igorot cosmo-vision. This point was clearly articulated in these words by Ama Macli-ingDulag,

> Such arrogance to say that you own the land when you are owned by it! How can you own that which outlives you?[31]

The matrix of resistance was deduced from the very word of Ama Macli-ing inheres in the earth and sky and all that dwell therein. This is not a raw statement or a thought that was constructed on the spot. This is an articulation of an Indigenous and collective ecotheological consciousness that has evolved from the Igorots' daily communion with the earth and sky. In between this utterance and the Igorots' everyday communion with the earth and sky are community rituals like the *podong*. What the *podong* and the Igorots are affirming is that the earth owns us. The politics of resistance is about the earth as *poon ti biag* (from where all life began), the womb from where life sprang. This is where the *podong* intersects with Christian worship and its sacraments: when the *podong* becomes, in Christian lingo, an "outward sign of an inward grace." The liturgical surfaces when the ritual performance becomes a "trans-formance"[32] (transgressive, transformative, and formative performance) by a community that is called back to its *adamic* ("of the earth") self and perform the ritual as a rehearsal for what the people must live out and do as the earth's very own. But here, the "transformance" in Indigenous rites like the *podong* would mean more than what both the high and low churches' liturgical theologies suggest. The *podong* does not need to go through some mystical ejaculations or some artificially induced subjective divination. *Podong* planting literally and organically enfleshes the link that connects "heaven" and earth. Its planting in a rite affirms the synergy between the movement of the gods and the struggles of the margins, meaning, that the *podong* rite reminds Indigenous peoples that the struggle is not simply a "temporal" and "profane" pursuit as seen by outsiders, but one that was conceived in the very womb of divinity (i.e., *Kabunianic*). The peoples' struggle for self-determination is the struggle of gods and spirits, too, to reclaim the "trinitarian" divinity-land-tiller *cultus* of the ancients— "for the beauty of the earth." "On earth as it is in heaven"? This Christian prayer is best understood in the Indigenous geo-theological sense.

---

31. BMBF. *Dulag, Macli-ing.*

32. The concept of "transformance," i.e., ritual performance that transforms one from one status, identity, or situation to another was a concept developed by Schechner. See Schechner, *Performance Studies*.

Bibliography

Alexander, Bobby Chris. *Victor Turner Revisited: Ritual as Social Change.* AAR Academy Series 74. Atlanta: Scholars, 1991.

BMBF. *Macli-ing Dulag.* Quezon City: Bantayog ng Mga Bayani Foundation. http://www.bantayog.org/dulag-macli-ing/.

Carino, Joanna. *The Chico River Basin Development Project Case Study in National Development Policy: An Update.* Unpublished transcriptions of the 1980 NPC-Pangat Dialogues, 1987. http://docplayer.net/164787550-The-chico-river-basin-development-project-a-situation-report-joanna-carino-jessica-carifio-and-geoffrey-nettleton-introduction.html.

Cawed, Carmencita. *The Culture of the Bontoc Igorots.* Manila: MCS Enterprises, 1972.

Cordillera Peoples Alliance Website. Archives. cpaphils.org/about%20us%20main.html.

Cordillera Schools Group. *The Igorots: People Who Daily Touch Earth and Sky.* Baguio City: Cordillera Schools Group, 1987.

Cox, Harvey. *Fire from Heaven: The Rise of Pentecostal Spirituality and the Reshaping of Religion in the Twenty-First Century.* London: Cassel, 1996.

———. *The Secular City: A Celebration of its Liberties and An Invitation to its Disciplines.* New York: Macmillan, 1966.

DKK. *Ti Daga Nagtaudan.* Baguio City: Dap-ayan ti Kultura ti Kordileyera. https://www.youtube.com/watch?v=HRvNcZTys94.

Herman, Edward, and Noam Chomsky. *Manufacturing Consent: The Political Economy of the Mass Media.* New York: Pantheon, 1988.

Hornedo, Florentino. *The Favor of the Gods: Essays in Filipino Religious Thought and Behavior.* Manila: University of Sto. Tomas Publishing House, 2001.

Lilburne, Geoffrey, "Land and Rainbow Spirit Theology: An Australian Method in Tribal Theology." In *In Search of Identity and Tribal Theology: A Tribute to Dr. Renthy Keitzar*, edited by A. Wati Longchar, 101–6. Jorhat: Tribal Study Center, 2001.

Longchar, A. Wati. "Tribal Theology: Issues, Method and Perspectives." In *In Search of Identity and Tribal Theology: A Tribute to Dr. Renthy Keitzar*, edited by A. Wati Longchar, 44–56. Jorhat: Tribal Study Center, 2001.

Longkumer, Atolah. "Not All Is Well in My Ancestors' Home: An Indigenous Theology of Internal Critique." *Ecumenical Review* 62 (2010) 406–10.

Rosa, Magali Rey. *Gold Fever Documentaries.* DVD, 2013. http://www.goldfevermovie.com/takeaction.

Scott, W. Henry. *On the Cordillera: A Look at the Peoples and Cultures of the Mountain Province.* Manila: MCS Enterprises, 1966.

Quitasol, Kimberlie. "Remembering Mother Petra, Bontoc Warrior." *Inquirer.Net*, April 30, 2019. https://newsinfo.inquirer.net/996382/remembering-mother-petra-bontoc-warrior.

Schechner, Richard. *Performance Studies: An Introduction.* London: Routledge, 2002.

Schroter, Sussane. "Rituals of Rebellion-Rebellion as Ritual: A Theory Reconsidered." In *The Dynamics of Changing Ritual*, edited by J. K. Kreinarth et al., 41–57. Oxford: Peterlang, 2004.

Turner, Victor. *The Ritual Process: Structure and Anti-Structure.* London: Routledge & Kegan Paul, 1969.

Van Gennep, Arnold. *The Rites of Passage.* Translated by Monika B. Vizedom and Gabrielle L. Caffee. Chicago: University of Chicago Press, 1960.

5

Eleele Interrupts the Eden Wedding

From Mother Earth to Mistress[1]

Faafetai Aiava

This essay operates within a threefold premise. First, that creation narratives offer particular insights into a given society and are highly treasured by its people whether in Palestine or in the Pacific. Secondly, that Indigenous creation stories can be read alongside the Christian narrative not as conflicting, as if the latter is divinely inspired and the former is not, but as complementary, expressions of the same God. Thirdly, as with many traditional customs and myths, none are laid out as strict manuals of how things ought to be observed for all time. This elusive nature of tradition and meaning suggests that even the most traditional of societies evolve. I put this forth as typical housekeeping etiquette and as an early disclaimer for what lies ahead. My intent is that it be treated as a foundation (think: preamble) for the overall discussion to follow.

This work comprises a ceremonial rearrangement of the second creation account (Gen 2:18–24) based on a skit that was performed through the perspective of Eleele (lit. dirt)—a character from one of Samoa's creation accounts. This rearrangement warranted another look at the suppressed

---

1. I am indebted to the help of Jewish scholar and colleague, Dr. Kathryn Imray, for her invaluable time and feedback put into this manuscript. The remaining errors are my own.

voice of the land within the text. While there are many ecological challenges in the Pacific worth investigating, the scope of this essay is limited to the problem of disinterest in these challenges and the debilitating legacy that it breeds. I argue that denial of our responsibilities to Eleele and her ongoing mistreatment as an unwanted mistress stems from a deeper misconception that she is not a living being. This problematic mindset will be critiqued as one of the leading factors behind the continuing depersonalization of Earth whereby what was once intimate to our Pacific worldviews has been dissolved into a fling, or what was once "source" has become "resource." Drawing from one of Samoa's creation narratives, I offer an alternative view about our relationship with creation and why discernment and radical engagement is no longer an option.

The offering here is divided in response to the acronym DARE (Discernment and Radical Engagement), an overarching theme highlighted by the Council for World Mission's international forums for which an earlier version of this essay was presented. In the *Dare to Discern* section I offer theological musings on the notion of "discernment" and God's overall creative work in both Genesis 1 and 2:18–24 (the creation of Eve in the garden of Eden). Here, I push the boundaries of discernment from an exercise in judgment to one of envisioning possibilities. In the *Dare to be Radical* section, I discuss the character of Eleele who is transplanted from one story (Samoan) into another (the Genesis creation story) as a thought provocation. This discussion does not mean radical in the sense of promoting the dreaded "eisegesis" that was forbidden in my formal theological training (although, if ever, I will not deny this accusation). "Radical," as it is used here, refers to the transgressive act of individuals speaking when they are not expected to and in places where they are not invited. In the *Dare to Engage* section, I address "engagement" not only in its external expression of inclusiveness and embrace, but also as having the inner courage to dare to become vulnerable. While many biblical stories have been re-engaged from the perspective of the marginalized and the less privileged, an issue that is seldom dealt with is the self-incriminating nature of reading texts in this way. I argue that allowing the self to become vulnerable when engaging texts not only helps us recognize the seriousness of a given issue, but also challenges readers to take up our shared responsibilities with those victimized in texts.

For the sake of clarity and cross-referencing, it is necessary for readers to familiarize themselves with the original text (Gen 2:18–24) before reading the dramatic dialogue inserted below.[2] The following skit was performed

---

2. A vote of thanks is in order to Craig Masaniai, Leinamau Seru, Ben Wea and the Late. Allan Walter who kindly agreed to perform the dramatic dialogue.

during worship by members of my Ecotheology course at Pacific Theological College in Fiji (October 2018).[3] My assigned passage according to the lectionary was the Genesis text (2:18–24) but instead of offering a homily, I wanted to find an alternative way to preach where it was not a monologue but a conversation. One of the greatest difficulties I faced in trying to produce an inclusive dialogue was that in the original text, only God and Adam spoke. The introduction of Eleele, a Gaia-like character from one of Samoa's creation accounts, provided me with an opportunity to combine pedagogy, or the lesson I had planned on Norman Habel's discussion of ecological voices, and the liturgy that was assigned to me.[4] Though the skit was initially written by me, the fruitful class discussions that followed inspired this essay to pay closer attention to those voices that have been silenced on all fronts, namely, in worship, in the halls of academia, and in the Bible itself.

Eleele

Officiating Minister (OM): Welcome all creatures of the garden. Gather around, for today is a very special day for Adam. It occurred to me after making all animals and living creatures, that it is not good for the man to be alone. I will make a helper suitable for him.

The rib is removed, and Eve is made. Adam wakes up.

Adam: Wow, beautiful . . . this at last is the bone of my bones and flesh of my flesh; she shall be called "woman," for she was taken out of me.

Eleele: Um . . . excuse me . . . can I say something?

OM: I am sorry Eleele; this is not that kind of service. But since you have our attention, please make it quick.

Eleele: Thank you, I have a question for Adam, if she is the bone of your bones, and flesh of your flesh—very romantic

---

3. The manner in which this skit has been coupled with the Genesis text resonates with Reuven Hammer's explanation of the rabbinic use of the Midrash together with Scripture. In his view the method of midrash explores "the possibility of adding meaning, of opening up texts, of probing the depth and the breadth of a text, of investing it with flexibility, of allowing it to fit the times without abandoning truth and simple meaning." Hammer, *The Classic Midrash*, 42.

4. Norman Habel is an Australian biblical scholar and key contributor to the *Earth Bible* Series (2000–2002) and its revival in 2011 as the *Earth Bible Commentary* series. Throughout the series, Habel has called for a major rethinking of the Earth within the context of the Bible.

vows by the way—where does that leave me? Were you not formed from my belly?

Eve: Adam, is she your mother? This is not a good way to introduce me to my future mother-in-law.

Adam: [asks OM] Can we continue with the service, please? I don't remember inviting her.

Eve: Wait not yet. Adam? Is she your ex? Let me check how many ribs you have left.

Eleele: [crying] You are right, I was not invited. I mean, how can I be a guest where I am the host? It is you who are the ones invited to the place in which you now stand.

OM: Alright, Eleele, if you have a valid reason to object to this union, speak now or forever hold your peace!

Eleele: What God has joined together, let no one put asunder, including me. My humble plea is this, as you begin your journey together, remember me. When you grow and multiply, be kind to me and I will continue to provide for your offspring and record their stories. Exploit my body and I become dry and infertile or consumed by oceans; your children and all living creatures will go hungry while my suffering becomes theirs. To my Son, Adam, Eve is not your subordinate; her name refers to life, something that only she and I have been blessed to conceive. Treat her with the same respect as you would me. For you are the bone of my bone and the flesh of my flesh; I shall call you both *tino*, which means family and body, because you were taken out of mine. This marriage is, therefore, the unification of all of our families, both human and non-human.

Eve: [Whispering to Adam] I like her, she sounds intelligent.

Adam: Ssshhh woman! I get it!

OM: Citizens of Eden, when a man leaves his father and mother and is united to his wife, the many tino become one flesh. On your behalf, I sincerely thank the tino of Adam and Eve for her blessings. For future weddings, we will try and make sure we invite the family members to say something.

Dare to Discern

This dramatized rearrangement of Genesis 2:18–24, especially the intrusion of the Samoan character of Eleele, is certainly not part of our collective memory as Christians. At the one end, the skit offers creative speculation designed for entertainment purposes. At the other, it is a syncretistic rearrangement of the story of creation with what some may consider as heretical leanings. The thought reflection here looks for a place in the middle, but accepts whatever radical end emerges. The irony here is that in the original story, the land of Eden acts as the theatre in which God's creative work reaches its climax. Within this context, the earth acts as a mere stage for the main characters of the story or, at best, a fundamental prop used by God to form other creatures including Adam. Despite the fact that a land motif is evident in God's dealings with Israel in the Old Testament,[5] land is nonetheless interpreted as non-living, causing us to miss its significant presence in the ensuing narrative.

In one of Fiji's Indigenous cosmogonies, the living status of land is never questioned. According to Fijian theologian Ilaitia S. Tuwere, the ancestor-god, Ratu-mai-Bulu, through whom all land and people come into being, can be translated as both Ratu "life" (Bula) and Ratu the "earth" (Bulu).[6] The faithful preservation of such cosmogonies, where there is no demarcation between life and land, is not only indicative of the Fijian worldview, but also of the way Indigenous communities, like those in the Pacific, perceive other deities and creation myths. This brings me to the more central question regarding the role of imagination in the act of discernment. In Samoan churches, it is not uncommon for Sunday school teachers and youth to perform scripts like the one above because they are a lot more fearless in their approach to the Bible than, say, the trained theologian. Is it because training somehow limits the imaginative possibilities of a biblical text? Or is it because the trained have formed a closed circle of biblical elites who think imaginative discourse is child's play? In agreement with Brandon O'Brien's assertion that the Christian life is not threatened by an "overactive imagination" but rather by a "lack of imagination,"[7] I contend that the severing of the link between "imagination" and what we call "discernment" has a lot to do with the assumption that imagination is baseless fantasy. I will return to this assertion below.

---

5. For an interesting reconstruction of Israel's history within the context of land, see Brueggemann, *The Land*.

6. Tuwere. *Vanua*, 41.

7. O'Brien, "Can you imagine," 4.

Imagination as it is employed in this study has to do with possibility-oriented-thinking or what I call "imaginative discernment." This process is one of envisioning alternatives beyond the limitations of one's concrete reality. This is perhaps what the Tongan anthropologist, Epeli Hau'ofa, had in mind when he re-imagined the Pacific not as "islands in a far sea" but as "a sea of islands."[8] Going beyond the land-locked characterizations of Pacific countries as small dots on a map, Hau'ofa preferred to begin his discernment with the enormity of the ocean and its possibilities. In like manner, the famous story of King Solomon's discernment in the case of the two mothers (I Kgs 3:16–28) ought not be attributed solely to Solomon's ability to judge right from wrong, but to his capacity to imagine the outcome and its potential impact on the most affected.[9]

For the purpose of this inquiry and in an effort to avoid a philosophical discussion on the role of imagination in theological hermeneutics,[10] I put forth two functions of imaginative discernment. First, it encompasses both the willingness to critique "what is" and the daringness to imagine "what could be." Given the history of colonialism in the Pacific and the legacies it continues to face, bridging this distance between "what is" and "what could be" is no easy task. In relation to the decolonization of education, Tongan poet and academic Konai Helu-Thaman fervently advocated that Pacific people need to be courageous enough to re-conceptualize education through our own Indigenous knowledge systems and not simply comply with those inherited from European colonists and missionaries.[11] Within this context, imaginative discernment is not a mere appeal to a utopian alternative or fantasy, but rather it serves as a critical dialogue of resilience against what has been normalized, or worse, imposed.[12]

Second, imaginative discernment is about engaging the Bible as a living text, as if hosting a conversation between persons, and not as a

---

8. Hau'ofa, "Our Sea of Islands," 6–7.

9. The same case might also be for the women involved who were asked to "image-ine" the outcome of cutting a child in half. While the false mother might have imagined it briefly, the real mother was the one who fully envisioned the double impact of either giving up motherhood to allow the child to live or permanently lose the child and a piece of herself in the process.

10. A detailed investigation of this topic can be found in Viljoen, "Theological imagination as hermeneutical device."

11. Helu-Thaman, "No Need to Whisper," 301–11.

12. Imaginative discernment should not be confused here with wishful thinking. Helu-Thaman's push for incorporating Indigenous knowledge systems into formal education was more than a case for making education relevant. It stemmed from the concrete reality of the increasing number of underachieving students from the Pacific being victimized by Western ways of learning and assessment.

passive object to be scrutinized. Within this context, imagination without discernment could result in an uncritical reading of the Bible, while discernment without imagination could result in a disinterested reading. Hebrew Bible professor Wilda C. Gafney likens this kind of discernment to "God-grappling," where readers have to seek the Word of God not just in texts but between the lines of the text.[13] This imaginative way of discerning texts is not about exhausting all the meanings but rather functions as a creative way of raising possibilities, even contradictory ones, hoping to incite further revelation.

Let me now address the drama and the imagined wedding bells. While it is more than likely an unconscious import from the constant use of the text in contemporary wedding ceremonies and the obvious husband-wife[14] references in verse 24, my reason for my use of the wedding scenario takes its cues from the first creation story in Genesis 1. That is, in the events leading up to Eden, there is a matrimonial weaving of light and dark, night and day, as well as land and ocean. Such acts provide what I think is a fitting prelude to what occurs in Eden. In Genesis 1, God's creative acts are followed by a judgment claiming that "it is good." However, the first time God's discernment was passed down as "not good" occurs in Genesis 2 in reference to Adam living alone.

Subscribing to the view that Adam refers to humankind and not a particular sex, God's discernment makes way for the imaginative conception of two people. This too is "imaginative discernment." It is imaginative in the sense that the first union between persons was instigated by separation; a realization of the other as distinct from the self. It is also imaginative in the sense that God's solution to the problem of loneliness was the result of God not clutching to "what is" but rather reimagining what the possibilities for humanity "could be."

Dare to be Radical

Now the characters of any story can be recast in light of the earth and the process of bringing them into the story can be humbly referred to as an experiment in hermeneutics. Norman Habel's attempt to capture the suppressed voice of Erets (earth) within the creation story is a case in point.[15] It

---

13. Gafney, *Womanist Midrash*, 5.

14. The husband-wife references from the Genesis account and from the Samoan creation story refer to the male-female relationship, but the reader is free to interpret the gender designations of husband, wife and mistress in light of his or her own preference.

15. For arguments that support the first human creature (Hebrew: *ha'adam*) as

certainly employs imaginative discernment in the way that he allows Erets to tell her own story like when Elohim blatantly ignored her as humans were being created. In this example, the biblical creation story is revisited through the eyes of Erets who watches helplessly as humans are made in a special celestial image and given the power to rule and subdue her.[16] While Habel's argument is persuasive indeed, I am curious if his treatment of Erets as subtext is radical enough to influence change in terms of today's climate injustices. Similarly, it is the trained theologian in me that privately appeals to scholars to treat my subtle rearrangement of the Eden text with the Samoan creation account as an example of intertextual criticism. But I fear that this might just end up having the Samoan creation text and the Genesis 2:18–24 text speaking "at" each other and not "with." On that note, I revert to my days as a Sunday school teacher when dramatizing biblical texts was about teasing out the possibilities in the story that resonate with one's lived context and not a mere reproduction of the same story.

Sri Lankan biblical hermeneuticist Rasiah S. Sugirtharajah shared similar sentiments about the Sepulchre Dance Drama where Jesus' infancy narratives were performed live. In his view, the performance was not "a lazy imitation of the canonical version of the Bible," but rather an unapologetic folk version embellished with Tamil rituals.[17] In one part of the drama, Joseph and Mary smear the tongue of Jesus with mashed rice according to Tamil custom. In another, the infant Jesus feeds his parents with broth which is one of the fundamental duties of a son in Tamil culture. Whilst it might be radical for an academic who is accustomed to applying a kind of interpretive modesty or seeking some form of external verification, for an Indigenous interpreter of the Bible, it implies a mutual coming together of two distinct stories.

This daringness to be radical is equally personified in this reflective piece through the character of Eleele who boldly speaks out of place[18] as a guest from a different narrative whilst simultaneously being the host in the Genesis 2 story. To get a better glimpse of her radical (mis)placement in Genesis 2:18–24, I will briefly describe her role in the Samoan creation account as a "behind the scenes" exclusive for audiences (think: readers) curious about the casting of her character.

---

being sexually undifferentiated, see Trible, *God and the Rhetoric*, 80; Bal, *Lethal Love*, 112–13; and Meyers, *Discovering Eve*, 81.

16. Habel, *The Birth*, 44–45.

17. See Sugirtharajah, *Exploring Postcolonial Criticism*, 183.

18. Radical theologies done from alternative places are engaged in Havea and Pearson's 2014 book, *Out of Place*. The book is part of a series that dialogues with unique and subversive voices from theology and across multiple disciplines.

Among other definitions, the noun *eleʻele* literally translates as land, earth dust, and blood.[19] In the Samoan creation story, Eleele was created by Tagaloa (a supreme deity in Samoan indigenous mythology) as a living being and not limited to land matter.[20] Corresponding with the matrimonial pairs created in Genesis 1, similar parallels can be found in the Samoan story regarding the relationship between *ao* (day) and *po* (night) as well as *ilu* (immensity) and *mamao* (space). According to Samoan theologian Amaʻamalele Tofaeono, the cosmological genealogy of the Samoans is said to have "originated from pairs of rock, [which] took the form of married couples and gave birth to the succeeding generations."[21] This might explain why Eleele was not created alone but alongside her husband, Fatu.[22]

Unlike the Genesis account where humankind is created after the emergence of land, in the Samoan version, the forming of land is also the origin of humans.[23] In other words, Fatu and Eleele were said to be the first intelligent beings infused with spirit, heart, will, and thought.[24] This common belief that traces human ancestry back to cosmic beings instead of human beings was recently affirmed in New Zealand when the Whanganui River was the first to be assigned the same rights as a person.[25] Such bold

19. As with the connection between blood and soil, there are many other parallels still evident in the Samoan language today. For instance, the word *fanua* refers to both land and to the placenta or womb of a woman; *palapala* means both blood and mud; and *tō* refers to the act of planting or cultivating and to a pregnant person or animal.

20. According to a Samoan account of creation, a place of habitation or land mass was required but it was not a central concern. John Fraser explains that after Tagaloa's initial forming of the earth, sea and sky from rock (*papa*) there was still no place for habitation as everything was still floating in the sea. See Fraser, "The Samoan story of Creation," 176–77.

21. Tofaeono, *Ecotheology—AIGA*, 157.

22. Fatu is literally translated as stone, heart or seed. The relationship between Fatu and Eleele is synonymous with that of a human couple. Fatu (male) is understood as being the seed and Eleele (female) as the receptacle of the seed (see Fraser, "The Samoan Story of Creation," 186). While Fatu is largely omitted in this essay, his presence alongside his counterpart Eleele is assumed. When the one flourishes so does the other; and when the other cries, the tears are mutual. Limiting the scope to Eleele is deliberate for reasons of space.

23. I admit this argument is oversimplified. Similar to the intelligent being mentioned in the Samoan account, the Hebrew translation of *adamah* (land) and *adam* (human) also connote a common ancestry. My emphasis is that in the Genesis account, there is an emphasis on the formation of the latter as being the only with the ability to procreate and with authority to dominate the former. In the Samoan creation account, there is no such hierarchy or partiality in relation to procreation.

24. Similar to the Hebrew *haʾadam*, the first intelligent being according to the Samoan creation account is singular. See Fraser, "The Samoan story of Creation," 177.

25. Roy, "New Zealand river granted same legal rights as human being."

recognition of the Indigenous worldview that humans are descendants of the cosmos is also echoed in Eleele's sentiments above. In reciting Adam's vows back to him, Eleele reverses Adam's lineage by reclaiming the fact that the first bone and first flesh actually came from her.

Yet the first bold move by Eleele was in her courage to speak in a story where she is not permitted to speak or be present, much less, considered a living being. In this new setting, she is the uninvited mother or the forgotten ancestor. Her interruption within this story is most radical because she is a stranger to the biblical story and unwelcome according to the biblical "conventions" of exegesis. In the dramatic dialogue that unfolded, we eventually find out that Eleele was always present in the Eden gathering but has been previously rendered silent. If that is the case, Eleele needs neither an invitation nor has to answer to anyone to make her presence known.

When she finally breaks her silence, we hear a certain pain in her voice. This yearning is expressed in Samoan as *ua tagi le fatu ma le elelele,* "the heart and land shedding tears." It is a Samoan lament attributed to those who have lost touch with their ancestral roots, lands and identity.[26] While Eleele's words are seemingly aimed at Adam and Eve, the officiating minister (God), who tries ardently to keep her silent throughout the proceedings, is by no means innocent. (This might even point to the contemporary problem regarding the way ministers like to assume the role of God in many public settings, but that is a topic for another study.) Be that as it may, what transpires from Eleele's courage to speak up was made evident in the officiating minister's change of heart when he announces that a space must be provided for unheard voices in future ceremonies.

Eleele might not have been radical enough to hold God responsible for her marginalization and exploitation,[27] but she was certainly no coward. She not only voices the concerns of the earth but also of Eve, who never actually gets to speak in the original text. Here, the cliché that "strong people stand up for themselves, but stronger people stand up for others" couldn't be truer. In the skit above, Eve speaks freely in the presence of Eleele, as if the boldness of the latter is what enables the former to chime in and find her voice. More importantly, Eleele's courage to turn and address Adam in her closing statement not only made her presence known, but also constituted an act that is profoundly radical, transforming the relations of power.

---

26. Aloali'i-Tēmese, "Ua tagi le fatu ma le eleele," 85–88.

27. For instance, the command in Gen 1:28, "to subdue and have dominion over the earth."

Dare to Engage

To engage in this usual outward manner is to be inclusive of the other. While this comes with many challenges of its own, it is hardly a new or daring enterprise. This study argues that the most daring part about engagement is not so much what happens to the other, but what happens to the self in the course of engagement. The parable of the Good Samaritan (Luke 10:30–37) illustrates what I mean about the risks to the self-involved in daring to engage. In that story, the characters of the priest and the Levite are notoriously remembered for their avoidance of the stranger. Dismissing them as heartless might be too easy a task given that parables are never meant to be taken at face value. Alternatively, it might also be true that the need to help the other was outweighed by the risks imposed on the helper. Even in today's context where altruistic acts are possible, one cannot ignore the fact that such acts come with risks to personal safety, financial status, reputation, and prestige.

In engaging Genesis 2:18–24 through the eyes of Eleele, I am appealing for readers not to cross over into safety, but to be willing to take a twofold risk. First, to engage a familiar story from an estranged worldview where the inanimate could speak and the human and cosmic realms are deeply intertwined. Second, to invest in an outsider like Eleele fully aware that her lament to her descendants is a lot more pressing today than ever. In this light, daring to engage is about reading the Bible in a self-incriminating way. Though Eleele's character is of Samoan and Pacific Island origin, such readers are not exempt from her message.

But there is another less radical twist. Engaging the Bible from the perspective of the voiceless, or in this case—Eleele, is commendable, but not enough. It can lead to a false self-confidence that being a voice for the voiceless is doing our part for the earth. Such confidence can inadvertently push the marginalized further into the margins. It could also excuse us from the teachable moment we are privy to as learners. What I propose in light of the Samoan rendition of the Eden text, is to re-engage it through the eyes of Adam. I have deemed this section the "least radical" in recognition of the fact that asking readers to resume the story from Adam's perspective might not sit well with women who typically have already been sidelined by the patriarchal dominance that has shaped the composition, transmission, and interpretation of the original Genesis text. However, the proposal to re-engage the text through the eyes of Adam (from the skit) is a communal appeal. Being true to the earlier disclosure about this re-reading having a self-incriminating dimension, I am proposing that we, descendants of Eleele or earth (*adamah*) communities, be open to dish out and receive her words of wisdom. This humbling of ourselves alongside Adam to the extent of being publicly humiliated by one's mother, might in fact drive home the seriousness of the consequences of our actions.

To that effect, I wish to add my own reservations on the supposed tension between deep ecology and social ecology as perpetuated in Murray Bookchin's "The Crisis of the Ecological Movement."[28] According to Murray, the transition by deep ecology (or the green camp) towards the "spiritual" dimension of ecology has slowed down environmental efforts. Murray is more convinced that focusing solely on society, not the alleged spirits of the land and other inanimate beings, would allow humans to realize that the major crisis of our times comes from within its social constructs. But I wonder if the two camps that Bookchin polarizes are actually in opposition or, like the story above, are, in fact, exemplary of a wedded pair. I have argued enough to be labeled by him as "green" or part of the deep ecology camp, even though I am not vouching that humanity is a mere species incapable of owning up to the climate injustices we have committed. I also agree that re-enchanting humanity from the perspective of social ecology has numerous benefits, including the advances of technology and how we, social beings, can be better equipped to identify both the exploitive tendencies within society and our joint responsibilities to the earth. But if there is anything both camps are guilty of, it is in the way that each manifests the tendency toward the depersonalization of the Earth and her beings. When social ecology continues to make the earth the object of social investigations, it betrays in effect its lack of a sense of urgency to engage the land on a personal level. Likewise, when deep ecology romanticizes nature through its tendency to reduce the human species to the level of living bacteria, it, too, has depersonalized and undermined real human efforts put into the conservation of the earth. The aforementioned proposal that we look at God's creation as both Adam and Eleele communities seeks to allow both perspectives to coexist in a reciprocal fashion and not as pitched against one another.

The obvious oversight by Bookchin is that ecology from a Pacific Indigenous perspective is not a movement but a life-world where everything is interconnected. It is not a return to a world of mysticism or (super)natural gods for the sake of revamping environmentalist efforts but rather a livelihood maintained over millennia by those societies that cannot be studied outside of this intimate relationship with non-humans and nature.[29] This has not prevented me from using Bookchin as an interesting conversation

---

28. Bookchin, "The Crisis in the Ecological Movement."

29. For a detailed explanation of the intimate bond between people of the Pacific and nature, see Bird, "Hermeneutics of Ecology and its relationship to the identity of the oikos in Oceania," 19–33.

partner. While harsh at times, I find his views to be complementary to deep ecology. I am equally convinced that his passion for the survival of the planet is no different from what we want in the Pacific.

From Mother Earth to Mistress

During its initial performance, there was a humorous segment in the skit that elicited an equal share of laughs and disapproving glances from the pews. This was in regard to Eve's suspicions about the identity of Eleele being a former lover of Adam's. While it served more as playful banter in the skit, I have radicalized its function as a climactic point of emphasis.

Eleele's identity in the skit as mother, host, and ancestor was never really questioned by Adam. The only thing he admits is that he did not invite her. This deliberate exclusion of mother-Eleele is interesting because it draws attention to the manner in which a man is meant to leave his parents as given in verse 24. The Hebrew verb *azab* translated as "leave" or "to leave behind" carries stronger connotations of forsaking or abandoning.[30] This is perhaps iconic of the way that Adam-communities are now, more than ever, further estranged from the land.

But this denial of connection and responsibility is in no way an isolated event. It continues every time land, earth, or the environment are referred to as non-living things or as properties ready to be owned and occupied. This dominant legacy of viewing land as inanimate is heard in the opening statement of Upolu Vaai's poem which contends, "we don't have oceans, we are the ocean . . . we don't have lands, we are the land."[31] Throughout the poem, the motives and mindsets between the "we ares" and the "we haves" are clearly distinguished. To the former, lands and oceans are both mother and source of life, whereas for the latter, the lands and oceans are like a desirable mistress, useful only as expendable resource.

This deep-seated misconception that Eleele is not a living being might not have been the central focus of the Genesis 2 passage, but it certainly vocalizes the many ecological concerns that continue to be silenced by theological discourse. While the painful cries of Eleele might not be audible in societies where the noise of global production persists, she still communicates to those cultures that have developed such sensitivity. Raimon Panikkar, a philosopher of Indian and Spanish descent and a prominent theologian at the forefront of interreligious dialogue, understands this

---

30. I am indebted to Jione Havea for pointing this out during the verbal presentation of this chapter draft.

31. Vaai, "We Are Because We Don't Have," 283.

self-communication as "*kosmos–legein*—that is, the self-disclosure of the cosmos as human consciousness 'hears' and 'sees' the cosmos 'speak' or 'manifest' itself."[32] This deep attentiveness which enables the earth to speak and allows us to decipher what the land is actually saying is where I think imaginative discernment complements science and technology.

Conclusion

In our daringness to discern, we envision what the planet could be when we are gone. We open up traditional texts in light of concrete realities and ask what else the text could be saying. In our daringness to be radical, we allow the object to talk back to the subject. We are uncomfortably interrupted and charged with disinterest, or, worse, making such disinterest a norm. In our daringness to engage, the pride of the self is exposed for the sake of taking ownership of our misdeeds. We are confronted with the tears of a mother, desired but not loved, host yet uninvited, longing for us to engage.

Bibliography

Aloali'i-Tēmese, Seuli V. "Ua tagi le fatu ma le eleele." *Measina* 6 (2013) 85–88. http://samoanstudies.ws/wp-content/uploads/2014/05/Ua-tagi-le-fatu-ma-le-eleele.pdf.

Bal, Mieke. *Lethal Love: Feminist Literary Readings of Biblical Love Stories*. Indiana Studies in Biblical Literature. Bloomington: Indiana University Press, 1987.

Bird, Cliff. "Hermeneutics of Ecology and Its Relationship to the Identity of the Oikos in Oceania." *Pacific Journal of Theology* 46 (2011) 19–33.

Bookchin, Murray. "The Crisis in the Ecological Movement." *Institute for Social Ecology* 6 (1988). http://social-ecology.org/1988/05/the-crisis-in-the-ecology-movement/.

Brueggemann, Walter. *The Land: Place as Gift, Promise, and Challenge in Biblical Faith*. 2nd ed. Minneapolis: Fortress, 2002.

Fraser, John. "The Samoan Story of Creation: A Tala." *Journal of the Polynesian Society* 1.3 (1892) 164–89. (http://www.jps.auckland.ac.nz/document//Volume_1_1892/Volume_1%2C_No._3%2C_1892/The_Samoan_story_of_creation%3A_a_tala%2C_p164-189/p1.

Gafney, Wilda C. *Womanist Midrash: A Reintroduction to the Women of the Torah and the Throne*. Louisville: Westminster John Knox, 2017.

Habel, Norman. *The Birth, the Curse and the Greening of Earth: An Ecological Reading of Genesis*. Earth Bible Commentary Series 1. Sheffield: Sheffield Phoenix, 2011.

Hammer, Reuven. *The Classic Midrash: Tannaitic Commentaries on the Bible*. New York: Paulist, 1995.

---

32. Panikkar. *The Rhythm of Being*, 186.

Hau'ofa, Epeli. "Our Sea of Islands." In *A New Oceania: Rediscovering our Sea of Islands*, edited by Eric Waddell, Vijay Naidu, and Epeli Hau'ofa, 2–16, Suva, Fiji: School of Social and Economic Development, USP, 1993.

Havea, Jione, and Clive Pearson. *Out of Place: Doing Theology on the Crosscultural Brink*. Adelaide: Openbook, 2014.

Helu-Thaman, Konai. "No Need to Whisper: Reclaiming Indigenous Knowledge and Education in the Pacific." In *Whispers and Vanities: Samoan Indigenous Knowledge and Religion*, edited by Tamasailau et al., 301–313, Wellington, NZ: Huia, 2014.

Meyers, Carol. *Discovering Eve*. England: Oxford University Press, 1991.

O'Brien, Brandon. J. "Can You Imagine? Why Imagination Is Crucial to the Christian Life." *Christianity Today*, 2011. http://www.christianitytoday.com/biblestudies/articles/theology/canyouimagine.html?start=1.

Panikkar, Raimon. *The Rhythm of Being: The Unbroken Trinity*. Gifford Lectures. Maryknoll, NY: Orbis, 2013.

Roy, Eleanor Ainge. "New Zealand river granted same legal rights as human being." *The Guardian*, March 16, 2017. https://www.theguardian.com/world/2017/mar/16/new-zealand-river-granted-same-legal-rights-as-human-being.

Sugirtharajah, R. S. *Exploring Postcolonial Biblical Criticism: History, Method, Practice*. Malden, MA: Wiley-Blackwell, 2012.

Tofaeono, Amaamalele. *Ecotheology—AIGA, the Household of Life: A Perspective from Living Myths and Traditions of Samoa*. World Mission Script 7. Erlangen: Erlanger Verlag für Mission und Okumene, 2000.

Trible, Phyllis. *God and the Rhetoric of Sexuality*. Overtures to Biblical Theology. Minneapolis: Fortress, 1978.

Tuwere, Ilaitia. *Vanua: Towards a Fijian Theology of Place*. Suva and Auckland: Institute of Pacific Studies, University of the South Pacific; and College of St John the Evangelist, 2012.

Vaai, Upolu L. "We Are Because We Don't Have." In *The Relational Self: Decolonising Personhood in the Pacific*, edited by Upolu L. Vaai and Unaisi Nabobo-Baba, 283–84. Suva: University of the South Pacific and the Pacific Theological College, 2017.

Viljoen, Anneke. "Theological Imagination as Hermeneutical Device: Exploring the Hermeneutical Contribution of an Imaginal Engagement with the Text." *HTS TeologieseStudies/Theological Studies* 72.4 (July 2016). http://dx.doi.org/10.4102/hts.v72i4.3172.

6

Dreaming Someone Else's Gods

A Cosmopolitics of Constructive Trespass

KATHRYN POETHIG

> When the spirit of place hatches dreams through mortals, it also dreams about us and for us as individuals, as a tribe, and as a race. . . . gods and human beings are the co-creators of dreams in the darkness of our mutual sleep.[1]

ON APRIL 16, 2013, I attended the 5th year celebration Mass for Our Lady of the Mekong, a Lourdes statue miraculously recovered from the confluence of rivers near Phnom Penh. It's a short ferry ride from Phnom Penh to Areyksat, the dusty ferry town in Kandal province where the mass was held. The Queen of Peace parish was choked with foreigners and ethnic Vietnamese Catholics, some of whom had arrived by bus from Vietnam. In truth, Vietnamese pilgrims had come for the *other* Mary, a graceful eight-foot mother with child who had been fished out of the same confluence in late 2012. She was stationed off to the side of the church portico, drawing devotees like a magnet. Unlike the badly ionized Lourdes statue, this Mary was less scarred, tenderly watching her infant Jesus. The faithful crushed around her, their palms in supplication, or draping rosaries and jasmine

---

1. Patton, "A Great and Strange Correction," 223.

garlands, and rubbing prayer cloths along her circumference to soak up her power. "Do you think Our Lady is jealous?" a new friend mused, turning to the solitary Mary we had come to celebrate.

The miracle stories of Catholic statue recoveries in Cambodia are part of a tradition of dream-inspired rescues of statues—what I call epiphany dreams—I have followed since the opening of Cambodia in the early 1990s. I first learned about the recovery of statues lost during the Khmer Rouge era when visiting Champa, one of the oldest Vietnamese settlements in Cambodia along the Mekong river. In 1994, just as Cambodia was opening to the international community, I visited this water-logged village with an American colleague. Our host, a Vietnamese priest who introduced himself as Fr. Peter, rowed us around in a small boat. At the end of his tour, he steered us to a small house and pointed to a small statue hidden in the eves, "see that statue, St Francis?" We peered up and he handed us an English translation of a miracle story. The statue had been recovered due to the dream of a *lok ta*, an old Khmer man, during the Khmer Rouge era. I have followed other examples—Buddhist statues found in a cave, and a Hanuman statue in a rice field. In these stories, the statue is ensouled, inhabited by the spirit that appears in the epiphany dream.

Because the statues ask for their recovery through dreams, I claim here that we consider dreams an oneiric ecumene, a multidimensional dream world inhabited by entities who traverse the "inside" and "outside" of the dreamer. In this cosmopolitics, if the "outside" world is an ontologically plural ecumene, then the self's internal world as represented by dreams is also porous and plural. In this Cambodian and Vietnamese oneiric ecumene, humans are necessary for the rescue of statues, who reassert their power once they are recovered to help the human community. I argue that these cases contribute to a cosmopolitics of *constructive trespass* in which gods themselves transcend cosmological allegiances and humans are expected to cross social and political divides.

What Is at Stake?

While I have been shuttling back and forth across the Pacific for most of my life, I am neither Cambodian, Vietnamese, nor Catholic. An American of European ancestry, I grew up as missionary kid in the United Church of Christ in the Philippines and have benefited from and struggled with the asymmetrical colonial politics of inclusion. As one who worked with resettlement and peacebuilding processes in the United States and Southeast Asia for thirty years, I heard many stories that didn't make it into formal refugee or conflict narratives, stories from the refugee camp where I worked, or on the streets of Oakland, about occult powers, dream warnings, divine apparitions, and family ghosts who assisted those fleeing and surviving disaster on both sides of the Pacific.

Decolonial theorist Santos attributes the absence of these narratives to abyssal thinking, the divide between North and South social realities and their epistemologies.[2] The epistemology of the North justifies its dominance through a coloniality of power—the power to decide what should be studied, civilized, patented, harvested, and litigated.

Beyond it, the South is only nonexistence, invisibility, non-dialectical absence.[3] Santos argues that the anti-imperial anti-capitalist, anti-patriarchal south is a "non-geographical south," composed of many epistemological souths which share an experience of knowledge born in struggle. His solution is a post-abyssal ecology of knowledge, a relationship of co-presence, where multiple epistemological communities are recognized, and rights acknowledged. In sum, there can be no global social justice without cognitive justice.[4]

An ecotheology can conjoin decolonial theory with cosmopolitical theorists who make different claims about the politics of environments and the entities that inhabit them. I have called us to "reassemble the oikouménē," the ecumene.[5] The ecumene is generally understood to be an inhabited realm in which the "terra incognita" (the expendable, uninvited, bizarre, invisible) is left on the margins. To reassemble the ecumene means to consider it ontologically plural with a wider range of the "incognita." Following from this, Stengers and Latour, offer a "cosmopolitics" that challenges the scientific and political truism of a single natural world.[6] Instead, we participate in an ontologically plural cosmos as an assemblage of entities with legitimate points of view—human and other-than-human: animal, plant, landscape, object, and spirit.[7]

Such a cosmopolitical position challenges our explanatory systems and those we privilege to speak. The methodological caution is to treat these "incognita" as they present themselves, "rather than immediately assuming that they signify, represent or stand for something else."[8] De la Cadena illustrates

2. Santos, *Epistemologies of the South*, 120.
3. Santos, "Beyond Abyssal Thinking."
4. Santos, *The End of the Cognitive Empire*.
5. Poethig, "Reassembling the Oikoimene;" See also Ingold, "What Is a Human Being?"
6. Stengers. "The Cosmopolitical Proposal"; Latour, "'Whose Cosmos, Which Cosmopolitics?" Blaser, "Is Another Cosmopolitics Possible?"
7. Descola. *The Ecology of Others*; Vivieros de Castro, "Perspectival Anthropology."
8. Langford, "Spirits of Dissent." See also Henare, Holbraad and Wastell, *Thinking*

this cosmopolitics in her ethnography of a coalition of environmentalists and local Indigenous activists resisting transnational mining concessions in the Andes.[9] The indigenous community claims that the sacred mountain is an "earth being" who would be endangered by extraction, which business personnel dismiss as "anti-capitalist nonsense."[10] De la Cadena argues that characterizing this as a struggle between the North and South for the same resources does not do justice to the claims of Indigenous actors. This cosmopolitical struggle involves two substantively different realities. In this study, I tease out the implications of this methodological caution by asking how ensouled statues (and the spirits that ensoul them) collaborate with humans both in the oneiric and waking ecumene.

Epiphany Dreams and Ensouled Statues

Let us first consider dreams as an oneiric ecumene, a multidimensional dream world inhabited by entities who traverse the "inside" and "outside" of the dreamer. The cultural sources of dreams and their interpretation are promethean. The dream phenomena I refer to here are most similar to Greek and Roman "epiphany dreams" in which a statue of a deity appears to the sleeper to offer guidance or demand a divine task. The notion of an oneiric ecumene is not new for many communities who regularly meet gods and other entities during sleep. The Bible also has examples of this.[11] These are sometimes referred to as "big dreams," in contemporary parlance, so there is modern oneiric space for divine inspiration.[12]

Contemporary dream theory indicates that we dream about five times each night and our dreams might include nightmares, lucid dreams, mutual dreams, dreams of dead loved ones, precognitive, prophetic and "big dreams."[13] Such classification of dream activity is not addressed by new neuroscience of dreaming which characterize dreams as sleep-dependent cognitions, what Windt terms, "immersive spaciotemporal hallucinations."[14] This takes as its cultural assumption what Charles Taylor refers to as a "buffered self." This self is Freud's psychocentric ego, where dreams are prompted by the unconscious so that the self dreams the self.[15]

---

through Things, 2.
9. De la Cadena, "Indigenous Cosmopolitics in the Andes."
10. De la Cadena, "Indigenous Cosmopolitics," 340.
11. Bar, *A Letter*; Miller, "Dreams and Prophetic Visions."
12. Bulkeley, *Big Dreams*.
13. McNamara, *The Neuroscience of Sleep and Dreams*, 171; Bulkeley, *Big Dreams*.
14. Windt, "The Immersive Spatiotemporal Hallucination."
15. Taylor, "Buffered and Porous Selves."

In the contemporary era, "big" dreamers balance notions of a psychocentric self with one that allows for more porous borders between the self and world.[16] Thus, Mittermaier, in her book on Egyptian Sufis' visionary dreams, indicates that even pious Muslims tack between the "rational mind" and the *ru'ya*, the divinely inspired dream or waking vision.[17] Mittermaier suggests, somewhat ironically, that ultimately all dreams come from "Elsewhere."[18] The "elsewhere" of an oneiric ecumene includes both the worlds to which dreamers travel and the places from which visitors appear. For example, because the soul wanders in Cambodian dreams, the dreamer might experience nightmares in worlds where family members who died in the Pol Pot period ask for assistance or "spirit attacks" from malicious supernatural beings.[19] In Muslim contexts, a saint or Muhammad visits the dreamer;[20] in Indigenous dreams, non-humans and the dead offer warning or blessing.[21] These multiple realms confuse and shift the boundary between waking and sleeping worlds.

If an oneiric ecumene is the venue for these spirit encounters, what then when a statue directs the dreamer to a task? Returning to the methodological caution, one might offer that if the statue appears in a dream asking to be found, the statue is agentive. Kendall, in her review of religious iconography in Korea and Vietnam, reflects on how religious iconography throughout Asia is ritually "ensouled" with the active presence of a god or spirit through ritual techniques and practices.[22] As Wei-Ping Lin has illustrated in Chinese contexts, once "awakened," the statues are personifications of divine compassion and power.[23] Kendall *et al.*'s study of both Vietnamese Catholic and Buddhist statues illustrates an "agentive" relationship between statues and human devotees and shows, in part, how a statue's vitality is transmitted to the objects devotees rub or place on them, as I observed in Vietnamese pilgrims' treatment of the Mary with Infant Jesus.[24] In Vietnam, Catholic statues blessed by priests are consecrated, what we might consider ensoulment. Some are miraculous, and thus endowed with stronger agency. These include the Weeping Madonna of Ho Chi Minh City, the Reproduction of Our Lady of Perpetual Help, Hanoi, and most prominently, Our

16. See Lohmann, "Supernatural Encounters"; Mageo, "Theorizing Dreaming and the Self"; Shulman and Stroumsa, *Dream Cultures*.
17. Mittermaier, *Dreams that Matter*.
18. Mittermaier, "Dreams from Elsewhere."
19. Hinton et al. "Nightmares among Cambodian Refugees."
20. Crapanzano, "Saints, Jnun, and Dreams."
21. Cecconi, "Dreams, Memory, and War."
22. Kendall and Yang, "What Is an Animated Image?"; Kendall, "Things Fall Apart."
23. Lin, "Conceptualizing Gods through Statues."
24. Kendall *et al.*, "Is It a Sin to Sell a Statue?"

Lady of La Vang.[25] It's important to note that all these statues are of Mary, and this comports with increased devotion to mother goddesses such as the Black Lady and Our Lady of the Realm in contemporary market-driven Vietnam since many seek her for financial success.[26]

Violence towards Ethnic Vietnamese Catholics in Cambodia

Cambodian antipathy towards Vietnam and to Vietnamese settlers has been attributed to Vietnam's expansionism, and a brief, violent period of occupation in the mid 1800s.[27] Hostility is so intense towards ethnic Vietnamese that they were almost annihilated through the Lon Nol (1970s) and Khmer Rouge eras (1975–79).[28] Thousands of Vietnamese were massacred or pushed into South Vietnam. Ethnic Vietnamese social and political isolation has continued to the present day. While largest of the ethnic communities in Cambodia, Vietnamese are considered the least assimilated.[29] Ethnic Vietnamese share poverty and fishing along Cambodian waterways with the Cham, ethnic Malay Muslims who have a long troubled history in Cambodia.[30] While the 1997 Nationality Law accords those born after 1996 to be eligible for citizenship, many ethnic Vietnamese are still unable to acquire it, and thus cannot vote though many have been in Cambodia for three generations.[31] Nearly 90 percent of the community do not have birth certificates, and cannot own land or access services.[32] Liv, an ethnic Vietnamese, laments, "Our ancestors lived and died here. I feel Cambodian. I don't know why I'm not being treated like

---

25. Ninh, "'Mother Looks Like Us!'" The apparition Our Lady of La Vang is particularly phenomenal. During Vietnam's persecution of Catholics (1798–1801) many beleaguered Catholics sought sanctuary in La Vang in central Vietnam. A woman in traditional Vietnamese clothes holding a child appeared on a banyan tree and claimed to be the Mother of God. She offered succor and recommended herbs for their ailments.

26. Fjelstad, "We Have Len Dong Too"; Taylor, *Goddess on the Rise*.

27. Osborne, *Phnom Penh*.

28. Goshal, Ku and Hawk, "Minorities in Cambodia."

29. Amer, "Domestic Political Change and Ethnic Minorities"; Ehrentraut, "Perpetually Temporary."

30. Filippi, "The Long Tragedy of Cham History."

31. Ehrentraut, "Perpetually Temporary"; Nguyen and Sperfeldt, "A Boat without Anchors."

32. Ang, Weill, and Chan, "Limbo on Earth."

a Cambodian."[33] In this sense, Vietnamese in Cambodia are "perpetually temporary."[34] In other words, trespassers.

This anti-Vietnamese sentiment explains why few Khmer convert to Roman Catholicism though Cambodia is the 9th fastest Christianizing country in the world.[35] As a legacy of the French colonial era, Cambodians associate Catholicism with the Vietnamese.[36] Indeed, two-thirds of Cambodia's estimated 30,000 Catholics are ethnic Vietnamese.[37] Two hundred years after its founding, the Catholic church in Cambodia is still an Apostolic mission.[38] The attempt of the church to adapt Khmer liturgies—Khmer versions of Mary and liturgical objects adapted to a Khmer aesthetic, has been a sore point for the Vietnamese who attend these masses.[39]

Ecumene as a Space of Cross-Border Interaction

In this brief retelling of the three statue recovery stories, I focus on aspects that signal the role of epiphany dreams in statue recovery and cross-border interaction. In the three narratives, different religious and ethnic communities rescued the Catholic statues:

St Francis / Ta Phao (1976?)
Khmer Buddhist
Dream instruction
Our Lady of Lourdes / Our Lady of the Mekong (2008)
Cham & Vietnamese Buddhists
Warned in a dream vision
Our Lady with infant Jesus / Mother of Providence (2012)
Vietnamese Buddhist
Dream instruction

33. The New Humanitarian, "Ethnic Vietnamese in Cambodia Face Discrimination."

34. Ehrentraut, "Perpetually Temporary."

35. Cogan, "Christianity in Cambodia." For more about Christianity in Cambodia see Chunakara, "Churches Together in God's Mission."

36. Chandler, A *History of Cambodia*; Ponchard, *The Cathedral of the Rice Paddy*.

37. Speciale, "In Cambodia, Khmer and Vietnamese Catholics remain disunited."

38. Ponchard, *The Cathedral of the Rice Paddy*. Fr Ponchard, a French MEP missionary and former Prefect Delegate of Kampong Cham, has written a definitive history of the Catholic Church in Cambodia. The three Catholic administrative regions in Cambodia Battambang, Kampong Cham, and Phnom Penh. Currently, French-born Bishop Destombes administers Phnom Penh, Spanish-born Kike Figaredo is Apostolic Prefect of Battambang and Indian-born Antonysamy Susairaj is Apostolic Prefect of Kampong Cham.

39. Ninh *Race, Gender, and Religion in the Vietnamese Diaspora*; Ninh "'Mother Looks Like Us!'"

The three statues were lost during the Khmer Rouge era, but it is critical to note that all religious communities suffered under the radical communist regime of Democratic Kampuchea.[40] The Khmer Rouge disrobed or summarily executed Buddhist, Muslim and Christian clergy. They desecrated religious sites, turning Buddhist wats into prisons and torture cells and sending pigs through mosques, and dynamiting the majestic Notre Dame Cathedral. Religious iconography was systematically vandalized. The fate of Catholic statues might have been less harsh than thousands of Buddhas that were toppled, vandalized, beheaded, or tossed into waterways. In the case of the Areyksat statues of Mary, Catholic clergy in Cambodia speculate that fleeing Vietnamese had loaded their statues on a boat, possibly during a Lon Nol purge, but the boat was so overloaded, the statues were dropped overboard. There is no community memory of this event.

St Francis Xavier

Champa is no longer subject to flooding. At its center is a Catholic church which first put the restored statue of Francis Xavier (the original wood had rotted) set first a glass case, then over the sanctuary doors (Figure 6.1).

Figure 6.1: St. Francis Xavier, Champa
Photo: Kathryn Poethig 2012

40. Chandler, *History of Cambodia*; Kiernean, *The Pol Pot*; Ponchaud, *Cathedral in the Rice Paddy*.

Fr. Peter—now Fr. Ting—and community members relay how, on three separate nights, the saint-as-statue appeared to the old Khmer and appealed to be rescued. In Fr. Ting's telling,

> On the third night he came down to the river and saw the statue in the water and stuck in the mud. He wrapped it in his krama and when he'd found a place, he cleaned it, and set it under a mango tree. In the morning, when he took coffee with the old men in the village (because the youth and adults were in work camps, so there were only elderly and children there), he told the old men in the village about the statue. So, everyone went over to worship the statue. This is the *Ta Phao*, protector of the village, they said. They would pour water on its head and collect it at its feet, and this water would be like medicine, healing many persons and animals. Nobody in that village was killed by the Khmer Rouge.[41]

When Catholic Vietnamese settlers returned to Champa after the Vietnamese had pushed back the Khmer Rouge, they were surprised to see their old statue of Frances Xavier venerated by Khmer living there.[42] For the subsequent decade, the statue was shared by both Cambodian and Vietnamese communities, easing a potentially troubled reintegration of Vietnamese settlers. But the story of St Francis has receded from importance in both the Vietnamese and Cambodia communities.

Our Lady of the Mekong: Protect My Body

Several years after the discovery of the first Mary in 2008, I met with the head of the Queen of Peace church council, his granddaughter, and Catholic clergy. Brochures of the miraculous recovery of the Marys are available at the Queen of Peace parish in Vietnamese and Khmer. More recently, the stories are now also posted on a small billboard with English translation.

The first statue of Mary is a five-foot, oxidized cast iron statue Our Lady of Lourdes, hands clasped in prayer, face turned upward (Figure 6.2a).

---

41. Interview with Fr. Ting, 2009 (Phnom Penh).

42. See Ninh, *Race, Gender, Religion*, for the difficult religious and ethnic politics in the revival of this Vietnamese Catholic community during and after the Vietnamese occupation, Fr. Ting's initial concerns about visibility and eventual leadership.

Figure 6.2a. Our Lady of the Mekong
Photo: Kathryn Poethig, 2012

Shortly after her recovery, French Vicar Apostolic Bishop Emile Destombes named her Our Lady of the Mekong and determined that the statue would not be restored so that the water-worn condition would remind visitors of the miraculous discovery (Figure 6.2b).[43]

---

43. Interviews with member of the Queen of Peace church council, his granddaughter, and Catholic clergy (2009, 2012 and 2013 in Phnom Penh). A French visitor tried to track down the factory where the Lourdes statue was produced, but it had burned down and all the receipts with it.

118 PART TWO: EARTH RITES

Figure 6.2b. Our Lady of the Mekong
Photo: Kathryn Poethig, 2012

The first Mary was recovered on April 16, 2008, *Choul Chnam Thmey* which is Khmer New Year, the most auspicious holiday in Cambodia. Cham fishermen (out on a day when no one is working) found a large metal object stuck in the river floor.[44] The Cham sold their rights to the metal to eight Vietnamese fishermen also out on the river that day. In this miracle story, when the Buddhist fishermen dragged the statue ashore in Areyksat, a Catholic bystander realized it was Mary and a frantic negotiation ensued. The fishermen set an exorbitant price and warned they would sell the metal to a foundry. Despairing, the parish council searched for the funds. But Mary had other plans. That night, her form—in the image of the statue—flew

---

44. Filippi, "The Long Tragedy of Cham History." Cham are a Malay people of the Kingdom of Champa for more than a thousand years in southern Vietnam and Cambodia which eventually annexed to Vietnam in the 1800s. In Cambodia, they have been further marginalized onto houseboats and fisherfolk, not unlike ethnic Vietnamese.

around the houseboat of one of the fishermen. Sleepless and terrified, they arrived at the church early morning, and knelt before the statue, begging her forgiveness. They offered the statue to the parish, refusing recompense. This Marian projection of spiritual power turned the eight Buddhist fishermen into her devotees. In a photo of the inaugural Mass, the eight men stand smiling beside Our Lady of the Mekong.

But the statue initiated a more important cultural shift in the struggle between a Vietnamese parish and foreign Catholic clergy intent on inculturating the Mass to draw in a Khmer congregation. Ninh has argued that Our Lady of the Mekong sparked a revival among the Vietnamese settlers in Cambodia. This included affirmation of their Vietnamese Catholicism by their Khmer neighbors, diaspora Vietnamese Catholic humanitarian and financial support, and global recognition of the small, beleaguered church.[45] Ninh suggests Mary's oxidized image has helped to mediate between "white" European statues and the "black" Khmer Mary. Furthermore, the style of her mountain grotto, towering alongside the church is modeled after grottos of Our Lady of the Realm and the Black Lady in Vietnam (Figure 6.3).[46]

Figure 6.3: Queen of Peace Parish, Our Lady of the Mekong Grotto
Photo: Kathryn Poethig, 2012

45. Ninh, *Race, Gender Religion*.
46. Ninh, "Mother looks like us!"

Her inscriptions and donation plaques are primarily in Vietnamese. In this way, she has initiated an acceptable mode of trespass back to a Vietnamese expression of Catholicism. She is a Lady for her people. But while keepers of her image have fashioned her as a Vietnamese rescue story, she is more slippery than that. Not only did she cross religious boundaries—from Cham to Vietnamese Buddhist, to Catholic, but she does so as a French-cast Vietnamese Mother Goddess.

Mother of Providence: Dream Instruction

I was in Cambodia three weeks after the second Mary was retrieved from the river on November 19, 2012. Surviving sisters of the Providence of Portieux, an order of primarily Vietnamese nuns, recognized the second statue, an eight-foot Mary with infant Jesus as their statue, the Mother of Providence (Figure 6.4).[47]

Figure 6.4: Mother of Providence

Photo: Kathryn Poethig 2013

47. Ponchard, *Cathedral*. The French order, which moved from Vietnam to Cambodia in the late 1800s, brought with them their patroness, Mary Help of Christians and helped to promote Marianism among Vietnamese Catholics.

The statue resided at the Providence of Portieux convent in Russey Keo, outside of Phnom Penh. On their Cambodia website, two sisters pose with the statue to affirm this connection.[48]

The ASEAN conference in Phnom Penh occurred November 18 and 19, 2012, the week before the annual Khmer Water Festival when the city is so packed with visitors one can hardly travel across town. President Obama's appearance at the ASEAN conference shut down traffic in Phnom Penh. A priest of St. Joseph Church in the diocese of Phnom Penh, said security was so tight, ferries were stopped, grounding working men in Areyksat. In this way, he conjectured, Mary was preparing able-bodied men to move her second statue to the church. He also considered it a lovely sign that the statue was found near the Feast of The Presentation of Virgin Mary on November 21st.[49]

A Maryknoll priest accompanied me to Areyksat to meet Phang Vaing Hou and his wife.[50] The story later posted in English on a bulletin board and brochure generally support Phang's narrative to us. Phang Vaing Hou and his wife were Buddhists living *"sans papiers"* in Areyksat. His wife had a terrible heart condition and had sought treatment without success. He was not much of a dreamer, he said, but in this epiphany dream, a "large statue of a large figure of a man" appeared to him and "the image," asked to be taken from the water, because, he said, "I am very cold." The image said that he had been under the Mekong for a long time, close to the other *preah mai* (Khmer, sacred mother is translated as Our Lady in the brochure).[51] Phang Vaing Hou woke and checked his watch: 2:55am. At 6:00 that morning, he descended to "get coffee" from the dark café under one of their houses, he said that "Jesus asked me to pick up his statue." and asked for assistance "from the Catholics." No one volunteered. At 7:00am, he and his two sons took two boats to the place where the first Mary was found. It took more than four hours, and eventually a crane, to dislodge the statue deeply embedded in the riverbed. It was so heavy with mud that it took up to fifty men to drag it from the shore to the church.

Phang Vaing Hou spoke to us in Khmer, not Vietnamese, and he hesitated as he interpreted the confluence between dream and discovery.

---

48. Child Jesus Parish, Sisters of Providence (https://childjesus.wordpress.com/activities/religious-communities/providence-sisters/).

49. Interview with Fr. Bruno Cosme, December 2012 (Phnom Penh).

50. Interview and assistance of Fr. Kevin Mahony December 2012 (Phnom Penh).

51. Interview with Phang Vaing Hou, December 2012 (Areyksat); Fr Gustavo Adrian Benitez, "Brief History of the statue of the Virgin Mary at the Mekong River 19th November 2012."

I brought the *preah mai* to the *preah vihear* and then I come back, so I felt happy to bring the *preah mai* back. But I also have a concern in my heart. Because in the dream—Jesus gave me a dream—I saw *preah mai* but I did not know this *preah mai*. I was happy but a little bit hopeless. When I came back, I met a Christian, Yu. I asked Yu, what is the life story (*prowat roup*) about the lady who is holding the baby? I want to know about. Yu told me that it was Jesus when he was a child. When I heard that answer, I was really glad. No matter how big the gift someone give me, it wouldn't make me as happy as this because I saved both the *preah mai* and him (Jesus). (He laughs a little).[52]

In the English brochure, his quote is italicized and in bold: *While taking her from the river onto the boat, I felt that it was not a statue but a person who was alive, like us. I was happy and afraid at the same time. I prayed to Her to heal my wife from her illness.*

For Phang, this unnamed statue is a *preah mai*—but not the one he expected to find. He thought he was sent to rescue Jesus and felt "a little hopeless" that he hadn't fulfilled the dream request. At the end of our talk, he speculated that there might be a statue of Jesus still left in the river, the figure he was supposed to find. But ultimately, both his message to us and to the chronicler of the public story indicate his joy and awe. She's "not a statue but a person who was alive," a form ensouled. And in truth, this water-worn statue of Mary peering at her child communicates such intimate tenderness that she seems more accessible than Our Lady of the Mekong (fig.4). In subsequent years, I learn, Phang offers a narrative of his dream to Vietnamese pilgrims who regularly visit the statue and celebrate Mass. Through that support and other gracious patronage, his wife has gone for surgery in Vietnam. Jesus and the *preah mai* have rewarded him. He and his wife converted to Catholicism and were subsequently baptized as Catholics.[53]

The brochure ends with this theological reflection on the auspicious day of the statue's recovery. But it also disrupts Phang's reference to the statue's personhood, subjugating her rescue to an omniscient God,

> God is truly wise and he knows everything. The finding of the statue, the day and time, is considered providential, because on, the same day 21st ASEAN Summit Day was held in Cambodia. Because of security reasons, the Government gave a day off to the nation and the public boats were not in operation which

---

52. Interview with Phang Vaing Hou, December 2012 (Areyksat).

53. Though beyond the scope of this study, see investigations on conversion dreams. See Bulkeley, "Dreaming and Religious Conversion"; Davis and Rambo, "Conversion Dreams in Christianity and Islam."

made the search of the statue easy. The fact proved that, God arranged everything and He wanted us to take the Statue of the Virgin Mary on that day to be placed in our Church.[54]

Dream Visitors from "Elsewhere" Seeking a "Here"

In the cases I follow here, I am asking what happens when dreamers dream someone else's gods? I argue that these exchanges are a cosmopolitics of constructive trespass in which gods themselves transcend cosmological allegiances. A cosmopolitics because humans are instructed with such authority that they obey these ensouled statues to cross social and political divides. I assert that this trespass is constructive because it slips over a cherished border and rewards the participants and us with a wider epistemological vista. As a cosmopolitics of constructive trespass, it takes everyone—the Cham, Khmer, Buddhist, Vietnamese, and Catholic—to trespass the boundaries of their cosmological (and ecumenical) allegiances and political loyalties to respond to the inner world of the dreams, the request of the statues, and the outer politics of the rescue.

These cases also challenge us about the nature of statues themselves. In the three cases I offer, the statues' ensoulment is attributed to their self-directed agency. This agency is not transcendent or omniscient, but personable, with needs and desires, as one who might enter into a contract. If there is succor in this story, it is that the statues have come "home" to a devoted community whose intimate sacred icons of worship were lost a generation ago in a terrible conflict. So, the Spirit introduces humans to statues who, like the Vietnamese settlers, have been displaced. But the humans who dream these statues are not left unrewarded. Dream visitors cross over the elsewhere to find a here, but there are many elsewheres and other heres. We can say now: the thing was hidden, and when it wanted to be "found," it crossed into human dreaming.

Do these "Christian" spirits have more than their own community at heart? I asked the young woman who lives across from the church, "why did Mary come now"? She says sweetly, "to show the world how she loves us."

Epilogue

In early 2011, before the second Mary had arrived, I had this dream:

---

54. Benitez, "Brief History of the Statue of the Virgin Mary."

In a house of hallways: I leave a room, walk down a long hall turn left, past a dingy empty room, and stop. No, not this way. I retrace my steps to the original door and glance to the left, Buddhist and Hindu statues are clustered on a low sandstone two-level shrine. Our gold-painted Burmese disciple with palms raised in a *wai* is asleep on the lower level. Above him, our familiar household statues: a *naga kanya*, a Khmer *apsara*, and buddha in a partial *parinirvana*, all bent from the waist in slumber, faces placid, enveloped in a sweet gold glow.

When I wake, I linger on these gods of sleep: golden, winged, nondual. Then in a flash, I understand—it's not the gods themselves but their statues who are sleeping. The slumber of things. Secret life of sandstone, bronze, wood, plaster. They are inside my dream, but what are they dreaming? Are they dreaming me, inside *their* slumber?

As I write in Spring 2020, statues—confederate and colonial—have generated much attention and pent up rage as memorials to historic injustice. They are toppled, dismantled, vandalized. I wonder, if, following the particular mindset I offer, about the agency of the statues themselves. Do they want to come down?

Bibliography

Amer, Ramses. "Domestic Political Change and Ethnic Minorities. A Case Study of Ethnic Vietnamese in Cambodia." *Asia-Pacific Social Science Review* 13.2 (2013) 87–101.

Ang, Chanrith, Noémie Weill, and Jamie Chan. "Limbo on Earth: An Investigative Report On the Current Living Conditions and Legal Status of Ethnic Vietnamese in Cambodia." *Stateless Vietnamese Investigative Report 2014*, no 2, Minority Rights Organization, Phnom Penh Cambodia, 2014.

Bar, Shaul. *A Letter That Has not Been Read: Dreams in the Hebrew Bible*. Translated by Lenn J. Schramm. Monographs of the Hebrew Union College 25. Cincinnati: Hebrew Union, 2001.

Barrett, Dierdre, ed. *Trauma and Dreams*. Cambridge: Harvard University Press, 2001.

Becker, Gay, Yewoubdar Beyene, and Pauline Ken. "Memory, Trauma, and Embodied Distress: The Management of Disruption in the Stories of Cambodians in Exile." *Ethos* 28 (2000) 320–45.

Blaser, Mario. "Is Another Cosmopolitics Possible?" *Cultural Anthropology* 31 (2016) 545–70.

Brandner, Tobias. "Emerging Christianity in Cambodia: People Movement to Christ or Playground for Global Christianity?" *International Bulletin of Mission Research* 44.3 (July 2020) 279–89. doi:10.1177/2396939319879556.

Brelich, Angelo. "The Place of Dreams in the Religious World Concept of the Greeks." In *The Dream and Human Society*, edited by Gustave Edmund von Greunbaum and Roger Caillois, 293–401. Berkeley: University of California Press, 1966.

Bulkeley, Kelly. *Big Dreams: The Science of Dreaming and the Origins of Religion*. Oxford: Oxford University Press, 2016

———. "Dreaming and Religious Conversion." In *The Oxford Handbook of Religious Conversion*, edited by Lewis R. Rambo and Charles E. Farhadian, 256–70. Oxford Handbooks. Oxford: Oxford University Press, 2014.

———. *Dreaming in the World's Religions: A Comparative History*. New York: New York University Press, 2008

Chandler, David. *A History of Cambodia*. 4th ed. Boulder, CO: Westview, 2007.

Cecconi, Arianna. "Dreams, Memory, and War: An Ethnography of Night in the Peruvian Andes." *Journal of Latin American and Caribbean Anthropology* 16 (2011) 401–24.

Chunakara, Mathews George. "Churches together in God's Mission—Cambodia II: Detailed Account of Christianity and Ecumenism." In *Asian Handbook for Theological Education and Ecumenism*, editded by Hope Antone, Wati Longchar, Hyunju Bae, Huang Po Ho, and Dietrich Werner, 473–99, Oxford: Regnum, 2013.

Crapanzano, Vincent. "Saints, Jnun, and Dreams: An Essay in Moroccan Ethnopsychology." *Psychiatry* 38 (May 1975) 145–59.

Cogan, Philip. "Christianity in Cambodia." *New Mandala*, Jan 21, 2016. https://www.newmandala.org/christianity-in-cambodia/.

Davis, Patricia M., and Lewis Rambo. "Conversion Dreams in Christianity and Islam." In *Dreaming in Christianity and Islam: Culture, Conflict, and Creativity*, edited by Kelly Bulkeley, Kate Adams, and Patricia Davis, 175–87. New Brunswick, NJ: Rutgers University Press, 2009.

De la Cadena, Marisole. "Indigenous Cosmopolitics in the Andes: Conceptual Reflections beyond 'Politics.'" *Cultural Anthropology* 25 (2010) 334–70.

Descola, Philippe. *The Ecology of Others*. Translated by Geneviève Godbout and Benjamin P. Luley. Chicago: Prickly Paradigm. 2013.

Doniger O'Flaherty, Wendy. *Dreams, Illusion and Other Realities*. Chicago: University of Chicago Press, 1984.

Edwards, Penny. "Imaging the other in Cambodian nationalist discourse before and during the UNTAC period." In *Propaganda, Politics, and Violence in Cambodia: A Democratic Transition under United Nations Peace-Keeping*, edited by Steve R. Heder and Judy Ledgerwood, 50–72. Armonk, NY: Sharpe, 1995.

Ehrentraut, Stefan. "Perpetually Temporary: Citizenship and Ethnic Vietnamese in Cambodia." *Ethnic and Racial Studies* 34 (2011) 779–98. doi:10.1080/01419870. 2010.537359.

Ewing, Katherine. "Dreams from a Saint: Anthropological Atheism and the Temptation to Believe." *American Anthropologist* 96 (1994) 571–83.

Filippi, Jean-Mitchell. "The Long Tragedy of Cham History." *Phnom Penh Post*, Nov. 4, 2011. https://www.phnompenhpost.com/post-plus/long-tragedy-cham-history.

Fjelstad, Karen. "'We Have Len Dong Too': Transnational Aspects of Spirit Possession." In *Possessed by the Spirits: Mediumship in Contemporary Vietnamese Communities*, edited by Karen Fjelstad and Hien Thi Nguyen, 95–110. Ithaca, NY: Cornell University Press, 2006.

Gell, Alfred. *Art and Agency: An Anthropological Theory*. Oxford: Clarendon, 1998.

Goshal, Bandas, Jae H. Ku, and David R. Hawk. *Minorities in Cambodia*. Minority Rights Group International Report 95/2. London: Minority Rights Group, 1998.

Guennou, Tan. "Catholic Church in Cambodia." In *New Catholic Encyclopedia*. Detroit: Gale Group, 2003. https://www.encyclopedia.com/religion/encyclopedias-almanacs-transcripts-and-maps/cambodia-catholic-church.
Harris, Ian. *Cambodian Buddhism: History and Practice*. Honolulu: University of Hawaii Press, 2005.
Henare, Amiria, Martin Holbraad, and Sari Wastell, eds. *Thinking through Things: Theorising Artefacts Ethnographically*. London: Routledge, 2007.
Hinton, Devon, Alexander Hinton,Vuth Pich, J. R. Loeum, and Mark Pollack. "Nightmares among Cambodian Refugees: The Breaching of Concentric Ontological Security." *Culture, Medicine and Psychiatry* 33 (2009) 219–65. doi:10.1007/s11013-009-9131-9.
Hinton, Devon, Vuth Pich, Dara Chhean and Mark Pollack. "'The Ghost Pushes You Down': Sleep Paralysis-Type Panic Attacks in a Khmer Refugee Population." *Transcultural Psychiatry* 42 (2005) 46–78.
Hollan, Douglas. "Selfscape Dreams." In *Dreaming and the Self: New Perspectives on Subjectivity, Identity, and Emotion*, edited by Jeannette Marie Mageo, 61–74. New York: State University of New York Press, 2003.
Horsfall, Sara. "The Experience of Marian Apparitions and the Mary Cult." *The Social Science Journal* 37 (2000) 375–84.
Ingold, Tim. "What Is a Human Being?" *American Anthropologist* 112 (2010) 513–14.
Kendall, Laurel. "Things Fall Apart: Material Religion and the Problem of Decay." *Journal of Asian Studies* 76 (2017) 861–86.
Kendall, Laurel, Vũ Thị Hà, Vũ Thị Thanh Tâm, Nguyễn Văn Huy, Nguyễn Thị Hiền. "Beautiful and Efficacious Statues: Magic and Material in Vietnamese Popular Religion." *Material Religion* 6 (2010) 60–85.
———. "Is It a Sin to Sell a Statue? Catholic Statues and the Traffic in Antiquities in Vietnam." *Museum Anthropology* 36 (2013) 66–82. https://doi.org/10.1111/muan.12005.
Kiernan, Ben, *The Pol Pot Regime: Race, Power, and Genocide in Cambodia under the Khmer Rouge, 1975–79*. 3rd ed. New Haven: Yale University Press, 2008.
Kwon, Heonik. *Ghosts of War in Vietnam*. Studies in the Social and Cultural History of Modern Warfare 27. Cambridge: Cambridge University Press, 2008.
Ladwig, Patrice. "Visitors from Hell: Hospitality to Ghosts in a Lao Buddhist Festival." *Journal of the Royal Anthropological Institute* 18 (2012) 90–102.
Ladwig, Patrice. "Ontology, Materiality and Spectral Traces: Methodological Thoughts on Studying Lao Buddhist Festivals for Ghosts and Ancestral Spirits." *Anthropological Theory* 12 (2013) 427–47.
Langford, Jean. "Spirits of Dissent: Southeast Asian Memories and Disciplines of Death." *Comparative Studies of South Asia, Africa, and the Middle East: Special Issue on Mourning and Memory* 25 (2005) 161–76.
Langford, Jean. *Consoling the Ghosts: Stories of Medicine and Mourning from Southeast Asians in Exile*. Minneapolis: University of Minnesota Press, 2013.
Latour, Bruno. "'Whose Cosmos, Which Cosmopolitics? Comments on the Peace Terms of Ulrich Beck." *Common Knowledge* 10 (2004) 450–62.
———. *Reassembling the Social*. Oxford: Oxford University Press, 2005.
Le Coz, Clothilde. "The Plight of Cambodia's Khmer Krom Community." *Diplomat*, (October 30, 2014). https://thediplomat.com/2014/10/the-plight-of-cambodias-khmer-krom-community/.

Lin, Wei-Ping. "Conceptualizing Gods through Statues: A Study of Personification and Localization in Taiwan." *Comparative Studies in Society and History* 50 (2008) 454–77.

———. *Materializing Magic Power: Chinese Popular Religion in Villages and Cities*. Cambridge: Harvard University Press, 2015.

Levine, Peggy. *Love and Dread in Cambodia. Weddings, Births and Ritual Harm under the Khmer Rouge*. Singapore: National University of Singapore Press, 2010.

Llewellyn, Sue. "Such Stuff as Dreams Are Made On? Elaborative Encoding, the ancient Art of Memory, and the Hippocampus." *Behavioral and Brain Sciences* 36 (2013) 589–607. http://dx.doi.org/10.1017/S0140525X12003135.

Lohmann, Roger Ivan. "Supernatural Encounters of the Asabano in Two Traditions and Three States of Consciousness." In *Dream Travelers: Sleep Experience and Culture in the Western Pacific*, edited by Roger Ivar Lohmann et al., 189–210. New York: Palgrave, 2006.

Mageo, Jeanette Marie. "Theorizing Dreaming and the Self." In *Dreaming and the Self: New Perspectives on Subjectivity, Identity, and Emotion*, edited by Jeanette Marie Mageo, 3–24. New York: State University of New York Press, 2003.

Miller, James E. "Dreams and Prophetic Visions." *Biblica* 71 (1990) 401–4. http://www.jstor.org/stable/42611121.

Miller, Patricia Cox. *Dreams in Late Antiquity: Studies in the Imagination of a Culture*. Princeton: Princeton University Press, 1997.

McNamara, Patrick. *The Neuroscience of Sleep and Dreams*. Cambridge Fundamentals of Neuroscience in Psychology. Cambridge: Cambridge University Press, 2019.

Mittermaier, Amira. "Dreams from Elsewhere: Muslim Subjectivities beyond the Trope of Self-cultivation." *Journal of the Royal Anthropological Institute* 18 (2012) 247–65.

———. *Dreams that Matter: Egyptian Landscapes of the Imagination*. Berkeley: University of California Press, 2010.

Nguyen, Lyma, and Christof Sperfeldt. "A Boat without Anchors: A Report on the Legal Status of Ethnic Vietnamese Minority Populations in Cambodia under Domestic and International Laws Governing Nationality and Statelessness." Cambodia: Jesuit Refugee Service, 2012. http://jrscambodia.org/aboat_without_anchors.html.

Ninh, Thien-Huong. "'Mother Looks Like Us!': Gender Convergences and Complexities in Marianism among Vietnamese Catholics in the U.S., Cambodia, and Vietnam." In *Alternative Intimate Spheres for Women in Vietnam*, edited by Kirsten Endres et al., 8–34. Kyoto: GCOE Kyoto University, 2012.

Ninh, Thien-Huong. *Race, Gender, and Religion in the Vietnamese Diaspora: The New Chosen People*. New York: Palgrave Macmillan, 2017.

Ong, Roberto K. *The Interpretation of Dreams in Ancient China*. Bochum: Studienverlag Brockmeyer, 1985.

Osborne, Milton. *Phnom Penh: A Cultural History*. Cityscapes. Oxford: Oxford University Press, 2008.

Patton, Kimberley. "'A Great and Strange Correction': Intentionality, Locality, and Epiphany in the Category of Dream Incubation." *History of Religions* 43 (2004) 194–223.

———. *Religion of the Gods: Ritual, Paradox, and Reflexivity*. Oxford: Oxford University Press, 2009.

Phan, Peter C. "Mary in Vietnamese Piety and Theology: A Contemporary Perspective." *Ephemerides Mariologicae* 51 (2005) 457–72.

Poethig, Kathryn. "Reassembling the Oikoimene." In *Mission and Context*, edited by Jione Havea. Lanham, MD: Fortress Academic, 2020.

Ponchaud, Francois. *The Cathedral of the Rice Paddy: 450 Years of History of the Church in Cambodia*. Paris: Fayard, 1990.

Santos, Boaventura de Sousa. *The End of the Cognitive Empire: The Coming of Age of Epistemologies of the South*. Durham: Duke University Press, 2018.

———. *Epistemologies of the South: Justice against Epistemicide*. London: Paradigm, 2014.

———. "Beyond Abyssal Thinking: From Global Lines to Ecologies of Knowledges." *Review* (Fernand Braudel Center) 30 (2007) 45–89. http://www.jstor.org/stable/40241677.

Shulman, David, and Stroumsa, Guy G., eds. *Dream Cultures: Explorations in the Comparative History of Dreaming*. New York: Oxford University Press, 1999.

Speciale, Alessandro. "In Cambodia, Khmer and Vietnamese Catholics Remain Disunited." UCANews.com, May 20, 2013. https://www.ucanews.com/news/in-cambodia-khmer-and-vietnamese-catholics-remain-disunited/68382.

Stengers, Isabelle. "The Cosmopolitical Proposal." In *Making Things Public: Atmospheres of Democracy*, edited by Bruno Latour and Peter Weibel, 994–1003, Cambridge: MIT Press, 2005.

Taylor, Charles. "Buffered and Porous Selves." *The Immanent Frame*, Sept. 2, 2008. http://blogs.ssrc.org/tif/2008/09/02/buffered-and-porous-selves/.

———. *A Secular Age*. Cambridge: Harvard University Press, 2007.

Taylor, Philip. *Goddess on the Rise: Pilgrimage and Popular Religion in Vietnam*. Honolulu: University of Hawaii, 2004.

———. "Modernity and Re-enchantment in Post-revolutionary Vietnam." In *Modernity and Re-enchantment: Religion in Post-revolutionary Vietnam*, edited by Philip Taylor, 1–56. Singapore: Institute of Southeast Asian Studies, 2007.

Viveiros de Castro, Eduardo, "Perspectival Anthropology and the Method of Controlled Equivocation." *Tipiti: Journal of the Society for the Anthropology of Lowland South America* 2 (2004) 3–22.

Wardel, Houn, and Justin Schaffner. "Introduction: Comopolitics as a Way of Thinking." In *Cosmopolitics: The Collected Papers of the Open Anthropology Cooperative*, Volume 1. edited by Justin Shaffner and Houn Wardel, 1–43. Scotland: Open Anthropology Cooperative Press, 2017.

Windt, Jennifer. "The Immersive Spatiotemporal Hallucination Model of Dreaming." *Phenomenology and the Cognitive Sciences* 9 (2010) 295–316. http://doi.org/10.1007/s11097-010-9163-1.

Part Three

Earth Politics
Practices and Movements
on the Ground

7

Truth, Reconciliation, and Climate Justice

Applications of Truth and Reconciliation Processes to Climate Debt and the Climate Crisis

Sheryl Johnson

AN OFFICIAL TRUTH AND Reconciliation Commission (TRC) has never been undertaken in regard to an issue as global, intergenerational, and inter-species as the climate crisis—an issue that is far from over and is, in fact, rapidly worsening. I will argue that aspects of TRC processes, generally speaking, can be helpful in addressing climate change, and, specifically, climate debt. Climate debt has been a key focus of the ecological work of the ecumenical movement, and I believe there is a great potential for a TRC-style process to enhance this work. As churches and the ecumenical movement have engaged both with climate debt and with various official TRC processes, there may well be openness to introducing insights and processes from the TRC framework in those contexts. Further, there are numerous ethical and theological connections that can enhance how Christians understand TRC processes and encourage Christians' participation in them. Toward the end of this essay, I will note the limitations of a TRC approach for this purpose, including the unlikelihood of a world-wide participation in an official TRC. However, I argue there is still great benefit from such a process both for those who actively participate and for societies and the world as a whole.

The Truth and Reconciliation Commission of Canada (TRCC) took place from 2008-2015, initiated to address the legacy of Indian Residential Schools and advance efforts toward reconciliation between Indigenous and non-Indigenous persons and communities. As a non-Indigenous person with European settler heritage (and privilege) born and raised in "Canada,"[1] my experiences of participation within the TRCC were profoundly moving, and appropriately destabilizing. As a person of Christian faith, I participated in the TRCC in many instances as part of my church communities. As a member of these communities, I hold particular accountability for the harms of Residential Schools and the wider colonial project due to the churches' active participation in, and practical and ideological/theological support of, both the Residential Schools specifically and the colonization and Christianization efforts of Indigenous peoples more broadly. While I recognize that this is not true for all or even many participants in the TRCC process, I understood my involvement to be a necessary expression of my Christian faith. Christianity and the Church must be interrogated due to their complicity in numerous injustices in regard to the treatment of Indigenous peoples. I also note the importance of not imposing Christian perspectives upon others' understanding of, and approaches to, the TRCC. Nevertheless, for me, I found great resonance between the TRCC process and my own faith, including in regard to Christian ethical methodology and theological and liturgical concepts particularly of confession, lament, repentance, metanoia, and conversion. I also found additional sacramental resonance in practices of ritually enacting and anticipating events that are to take place on a broader and a fuller level and in a future time. While the TRCC was/is not without criticism and limitations, my connection and involvement with the TRCC provoked me to consider the possibilities for a Truth and Reconciliation Commission (TRC) to address other broad-scale situations of oppression and injustice such as the present global climate crisis.

What Is Truth and Reconciliation?

Historian Sherry L. Smith describes Truth and Reconciliation processes as emerging out of the post-World War II context, where Germany accepted some responsibility for the Holocaust and compensated victims. This was part of a growing movement of perpetrators being willing to admit

---

1. I employ quotes around the name Canada to identify that I am aware that the name, construct, and identity of the nation-state of Canada was and is a colonial imposition by European settlers.

responsibility for their crimes and human rights violations.² TRCs are established to respond to specific human rights abuses and are influenced by political culture and public opinion in a specific location. Truth and Reconciliation processes can be sponsored by a range of organizations including governments, NGOs (local or international), and the UN, and in some cases, by civil society, which can be involved in creating the commission itself. The period of time they investigate may be quite limited around a specific incident or may be broader, and they are generally established soon after the conclusion of the incident or a regime change. The mandates of TRCs also vary: they may be comprehensive or selective in the types of abuse they consider, broad or limited in geographic location, their legal powers and connections to traditional courts diverse, the naming of perpetrators allowed or not, information and records made widely available or not, and the purpose and scope of recommendations from the TRC more descriptive, punitive, restorative, or prescriptive/reformative. Commissioners representing and leading the TRC may have a variety of backgrounds/social locations and may be local, international, or a combination of both. Activities may include investigations, hearings and interviews (which may be public/with media coverage), public rituals, allocation of reparations, granting of amnesty to perpetrators, and preparation of a report (which may include recommendations). While TRCs may vary widely, generally they are intended to create closure in a post-conflict situation, mute recrimination, and allow the nation-state to (re-)build[3] by creating (new) narratives of what happened and a pathway to heal and move forward together.

Although TRCs (and other related processes) have taken place all over the world, the most studied and well-known is that which took place in South Africa after Apartheid.[4] Political scientist Robert I. Rotberg argues that this was because it was wide-reaching, televised, and contained a broad mandate that allowed South Africans (and others) to understand Apartheid from the side of both victims and perpetrators.[5] Although many TRCs have a spiritual component, and some might argue that such work is inherently spiritual, the South African process is said to have been particularly so, bringing not only different ethnic/racial groups together but also different religious groups particularly through the concept of *ubuntu* (often translated as "humanity towards others").[6] White South Africans found affirmation of

2. Smith, "Reconciliation and Restitution," 7.
3. Rotberg, "Apology, Truth Commissions, and Interstate Conflict," 33.
4. Smith, "Reconciliation and Restitution," 8.
5. Rotberg, "Apology, Truth Commissions, and Interstate Conflict," 42.
6. Barkan and Karn, "An Ethical Imperative," 15.

this principle in their Christian faith and Black South Africans saw it as an affirmation of their traditional culture/beliefs.[7]

A central feature of Truth and Reconciliation processes is a broad, intentional, and honest conversation between victims and perpetrators of a situation (which may be quite complex and have occurred over a long period) about what happened. It is comprised of testimonies from individuals, and in many cases, also groups such as institutions and organizations, on both "sides." Smith refers to this as constructing the macro truths of the situation, but also notes that micro truths about specific incidents, also need to be (re)constructed.[8] It is important to remember that truths are always multiple and contested, and that voices (particularly marginalized ones) should not be silenced or homogenized in narrative creation and (re-)construction. Therefore, the title *Truths* and Reconciliation might be more appropriate. Broadly, I would argue that several key components of Truth and Reconciliation processes are: individual cases are linked to wider, systemic factors and realities; perpetrators and victims are brought together and enter into dialogue; they, together, begin to create a vision for a more positive future; and reparations and reconciliation projects, arising from the particularities of the situation and context, address at least some of the injustices and help to create that better future.

The truth-telling and narrative re-construction element examining what took place is generally referred to as the "truth" component in TRCs, and some aspect of restitution (often comprised in part by individual financial settlements to victims) generally comprises a large part of the "reconciliation" component, but it may also include other aspects such as policy changes and educational and cultural projects. In the South African process, the state paid initial reparations of $450 and later $3000 to victims, but these amounts and the ideology behind the method overall has been criticized.[9] For example, some argue that these amounts are insufficient for those who experienced serious crimes and also that these payments have not transformed the overall situation of inequality in South Africa as severe poverty amongst Black South Africans persists.[10] Smith notes that some argue that no amount of money can take away the pain of the injustice, while others believe that it does serve a role but needs to be part of a larger process of reconciliation.[11] Many authors make the point that individual financial

---

7. Barkan and Karn, "An Ethical Imperative," 15.
8. Smith, "Reconciliation and Restitution," 9.
9. Smith, "Reconciliation and Restitution," 9.
10. Smith, "Reconciliation and Restitution," 10.
11. Smith, "Reconciliation and Restitution," 10.

settlements are not sufficient to address the wide-ranging impacts of the situations that led to the TRCs, not to mention the underlying, systemic issues that may also have contributed to those situations. Bruce Granville Miller, for example, raises the critique that many have noted about the Canadian context where, despite an official TRC to address Residential Schools, Indigenous people continue to experience profound injustices that the TRC has not (sufficiently) addressed. These include issues related to Indigenous land rights and sovereignty, resource extraction, and ongoing instances of children being taken away from parents through child welfare policies and practices.[12] While reconciliation is a key component of TRC processes, what it entails and how it is enacted is highly contested.

The Concept of Climate Debt

While the concept of "climate debt" is in many ways quite different from the ideology and practices of Truth and Reconciliation, I would argue that there are some significant underlying connections that can be made. Climate debt is a concept that places climate change in the historical trajectory of colonialism and globalization. As Global North per capita usage of atmospheric space for carbon sinks is and has been severely disproportionate to that of the Global South (due, for instance, to higher energy and resource usage), the primary actions to address climate change must come from the Global North.[13] As a subset of broader ecological debt, the concept of climate debt was created and posed as a challenge to the realities of economic indebtedness in many countries of the Global South. This concept reveals not only the severe impacts of these economic debts on the abilities of these countries to deal with climate change but also suggests that there is a moral imperative to cancel these economic debts by understanding them within a broader context of other forms of credit/indebtedness between the Global North and South. Cynthia Moe-Lobeda details many of the benefits of the concept of climate debt, including its calls for reparations and compensation and the naming and challenging of systems of privilege.[14] Many of the frameworks to address climate change conceptualize the contributions of the Global North to the Global South as "benevolent aid" rather than obligations arising from harms that we in the Global North have created and inflicted on the world.[15] Climate debt is a concept widely used in many

12. Miller, "Bringing Culture In," 4.
13. Moe-Lobeda, *Resisting Structural Evil*, 3–4.
14. Moe-Lobeda, *Resisting Structural Evil*, 7.
15. Moe-Lobeda, *Resisting Structural Evil*, 7, 25.

of the World Council of Churches and other ecumenical documents as well as Pope Francis's *Laudato Si* and has been submitted to the UN's Framework on Climate Change by over fifty countries.[16]

The concept of ecological debt is attributed to the work of Latin Americans in the 1990s who were focused on the issue of ozone depletion.[17] They proposed that their foreign debts be forgiven in recognition of the ecological losses they have suffered from colonial processes and exploitative foreign investment. Not only did they consider the demand that they pay off their foreign economic debts to be unfair, but they also asserted that they represented a continuation of colonial relationships and directly and indirectly limited the abilities of their nations to "develop." Legal scholar Karin Mickelson notes several benefits of utilizing the framework of climate debt, including its quantification of the cost of environmental damage and abatement as well as its potential for initiating a broader conversation about compensation that also connects to the need for debt relief.[18] Mickelson also notes how climate debt links wealth and poverty[19] in that it shows how larger systems operate and how poverty has been created and is perpetuated. Loosely speaking, climate debt could be understood as a sort of approach to "Common but Differentiated Responsibilities" (CBDR) for addressing climate change, which has been widely accepted as a framework in many international agreements (for example, in the 1992 Rio Declaration) although it is much weaker than climate debt.[20] CBDR acknowledges the greater ability (and responsibility) of the Global North to pay for the costs associated with climate change and generally to assist countries of the Global South (for example, through technology transfers), but it fails to connect the obligations of the Global North to larger dynamics such as (neo)colonialism and the environmental impacts of Global North policies on countries of the Global South. There is no precise consensus about how CBDR is to be enacted and what those responsibilities are for those in either the Global North or the Global South and there are very different ideas about what the historical culpability of those in the Global North is or should be.[21] While climate debt could also be argued to lack some clarity and precision, it does at least connect to historical realities and broader systems (i.e. economic, colonial) and more clearly identifies responsibility and culpability for climate change.

16. ClimateDebt.org, "Climate Negotiations."
17. Mickelson, "Leading Towards a Level Playing Field," 150.
18. Mickelson, "Leading Towards a Level Playing Field," 156–57.
19. Mickelson, "Leading Towards a Level Playing Field," 156–57.
20. Moe-Lobeda, *Resisting Structural Evil*, 25–26.
21. Brunnee, "Climate Change," 326–27.

Connections between Climate Debt and TRCs

I will now consider some of the underlying connections between climate debt and TRCs by noting their similarities. The most noticeable similarity may be the notion of reparations as a means to address injustice. While reparations tend to be considered on a national scale in climate debt and often on an individual or community scale in TRCs, in both instances, reparations are deemed imperative to address the injustices suffered by those who have been on the underside of power and those who have been directly impacted by injustice. In using the TRC methodology to address climate debt, it would be important to emphasize the role of nations (and corporations, etc.) and not be overly focused on the roles of individuals (particularly in the case of those on the side of privilege/perpetration). Still, individual stories can be valuable if they are linked to wider systemic issues and themes and if connections are drawn between individual stories and broader trends. For example, the story of an individual farmer personally dealing with the impacts of climate change in the Global South could connect with themes such as colonization and neocolonialism, national and global policy, race and racism, gender and gendered oppression, etc. Further, the possibility of individual participation is valuable with regard to agency, as this allows individuals and smaller communities to participate even if the broader groups (i.e., nations) that they belong to refuse to do so. For example, a business executive in the Global North could participate even if the corporation they work for, or the religious organization they belong to, or, for that matter, the nation-state they hold citizenship within, does not.

In both TRCs and climate debt, victims and perpetrators are linked theoretically and, particularly in the case of TRCs, interpersonally, and systemic injustice is exposed by revealing the ways that perpetrators are culpable for the impacts experienced by victims. This theoretical linkage exists in spite of the possibility (and perhaps tendency) of focusing more narrowly on the situation of the victim in isolation from other factors, thus de-emphasizing the role of the perpetrator and the nuances of the systemic injustice in considering various social and ecological concerns. In both TRCs and climate debt, the role of the dominant party/perpetrator shifts from that of a "benevolent observer/assistant" to an implicated party whose role in creating the situation of injustice is, at least, somewhat exposed. Reparations have an economic component in both instances, which may not completely resolve the issues, but, at some level, acknowledges that some resources do not rightfully belong to the dominant group (and may suggest that some wealth was generated through the unjust situation perpetrated by the dominant group). The focus in both TRCs and climate debt is on the future and on different groups being able to live together in a future built on greater justice. Additionally, the victim is given a central role in determining what reparations might mean and look like. This is very critical given the many problematic means that have been pursued, particularly by those in the Global North, to address climate change. These include bio-fuels (which can, for example, cause food crops to be replaced and food prices to rise), carbon credit schemes (which can allow high carbon emitting activities by simply purchasing credits), and various forms of "green-washing" or "green" capitalism. Finally, both TRCs and the concept of climate debt have garnered support from various religious communities and, specifically, ecumenical movements, which suggests that these communities might be open to bringing aspects of these projects together.

What Could be a Truth and Reconciliation Approach to Climate Debt?

While I do not have space, nor is it my place, as one individual privileged North American of European heritage, to respond fully to this question, I would like to briefly consider what such a process could look like in practice. While a traditional TRC would not be possible on a global scale for a variety of obvious reasons, I do believe that some aspects of the methodology could be used to address a global issue such as climate debt. The process could be initiated by a group of NGOs or perhaps a faith-based or interfaith organization. Commissioners could be given the mandate of leading the process and helping to facilitate widespread participation. Truth-telling could be done by individuals and groups of people, likely not in an in-person context, but through technology (including text and video) where testimonies could be shared in an online platform with public access. A benefit of technology in this regard is the broader public accessibility of the process and the decreased need for carbon-intensive travel, although not everyone has the same access to technology and that must be considered and addressed, in addition to concerns related to privacy and the practices and impacts of technology companies, broadly speaking. People who have been both impacted by climate change and are contributors to it could share their stories and name their needs, describing what reparations would look like for them. Creative means could be used to share "testimonies" from non-human parts of creation, such as through various artistic media or the sharing of scientific information about the impacts of climate change on non-humans. Part of the TRC process is listening to and acknowledging what has been shared, which could be done through (moderated) on-line comments as well as brief responses from Commissioners and other leaders. Technology could also create opportunities for groups and individuals to connect in real-time and to build more direct relationships. Opportunities for in-person sharing of testimonies could be created around specific events (i.e., global religious gatherings) where people are already travelling to a common location, but because of the environmental impact I would not advocate for additional travel to be created for this process.

With respect to reconciliation, the on-line platform could also play a strong role, as well as linking to other platforms that already exist. Groups and individuals impacted by climate change could share descriptions of what actions might constitute reconciliation for them, which could then be funded or otherwise enacted by those who are able to shoulder such directly, or through funds collected generally through the TRC process, given by those wanting to express reconciliation. Projects also do not need to be limited to those that can be undertaken by individuals or small groups; larger projects could also be shared online, and others invited to take part. With respect to climate change, many of the actions may also need to be inactions, i.e., commitments to *not* do certain things (i.e., buy from certain companies, engage in carbon-intensive practices). Reconciliation need not be limited to concrete actions, and much of this work may well take a more political form, such as advocating for specific policies or working to pressure governments to commit to the much larger sums needed for reparations through a framework such as the concept of climate debt. Finally, Commissioners and other leaders can have a strong role in offering observations from their perspectives and making recommendations not only to those who have participated but also to governments and even intergovernmental organizations based on what they have heard.

Limitations of a Truth and Reconciliation Framework

Truth and Reconciliation Commissions and processes generally, and specifically with respect to issues such as climate change/climate debt, have real limitations. These include the fact that climate change is not a past situation, but an ongoing and intensifying situation with an uncertain outcome implicating not just humanity but the whole planet. Climate change (and climate debt) is at once inter-generational, intra-generational, and inter-species in scope, with all of these dimensions needing to be attended to. Also, unlike many situations that TRCs have dealt with, the distinction between "victim" and "perpetrator" is far more complicated. As has been noted by many, there are many in the Global North who can be understood to be positioned more as victims and some in the Global South positioned as perpetrators, with some people falling in both categories. In some cases, TRCs have been a mechanism used to foreclose on claims of injustice and wrongdoing with the payment of reparations deemed to be an end to moral culpability. For example, in the Canadian context, some tried to shift conversations about reparations to minimizing Indigenous' peoples perceived dependence on taxpayer dollars.[22] Despite approaching reconciliation from a broad perspective not limited to financial reparations, I do acknowledge the possibility for other agendas to play into TRCs with the primary motivation being to put an end to accountability. Even apologies (and promises for reconciling actions) that are made can be largely empty and unfulfilled, although this is less likely if they are coming from individuals and groups that have actively chosen to participate in the process. Another limitation in the TRC process in regard to climate debt that I am proposing is the dubious capacity of individuals and groups (and perhaps even some smaller-scale governments) to make a profound impact on climate change, global inequality, and climate debt. Finally, although I acknowledge that true and universally satisfying reconciliation may be unlikely, given the enormity of the challenge of climate debt, still, I would argue that the process and striving is nevertheless worthwhile.

Theo-Ethical Methodology in a Truth and Reconciliation Approach to Climate Debt

I will now briefly attend to some elements of the ethical methodology that is present in a TRC approach to climate debt to demonstrate the ways that this approach can embody some key principles of a Christian ethical framework. This might be helpful to those working to promote such an approach within the ecumenical community, which I imagine might be key in facilitating a TRC-related response to climate change/debt. Ethical methodology does not only include the process used to perform moral deliberation but also relates to moral formation and agency. This is key, given that while TRCs may lead to ethical deliberations and decisions, they are less focused on specific choices and more on forming and re-forming moral communities who, having acknowledged and repented for the past, are then empowered and able to address the future together.

With respect to moral epistemology, the primary sources of knowledge are the voices of those who have suffered through their testimonies, particularly as these may challenge mainstream information or silence on

22. Henderson, "Residential Schools," 11.

an issue. Another source, however, may consist of the testimonies of those who have perpetrated the abuse, particularly the self-reflective contributions that express repentance and regret. Theologically, this places the practice of confession as central—leading to acts of repentance, metanoia, and new life. People living carbon-intensive lifestyles of privilege in the Global North, with respect to theological anthropology,[23] can be understood as both sinful, particularly as we are entwined in structural sin such as the climate crisis, but also as agents capable of transformation and participation within salvation, of envisioning possibilities and making bold, challenging commitments to change.

The ethical starting points in TRCs are diverse and varied, but generally begin with the testimonies of those who have suffered most. Criticisms of this approach, however, might be that it is quite anthropocentric as it relies on articulated testimonies which only humans are capable of and will likely miss many of the non-human impacts of climate change. However, these perspectives could be shared, as noted previously, through various creative forms (such as image and video, artistic creations that imagine what the more-than-human beings might say if they could speak, etc.), or through information about the impacts that various species and ecosystems have experienced. While a TRC could also be critiqued as a somewhat individualistic, bottom-up approach, I would argue that there is nothing inherently preventing governments or larger groups of people from participating and it could contribute to systemic change. It would create a mechanism for people to participate on multiple levels, including both on an individual and as part of a group, and to be able to respond even if larger communities they are a part of do not. Overall, I believe that the ethical method embodied in a TRC response aligns well with many of the values and frameworks of justice-oriented Christianity and therefore would largely be supported by those communities, even if it does not end up fulfilling every commitment.

With respect to liturgical theology, participation in a TRC might be similar to that of partaking in the Eucharist or other sacraments. Sacraments are often understood as making visible and tangible something that is difficult or impossible to express or experience in its entirety, yet that small expression can foretell, anticipate, or point toward that larger reality, or what is to come. Therefore, although a TRC may not fully create all of the material circumstances needed to resolve climate debt, value still exists in smaller-scale ritual and practical enactments of confession and

---

23. "Theological anthropology" refers to considerations of humanity within Christian theology.

truth-telling, and acts of reparations and reconciliation.[24] Ritual acts do not only reflect commitments and beliefs that already exist but they may, in themselves, help to change hearts and minds and strengthen commitment and embolden communal resolve for justice. The particular aspects of truth-telling or confession and repentance or reconciliation are well-aligned with a Eucharistic model, as this sacrament often begins with confession of sin as well as story-telling—narratives that tell of God's creation, Jesus' life, and the Spirit's ongoing presence throughout all of time and all of creation. Brokenness is seen in the bread and wine, in addition to serving as symbols of sustenance, communal connection, and reconciliation. At an open table that invites people to come together in receiving the elements in a spirit of equality and a commitment to go forth to serve as we have been served, the spirit and promise of reconciliation can be experienced. The metanoia that can be experienced through ritual action may well serve as a preparation and rehearsal for transformation on a much broader scale.

Conclusion

Support for the concept of climate debt is widespread in ecclesial contexts. However, most churches are not well equipped to enact the scale of reparations payments that climate debt calls for. I believe that facilitating a process that draws on Truth and Reconciliation methodology could be a helpful contribution to move governments, groups in civil society, and individuals toward recognition of climate debt and the enactment of reparations (and ultimately, deeper reconciliation). Ecclesiologically, one understanding of the church is as a seed or a foretaste of the kingdom of heaven—a body which can initiate and also, on a small scale, enact the future we believe in and for which God yearns. Similarly, TRCs also strive to initiate reconciliation on a large scale and to enact and inspire actions at all levels of society. While climate science provides critical data about what is taking place and UN mechanisms and negotiations can create political commitments for reparations, neither has the ability to garner broad-based moral support. Both faith communities and TRCs, as values-based mechanisms (and, arguably, a spiritual process), can change hearts, minds, and actions, raise hope and imagination, build political will, give voice and agency to the marginalized, and build connections across difference and divides. Barkan and Karn purport that, in TRCs, victims restore humanity to perpetrators and apologies can release us from the grip of history.[25] Even if only partially embodied, the possibil-

---

24. A very interesting and helpful example of such a ritual was created by artist/activist/theologian Claudio Carvalhaes and is described in Carvalhaes, "Why I Created a Chapel Service Where People Confess to Plants."

25. Barkan and Karn, "An Ethical Imperative," 25.

ity of healing that the TRC process could offer may provide a measure of hope and agency in a situation of climate change that can be so demoralizing and overwhelming. Examples from many successful TRCs where former enemies, oppressors, combatants, and victims have learned not only to speak their once silenced truths but listen deeply to one another and find genuine reconciliation can be spiritual guides in this work.

Bibliography

Barkan, Elazar and Alexander Karn. "An Ethical Imperative: Group Apology and the Practice of Justice." In *Taking Wrongs Seriously: Apologies and Reconciliation*, edited by Elazar Barkan and Alexander Karn, 3-32. Stanford: Stanford University Press, 2006.

Brunnee, Jutta. "Climate Change, Global Environmental Justice and International Environmental Law." In *Environmental Law and Justice in Context*, edited by Jonas Ebbesson and Phoebe Okowa, 316-32. Cambridge: Cambridge University Press, 2009.

Carvalhaes, Claudio. "Why I Created a Chapel Service Where People Confess to Plants." *Sojourners*, September 26, 2019. https://sojo.net/articles/why-i-created-chapel-service-where-people-confess-plants.

ClimateDebt.org. "Climate Negotiations." http://climate-debt.org/climate-negotiations/.

Craig, Robert H. "Institutionalized Relationality: A Native American Perspective on Law, Justice and Community." *Annual of the Society of Christian Ethics* 19 (1999) 285-309.

Francis. *Laudato Si* [Encyclical On Care for Our Common Home]. May 24, 2015, Vatican Website. http://w2.vatican.va/content/francesco/en/encyclicals/documents/papa-francesco_20150524_enciclica-laudato-si.html.

Granville Miller, Bruce. "Bringing Culture In: Community Responses to Apology, Reconciliation and Reparations." *American Indian Culture and Research Journal* 30.4 (2006) 1–17.

Henderson, Jennifer. "Residential Schools and Opinion-Making in the Era of Traumatized Subjects and Taxpayer-Citizens." *Journal of Canadian Studies* 49 (2015) 5–43.

Mickelson, Karin. "Leading Towards a Level Playing Field, Repaying Ecological Debt, or Making Environmental Space: Three Stories About International Environmental Cooperation." *Osgoode Hall Law Journal* 43.1-2 (2005) 137–70.

Moe-Lobeda, Cynthia D. *Resisting Structural Evil: Love as Ecological-Economic Vocation*. Minneapolis: Fortress, 2013.

Rotberg, Robert I. "Apology, Truth Commissions, and Interstate Conflict." In *Taking Wrongs Seriously: Apologies and Reconciliation*, edited by Elazar Barkan and Alexander Karn, 33-49. Stanford: Stanford University Press, 2006.

Smith, Sherry L. "Reconciliation and Restitution in the American West." *Western Historical Quarterly* 41 (2010) 5–25.

Truth Commissions Project. "Strategic Choices in the Design of Truth Commissions." http://www.truthcommission.org/commission.htm.

8

Where Earth and Water Meet

Development, Displacement, and African Spirituality in Zimbabwe[1]

Sophia Chirongoma

EMPLOYING THE LIFE HISTORY approach, this chapter illustrates how the experiences of Karanga communities are a living testimony of the magnitude of disruption on African spirituality caused by mega development projects such as the Tokwe-Mukosi dam in Chivi and Masvingo districts of Zimbabwe. The chapter foregrounds and bemoans how the displaced Karanga communities were hurriedly displaced without adequate compensation. Intended to provide irrigation and electricity to communities in the semi-arid southern Masvingo province and all the other provinces in Zimbabwe, the government initiated 1.8 million cubic liter Tokwe-Mukosi dam has been under construction since 1998. The vast project remains incomplete in December 2020 even though it was initially intended to have been completed by the end of 2015. Whilst the construction of the dam will present long term benefits for the business fraternity, particularly the sugar cane farmers in Triangle who will be assured of constant irriga-

[1] The field research for this article was made possible through the funding awarded to the author by the Tugwi-Mukosi Scientific Research Institute at Midlands State University to conduct a baseline survey on the topic "Rethinking Tokwe-Mukosi displacement in light of African Spirituality and Religion in Zimbabwe"

tion water supply as well as the various industries and business personnel dependent on hydro-electric power, for the forcibly displaced Karanga communities, all this pales into oblivion because these benefits do not filter through to them.

Although my own ancestral home is not within the vicinity of the geographical area directly affected by the Tokwe-Mukosi dam displacements, being a member of the Karanga community whose neighbors' and friends' lives were turned upside down in the wake of the construction of Tokwe-Mukosi dam, the pain, loss and trauma endured by the affected communities remains indelibly etched in my heart. Hence, the writing of this essay is an attempt to lay bare how displacements and relocations have a deeply negative effect on African spirituality using the lived experiences of the displaced Tokwe-Mukosi community as a case study.

Cognizant of the fact that just like any other African Indigenous community, the Karanga people's philosophy and spirituality is rooted in their closely knit communal society, inevitably, being displaced to make way for the construction of Tokwe-Mukosi dam and the attendant development projects around the dam had far-reaching repercussions on their communal mode of existence. Using an emic approach, the essay seeks to provide a platform whereby the affected communities share their experiences of how the displacements severely disrupted the integrated and harmonious tripartite Karanga communal society comprising of the living members (including humans, animals, birds, water bodies, vegetation and forestation); the ancestral spirits (commonly referred to as the living dead) and the yet-to-born community members. Hence, the construction of Tokwe-Mukosi dam interrupted the Karanga community's solid communal unison throwing them into a real quandary.

The chapter also unpacks how the construction of Tokwe-Mukosi dam and the consequent displacements contravened animal and human rights, flouted justice, as well as scorned the cultural and Indigenous values of the affected Karanga community. Drawing from the African and Christian principles of radical love, compassionate care and hospitality, the host communities are also invited to "spread their welcome mats" and embrace the displaced people so as to journey with them towards the path "of healing, restoring, nurturing and caring for life."[2] The churches are also reminded of their fundamental mission of serving as "a beacon of hope,"[3] ushering in

2. Chirongoma, "In Search of a Sanctuary," 120.

3. In most African communities, particularly in Zimbabwe, whenever there is a crisis, people turn to the church for guidance. Hence, when this disaster occurred, the various Christian denominations responded by donating food, clothing and other household items to alleviate the suffering of the displaced communities.

"exceptional acceptance and reception" towards the displaced communities.[4] In order to effectively minister to the needs of the displaced communities, the church is also implored to reclaim its public voice and identity in its theologizing so that it preaches a message of unconditional love, hope, justice, restoration and solidarity. More importantly, the displaced communities are also urged to reject victimhood; instead, the essay prompts them to embrace a survivor mentality, persistently pressing for justice and relentlessly demanding for the restoration of their humanity and dignity in the form of compensation and allocation of adequate, arable, habitable, and productive land. Their tenacious creativity in reinventing Indigenous traditions, spirituality and philosophy in an endeavor to preserve their cherished vision of communal interrelatedness is being galvanized here. Below we now turn to listen to the voices of the Karanga Indigenous community as they bare their souls on how the Tokwe-Mukosi dam displacements disrupted their family and communal ties.

Disruption of Family and Communal Ties

As observed by Steve de Gruchy and Sophia Chirongoma, African spirituality is an "all pervasive reality which serves to interpret society and give wholeness to the individual's life and community."[5] Key elements include belief in a world of spirits and divinities and usually a supreme being or high God, the importance of rites of passage, belief that life is stronger than death (therefore the living dead continue to play a role in the present), and a focus on predicting and controlling divine causality around such matters as rain-making and human health.[6] A communal existence that finds expression in the extended family institution is highly prized. The family institution in this regard is sacred since it includes the spirit elders as its indispensable constituents. Unfortunately, most families and communities affected by the Tokwe-Mukosi dam were fragmented as some individuals decided not to go and settle in the designated relocation sites. Several study participants lamented the level of disintegration caused, as some of their family members who could afford to purchase their own pieces of land went on to settle in faraway places such as Mvuma, Chivhu, urban Masvingo, and Mwenezi. An elderly man who had been moved from Chikandigwa village after their village had been flooded bemoaned such a breakdown:

---

4. Boyo, "Of Penguins and Immigrants," 106–8.
5. De Gruchy and Chirongoma, "Earth, Water, Fire and Wind," 295.
6. De Gruchy and Chirongoma, , "Earth, Water, Fire and Wind," 295.

> Our family fiber and communal ties have been torn asunder. One of my brothers migrated with his family to join his in-laws in Mvuma after realizing that the government's promises of allocating us productive land were taking longer to be fulfilled. Another brother moved to Chivhu where his eldest son had bought a farm. Several families from our community have either moved to Ngundu Growth point or Masvingo urban where they bought stands and built homes, whilst others were resettled in Masangula. I am here in Mwenezi with my immediate family which means I have lost touch with my extended family and several members from my village are scattered all over. This leaves such a sour taste in my mouth because I will die a lonely man *kuita sendisina hama* (as if I do not have relatives).[7]

This is a clear illustration of how the much-cherished communal existence was suddenly disrupted. When relatives live far apart; family, social and religious functions become difficult to manage. The wholeness enshrined in the notion of communal existence becomes hollow as the social and religious rallying point is lost. Kofi Asare Opoku aptly illustrates this understanding through the common African proverb, "Life is when you are together, alone you are an animal."[8] Family ritual activities were also dealt a heavy blow. Canisius Mwandayi elucidates the dilemma presented by the tearing apart of families and communities in light of ritual performance:

> Rituals are powerful vehicles of meaning on life's events, they offer the opportunity to contain and express emotion. Such a transcendental significance of rituals is usually shared within a group. Thus a community is allowed to come together, witness and interpret an event for its own survival. A ritual enforces a particular collective identity. It is no mistake then to say that one of the recognitions shared by humans the world-over and over time is the importance of ritual.[9]

It is therefore apparent that the displacements impacted heavily on the Karanga people's understanding of existence by robbing them of their family and communal ties which are a crucial component of their lives. The impact of displacement and relocation did not only entail the disruption of family and communal ties, what is even worse is that they were forcibly separated from the graves of their loved ones whom they consider as part of the community (the living dead). Below, we will proceed to discuss how the study

---

7. Tendai Gono, personal Interview (20 July 2018).
8. Opoku, *West African Traditional Religion*, 28.
9. Mwandayi, *Death and After-life Rituals*, 55.

participants bemoaned the severing of ties with the ancestral cult and their sacred sites as a major blow to their Karanga Indigenous spirituality.

Forced to Sever Ties with Sacred Groves and Interference with Ritual Performance

For most Africans, particularly the Karanga people who were affected by the Tokwe-Mukosi displacements, graves and burial places are considered as sacred groves. They are regarded as the final resting place for their loved ones, and hence they revere such sacred sites and take special care to maintain them. Unfortunately, the relocated families had to leave the graves of their dearly departed ones behind, rendering maintenance of the grave sites impossible. In some cases, the remains of their deceased were exhumed and reburied in a common cemetery away from the site of the dam wall. The worst-case scenario is that other graves in the Tokwe basin were not exhumed but left to be submerged under water. This state of affairs left the relocated communities vulnerable and disturbed since the development robbed them of their bastion of security and exposed them to the eventuality of all sorts of challenges striking at them. Shoko puts it succinctly:

> The basis of the Karanga religion is the ancestor cult. They believe their lives are controlled by *vadzimu* (ancestor spirits). *Vadzimu* are spirits of people who died but exist in a spiritual form. The dead include family elders like fathers, mothers, grandmothers, uncles, cousins, aunts, etc. These are family spirit elders who deal with family affairs.[10]

Michael Bourdillon[11] and Michael Gelfand[12] concur that the ancestral spirits are referred to as *vari pasi* (those who inhabit the underworld), they dwell in *nyikadzimu* (the spirit world) and they are the guardian spirits who are influential in the lives of their descendants.[13] Clearly, the displacements caused them severe agony since the direct link with their ancestral graves was disconnected. An elderly woman who was displaced from Neruvanga village and moved to Chisase bewailed:

> Being cut off from accessing the graves of our loved ones presents a major challenge for us. We were used to visiting the graveyard to communicate with our ancestors especially

---

10. Tabona, *Karanga Indigenous Religion in Zimbabwe*, 33.
11. Bourdillon, *The Shona Peoples*, 89.
12. Gelfand, *Shona Religion*, 51.
13. Taringa, *Towards an African-Christian Environmental Ethic*, 49.

in times of crises. Now, such contact is no longer possible because some of the graves are buried under the vast expanses of water and the other burial sites have been turned into a wildlife sanctuary, hence, we cannot access them. Just the thought that the remains of our loved ones are lying at the bottom of the dam makes my stomach turn.[14]

In the Karanga people's worldview, any misfortune and mishap is interpreted as a direct result of the separation between the living and their spirit elders. In crude terms, relocating from one's ancestral land may be interpreted as abandoning the ancestors. Some of the study participants lamented the void left in their constant need to "talk" to their ancestral spirits so as to explain to them that the mishap was not by choice and should not be interpreted as neglecting them since this was a government project which they had no control over. This invocation was intended to maintain good relations with their ancestors to mitigate against the ancestral wrath. In order to address the separation and the vacuum created by the relocation, people carry some soil from their relatives' graves to sprinkle in their new relocation sites. This ritual affirms the Karanga people's belief in maintaining an abiding bond with their living-dead for healthy relations.

Sacred places used by the traditional leadership such as sacred mountains were submerged in water, leaving the community in limbo as the meeting places with their spiritual powers disappeared. This has far reaching repercussions on their spirituality since such a separation clogs lines of communication between the physical and the spiritual world. Furthermore, the community is thrown off balance as they are left without a claim to their space. People experience mysterious events as a result of a disturbed social and religious order. They interpret the appearances of mysterious snakes as a sign of the ancestors' displeasure with the displacement of the communities. A middle-aged man who was displaced from Zunga and moved to Chisase lamented:

> Our sacred mountains where the traditional leadership lie buried have all been swallowed by the dam. We would regularly offer sacrifices and perform important rituals on these mountains but now we have been cut off from them. A number of sacred trees and sacred animals with a fundamental religious significance to our lives which lived on these mountains were either trapped by the game reserve officials and are now part of the game park or drowned during the floods. The numerous misfortunes we are experiencing as well as the appearance of

14. Shanangu Maphosa, Personal Interview (22 July 2018).

> mysterious animals and snakes in our midst are a result of the ancestral vengeance; they are angry with us for deserting them. Failure to perform the cherished rituals on the mountains and failing to maintain constant contact with our communal spirits causes us continual distress and frustration.[15]

Clearly, the displacement has presented a major predicament for the affected communities. Having no access to the sacred sites is tantamount to being cut off from their source of security and identity, exposing them to all sorts of adversities. This is clearly explained by Shoko who proffers:

> Periodical rituals take place in connection with agriculture. At planting, sowing and harvest, people consult the spirits. Before planting, people gather and offer prayers to bless the seeds. The first fruits of the field are dedicated to the spirits before anyone eats them. At harvest, samples of crops like maize and millet are dedicated to the spirits at the shrine. Periodical rituals are vital. They are meant to ensure bumper harvest, prevent pestilences and plagues, and to thank the spirits. Life-crisis rituals occur in the event of illness and disease.[16]

The Karanga people believe that the deceased will remain perpetually attached to their homestead where the umbilical code lies buried.[17] They also have a nostalgic connection especially with the rituals performed in burying one's umbilical cord. An elderly woman relocated from Zunga to Chisase articulates the significance of rituals performed before and after one's birth illustrating how the umbilical cord connects an individual with the tripartite Karanga communal entity:

A few days after birth, once the umbilical cord has dried and fallen, a special ritual is performed to safely bury the umbilical cord within the family homestead. This facilitates a connection between the newly born baby and his/her progenitors, the family elders whose umbilical cords lie buried within the homestead as well as the living-dead who lie buried around the homestead. The safe disposal of the umbilical cord within the homestead is also very significant because if anyone wants to inflict harm on you, they can use the umbilical cord to administer lethal charms which will directly endanger your life. Furthermore, if one migrates to a land faraway, whenever they encounter a major life crisis such as being struck by unusual sickness or other natural calamities, they are usually advised to return to

---

15. Rangarirai Murambwi, personal interview (21 July 2018).
16. Shoko, *Karanga Indigenous Religion*, 37.
17. Mwandayi, *Death and After-life Rituals*, 62.

their original homestead *kundotsika ivhu* (a ritual performed to reconnect an individual with their ancestral land); usually, once they have done that, all will be well. Upon death, one will be buried within the family homestead around the same place where their umbilical cord was buried. This is done to complete one's life cycle and to reunite them with their ancestors whilst awaiting another ritual which will be performed after a year, *kurova guva* (bringing back the spirit of the dead) ceremony whereby the deceased's spirit is eventually turned into an ancestor.

People who were moved from Zunga to Chisase expressed major disgruntlement regarding the fact that since they settled in Chisase, they have been suffering from several ailments and calamities which they never used to experience before the displacement. Since agriculture has always been their major source of livelihood, crop failure and outbreak of diseases among their livestock really struck them where it hurt the most. All these calamities were interpreted as a sign of their having lost protection from their guardian spirits. Shoko articulates this Karanga understanding of spirituality as follows: "Neglecting ritual duties . . . breaking rules of respect . . . exhibiting antisocial behavior . . . abrogating social and religious norms . . . all make an individual physically indisposed."[18] Such exposure and vulnerability due to the displacement is also closely related to their sense of uprootedness from their land of origin and loss of identity which we now turn to discuss below.

Uprooted from Their Land and Robbed of Their Identity

For many Africans, the land symbolizes belonging, connectedness and continuity. As Taringa elucidates:

> The Shona[19] share with most Africans the belief in land as sacred. It is ancestral land. Land is sacred because it bears the remains of the ancestors particularly in the form of graves of the chiefs. Shona religion is based on the grave. In the central rituals of *kumutsa mudzimu* (rituals in honour of ancestors), the point of entry is the grave. In other rituals, libations are poured on the ground.[20]

Bakare also foregrounds this Karanga conception of land use and importance:

---

18. Shoko, *Karanga Indigenous Religion*, 67.

19. The Karanga are a sub-group of the Shona, the term Shona is a blanket term comprising of several sub-groups.

20. Taringa, *Towards an African-Christian Environmental Ethic*, 49.

> Land (house) is a place of connection with mother earth, where one's roots are, where one's umbilical cord has been buried, where one's ancestors are deposited, a place of connection and orientation. To sum up, *land for Zimbabweans consists of things that can be qualified and not quantified. It offers them identity, a livelihood and it is sacred.*[21]

In this regard, Frans Verstraelen reiterates:

> The land forms a close and enduring bond between the living and the dead: through their control of the fertility of the land they once cultivated, the spirits are believed to continue to care for their descendants and the descendants are forced to remember and honour their ancestors.[22]

Clearly, for the Tokwe-Mukosi communities, being displaced from their ancestral land impacted heavily on their spirituality and disenfranchised their sense of identity. Shoko elucidates:

> The land is regarded as a special gift from the ancestors. All the products of the land such as crops, trees, and animals emanate from the spirits who own the land. Key products such as maize which provide food come from the ancestors. Millet and rapoko are essential for ritual beer. Trees such as *muchakata* are assembly points for ritual occasions . . . The land is essential as it provides sustenance to the people.[23]

People bewail the hostility, dehumanization, and suspicion they suffer at the hands of the host communities where the government resettled them. An elderly male relocated from Zifunzi to Chisase moaned:

> Being rendered landless after having been uprooted from our vast and fertile ancestral land, then being allocated only one hectare of land per family unit in a community so hostile to us is an extremely bitter pill for us to swallow. We have been stripped off our identity and we can barely participate at social gatherings since the local people treat us as *vatogwa* (outsiders/intruders). They resent us for encroaching on their land. They label us as *vanhu vedhamu* (people of the dam/victims of the dam project) or *mavhakanzi/vakashanya* (visitors/passersby). We have no other recourse except to endure such demeaning and dehumanizing treatment, being constantly reminded that

---

21. Bakare, *My Right to Land*, 57 (my italics).
22. Verstraelen, *Zimbabwean Realities*, 98.
23. Shoko, *Karanga Indigenous Religion*, 35.

we are a people uprooted from our ancestral land as if we chose to be in this situation.[24]

Feeling unwelcome and being treated as impostors by the host community is a common experience of the people who were displaced to make way for the dam. A middle-aged woman displaced from Gunikuni nostalgically expounded:

> Before the displacement, we had vegetable gardens, some of the vegetables were for domestic consumption, then we sold the rest to generate income. Throughout the year, we enjoyed picking a wide range of fresh fruits from the orchards planted by our ancestors. There were also numerous delicious and nutritious wild fruits. Unfortunately, the land allocated to us here does not have adequate water sources for growing vegetables and the land is inadequate for growing all that we need to subsist. What is even worse is that we have been cut off from our precious fruit trees (domestic and wild). We cannot just walk into our neighbors' homesteads to pick fruits, neither can we go into their forests in search of wild fruits. Some of the forests are their sacred sites, we are afraid of trespassing and invoking the wrath of their guardian spirits.[25]

The displaced people are blamed by the host community for invading their land as if the displacement was something out of their own volition. They express a heartfelt wish for their hosts to understand their plight of having been forced off their land to make way for the dam. The central issues raised by the Karanga people forcibly displaced to make way for the construction of Tokwe-Mukosi dam resonate with the outcomes of a study conducted by Konyana and Sipeyiye in Chisumbanje, Chipinge district, Zimbabwe where the local people were forcibly relocated to make way for an ethanol project. Upon interacting with the displaced people, they established that, in essence, the affected groups are not outrightly opposed to development initiatives. However, what infuriated the displaced groups most is that they:

> were not consulted prior to the establishment of the development project, but were forced to create space for the project. It is this approach that has given rise to so much resistance to the establishment of development projects in a number of rural areas in African communities. The socio-ethical sources of

---

24. Takatadzei Mupfuuri, personal interview (24 July 2018).
25. Musiiwa Wezhira, personal interview (25 July 2018).

this resistance are attached to the local people's concept of land ownership.[26]

An apparent lack of respect for animal rights and the massive loss of livestock through flooding, and the sustaining of injuries during the repatriation process, as well as the difficulty of adjusting to the unfamiliar environment was another major blow suffered by the displaced communities. We will now turn to discuss that aspect below.

Animal Rights Infringements and Loss of Livestock during the Displacements

For the Karanga people, "important animals such as the lion and the baboon are representations of the spirits. The entire kinship system is based on respect for totem animals."[27] Taringa illuminates:

> The Shona like many other African people recognise that spirits operate in the human world through animals, birds and fish. Each Shona subgroup has its own taboos and restrictions towards particular animals. Certain animals and birds like *mvuu* (hippo), *hove* (fish), *mheta* (waterpython), *garwe* (crocodile), *hungwe* (fish-eagle), *mbiti* (otter), *soko* (monkey), *shava* (antelope), *beta* (termites), *humba* (wild-pig/warthog), *nzou* (elephant), *shumba* (lion), and *nyati* (buffalo) are considered totems. The animals related to aquatic life are associated with the beginning of the Karanga- Shona. As a result, the Mwedzi myth of creation is often associated with the Karanga. They trace their origin from *dzivaguru* (the great pool). The Shona believe that if totemic animals are killed, mysterious diseases and wounds will catch up [with the] children.[28]

The abrupt relocation of communities due to the floods exposed fauna and flora to adverse suffering and death. Due to the sacred value attached to animals, the villagers tearfully and helplessly watched as their livestock and several wild animals were being swallowed by the floods due to delayed rescue operations. Disoriented by the floods, some of the animals (both wild and domestic) evaded the rescue teams and eventually drowned. The few that survived suffered from injuries and disease outbreak during and after the relocation process. Losing their treasured domestic animals,

---

26. Konyana and Sipeyiye, "Complex Moral Dilemmas of Large Scale Projects," 356.
27. Shoko, *Karanga Indigenous Religion*, 35.
28. Taringa, *Towards an African-Christian Environmental Ethic*, 50.

particularly cattle which is regarded as a measure of wealth and a status symbol wounded the displaced villagers to the core. Also, cattle and goats are used for performing most of the traditional rituals, hence, losing these domestic animals threatens their capacity to adhere to the long cherished ritual performance ceremonies. They are indignant and nostalgic over the loss of family members, household property, and other family treasures passed down from generation to generation. Inadequate or no compensation for the severe losses incurred due to the displacement exacerbated a sense of injustice, hopelessness, and despair.

Having chronicled how the Karanga people's spirituality and worldview were heavily impacted by the Tokwe-Mukosi displacements, it seems befitting to raise a clarion call to the key stakeholders to heal the wounds of trauma inflicted on the communities which is the focus of the proceeding section.

Reclaiming the Humanity, Dignity, and Identity of the Displaced Communities

The timely intervention of various churches in providing material assistance to the displaced communities during the time they were squashed in transit camps is commendable. However, the church should continue exercising its prophetic voice and demand justice for the displaced communities by advocating for adequate and equitable land distribution and fair compensation. Embarking on "prophetic criticism" and "prophetic story-telling," the church should "give voice especially to the pain and cries of the marginalized, outcasts, and silenced peoples and creatures of society."[29] Engaging in "policy discourse," churches should collaborate with policy makers "in the quest to make, implement and monitor policies that will enhance the plight of the most vulnerable in society."[30] Together with the displaced communities, churches should speak "truth to power" and hold the government accountable so that it fulfils the promises made to the displaced communities. Drawing from the wells of African and Christian ethics, the host communities should offer hospitality, love, compassion, and solidarity to the displaced communities. Although the church and the government authorities are important stakeholders in redressing the damage caused by the Tokwe-Mukosi dam displacements on the Karanga people's religiosity, spirituality, and worldview, the agency, creativity, and tenacity of the displaced people is equally important in keeping alive and restoring their Indigenous

29. Koopman, "Public Theology," 1145.
30. Koopman, "Public Theology," 1145.

ecological worldview as they continue envisioning an integrated Karanga tripartite worldview. Below, the discussion turns to focus on celebrating and reigniting the Karanga people's alternative ecotheological paradigms in their newly settled land post-Tokwe-Mukosi dam.

Ecotheological Reflections in the Context of the Tokwe-Mukosi Dam: Karanga Indigenous Worldviews, Religiosity, Rituals, and Spirituality

As noted above, the Indigenous worldviews, religiosity, rituals, and spirituality of the Karanga community is blended within their tripartite understanding of existence. As such, the neo-liberal development paradigm adopted by the government and other influential stakeholders who stand to benefit from the construction of Tokwe-Mukosi dam infringes on the displaced community's perspective on what is regarded as life-giving and life-affirming. Overlooking the Karanga communal values, religiosity, and spirituality is tantamount to eliminating them from the face of the earth. The Karanga people uphold and cherish their symphonic interrelatedness with their land, water bodies, animals, trees, and vegetation; they believe that their guardian spirits inhabit all these natural phenomena. As such, the construction of a mega development project such as Tokwe-Mukosi dam should not have commenced without following due diligence in performing the requisite rituals in order to seek permission from the spiritual realm as well as properly informing the ancestral spirits who are perceived as the real owners of the land by the Karanga people. Furthermore, while the Karanga people revere water as a sacred resource, a divine gift, as well as the source of abundant living, unfortunately, the floods that followed the construction of Tokwe-Mukosi dam, covering and destroying their sacred groves while denying them the opportunity to perform their sacred rituals, inadvertently became a source of anguish, death, displacement, and devastation. Instead of celebrating and enjoying the benefits wrought by Tokwe-Mukosi dam, the displaced Karanga people are languishing in poverty and disintegration.

Refusing to wallow in their misery, hopelessness and dejection, the displaced communities should be motivated to exercise their agency in adopting "strategies and struggles for survival, adaptation and freedom."[31] Restoring their humanity, dignity, and identity will remain a far-fetched dream if displaced communities fail to shake off victimhood and embark on a journey towards healing and integration within the host communities.

31. De Gruchy, "Of Agency," 22.

There is hope when some displaced individuals are repudiating the feelings of hopelessness and futility by proactively adopting alternative ecotheological paradigms. For instance, some families performed rituals that allowed them the opportunity to carry a portion of the soil from their homesteads and their ancestral grave sites in their new relocation sites. Upon their arrival in the new land, they safely buried some of the soil in a clay pot and sprinkled some of the soil around their new homesteads. Others have also carried branches of some sacred trees and some herbs believed to have spiritual significance and planted them in their newly settled homesteads. In so doing, they are ensuring the continuation of their relationship with the spirit realm since the soil and vegetation which they carried are believed to be representing the constant presence of their ancestors. As such, the newly resettled land is turned into a sacred site in the same manner that the old site which they were forcibly separated from was. This signifies an Indigenous community's passive resistance to being cut off from their religiosity and spirituality. Using the locally available resources in their newly allocated land, some of the displaced communities have also rallied together to propitiate their ancestors, informing them that the displacement was beyond their control. During such rituals, they entreat their ancestors not to abandon them, rather they invite the ancestral spirits to continue watching over them and blessing them.

Conclusion

Clearly, the Tokwe-Mukosi displacements caused pain beyond measure to the affected communities. Their livelihoods, their sense of community, and their spirituality was thrown in disarray. The concerns raised by the Karanga people displaced from the areas surrounded by Tokwe-Mukosi dam resonate with Tarisayi who echoed:

> Traditional management systems tend to lose their leadership as a result of forced relocation. The dismantling of households and villages destroys some traditional leadership. People from Tokwe-Mukosi dam were relocated to places which already have their traditional leaders such as Chisase and Mpapa areas and they were randomly displaced such that they now no longer reside as groups or collectives which can fall under one authority. Local authorities in the area complained that the relocation exercise has affected their powers because now they are stripped

of their duties because their people have been moved to different areas where they are now under some authorities.[32]

Mutangi and Mutari concurred:

> The programme has excluded the cultural values and made the graves valueless and they were exhumed. The moved individuals complained about the history of their families being distorted as a result of the fact that their children will be distanced from their ancestors. Therefore, there was a clash of cultural paradigms and no clear interface situations at Tokwe-Mukosi resettlement program since local people's cultures, values and beliefs were sidelined in the project.[33]

Granted, compensation for material losses is fundamental to soothing the wounds inflicted by the displacement. However, no amount of compensation can completely heal the emotional and spiritual scars that remain ineradicably engraved on the hearts of the displaced communities. While acknowledging their woundedness, this chapter has also foregrounded the importance of how the displaced Karanga people might refuse being pushed into a cleft stick, but encouraged rather to exercise their agency and determination to dig deeper into their rich Indigenous knowledge systems as they continue to preserve their ecological, religious, and spiritual perspectives against all odds.

Bibliography

Bakare, Sebastain. *My Right to Land in the Bible and in Zimbabwe: A Theology of Land in Zimbabwe*. Harare: Zimbabwe Council of Churches, 1993.

Bourdillon, Michael F. C. *The Shona Peoples: An Ethnography of the Contemporary Shona, with Special Reference to Their Religion*. Gweru: Mambo, 1976.

Boyo, Bernard. "Of Penguins and Immigrants." In *Walking Together: Christian Thinking and Public Life in South Africa*, edited by Joel Carpenter, 105–19. Abilene, TX: Abilene Christian University Press, 2012.

Chirongoma, Sophia. "In Search of a Sanctuary: Zimbabwean Migrants in South Africa." In *Walking Together: Christian Thinking and Public Life in South Africa*, edited by Joel Carpenter, 150–75. Abilene, TX: Abilene Christian University Press, 2012.

De Gruchy, Steve. "Of Agency, Assets and Appreciation: Seeking Commonalities between Theology and Development." *Journal of Theology for Southern Africa* 117 (2003) 20–39.

---

32. Tarisayi, "Traditional Leadership."
33. Mutangi and Mutari. "Socio-cultural Implications," 75.

De Gruchy, Steve, and Sophia Chirongoma. "Earth, Water, Fire and Wind: Elements of African Ecclesiologies." In *The Routledge Companion to the Christian Church*, edited by Gerard Mannion and Lewis S. Mudge, 291–305. New York: Routledge, 2008.

Gelfand, Michael. *Shona Religion*. Cape Town: Juta, 1962.

Konyana, Elias G., and Macloud Sipeyiye. "Complex Moral Dilemmas of Large Scale Projects: The Case of Macdom-ARDA Chisumbanje Ethanol Plant Project in Chipinge, Southeastern Zimbabwe." *International Journal of Sustainable Development* 18 (2015) 349–360.

Koopman, Nico. "Public Theology in African Churches." In *Anthology of African Christianity*, edited by Isabel Apawo Phiri et al., 1142–48. Oxford: Regnum, 2016.

Mutangi, Gumisai Tinotenda and Mutari Wellington. "Socio-cultural Implications and Livelihoods Displacement of the Moved Communities as a Result of the Construction of the Tokwe Mukosi Dam, Masvingo." *Greener Journal of Social Sciences* 4.2 (2014): 071–077.

Mwandayi, Canisius. *Death and After-life Rituals in the Eyes of the Shona: Dialogue with Shona Customs in the Quest for Authentic Inculturation*. Bamberg: University of Bamberg Press, 2011.

Opoku, Kofi Asare. *West African Traditional Religion*. Accra: FEP International, 1978.

Shoko, Tabona. *Karanga Indigenous Religion in Zimbabwe: Health and Well-Being*. Vitality of Indigenous Religions. Aldershot, UK: Ashgate, 2007.

Taringa, Nisbert Taisekwa. *Towards an African-Christian Environmental Ethic*. Bible in Africa Series 13. Bamberg: University of Bamberg Press, 2014.

Tarisayi, Kudzayi.S. "Traditional Leadership and the Tokwe-Mukosi Induced Displacements: Finding the Missing Link." *Jàmbá: Journal of Disaster Risk Studies* 10 (2018) a592. https://doi.org/10.4102/jamba.v10i1.592.

Verstraelen, Frans. J. *Zimbabwean Realities and Christian Responses*. Gweru: Mambo, 1998.

9

Eschatology and Creation Care in the Context of the Israeli Colonialization of Palestine

Yousef Kamal AlKhouri

> On this land,
> There is what makes life worth living
> On this land
> The lady of our land
> The mother of all beginnings
> And the mother of all ends
> She was called Palestine
> Her name later became Palestine
> My lady...
> Because you are my lady
> I deserve life. (Mahmoud Darwish, *On This Land*)

The words of Mahmoud Darwish's poem resonates with Palestinians in their pursuit to decolonize their land from Israeli colonialism. Land for them is the source of life. Growing up in Palestine, I had more interest in the political aspect of Israeli colonization and had very little awareness of the ecological challenges which threaten the Palestinian land and environment. In 2015, I moved to the northeastern region of the United States for my theological education. The abundance of green spaces, national parks, and water triggered my fascination with nature. I began a personal journey of developing an appreciation for mother earth and experiencing her profound impact on the human soul and spirit. Caring for creation and enjoying its beauty have become fulfilling spiritual disciplines in my life. Returning to Palestine and being confronted with the reality of the ecological menace created by Israeli colonization and the silence of the church galvanized my theological reflection on the issue of creation care.

Colonization of Palestine is certainly a political and socioeconomic issue, but its theological and ecological roots and implications must not be overlooked. Certain eschatological views, especially that which Christian Zionism upholds, have become an ideology that supports the colonization of Palestine and ignores the ecological injustice committed against the Palestinian land and environment. This chapter investigates the ways eschatological convictions of Christian Zionism informs and shapes the teaching and activism for creation care in the context of occupied Palestine. First, I survey the ecological reality in Palestine in the context of Christian Zionist history and eschatological convictions. Then, I demonstrate the role that Christian Zionist eschatology plays in ignoring ecological threats imposed by the Israeli occupation. I conclude with a biblical and missional view with suggestions for creation care, particularly in the context of colonized Palestine.

Ecological Reality in Colonized Palestine

Ecological threats are an imminent concern for Palestinians. Every morning, Palestinian farmers wake up to discover that their lands are either being set ablaze by the Israeli settlers, and their fruit-bearing trees are being uprooted, and/or confiscated by the Israeli military. In Gaza, Israel continues to control the natural resources of the Palestinians. It also does not supply sufficient power for their day-to-day needs. Consequently, the Palestinians in Gaza are unable to dispose of their sewage water in a safe and environmentally friendly manner. Instead, the local authorities drain out the wastewater into the Mediterranean Sea. That seems to be their only option, as the Gaza Strip has been under complete Israeli siege for over twelve years.[1] The direct consequence of this is the pollution and de-

1. The United Nations Office for the Coordination of Humanitarian Affairs states

struction of the sea, its ecosystem, and its many living creatures. It is also important for us to recognize the ecocide that is inadvertently inherent in the non-violent resistance of the Palestinians. For instance, Palestinian protestors burn car tires in their clashes with the Israeli army. Although they are seeking to protect themselves from the danger of Israeli snipers, the pollution and emission of carbon dioxide through burning tires affects the quality of air and contributes to the depletion of the ozone layer. Furthermore, since 2003 Israel has been constructing an eight-meter-high and 760 kilometer-long separation wall around the Palestinian Territories, and we are yet to assess the environmental impacts it has on the people and their ecosystems. These issues, and many others, are rarely discussed and addressed by mainline and evangelical churches in Palestine. The silence of the Church—both locally and globally—on the ecological consequences of Israeli colonialism is profoundly theological.

Re-reading the Israeli Colonialism of Palestine through the Eyes of the Earth

Palestinians have been suffering from diverse, yet interconnected forms of injustice under Israeli rule, such as the confiscation of their lands, the detention of people, and the displacement of over six million people. In the mainstream narratives of the Israeli occupation of Palestine, we seldom recognize and address the ecological injustice perpetrated. Ever since the war of 1948, the Israeli militia and army have destroyed dozens of Palestinian towns and villages. Along with the displacement of the Palestinians, animals were also displaced and made extinct. Farmlands and national parks were confiscated, and natural habitats, turned into cities for the Israeli colonizers. Since 1967, the Israelis have taken over hundreds, if not thousands of acres, of land to establish settlements and colonies. According to B'Tselem, the Israeli Information Center for Human Rights in the Occupied Territories, about two hundred illegal settlements have been built on Palestinian land which approximately 620,000 Israeli settlers now occupy.[2] Furthermore, the Israeli government has been building a wall which

---

that "The immense electricity deficit affecting the Gaza Strip, alongside the longstanding shortage of adequate sanitation infrastructure, continues to result in the discharge of 100-108 million litres of poorly treated sewage into the sea every day." See, "Seawater pollution raises concerns of waterborne diseases and environmental hazards in the Gaza Strip," *The Monthly Humanitarian Bulletin*, July 2018, OCHA, posted August 2018, https://www.ochaopt.org/content/seawater-pollution-raises-concerns-water-borne-diseases-and-environmental-hazards-gaza-strip.

2. "Settlements," *B'TSELEM*.

separates the Palestinian Territories from Israel. The Wall has a disastrous impact on people, and also on animals that used to move freely between the two sides of the land. It is meant to divide people, yet it also divides animals and severely affects the wildlife. As Miriam Deprez frankly states, "[The wall] divides ancient ecological corridors; the Wall has a devastating effect on the environment and the population of land-dwelling mammals."[3] In the same article, Deprez quotes Imad Atrash, a Palestinian wildlife expert and the Director of Wildlife Society, "The flora and fauna in Palestine are threatened not only because of the Separation Wall, but also [by] the bypass roads and the Israeli settlements." Atrash notes, "we can replant the area around the Wall to keep the habitat and vegetation the same as before, but this is long term, and it is not easy when the Israelis only follow environmental implementations for Israel, and not for the West Bank."[4]

Such dangerous interventions on the Palestinian ecosystem continues today as Israeli settlers regularly release wild animals to destroy the Palestinian farmlands. They intentionally uproot fruit-bearing trees planted by the Palestinians, and at times, they set them on fire. According to B'Tselem, thousands of Palestinian-owned trees and vines were either broken, cut down, or burned. In fact, B'Tselem's report covers only the incidents reported between the months of May and June 2018.[5] The Applied Research Institute in Jerusalem (ARIJ) study reports that Israeli settlers and forces have uprooted 1,405,658 trees from September 2000 to December 2006.[6] These numbers are alarming, as it illustrates the massive destruction of the natural habitats of many animals and birds, and adds to the global concern over the significant decrease in forest and green spaces.

The Israeli violations continue by turning lands owned by Palestinians into landfills. For instance, according to ARIJ, the Israeli authorities created a landfill on the Palestinian village of Burin.[7] Many Palestinian towns and villages also suffer since sewage water is drained into their fields. These violations not only affect the livelihood of the Palestinians but also increase the pollution of the land and soil. The Israeli government has been controlling all the water resources in the Palestinian Territories, which leaves Palestinians with barely the minimum supply. Additionally, Israeli settlers dump hazardous materials in the Palestinian water-bodies,

3. Deprez, "Even Animals Are Divided by Israel's Wall."
4. Deprez, "Even Animals Are Divided by Israel's Wall."
5. "Settlers Destroy 2,000+ Palestinian-Owned Trees and Vines."
6. Applied Research Institute Jerusalem, "Environmental "Ecocide."
7. Land Research Center, "New Israeli Landfill on Lands of Burin Village in Nablus Governorate."

which they use for household and farming purposes. According to an Al-Jazzera report, Israeli settlers were suspected of poisoning the only water source for the Palestinian village of Madama.[8] There are numerous other cases of water contamination yet to be properly documented. These narratives offer us glimpses of the ecological dangers in the West Bank. For the Gaza Strip, the situation seems to be much more complicated. Since 2008, the people of Gaza have endured several brutal Israeli wars, where the Israeli Defense Forces (IDF) used weapons prohibited globally for their toxic effects on people and the environment.

These acts of terror against the Palestinians and their lands, have endangered the ecosystem in the Palestinian Territories. Sadly, Christian Zionist organizations from the West have largely endorsed and financed such activities. Haaretz, an Israeli news agency, states that Christian evangelicals in the US have been one of the main financial supporters of the Israeli settlement and takeover of Palestinian lands. According to Haaretz, Christian evangelicals have raised somewhere between $50-65 million in funds for Israeli settlements and settlers in the past ten years.[9] Many Christian Zionists in the Western churches are eager to support Israeli colonialism. Stephen Sizer, quoting from a Pew Research Center study, states that 63 percent of white evangelicals support the State of Israel.[10] This number only includes the evangelical Christians from the US. They base their blind support for Israel on their particular understanding of the Bible and eschatology. Thus, it is crucial to critique those beliefs and convictions especially as some Palestinian evangelical churches are likewise being influenced by them.

Christian Zionism

As stated by Mitri Raheb, Israeli colonialism is an extension of western colonialism.[11] Christian Zionist eschatology is an integral part of the theological "software"[12] that feeds into the Israeli colonial narrative of Palestine. Therefore, it is important at this point to define Christian Zionism and how it relates to the issue at hand.

8. Amayreh, "Settlers Poison Palestinian Well."
9. Maltz, "Inside the Evangelical Money Flowing into the West Bank."
10. Sizer, "Christian Zionism."
11. Raheb, *Faith in the Face of Empire*, 17.
12. Ibid, 30. Raheb discusses the concept of dominant culture and states that "It is not only the flow of hardware, military equipment, and advanced technology that provides the fuel to maintain the occupying power, but it is also the 'software'—the culture, the narrative, and the theology—that helps to power the state of Israel."

What Is Christian Zionism?

There is no one, all-time, singular definition for Christian Zionism. Some scholars attempt to simplify it, and others would suggest more complex theological and biblical connotations. Colin Chapman in his book *Whose Promised Land?* (2015) gives a simple definition. He states that Christian Zionism is "Christian support for Zionism that is based on theological reasons."[13] On the other hand, Michael David Evans adds some theological and biblical dimensions to the definition. He states in his book, *The History of Christian Zionism*, that it is "the support of the return of the Jewish people to Zion (Jerusalem or Israel) by Christians."[14] What most scholars do agree on is on the global nature of Christian Zionism. Hence, it can be suggested that Christian Zionism is a global movement among Christians which supports the colonization of Palestine by the modern state of Israel for the purpose of creating a national homeland for the "Jews" and as a fulfillment of what are believed to be the Old Testament promises and prophecies purporting to restore the Jewish people to 'the Promised Land.'[15]

Brief History of Christian Zionism

The restoration of the Jews to the land is a topic that was never dismissed in the history of the Church. Augustine and other Church Fathers did not expect that the Jews will be restored to the land physically.[16] Although the question about the restoration of the Jews arose many times in the Church's history, the era after the Reformation had a significant role in planting the first seed for Christian Zionism.[17] Reformed Protestants in the sixteenth century developed a new understanding of the Old Testament promises. They insisted that the physical return of Jews to their "homeland"—Palestine—is

---

13. Chapman, *Whose Promised Land?*, 369.
14. Evans, *The History of Christian Zionism*, 27.
15. The concepts of "Promise Land," and "Jews" remain debated. For example, some would ask, which Jews? Many Jews refuse to endorse Israeli colonialism of Palestine. Jewish Voices for Peace is a Jewish-led organization which advocates for the liberation of Palestine from Israeli colonialism. See https://jewishvoiceforpeace.org/mission/. The meaning of "the land" is also controversial. Many Palestinian theologians discuss the meaning of the land by posing questions, such as, which land? What are the boarders of the land? And how to interpret the promises related to the land? See, for example, Raheb, *Faith in the Face of Empire* (2014), Katanacho, *The Land of Christ*, Isaac, *From Land to Lands*.
16. Lewis, "A Very Short History of Christian Zionism," 3.
17. I acknowledge that the term "Christian Zionism" emerged in the twentieth century. However, it also reflects an ideology that goes back in history to the Reformation.

a prophecy of an event to be fulfilled in the future. The Christian Zionist perspective continues to emerge in response to potential threats from Islam and the Catholic Church.[18] This emergence can be dated back to John Bale in the late fifth century to the middle of the sixteenth century, and through the Puritan revolutionary period until the nineteenth century.[19] In the nineteenth-century, British evangelicals worked vigorously to realize the physical return of the Jews to Palestine. Through the influence of the Christian Zionist lobby in Britain, the British government established a vice-consulate in Jerusalem in 1838. William Blackstone, the author of *Jesus Is Coming* (1878), John Nelson Darby, a founder of Plymouth Church, and C. I. Scofield, a contributor of marginal notes to the *Scofield Reference Bible* had great influence on the British and American Protestants that made the restoration of the Jews to Palestine embedded in their minds.[20] Christian Zionists had a major role in issuing the Balfour Declaration in 1917, which declares the commitment of the British government in establishing a Jewish homeland in Palestine.[21] That role continued as the British and American governments pushed for the partition plan in the United Nations in 1947 and later backed the Zionist military in colonizing Palestine and establishing the modern state of Israel. Since then, the Christian Zionist support for Israel has been unconditional and never ceased.

Christian Zionist Eschatological Convictions

Most of Christian Zionists commit to a literal interpretation of the prophecies in the Old Testament and future apocalyptic fulfillment. There are different schools of thoughts regarding the interpretation of the eschatological prophecies and events. However, Pre-Millennial Dispensationalism is considered the most influential eschatology that shapes the agendas of Christian Zionism. It is proper to suggest that Pre-Millennial Dispensationalism is a dominant form of eschatology in the Western Church. Philip A. E. Church makes an explicit statement, noting, "Many Christian Zionists would also describe themselves as dispensationalists."[22] Therefore, the question to address here is, how does dispensationalism shape its view of Palestinian ecological concerns and the ecological injustice committed by the Israeli colonialism?

18. Lewis, "A Very Short History of Christian Zionism," 4.
19. Lewis, "A Very Short History of Christian Zionism," 4.
20. Lewis, "A Very Short History of Christian Zionism," 4.6.
21. Lewis, "A Very Short History of Christian Zionism," 4.7.
22. Church, "Dispensational Christian Zionism," 377.

Many Christian dispensationalists would argue that Christians should not attach themselves to this world because annihilation is the ultimate destiny of the universe. The dispensational conviction that the world is evil, and the Church is a heavenly entity waiting to escape it implies a dualistic worldview. The dispensational emphasis on an otherworldly eschatology is leading many of its followers to neglect the ecological issues, particularly in the context of Palestine. They are convinced that, "If the earth is inevitably coming to an end, there is no need or responsibility for us to develop any programs or practices of sustainable use of natural resources."[23] Sadly, several Palestinian evangelical churches have also adopted dispensationalism. They encourage believers to detach themselves from the world and its concerns, because they are heavenly beings, and their home is in heaven and not on earth. An Arabic worship song illustrates that very well. It states "Ānā ḏāhb ll sāmā ānā ḏāhb ll sāmā mābsūwt," which translates as, "I am going to heaven, I am going to heaven rejoicing." Those types of worship songs are earth-denying and escapist. For dispensationalists, heaven is their destination, to escape from the destruction of the cosmos. Afterall, the world is a sinking ship.

Moreover, dispensationalists and their escapist eschatology imply a negative view of the material world and the cosmos. Ilsup Ahn states it well when he says, "At the center of these types of eschatology [dispensationalism] lies a skewed perspective which encourages us to live oriented toward a spiritualized heavenly home while turning away from this world."[24] Some Church Fathers have developed and claimed dualistic eschatology, such as Origen. However, many others rejected this Gnostic notion, such as Augustin and Irenaeus.[25] Ilsup quotes Irenaeus in response to the dualistic eschatology, "Neither the substance nor the matter of the creation will be annihilated . . . but the form of this world passes away, that is, in those things in which transgression was committed."[26] N.T. Wright in his book *Paul: A Biography* (2018) makes a very provocative observation that the dualistic eschatology, which emphasizes the view that the end of the world is catastrophic, is alien to Judaism and early Christianity. He says, "The irony of this position [annihilation of the creation] is that the idea of the end of the world is neither biblical nor Jewish nor early Christian."[27] The early church in the first five centuries rejected all forms of dualism and Gnostic beliefs

---

23. Ahn, "Deconstructing Eschatological Violence," 459.
24. Ahn, "Deconstructing Eschatological Violence," 459.
25. Ahn, "Deconstructing Eschatological Violence," 460.
26. Ahn, "Deconstructing Eschatological Violence," 460.
27. Wright, *Paul*, eBook, 686.

that disregard matter. The Nicene Creed which institutes orthodoxy in the church for centuries, stresses the goodness of creation as made by God and the hope for a life in a renewed earth.

Towards a Contextual Biblical and Missional Eschatology of Creation Care

After demonstrating the danger of dispensationalism and its dualistic worldview, it is quite clear that the eschatology of Christian Zionism has an adverse effect on the Church's view and teachings of ecological responsibility and activism. In agreement with Catherine Keller's argument that the Church has to develop "a responsible Christian eschatology" which is also "an ecological eschatology,"[28] I suggest that a responsible ecological eschatology has to be biblical and missional. Therefore, in this section I offer a biblical eschatology for creation care, and conclude with a missional eschatology of creation care.

Biblical Eschatology of Creation Care

The goodness of God is an indisputable matter. A good God creates good creation. The creation with every creature within it, is created to reflect the goodness of the One who through Him everything was created (John 1:3). From Genesis to the Revelation, all of creation is in an active act of worship to God as the Psalmist declares (Pss 19:1; 96:11–12, etc.) and Paul in his epistle to the Church of Corinth (1 Cor 10:26). In the first chapter of Genesis, God creates and declares goodness on His creatures. Six times in the first six days, God declares His delight in what He does, and then, on the sixth day, He once again reaffirms the same. When God created humankind, He invited them to rejoice and enjoy creation. As Richard Bauckhman observes, "The [Genesis 1] narrative is inviting us to share in God's delight in his creation."[29] Interestingly, the first commandment God gives to humanity is not to worship Him, but to care for His creation and the earth (Gen 1:26-28). Caring for God's good creation is a loving act of worship, i.e., "We care for creation because we love the God to whom it belongs and because we long to see God's glory enhanced through creation and God's pleasure in creation served through our loving care."[30]

---

28. Keller, "Eschatology, Ecology, and a Green Ecumenacy," 87.
29. Bauckham, "Reading the Bible in the Context of the Ecological Threats."
30. Wright, *Old Testament Ethics*, 127.

Despite the fall, the command of God does not lose its validity for humanity. The command to care for God's creation never fails. One of the most significant issues in understanding God's command is the notion of defining the concept of dominion as ownership. The Bible vividly demonstrates that the whole creation is under God's ownership, i.e., "The whole earth is both the gift of God to humanity but the whole earth is also still held in God's ownership."[31] Creation is God's gift for humanity to enjoy, not to exploit. It is a gift that comes with a responsibility, rather than arbitrary possession. Dominion over creation means a responsibility for caretaking not possession because creation is not a human possession but God's.[32] It is even more obvious in God's covenant with Abraham and Israel. God entrusts the biblical Israelites in the Old Testament to take care and to do justice to their land.

The Levitical Law reminds them that the Land is not their possession but God's (Lev 25:23–28). The Old Testament and the Israelites have a significant attachment to the land and the world that they never look forward to otherworldly unearthly consummation. In fact, they anticipated the full restoration of God's creation and cosmos. The prophet Isaiah declares God's word to His people: "For behold, I create new heaven and a new earth; And the former things will not be remembered or come to mind" (Isa 65:17). Likewise, Jesus and the disciples envisioned the consummation to be the fullness of God's Kingdom presence on earth. The message of Jesus, since the launching of his ministry, is for people to "repent for the Kingdom of God is here, at hand" (Matt 4:17; Mark 1:12). By this, he is referring to God's redeeming presence on earth, i.e., "God saves us not by snatching us out of the world, but by coming into the world to be with us."[33] When Jesus teaches his disciples to pray, he does not urge them to escape earth, but to pray for God's Kingdom to come, "on earth as it is in heaven" (Matt 6:10). In the Sermon on the Mount, Jesus declares that the humble would inherit the land (Matt 6:6) echoing the psalmist in Ps 37:11 "But the humble will inherit the land."

Biblical Israelites, Jesus, the disciples, and the early church never considered the earth and the world as evil, but rather affirmed its goodness. The resurrection of Jesus Christ is a significant example of how God intends to renew His creation and the cosmos in the here and now. The resurrection of Jesus is a prototype of restoration of creation. Thus, N. T. Wright, in his article, "Jesus is Coming," states, "the resurrection of Jesus

---

31. Wright, *Old Testament Ethics*, 143.
32. Keller, "Eschatology," 87.
33. Rossing, *The Rapture Exposed*, 35.

is the reaffirmation of the goodness of creation."[34] As the human physical bodies will resurrect and be restored, earth as well will experience the renewed power of resurrection.[35] The resurrection of Jesus and the sending of the Holy Spirit are signs meant to empower the Church for the mission to expand God's Kingdom with the anticipation of God's act of redemption for the entire world and creation. Wright states, "The resurrection of Jesus and the gift of the Spirit mean that we are called to bring forth real and effective signs of God's renewed creation even during the present age."[36] Apostle Paul assures that creation has a part in God's salvific purpose, and creation is groaning for God's act of redemption as it states in Romans 8: "Creation itself would be freed from its slavery to decay, to enjoy the freedom that comes when God's children are glorified."[37] Clearly, the Church's mission is to participate in God's work of restoration of creation, not to be awaiting an escape to heaven. Munther Isaac, a Palestinian theologian and minister, in *From Land to Lands, from Eden to the Renewed Earth* (2015), develops a Christ-Centered Biblical theology of the Promised Land. He criticizes the escape eschatology and observes that "The theology of the land . . . realizes the goodness of God's creation. God's intention is to redeem this world, not to annihilate it."[38]

John envisions the consummation of the creation in a state of renewal when he writes, "Then I saw a new heaven and a new earth . . . and I saw the holy city, New Jerusalem, coming down out of heaven from God" (Rev 21:1–2). John's apocalypse envisions a New Jerusalem, which illustrates "radical renewal of this creation."[39] In fact, John in Rev 11:18 warns that the destroyers of the earth are subjected to God's judgment and destruction. "The divine judgement is for the destroyers of the earth not the earth itself."[40] This section has demonstrated that the whole Bible and the teachings of the apostles assures the renewal and restoration of the cosmos, and the Church mission is God's act of redemption to the people and creation. The concept of unearthly, otherworldly consummation is consequently foreign to the people of the Old Testament and New Testament, the early church, and the mission of God globally.

34. Wright, "Jesus Is Coming."
35. Rossing, *Rapture Exposed*, 7.
36. Rossing, *Rapture Exposed*, 7.
37. Rossing, *Rapture Exposed*, 7.
38. Isaac, *From Land to Lands*, 371.
39. Keller, "Eschatology," 94.
40. Keller, "Eschatology," 94.

Missional Eschatology of Creation Care

Realizing the impact of eschatology in shaping the Church's ecological teachings and activism invites the Church to be careful of sliding to Gnosticism and its dualistic and otherworldly eschatology. Wright warns the Church against taking that route, thus: "If you suppose that the present world of space, time, and matter is a thoroughly bad thing, then the task is to escape from this world and enable as many others to do so as possible. If you go that route, you will most likely end up in some form of Gnosticism."[41] Gnosticism and dualism endanger the Palestinian church's mission to be salt and light in the land of Palestine and to the Palestinian people.

Furthermore, the Church in Palestine must think about its ecological eschatology missionally. The message of the Church, especially in colonized Palestine, is one of hope, not despair, and of life, not death. Keller stresses that "our mission is not to a life after life but to life itself."[42] To add to Keller's statement, the mission of the Church is also to bring life to the world through the redemptive work of Christ. Ecology is not a marginal issue. Isaac rightly insists that "ecological concerns can never be merely a 'side-issue' for the church."[43] Creation care is an integral part of the mission of the Church and God's people; in other words, "the Christian mission cannot exclude our primal human mission, which is to exercise godly rule over creation by serving and keeping it."[44] In the context of Israeli colonialism of Palestine, caring for creation, on the one hand, is an exercise of creative resistance against colonialism and environmental injustice. On the other hand, it exemplifies a commitment to God's command to care for His creation.

I shall not overlook that many Palestinian theologians have written extensively on the issue of land with a focus on the goal of political and socio-economic liberation from Israeli oppression and colonialism. However, the land is rarely being discussed in terms of ecological colonization. Thus, I suggest a move from a theology of the land to theology *for* the land. A theology *for* the land which advocates for ecological justice, critiques escapism and colonialism, and brings awareness to the importance of creation care.

In conclusion, a responsible eschatology of creation care urges the Church, particularly in Palestine, to stand prophetically against any act of exploitation of Mother Earth and its beings. "Human societies [the Church, in particular] which seek to revere God and to mirror his justice will also

---

41. Wright, "Jesus Is Coming."
42. Keller, "Eschatology," 85.
43. Isaac, *Land to Lands*, 372.
44. Wright, *Five Marks of Missions*, 31.

produce the fruits of justice and equality in human moral order and harmony in the natural world."[45] Thus, a holistic view of the Church's mission involves reflecting God's justice for people and creation as it prays "your Kingdom come," and awaits the age to come.

Bibliography

Ahn, Ilsup. "Deconstructing Eschatological Violence against Ecology: Planting Images of Ecological Justice." *Cross Currents* 67 (2017) 458–75.

Amayreh, Khalid. "Settlers Poison Palestinian Well." *AlJazeera*, Feb 21, 2005. https://www.aljazeera.com/archive/2005/02/2008410134142919210.html.

Applied Research Institute-Jerusalem. "Environmental 'Ecocide': The Undeclared Israeli War against the Palestinian Trees." *POICA* (Jan 26, 2007). http://poica.org/2007/01/environmental-ecocide-the-undeclared-israeli-war-against-the-palestinian-trees/.

Bauckham, Richard. "Reading the Bible in the Context of the Ecological Threats of Our Time." *64th Annual Meeting of the Evangelical Theology Society*, "Caring for Creation." Nov 14–16, 2012, Milwaukee, WI.

Bulman, Raymond F. *The Lure of the Millennium: The Year 2000 and Beyond*. Maryknoll, NY: Orbis, 1999.

Chapman, Colin. *Whose Promised Land?* Oxford: Lion Hudson, 2015.

Church, Philip A. E. "Dispensational Christian Zionism: A Strange but Acceptable Aberration or a Deviant Heresy?" *Westminster Theological Journal* 71 (2009) 375–98.

Deprez, Miriam. "Even Animals Are Divided by Israel's Wall and Occupation Threats to the Local Environment." *Middle East Mentor*, Aug 20, 2018. https://www.middleeastmonitor.com/20180820-even-animals-are-divided-by-israels-wall-and-occupation-threats-to-the-local-environment/.

Evans, Michael David. *The History of Christian Zionism*. Vol. 1. Phoenix: TimeWorthy, 2013.

Issac, Munther. *From Land to Lands, from Eden to the Renewed Earth*. Carlisle, UK: Langham, 2015.

Keller, Catherine. "Eschatology, Ecology, and a Green Ecumenacy." *Journal for the Study of Religion, Nature and Culture* 1 (1996) 84–99.

Land Research Center. "New Israeli Landfill on Lands of Burin Village in Nablus Governorate." *POICA* (May 2, 2017). http://poica.org/2017/05/new-israeli-landfill-on-lands-of-burin-village-in-nablus-governorate/.

Lewis, Donald M. "A Very Short History of Christian Zionism from the Reformation to Today." *Crux* 51.3 (2015) 2–11. http://search.ebscohost.com/login.aspx?direct=true&db=a6h&AN=ATLAn3971307&site=ehost-live.

Maltz, Judy. "Inside the Evangelical Money Flowing into the West Bank." *Haaretz* (Dec. 9, 2018). https://www.haaretz.com/israel-news/.premium.MAGAZINE-inside-the-evangelical-money-flowing-into-the-west-bank-1.6723443.

Raheb, Mitri. *Faith in the Face of Empire: The Bible through Palestinian Eyes*. Bethlehem: Diyar, 2014.

---

45. Wright, *Ethics*, 142.

Rossing, Barbara R. *The Rapture Exposed: The Message of Hope in the Book of Revelation.* Boulder, CO: Westview, 2004.

"Settlements." *B'TSELEM* (Jan 16, 2019). https://www.btselem.org/topic/settlements.

"Settlers Destroy 2,000+ Palestinian-owned Trees and Vines, Backed by Israeli Authorities." *B'TSELEM* (Aug 5, 2018). https://www.btselem.org/settler_violence/20180802_settlers_destroy_2000_palestinian_owned_trees.

Sizer, Stephen. "Christian Zionism: The New Heresy that Undermines Middle East Peace." *Middle East Mentor* (Jan 29, 2014). https://www.middleeastmonitor.com/20140129-christian-zionism-the-new-heresy-that-undermines-middle-east-peace/.

Wright, Christopher. *Five Marks of Mission: Making God's Mission Ours.* n.p.: Micah Global, 2015.

Wright, Christopher J. H. *Old Testament Ethics for the People of God.* Downers Grove, IL: InterVarsity, 2004.

Wright, N. T. *Paul: A Biography.* New York: HarperCollins (eBook), 2018.

———. "Jesus Is Coming—Plant a Tree." *Plough Quarterly Magazine* 4 (March 9, 2015). https://www.plough.com/en/topics/justice/environment/jesus-is-coming-plant-a-tree.

10

Decolonizing the Privileged

*Resistance and Re-building
the New Economy*

Cynthia D. Moe-Lobeda

> "In ecclesiological terms, if the church is the one universal body of Christ, this body of Christ is divided among active thieves, passive profiteers, and deprived victims" and courageous resilient resisters/rebuilders.—African American theologian Peter Pero

How might the "passive profiteers" of the corporate-and-finance-driven global economy become resisters to it and builders of the "new economy"? This question was seared into my soul and began to shape my life journey at age fourteen when I was exposed to the brutal exploitation of Caribbean and Central American workers by multinational corporations using workers' bodies and land to make vast profits and to produce inexpensive fruit and sugar for North American tables. I was aghast at the suffering rendered by this quest to maximize profit and at the links between those workers' suffering and what we North Americans eat. I soon learned, to my horror, that this was but one instance in the complex webs of exploitation enabling "our" extravagant acquisition and consumption. (In this essay, unless otherwise indicated, "our" and "we" refer to U.S. citizens of relative economic privilege.[1]) In the ensuing years, working with people of Africa, Latin America, and Asia, I have learned that our ways of life and the economic policies that make them possible, contribute to severe, even deadly, poverty and ecological degradation on massive scales. We are colonized by the mindsets and lifeways of neoliberal capitalism—in particular its economic practices, policies, norms—that seem to bind us into these relations of exploitation and to hide them from our consciousness. We are—albeit, for many of us, unwittingly—"profiteers" of the global economy. This reality has haunted me for decades and has motivated my work toward economic and racial justice. I have learned too that, while profiting from the global economy, we also are deeply damaged materially and spiritually by it.

My purpose in this essay is to foment moral-spiritual agency for economically privileged citizens of the United States who currently comply with the demands of advanced global capitalism ("passive profiteers") to, instead, engage in efforts to subvert and transform it. While I am tempted to despair in the face of this challenge, especially in light of its links to the climate catastrophe, I have been converted to radical hope by working with people of Latin America, Africa, Asia, and North America who, despite living on the underside of power and privilege and facing seemingly impossible situations of oppression, have not allowed despair to undo their commitments to life and liberation.

This essay proceeds in two parts. First, I lay the contextual, theological, and epistemological groundwork by identifying six presuppositions regarding the current socio-ecological context that ground the analysis and four presuppositions regarding economic change, noting the study's theological and epistemological grounding, and articulating the paradox at the heart of the enquiry. Secondly, I sketch a preliminary, practical framework for engagement by economically privileged people of the Global North, to radically reconstruct economic life.[2]

---

1. While this category is admittedly ambiguous and porous, it remains useful as a general indicator.

2. This study is part of a lager project that elaborates each of these more fully and builds on them.

PART ONE: Presuppositions, Theological and Epistemological Grounds, and a Deadly Paradox

Presuppositions regarding the Socio-Ecological Context

The first presupposition is highly evident to many readers of this volume. Corporate-and-finance-driven fossil-fueled global capitalism is concentrating obscene levels of wealth in very few hands while destroying: 1) the lives, livelihoods, lands, and communities of countless people around the globe; 2) Earth's fragile life-support systems; and 3) democratic trajectories where the term "democratic" refers to power that is accountable and equitably distributed.

Second, the climate catastrophe (to which I refer as climate colonialism[3]) is inseparably linked to economic violence and to white supremacy.[4] The links are multiple and pernicious. Here we note just one—climate change may be the most far-reaching manifestation of white privilege and class privilege yet to face humankind. Caused overwhelmingly by the world's high-consuming classes, climate change is wreaking death and destruction first and foremost on economically impoverished people who also are disproportionately people of color. Many voices of the Global South recognize this as climate debt or climate colonialism and situate it as a continuation of the colonialism that enabled the Global North to enrich itself for five centuries at the expense of Africa, Latin America, Indigenous North America, and parts of Asia.

The third presupposition is about geo-physical reality. The extractive fossil-fueled corporate-and-finance-driven global economy will not continue long into the future.[5] This is a statement about the physical reality of

---

3. This term I learned from colleagues in India. The National Council of Churches of India declares, "Climate change and global warming are caused by the colonization of the atmospheric commons. The subaltern communities are denied of their right to atmospheric commons and the powerful nations and the powerful within the developing nations continue to extract from the atmospheric common disproportionately. In that process they have emitted and continue to emit greenhouse gases beyond the capacity of the planet to withstand. However, the subaltern communities with almost zero footprint are forced to bear the brunt of the consequences of global warming."

4. I have elaborated this somewhat more fully in Moe-Lobeda, "From Climate Debt to Climate Justice."

5. As articulated by the Indigenous Environmental Network, "After centuries of global plunder, the profit-driven, growth-dependent, industrial economy is severely undermining the life support systems of Mother Earth. An economy based on extracting from a finite system faster than the capacity of the Earth to regenerate will eventually come to an end" (https://www.ienearth.org/justtransition/).

Earth's limits. Earth can no longer provide for what this form of economy requires, namely:

- Unlimited growth.

- Unlimited "Earth services" required for unlimited growth such as "soil formation and erosion control, pollination, climate and atmosphere regulation, biological control of pests and diseases," and more.[6]

- Unlimited "resources" (required for unlimited growth) such as oil, timber, minerals, breathable air, cultivable soil, oceans with a balanced pH factor, the ocean's food chain, potable water, etc.

- An unregulated market in which the most powerful players are economic entities having a mandate to maximize profit; the legal and civil rights of a person; limited liability; the legal right and resources to achieve size larger than many nations; very little accountability to bodies politic be they cities, states, nations, or other; the right to privatize, own, and sell goods long considered public.

- Freedom of individuals to do as they please with economic assets (including nearly unlimited carbon emissions and speculative investment that may result in the economies of nations crashing).

In other words, the Earth can no longer provide or support these requirements of unregulated corporate- and finance-driven global capitalism. Hence, carrying on indefinitely with this form of economy is not an option.[7] The option is something different. While human beings have no choice in *whether* economic life will change dramatically, we have tremendous choice about the *direction* of that change.

Fourth, I presuppose that four overarching norms ought to guide the direction of this change. They are economic equity, environmental equity, ecological regenerativity, and economic democracy.[8] These norms call for

6. Abramowitz, "Putting a Value on Nature's 'Free' Services," 14–15.

7. Historically the question has been "can capitalism as we know it change substantively?" The question no longer pertains, because capitalism as we know it cannot *not* change. The question has become, "In what direction? And by whose directions?

8. The significance of these norms depends upon the meaning behind the terms. In short, the norms of economic equity, environmental equity, environmental regenerativity, and economic democracy refer to economic practice, policies, and principles that:

- move toward an ever-decreasing gap between the world's "en-riched" and "impoverished" people and peoples, and prioritize need over wealth accumulation (economic equity),

- move toward more equitable "environmental space" use (environmental equity),

- operate within, rather than outside of, Earth's great economy (environmental

resisting and transforming the exploitative, extractive, wealth-concentrating economies that currently reign on a global level as well as in many nation-states.

The fifth presupposition pertains to the controversial matter of high consuming classes' (in this case in the United States) moral accountability for participation in structural evil. Three questions point to moral accountability: 1) Do we, relatively economically privileged U.S. citizens, play an indirect role—through public policy or U.S. based corporate activity—in causing or perpetuating others' poverty here in the U.S. or in other lands? 2) Do we benefit from that poverty or the factors that cause it? 3) Do we have tools and capacity for contributing to a changed situation? In large part, the response to these queries is yes. These three "yeses" held together render us morally responsible to challenge systemic economic injustice. Assistance to those who suffer from ecological or economic injustice, while a moral imperative, is not a morally adequate response.[9]

Finally, a tendency in liberal and progressive circles in the United States is to frame the need for change in terms of moral responsibility to the other—the other who is damaged by the economy that renders material benefit for high consumer sectors—and to the Earth. I presuppose that this moral responsibility to others and to the Earth is indeed binding. However, I presuppose that it is joined by self-interest as another compelling reason for change. It is in our self-interest to live in ways that Earth can sustain, and to decolonize our lifeways and consciousness. This includes surfacing the racism and classism that shape economic life as we know it in the United States and damage all of us, and seeking to live in ways that dismantle such structures of injustice.

Presuppositions Regarding Economic Change in the Current Context

The first presupposition is born of my work in Central America beginning in the late 1970s through the mid-1990s. Arguably, the most powerful

---

regenerativity), and

- are accountable to bodies politic (be they of localities, states, nations, or other), and favor distributed power over concentrated power (economic democracy).

9. As expressed by Thomas Pogge, "If affluent and powerful societies impose a skewed global economic order that . . . makes it exceedingly hard for the weaker and poorer populations to secure a proportional share of global economic growth . . . such imposition is not made right by" assistance from the former provide (Pogge, "Priorities of Global Justice," 16–17).

configuration of human players, systems, and other forces the world has ever known are lined up against change toward more equitable, ecological, and democratic economies. These forces are economic, political, military, and ideological (wedding white supremacy, American exceptionalism, moral oblivion, privatized morality and spirituality, domesticated understandings of Jesus, and more.) Recent decades reveal that some of these forces are willing to kill in large numbers, torture, and lie in order to maintain the concentration of wealth and power in few hands.

The next presupposition counters the previous and pertains to moral agency for economic restructuring. It is this: the reigning form of global economy was constructed by human decisions and actions and therefore can be changed by other human actions and decisions. This vital understanding wields subversive power.

Thirdly, the present historical moment is ripe. As Michael Hardt and Antonio Negri in their most recent book *Assembly* note, movements have emerged with the potential to wrest power from the concentrated hubs of finance and corporate entities to the multitudes.[10]

Finally, of the many paradigms for describing the shift into the new economy, I find most promising the concept and practices developing around the notion of "just transition," because it prioritizes the well-being of people most vulnerable to economic marginalization and exploitation. As described by the Indigenous Environmental Network:

> Just Transition strategies were first forged by labor unions and environmental justice groups who saw the need to phase out the industries that were harming workers, community health and the planet, while also providing just pathways for workers into new livelihoods. This original concept of Just Transition was rooted in building alliances between workers in polluting industries and fence-line and frontline communities . . . A Just Transition requires us to build an economy for life in a way that is very different than the economy we are in now. This calls for strategies that democratize, decentralize and diversify economic activity while we damper down consumption, and redistribute resources and power.[11]

---

10. Hardt and Negri, *Assembly*, 286.
11. https://www.ienearth.org/justtransition/.

Epistemological Grounding

Tremendous change in modes of knowing must occur among the world's high consuming people and societies, in particular within the United States, if motivation and capacity for radical change are to grow. That is because our knowing is, to varying extents, shaped by worldviews of profit-maximizing capitalism, anthropocentrism, male supremacy, and white supremacy at the heart of colonialism. Therefore, while we (economically privileged U.S. citizens) must change dramatically, we cannot do so adequately without a dramatic epistemological shift that seeks out and privileges subaltern knowledges and moral wisdom. In particular, and most challenging, we must learn to learn from people who suffer from the systems that bring our material wealth.

The obstacles to this calling are daunting. The call to learn from people on the margins of power and privilege has become common in some strains of theology. Yet operationalizing it requires facing the obstacles to such an epistemological revolution, and naming some paths into it. How are we to learn from people who are, in George Zachariah's terms, "uprooted from life"?[12] How am I to learn from people whose lives are threatened by mine when I do not even know who most of them are? How do I "learn from" people without repeating the colonizing assumption that "I" have the right to possess what is theirs, in this case, knowledge?

Mercy Kappen, a highly accomplished feminist leader in India's people's movements suggests one (but not the only) pathway. She accompanied me for two days as I listened to her and her colleagues. They talked of their struggles on behalf of children, women, workers, and others. "Mercy," I asked her, "What would you advise U.S. citizens to do to support your struggles for justice?" "U.S. citizens," she responded, "who want to support our struggles for justice should get to know us and our social movements." Indeed, few things have more power to spawn moral agency than witnessing the courage and fierce tenacity of people on the underside of the global economy and their social movements toward justice, and then guided by their leadership, being present with them. Such movements are erupting here in the Unites States and around the world as never before, inviting such presence.[13]

---

12. Zachariah, *Alternatives Unincorporated*. This paragraph and the next are drawn from Moe-Lobeda, *Resisting Structural Evil*, chap. 9.

13. In *Why Civil Resistance Works*, Erica Chenoweth demonstrates that we are experiencing an unparalleled time of progressive social movement activity around the globe.

Theological Grounding

Living in ways that kill is not only a political, material, economic, and moral problem. It is a profoundly spiritual and religious problem. From Jewish, Christian, and Muslim perspectives, it defies the fundamental spiritual and moral calling of the human being—to love God and to love neighbor as self with a love that is both justice-seeking and Earth-honoring. From a perspective of Buddhism and other dharmic traditions, living in ways that kill or damage others defies the central precept of living with compassion. From many Indigenous perspectives, it defies the call to honor Earth's web of life and to live as kin with other-than-human parts of creation.

Christian traditions bear a unique moral accountability due to the church's role in establishing both the colonial enterprise and the norms of western society that have undergirded the extractive and exploitative form of economic life. The church is called, in the name of a dark-skinned Palestinian Jew named Jesus, to resist economic and ecological violence and to rebuild economies that are more consistent with the "kindom" of God into which Jesus calls us—a world in which all people have the necessities for fullness of life, none gain great wealth at expense of others, and Earth's life systems flourish.

This calling may be situated theologically in myriad ways. To illustrate, it may be seen as heeding God's two great economic rules for human life—to serve and preserve God's garden Earth (Genesis 2:15) and to "love thy neighbor as thyself" (Lev 19:18 and Matt 22:39). Alternatively, the call to economic "right relations" may be seen as a framework for living the resurrection, as an essential ingredient of discipleship, as embodying the biblical call to justice, as integral to being the church in the context of empire, or as realizing a number of other dimensions of faith life.

Many voices of the secular society have called for religion to step up to the plate in facing climate change and the economic practices that fuel it.[14] Indeed, religious traditions are rife with resources to offer to the movement to build the new economy.[15] Iterating and developing them cannot be my purpose here—although I have done so elsewhere—because my intent in this chapter is to explore pragmatically a framework for what we are to DO in order to heed this calling.[16]

---

14. Notable among them is the Indian literary figure Amitav Ghosh in *The Great Derangement*.

15. See for example the succinct summary of religious resources identified by Roger Gottlieb in *A Greener Faith*, chap. 1. See also the extensive resources catalogued by the Yale Forum on Religion and Ecology at http://fore.yale.edu/.

16. In previous work, I have developed theological resources. See for example

The Paradox

Global ecumenical networks, theologians, ethicists, activists, and others have argued vividly for decades that people of faith are called to challenge and work toward transformation of the exploitative extractive global economy. Yet—at least in the United States—a ubiquitous assumption that this form of global economy is beyond citizen power to reign in pervades the public consciousness; radical change in economic and financial power structures, policies, and practices at the macro level is widely presupposed to be impossible. "The exploitative extractive economy is inevitable," whispers convincingly in people's ears. Simply stated, the paradox is this: The viability of life on Earth as well as the call to equity among people requires radical economic change; yet, for many people, that change is assumed—on some unspoken level—to be impossible. A related paradox of knowledge bakes this initial contradiction into the collective psyche: people of relative economic privilege in the United States need to recognize more fully and on a deep level, the extent of the economic-ecological violence wrought by advanced global capitalism in order to challenge it; yet the more people know, the more powerless and hopeless they tend to feel and act.

This essay responds to this paradox, and does so based on the aforementioned presuppositions, epistemological claims, and theological grounding. My aim in this essay and the larger project of which it is a part is to foment transformative action by relatively economically privileged people of the United States who may be liberal or progressive in their desire for more equitable, ecological, and democratic economic structures and lives, *but who are at the same time profoundly inactive or ineffective in seeking it and are effectively resigned to "the way things are."*

Within that broader purpose and project, the limited focus of this essay is: 1) to outline a practical, operational framework for engagement by these people in efforts to radically re-direct economic life, and 2) to test the framework by receiving critique and constructive response from others, especially from people keenly aware of the underside of the economic and ecological violence that has—for over five centuries—normalized an extractive consumption orgy by the world's high consumers, a deadly and growing wealth gap, a white supremacist infrastructure and consciousness, and a threat to Earth's life systems.[17]

Moe-Lobeda, *Resisting Structural Evil*, chaps. 6 and 7; Moe-Lobeda, *Healing a Broken World*, chaps. 4 and 5; Moe-Lobeda, "From Climate Debt to Climate Justice"; Moe-Lobeda, "Love Incarnate."

17. This essay does not identify policy moves required for a more equitable, ecological, and democratic economy. One fine source is the NIFEA process organized by

PART TWO: A Framework Sketched

The *desire* for radical change in economic life at the societal (macro) level is easy. The *commitment to act* in that direction, however, is easily thwarted. Identifying and demystifying the many dynamics that thwart it is crucial.[18] This essay identifies and addresses just one such dynamic. Virulent in the United States, it is the seductive lure of doing relatively little to effect macro level change because one is governed unconsciously by two mutually reinforcing voices. One voice whispers, "The changes required are too complex to grasp and therefore too complex to address." The other voice joins in with: "What I do cannot really make a difference in social structural injustice."

This second voice is born in part of the extraordinarily individualistic ideological context that perceives agency in terms of individual action rather than assuming a collective notion of moral agency. This perception is fed by widespread unawareness of the vast and growing global body of organizations, networks, and initiatives at work in multiple areas of human endeavor to reconstitute economic life along the lines of equity, Earth's health, and democracy. Unawareness of this movement, wedded to the individualistic sense of moral agency, breeds a conclusion, largely unconscious that says, "On a macro level, things will go on as they are despite whatever I might try to do, so I will limit my efforts to the micro level at which I can make a difference—by providing direct aid to people who are suffering." Structural change, thus, is effectively ignored.

The impact of these voices in concert is cruel and evil. It seduces people to continue living in ways (that is, enacting economic principles, policies, and practices) that kill people around the globe and destroy Earth's life systems. Not only cruel and evil, the impact also is tragic, for living in such ways violates the dearest and deepest values of many people in the United States who, nevertheless, continue in these lifeways—values such as compassion for the suffering and enabling one's children to have a future. These values may be honored in private life, but ignored in relationship to the impact of collective life.[19]

The framework attempted herein defies these two voices by creating a partial map for swimming the sea of complex change required in order to

---

the Council for World Mission, the Lutheran World Federation, the World Council of Churches, and the World Communion of Reformed Churches.

18. Doing so is beyond the scope of this essay, and I have done so in previous work. See Moe-Lobeda, *Resisting Structural Evil*, chap 4, and "From Climate Debt to Climate Justice."

19. For treatment of this dynamic, which I call privatized morality, see Moe-Lobeda, *Resisting Structural Evil*, 88–93 and 117–24.

bring in the new economy. My hope is that the map will: 1) make the complexity manageable (or even a valued resource) rather than a block to action, and 2) clarify how one's engagements may indeed contribute toward systemic change. This combination may help to pave the way for active commitment to subvert and transform the exploitative and extractive economies.

The disempowering complexity is multi-faceted. The requisite changes are diverse, multi-dimensional, constantly emerging, and often contradictory. They involve multiple *kinds of players* and diverse *forms of action* in all *spheres of social organization*. People—at least in my context—tend to avoid acknowledging that complexity by landing on one form of action in one sphere of social organization, perceiving this as the only or most important and vital area for change, and failing to link it to other forms of action and spheres for effort.[20]

In contrast to this tendency, it is crucial to recognize that no form of action or arena of change alone is adequate. Change of the radical nature required at the macro level will happen only by recognizing that it happens: 1) though various forms of action, 2) in multiple arenas of social organization, 3) by varied kinds of payers, 4) by wedding resistance and rebuilding, and 5) through the interplay of material change with change in consciousness or worldview. To these five elements, we move in a moment.

First, note that long-term efforts at systemic change in the political economy are more powerful if carried out with awareness of the following key connections. One is that resistance and rebuilding are interdependent. Another link is between various forms of action; each form of action opens doors to and depends upon other forms. The next vital connection is that change in one arena of social organization enables and depends upon change in the other arenas. Finally, we note the link between action at the grassroots or local level and action at the macro level. Actions at these two levels can be mutually enabling and supporting; work at the local/grassroots level should always ask: "How is this a part of the broader movement to enact societal change?"

The challenge is to make these connections and to navigate this complexity with creativity and tenacity in a community of communities that

20. For example, some people insist that what is needed is change in the individual or household sphere through the action of lifestyle change (eat local, organic, and vegetarian; bike or use public transport instead of cars; etc.) Others will argue that this is naïve. What we need is public policy change. Others will say, "No, lifestyle change and public policy are too slow; we need direct action to block the power of large corporation." Still others assert that we ought focus on changing the stories by which we live; we need a defining story that decenters the human, holds creation itself as sacred, undoes dominion theologies, re-politicizes Jesus, recognize sin as social structural, and redemption as cosmic.

transcends geographic and social location. This calls for a "map" for movement-building toward a new economy. It is necessarily provisional, fluid, and incomplete. While such a map could take many forms, here I construct a simple one with the five overlays or elements noted above:

- the relationship of resistance to rebuilding,
- spheres of social organization in which change is required,
- the relationship of material change to change in consciousness/worldview/attitude/ideology/ analysis,
- forms of action, and
- agents of change.

First Overlay: Relationship of Resistance to Rebuilding

One overlay is the necessary interdependence and intertwining of resistance and rebuilding or in Gandhi's terms "two strings [in the] nonviolent bow" of *satyagraha*. For Gandhi, they were *non-cooperation with evil* and *cooperation with good*.[21] "Resistance" includes refusing to participate in some aspects of an economic system that is fast destroying earth's atmosphere and countless livelihoods, communities, and lives. Resistance also includes such things as challenging institutional and public policy that undergirds that system; artistic expression, social analysis, and prophetic witness that expose the lies supporting the hegemony of global capitalism; blocking the entry of mega corporations into communities, etc.

"Rebuilding" signifies building or supporting more socially just and ecologically healthy alternatives that are accountable to a "triple bottom line" (social, ecological, and financial). Many of these alternatives will be small-scale and local/regional business and agriculture. Rebuilding also includes advocacy and organizing to generate public policy that holds capital accountable for its impact, redistributing wealth and power, replacing fossil fuel with renewable energy, etc. "Resisting and rebuilding" are anchored in Christian theology as *denouncing* that which thwarts the in-breaking reign of God and *announcing* that which furthers it.

21. Nagler, *The Search for a Non-Violent Future*.

Second Overlay: Change in Four Spheres of Social Organization

A second overlay is four spheres of social organization in which change is required. They are individual/household, institutions of civil society, large corporations and other business, and government (local, state/provincial, national, global).[22]

Three points are vital. First, radical change in all of these spheres is necessary to systemic change. Secondly, change in any of them alone is inadequate to render systemic change. Finally, change in any of these spheres can open doors to change in the others. To illustrate, public policy (*government sphere*) that penalizes speculative investment and investment in extractive industry would encourage *institutions of civil society* and *households* to invest for the long-term in renewable energy.

Third Overlay: The Relationship of Material Change to Change in Consciousness/Worldview/Attitude/Ideology/Analysis

Practice shapes and is shaped by our perspectival lenses, the eyes through which we perceive and interpret reality.[23] By "perspectival lens," I mean the overarching—partly conscious but also largely unconscious—presuppositions, social analyses, value systems, and belief systems that govern decisions and actions. For purposes of this essay, I use "perspectival lens" interchangeably with "worldview."

Not long ago, a young college student spoke with me after an address I had given on her campus. She declared her deep concern that her generation had lived their entire lives in the worldview and lifeways established by neo-liberal capitalism. She was dedicating her studies to understanding the implications of this and how to respond to it.

This young student provoked me to face more deeply the colonization of consciousness and material life by the mindsets, norms, desires, and lifeways of neoliberal capitalism. Unwittingly, our desires, economic actions, other daily activities, and relationships are controlled by its precepts, serve its purposes, and reinforce its power alignments. While we cannot here unravel the constellation of implications, we illustrate a few that are particularly salient to this project, using a vignette in the voice of a companion named Freddie. The

---

22. An alternative conceptual frame is to identify change in the behavioral and structural spheres. In Ulrich Duchrow's terms, this is a "double strategy" (Duchrow, *Alternatives to Global Capitalism*, 278).

23. See Birch, Lapsley, Moe-Lobeda, Rasmussen, *Bible and Ethics*, chap 7.

vignette reveals the power of the petroleum industry—one of the most potent players in neoliberal economy—to colonize our lives.

The Power of the Petroleum Industry: Two Vignettes[24]

FREDDIE'S OILY MORNING

In the first hour of my day, I have served the interests of the fossil fuel industry and its profit maximizing policies. By living according to its mandates, I have reinforced its hegemony.

I awaken between sheets of a cotton polyester blend; the cotton was grown in fields dependent upon petroleum-based fertilizers, pesticides, and fungicides. The frames of the glasses that I sleepily don are made of petroleum-based plastics and covered with a petroleum-based varnish. Nearly all plastics are derived from oil, and the plastics industry was "fueled" by the petroleum industry.[25]

Before consuming my cereal—also grown through petroleum-based fertilizers, pesticides, and fungicides—I fill a plastic container with lunch food that is kept from expiring by petroleum-derived preservatives. While eating, I peruse information on my laptop about my upcoming flight across the country to see my family for Thanksgiving. Little do I know that the round trip flight will consume about 30,000 gallons of fuel and produce a total of about 0.68 metric tons / 650,000 pounds of greenhouse gases.[26] Divided by some 200 passengers, my share is about 3,250 pounds.

As I step outside, my first inhalation sends traces of traffic-produced petroleum fumes and microscopic particulate matter into my lungs. My car pulls out of the driveway and onto pavement: twelve inches of asphalt from Texas petroleum poured over a graded roadbed. Petroleum fuels my car and about 87% of the cars I see on the road, as well as the airplanes flying over my head.[27] The rubber tires of my car came from oil, and the petroleum-based engine lubricant and antifreeze trace my path with a drip line that will end

---

24. These vignettes are excerpted with modification from Moe-Lobeda, *Resisting Structural Evil*, chap. 3. They were written primarily by the research associate for that book, Frederica Helmiere.

25. https://www.ecowatch.com/oil-industry-is-pushing-plastic-2581507770.html.

26. The Energy Information Association of the US provides the emission coefficient of greenhouse gases for certain types of fuel. A 747 jet releases 30.638 kg/km of flight.

27. "Energy: Alternative Fuel: Alternative Vehicles" from Project America website: http://www.project.org/info.php?recordID=237; Also: Melissa Hinca-Ownby, "Predicting Sales of Alternative Fuel Vehicles" *Mother Nature Network*, March 8, 2010. http://www.mnn.com/transportation/cars/stories/predicting-sales-of-alternative-fuel-vehicles.

up in the water system after the next rain. The voices on my radio include politicians who are heavily influenced by oil lobbies, reporters announcing a catastrophic oil spill, and guests commenting on a war that depends upon and arguably is fought over, oil. I am inundated by advertising telling me I will be a better person if I buy this or that; all of the products will depend on petroleum to arrive at my home or at the nearby store.

Living on the outskirts of a city, commuting by car is almost a necessity. Decades ago, the powerful automobile industry influenced public policy away from investing in public transportation.[28] Transportation is the primary use of oil in the U.S. $2700 is the estimated cost of financial aid given directly or indirectly to the auto and oil industry by each American every year.[29]

In short, my society and I are petroleum addicts, and we consider it normal. Our addiction is strategically cultivated by the petroleum industry. Our actions and consciousness are colonized by it. The moral implications are due not to the impact of my individual actions, but the collective actions of many people. Facing the moral implications of this collective impact means asking: "How do we acquire that oil? What happens to people and the earth in the extraction and refining process?" "What convinces me to think this way of life is acceptable?" Of course, the impacts are widespread, and two commonly recognized are climate change and wars fought to protect oil resources, but consider another.

Niger River Delta

Nigeria exported 962,000 barrels of oil per day to the US in 2010.[30] Cheap and abundant petroleum is necessary for a distinctly American way of life. As a result, writes security expert Michael Klare, oil shapes government policy and military force is used to protect American oil interests overseas. "Petroleum is unique among the world's resources," writes Klare. "It has more potential than any of the others to provoke major crises and conflicts in the years ahead."[31] This sentiment plays out powerfully in the Niger River Delta.

---

28. The automobile industry and related industries have exercised considerable control over transportation policies in America over the past century. The 1920s and 1930s saw auto and oil companies (specifically GM, Standard Oil, and Goodyear Tire) purchase and disassemble public transportation and light rail systems in several major American cities in order to eliminate competition for the car.

29. Tamminen, *Lives Per Gallon*, 54.

30. US Energy Information Administration, Country Analysis Brief on Nigeria. http://www.eia.doe.gov/cabs/Nigeria/Oil.html.

31. Klare, *Blood and Oil*, xiii.

Oil and violence travel hand in hand in Nigeria, Africa's leading petroleum producer. The Ogoni are a minority ethnic group that have lived in the Niger River Delta for centuries. Today they live daily with oil spills, gas flares, seepage from drilling, soot spewing from the methane gas flares, and constant noise and flickering lights. Their aquatic life is decimated, their waterways are infused with oil, and their mangrove forests are destroyed. They suffer from elevated rates of asthma, bronchitis, pneumonia, skin diseases, and emphysema. Food shortages, limited health services, and educational opportunities are their reality.[32] In the industrial city of Port Harcourt, natural gas flares dot the land, acid rain rusts the galvanized iron roofs within two years, and miles of pipeline often burst, sending sticky back oil into the fields. Meanwhile, since 1958, 30 billion dollars in petroleum has been extracted from the 400 square miles that the Ogoni people occupy. They have seen none of the money but experience all of the devastation. The development of oil resources in Nigeria is undertaken by several multinational oil companies (the biggest of which is Shell), the federal government of Nigeria, and a small handful of local elites.

Opposing the oil production on the land has proven dangerous—even deadly—to the Ogoni people. In May 1994, four prominent Ogoni chiefs were brutally murdered in a clash between federal government soldiers and Ogoni activists. Nine environmental activists, members of the Movement for the Survival of the Ogoni People, were framed and tried by a federal military tribunal that sentenced the innocent men to death by hanging. Prosecution witnesses in the trial later confessed to accepting bribes and job offers at Shell from the Nigerian government. The incident provoked international outrage and talk of sanctions against Nigeria, but Shell Oil proceeded with its drilling and extraction and admitted no responsibility for the events. In response to lawsuits, 2009 Shell paid $15.5 million to the victims' families in an out-of-court settlement.[33]

If drilling were to be done in a manner that did not damage the life and land of the Ogoni people, we would most likely pay a steep price per gallon and buy less gas.

Our daily habits, desires, and consciousness about what is normal for life are significantly controlled by the neoliberal precepts that maximizing profit, consumption, and growth is acceptable and even good regardless of the social and ecological costs. The petroleum industry and our captivity to its mandates exemplify such, but that industry is not alone. (Agriculture and the fashion industry are also potent illustrations.) All "forms of action" in the subsequent section of this essay have more transformational

---

32. Wright, "Race, Politics, Pollution," 137.

33. Agbola and Alabi, "Political Economy," 269, 283. See also http://www1.american.edu/ted/ogoni.htm.

power if intentionally aimed not only at material change but also at change in consciousness and, more specifically, at gaining freedom from the colonizing control of neoliberal capitalism and the corporate and financial powers that drive it. We note here four perceptual lenses that may aid in that decolonizing.

Seeing through a Socio-Ecological Lens

This means linking social inequity (in particular economic, racial, and gender inequity) inseparably with ecological matters. This crucial lens undergirds the climate justice movement(s), the environmental justice movement to counter environmental racism, and the just transitions movement.[34] Without this linkage, efforts at ecological well-being will almost inevitably (albeit not necessarily intentionally) serve the good of privileged sectors and neglect or counter the good of sectors marginalized by race/ethnicity, class, and gender.

Seeing through a Racial Justice Lens, a Gender Justice Lens, and an Economic Justice Lens Held Together

Justice movements among women of color have revealed the danger of any work toward economic justice that does not also see reality through racial and gender justice lenses. As noted by African-American justice organizer Rinku Sen, "If the world became socialist today, racism would still vilify certain people, and women would still get raped."[35] This is in part because the worldview of white supremacy pervades white America and unconsciously influences even the progressive and justice oriented endeavors.

Seeing through a Systemic Lens

Morality—at least according to Jewish, Muslim, and Christian traditions—requires assuming some form of moral accountability for the systemic impact of our lives. That accountability is possible only if systemic impact is

---

34. Just transitions "centers those most impacted by climate change as leaders in a fair shift from an extractive economy to one that is ecologically sustainable and equitable for all. It aims to democratically transition whole communities to build thriving economies that provide workers with dignified livelihoods that are ecologically resilient." Institute for Food and Development Policy, "Food First Backgrounder," 4.

35. Sen, *Stir It Up*, 11.

recognized. However, North American economically privileged people are socialized to perceive through lenses of individualism. (Thus, for example, people who are not greedy and who would never choose in individual life to destroy the homes of a coastal community in another land or to starve a child, nevertheless are doing exactly that without knowing it, through economic systems.) The roots of this isolated individualism are many. One is the colonizing mentality that must ignore the collective impact of individuals' lives. Economic restructuring requires learning to recognize the life and death impact that we have on other people by virtue of the systems of which we are integral parts. The Rev. Dr. M. L. King Jr. said as much. In his last presidential address to the Southern Christian Leadership Conference, he called upon people to

> honestly face the fact that the movement must address itself to the question of restructuring the whole of American society. There are 40 million poor people here. And one day, we must ask the question: "Why are there 40 million poor people in America?" And when you begin to ask that question, you are raising questions about the economic system, about a broader distribution of wealth. When you ask that question, you begin to question the capitalistic economy . . . We are called upon to help the discouraged beggars in life's marketplace. But one day we must come to see that an edifice which produces beggars needs restructuring.

Seeing through a Lens of Collective Moral Accountability

Collective moral accountability for systemic sin is not yet commonly considered in the dominant discourse of the US. However, key concepts are appearing, partly due to work arising from the Global South. These concepts include reparations, restorative justice, ecological debt, and carbon debt. Macro level economic restructuring toward the new economy must develop the action implications of these concepts. Worldview will shift to see them as normal and viable, rather than marginal and unrealistic.

Fourth Overlay: Forms of Action

The next overlay is forms of action. The key point here is not to construct a perfect comprehensive typology. That is impossible because forms of action are rapidly emerging and shifting due to the dynamism and creativity of global people's movements at this point in history.[36] Rather my key points are two: First is that multiple forms of action are *necessary, interdependent, and inadequate apart from other forms*. A dangerous mistake is made when practitioners or theorists of one form imply or assume that it alone is adequate. The second point is that, while most of these forms of action are commonly understood to be aimed at material impact, they also wield power for decolonizing consciousness. Each of these forms of action can be practiced consciously as a ritual of resistance. Here we note twelve interrelated forms of action.

1. **Lifestyle changes** refers to changes in transportation, eating, consumption levels, housing, travel and recreation, and other daily activities. To illustrate: One family determined to make one new lifestyle change each month while retaining the previous changes. Ten years later they celebrated 120 ways in which their lives contributed to the new economy. They were masters of public transportation, used very little plastic, had a small carbon neutral home, ate delicious largely plant-based meals, and more.

2. **Economic advocacy** includes such things as boycotts, investing in companies engaged in economic and racial justice or renewable energy, divesting from fossil fuels and exploitative unaccountable corporations, shareholder advocacy, and socially/ecologically responsible buying. The Indigenous Environmental Justice Network articulates the value of economic advocacy: "Exercise your moral authority through your investments and the banks you use.... These banks are funding a future that will cost the lives of the next seven generations of life and beyond. Indigenous knowledge and western science both clearly demand that we must rapidly divest from fossil fuels in order to avoid complete climate disaster."[37] Many universities and faith organizations have pledged to divest from the fossil fuels and to reinvest in clean energy.[38]

3. **Public policy advocacy** works on local, state, and national legislation, seeking to impact both outcomes and processes of public policy formation. (Processes here refers to building more participatory, accountable,

---

36. See for example the paradigms described in *Emergent Strategy: Shaping Change, Changing Worlds* by adrienne maree brown; *Stir It Up* by Rinku Sen; *This Is an Uprising: How Nonviolent Revolt Is Shaping the Twenty-First Century* by Mark Engler and Paul Engler; and *Why Civil Resistance Works* by Erica Chenoweth.

37. https://www.ienearth.org/?s=divest.

38. For a list, see https://greenfaith.org/programs/divest-and-reinvest#.

and transparent decision-making processes) The illustrations are endless. Consider local legislation to require a living wage and paid parental leave for all, state legislation to protect workers in dangerous industries, and national legislation to build a Green New Deal.

4. *Electoral advocacy* aims not only at electing particular people but also at re-forming electoral processes to be more equitable, accountable, transparent, and free from the strong influence of money.

5. *Art for social change* (music, theatre and other performance art, poetry, visual arts, etc.) takes countless forms. Among them are protest music, theatre, poetry, murals, and more; artistic expression of lament, anger, grief, and power; and artistic portrayal of the "beloved community," the "new economy," and peoples' struggles for justice. All of these disclose the beauty and power of art to inspire, motivate, instruct, reveal hidden histories, cultivate courage, pass on ancestral knowledge, and more. Resistance art is a vital tool for decolonizing consciousness and actions.

6. *Education, consciousness-raising, and desire-shifting* also assumes myriad forms.[39] One is socio-ecological analysis that demystifies power dynamics, uncovers the links between issues, situates contemporary justice work in its historical trajectories, and discloses the structural nature of problems that people often privatize and personalize. Educating self and others about tools for democratic engagement is crucial, as is frequenting alternative sources of news and information that give voice to people on the margins of power and privilege. Yet another means of educating self and others for life-giving change is regularly investigating the social and ecological costs of a product or activity rather than only the monetary price to be paid for it. Creative effort to perceive and resist the lure of advertising and corporate PR is yet another form of consciousness-raising education. Illustrations of education as a form of action abound in the emerging movement toward the new economy. Movement Generation (an organization led by low-income communities and communities of color and committed to a "just transition" towards more equitable and ecological economies), for example, created *"Propagate, Pollinate, Practice: Curriculum Tools for a Just Transition."*[40]

---

39. Hardt and Negri in *Assembly* argue that rule by the multitudes requires multitudes with "capacities for necessary cooperation and collective political action" (286).

40. https://movementgeneration.org/propagate-pollinate-practice-2/.

7. **Public protest** is a multi-faceted form of action including non-violent demonstrations and marches, non-violent civil disobedience, silent vigils, and more.

8. **Building small-scale local/regional economic and agricultural alternatives**, a centuries old form of action, is gaining enormous momentum in the last two decades. Alternatives include food and agricultural systems that build economic equity, ecological well-being, and democratic control such as community supported agriculture (CSA's), small scale organic farming, farmers' markets, and farm-to-school programs; local and regional socially and ecologically accountable finance and banking; worker-owned business; municipality-owned or community-owned services such as cable, telephone, and internet services; consumer coops; local and regional socially and ecologically accountable business; etc. Emerging with blazing energy, these alternatives are a "moving river of alternative systems that are operating, growing, and being imagined around the world."[41] Kessler refers to them as the "germ cells" of an equitable economy.

9. **Community organizing campaigns** aim at building people's capacity for enacting their shared values powerfully and collectively in the public arena. Illustrations are plentiful. They range from neighborhood (to prevent a corporate big-box retailer from displacing local businesses) to citywide (living wage campaigns), to national (Immokalee tomato growers), to global (Jubilee Campaign to cancel the debt of highly indebted and impoverished nations).

10. **Worship and prayer** serve to inspire, en-courage, motivate, and spiritually ground many other forms of action, and to form people for engaging in them.[42] Worship as a form of action for life-giving social change may include Earth-honoring liturgy, hymnody, and art;[43] public lament over social and ecological suffering; celebrating religious heritages of resistance; liturgies and prayers of repentance and for courage and wisdom; and more.

11. **Biblical and theological education** hone skills for practicing the three tasks of theology in relationship to economic and ecological justice.

41. Cavanaugh and Mander, *Alternatives to Economic Globalization*, 267.

42. Walter Brueggemann, in his classic *Prophetic Imagination*, argues that public liturgically enacted lament can be a catalyst for building communities and consciousness that are alternative to the dominant consciousness and norms; see also: Carvalhaes, *From the Ends of the World*; and Moe-Lobeda, "Liturgy Reshaping Society."

43. Multiple websites provide liturgical resources. See for example: https://www.webofcreation.org/ and https://lutheransrestoringcreation.org/worship/.

Those tasks are: a) critiquing beliefs and practices that have undergirded exploitative and extractive economic relationships, practices, and structures; b) rediscovering and reclaiming hidden, ignored, or repressed voices of liberative streams in the religious tradition; and c) reconstructing theologies and biblical interpretations that serve economic justice and Earth-honoring ways of life.[44] Illustrations abound and are being generated around the globe. Just one example is the *Earth Bible* series that constructs a hermeneutical lens for reading the Bible from perspectives of the Earth.

12. ***Transgressing the boundaries of privilege** to have a foot in a world on the margins* is another form of action that appears in many shapes. Examples include building coalitions across "class lines" and national borders; listening to and "companioning" movements domestically or in the Global South that are resisting exploitative enterprises; and finding ways to disavow some of the unwarranted "advantages" that come with privilege based on class, caste, race/ethnicity, or gender (e.g. the race traitor movement, dismantling racism work, etc.).[45] A central guideline for people in positions of privilege is to learn from and be informed by social movements that are led by people who have been flung from their homes, lands, livelihoods, or lives by the economic systems that put food on our tables and money in our pockets.

These actions are means of resisting economic and ecological violence and rebuilding the "new economy" (far more equitable, ecological, and democratic economic life). Theologically these forms of action may be seen in multiple ways, including but not limited to: practicing loving neighbor as self, living the resurrection, moving in the already but not yet "kinship" of God revealed in Jesus, or embodying hope.

Fifth Overlay: Agents of Change

Previously we identified four spheres of social organization in which change is required. They were individual/household, institutions of civil

---

44. Tremendous work has been done in generating justice-seeking Earth-honoring theologies, especially since the rise of the initial liberation theologies in the mid-twentieth century. Far less progress has been made in uncovering the power to enact these theologies in the lives of faith communities, at least in the US context. That step is crucial theological work for the current time. It is one intent of this essay and the project of which it is a part.

45. Excellent work exists on disavowing white privilege and male privilege. Similar work could be done regarding economic privilege.

society, large corporations and other businesses, and government (local, state/provincial, national, global). Each of these, however, has potential to be not only the object of change toward the new economy, but also the agent of change in that direction. For example: a faith community can advocate for more just public policy.

In Closing

In this essay, I have sought to outline keys to overcoming the moral inertia of relatively economically privileged citizens of the United States in the face of advanced global capitalism and the structural evil it generates. My aim is to help those who currently acquiesce to the demands of the neoliberal economy to become deeply engaged in efforts to resist and transform it.

After identifying presuppositions and epistemological and theological grounding, I named a deadly paradox: Morality and faith in the God revealed in Jesus call for resisting corporate-and-finance-driven capitalism, and building more equitable, ecological, and democratic alternatives; yet—at least in the United States—many people who long for that change continue to act as though this exploitative extractive economy is inevitable. This moral-spiritual inertia has many roots. We considered two that intertwine. They are the assumptions that the changes required are too complex to engage, and that people cannot really have an impact on systemic economic injustice.

In response, I have outlined a practical framework for engagement—for these people—to radically re-direct economic life toward equity, ecological regenerativity, and democratic accountability.[46] This entails transgressing the norms, ideologies, practices, and power structures that produce the hegemony of trans-national corporate-and-finance-driven global capitalism. Said differently, it entails decolonizing our material lives and our consciousness.

Now we return to my story. Healing from the shame that burned my soul at age fourteen upon learning that I was a "beneficiary" of brutally exploitative economic systems has come through many wise companions, the great Spirit working through them, and action. Among other things, I have learned that moral power in the midst of horrific economic and ecological violence requires the capacity to live in paradox. In particular, I

---

46. It remains to be said that many pieces of a framework for action, and questions raised by it remain unaddressed in this essay. One piece has been mentioned. It is the kinds of public policy moves required to bring in the new economy. Another is the daunting question of just who within the US ought to be held morally accountable for the ravages of American economic imperialism.

mean the paradoxes of holding together without allowing the one to wipe out the other:

- The stunning beauty of this world with its brutality,
- Hope with despair,
- Profound sorrow with profound joy,
- Anger as a holy companion of love and tutored by it.

Bibliography

Abramowitz, Janet. "Putting a Value on Nature's 'Free' Services." *World Watch Magazine* 11.1 (1998) 10–19.

Agbola, Tunde and Mouruf Alabi. "Political Economy of Petroleum Resources Development, Environmental Injustice and Selective Victimization: A Case Study of the Niger Delta Region of Nigeria." In *Just Sustainabilities*, edited by Julian Agyeman, et al., 246–66. Cambridge: MIT Press, 2003.

Anthony, Carl. *The Earth, the City, and the Hidden Narrative of Race.* Oakland, CA: New Village, 2017.

Birch, Bruce, Jacqueline Lapsley, Cynthia Moe-Lobeda, and Larry Rasmussen. *Bible and Ethics: A New Conversation.* Minneapolis: Fortress, 2018.

brown, adrienne maree. *Emergent Strategy: Shaping Change, Changing Worlds.* Stirling, UK: AK, 2017.

Brueggemann, Walter. *The Prophetic Imagination.* 2nd ed. Minneapolis: Fortress, 2001.

Carvalhaes, Claudio, ed. *From the Ends of the World: Prayers in Defiance of Empire.* Nashville: Abingdon, 2020.

Cavanaugh John, and Jerry Mander, eds. *Alternatives to Economic Globalization: A Better World Is Possible.* San Francisco: Berrett-Koehler, 2004.

Chenoweth, Erica. *Why Civil Resistance Works.* New York: Columbia University Press, 2012.

Day. Keri. *Religious Resistance to Neoliberalism: Womanist and Black Feminist Perspectives.* Black Religion/Womanist Thought/Social Justice. New York: Palgrave Macmillan, 2015.

Dorrien, Gary. *Economy, Difference, Empire: Social Ethics for Social Justice.* Columbia Series on Religion and Politics. New York: Columbia University Press, 2010.

Duchrow, Ulrich. *Alternatives to Global Capitalism.* Utrecht: International Books, 1995.

Engler, Mark, and Paul Engler. *This Is an Uprising: How Nonviolent Revolt Is Shaping the Twenty-First Century.* New York: Bold Type Books, 2017.

Ghosh, Amitav. *The Great Derangement: Climate Change and the Unthinkable.* Randy L. and Melvin R. Berlin Family Lectures. Chicago: University of Chicago Press, 2017.

Gottlieb, Roger S. *A Greener Faith: Religious Environmentalism and Our Planet's Future.* Oxford: Oxford University Press, 2006.

Hardt, Michael, and Antonio Negri. *Assembly.* Oxford: Oxford University Press, 2017.

Hinca-Ownby, Melissa. "Predicting Sales of Alternative Fuel Vehicles." *Mother Nature Network* (March 8, 2010).

Indigenous Environmental Network. "Divest and Starve the Black Snake." https://www.ienearth.org/divest/.

———. "Just Transition." https://www.ienearth.org/justtransition/.

Institute for Food and Development Policy. "Food First Backgrounder." 25.2 (Summer 2019; https://foodfirst.org/wp-content/uploads/2019/05/Backgrounder_SUMMER_2019-05-18-Final-1.pdf).

Kelly, Marjorie, and Ted Howard. *The Making of a Democratic Economy: Building Prosperity for the Many, not Just the Few.* Oakland, CA: Berrett-Koehler, 2019.

Klare, Michael. *Blood and Oil: The Dangers and Consequences of America's Growing Petroleum Dependency.* New York: Metropolitan Books/Henry Holt, 2004.

Lee Boggs, Grace. *The Next American Revolution: Sustainable Activism for the Twenty-First Century.* Berkeley: University of California Press, 2011.

Lummis, Douglas C. *Radical Democracy.* Ithaca, NY: Cornell University Press, 1997.

Moe-Lobeda, Cynthia D. "From Climate Debt to Climate Justice: God's Love Embodied in Garden Earth." In *The Wiley Blackwell Companion to Religion and Ecology,* edited by John Hart, 203–19. Wiley-Blackwell Companions to Religion. Hoboken, NJ: Wiley, 2017.

———. *Healing a Broken World: Globalization and God.* Minneapolis: Fortress, 2002.

———. "Liturgy Reshaping Society." In *Ordo: Bath, Word, Prayer, Table: A Liturgical Primer in Honor of Gordon Lathrop,* edited by Dirke Lange and Dwight Vogel, 164–87. Akron, OH: OSL, 2006.

———. "Love Incarnate: Hope and Power for Climate Justice." In *Ecotheology: A Christian Conversation,* edited by Alan Padgett and Kiara Jorgenson, 67–105. Grand Rapids: Eerdmans, 2020.

———. *Resisting Structural Evil: Love as Ecological-Economic Vocation.* Minneapolis: Fortress, 2013.

Movement Generation: Justice and Ecology Project. "Announcing: Propagate, Pollinate, Practice!" https://movementgeneration.org/propagate-pollinate-practice-2/.

Nagler, Michael N. *The Search for a Nonviolent Future: A Promise of Peace for Ourselves, Our Families, and Our World.* Novato, CA: New World Library, 2010.

Nixon, Rob. *Slow Violence and the Environmentalism of the Poor.* Cambridge: Harvard University Press, 2011.

Pogge, Thomas. "Priorities of Global Justice." *Metaphilosophy* 32.1/2 (2001) 6–24.

Powell, John A. *Racing to Justice: Transforming Our Conceptions of Self and Other to Build an Inclusive Society.* Bloomington: Indiana University Press, 2015.

Sen, Rinku. *Stir it Up: Lessons in Community Organizing and Advocacy.* Chardon Press Series. San Francisco: Jossey-Bass, 2003.

Tamminen, Terry. *Lives per Gallon: The True Cost of Our Oil Addiction.* Washington, DC: Island Press/Shearwater Books, 2006.

US Energy Information Administration. "Country Analysis Brief on Nigeria." 25 June 2020. https://www.eia.gov/international/analysis/country/NGA.

Wright, Beverly. "Race, Politics, Pollution: Environmental Justice in the Mississippi River Chemical Corridor." In *Just Sustainabilities,* edited by Julian Agyeman, et al., 105–26. Cambridge: MIT Press, 2003.

YES! Magazine. "Infographic: How the Oil Industry Is Pushing Plastic." *EcoWatch* (26 June 2018). https://www.ecowatch.com/oil-industry-is-pushing-plastic-2581507770.html.

Zachariah, George. *Alternatives Unincorporated: Earth Ethics from the Grassroots.* Cross Cultural Theologies. Oakville, CT: Equinox, 2014.

Part Four

Earth Uprisings

Decolonization and a Return
to the Commons

11

Whose *Oikos* Is It Anyway?

Towards a Poromboke *Ecotheology of "Commoning"*

GEORGE ZACHARIAH

CONTEXTUAL THEOLOGIES ARE THEOLOGICAL reflections emerging from particular communities in response to the realities around them. In that sense, Ecotheology is a contextual theology, as it engages in theological reflections and praxis in response to the ecological crisis. However, in recent times, ecotheology has emerged as a mainstream theology with universal categories and metanarratives. A common metaphor that we come across in the dominant strands of ecotheology is *Oikos* or *our common home*. Such metaphors are certainly important as they can inspire us to restore the beauty and integrity of the earth. However, the very perception of the earth as *our common home* is problematic. Often, we valorize terms such as *Oikos* while engaging in the politics of enclosing and privatizing the earth. When corporate forces and settler colonialism continue to colonize the commons by dispossessing the indigenous and subaltern communities who live in communion with the commons, the question is not whether we are concerned about the future of the earth, but "Whose *oikos* is it, anyway?" This disturbing discernment is an invitation to go beyond our dominant feel-good ecotheological discourses and practices of romanticizing the earth, and to perceive ecological crisis in a trans-sectional way, privileging the voices of the communities that are disproportionally affected by different manifestations of ecological injustice.

The Indigenous and subaltern engagement with the ecological crisis interprets the crisis as the colonization of the "commons." The commons here signify the commonwealth of the community of creation that births, sustains and nurtures the movement of life—the land, water, forests, seeds, biodiversity, atmosphere and the commoners who live in communion with these commons. This discernment calls for a new problematization of the current ecological crisis as ecological injustice and ecological racism and casteism. The crisis of the earth is more than some changes in the mercury level, extinction of different species, and the decrease in the natural green canopy of the earth. Rather, it is the colonization of the commons, thanks to corporate appropriation of the commonwealth, which destroys the integrity of creation and uproots the commoners from their traditional abodes: *jal, jungle* and *jamin* (water bodies, forest and land).

For the subaltern communities in India, *Poromboke* is their commons—burial grounds, grazing lands, and wetlands. As commoners, they are organically connected with the *Poromboke* geographies. In colloquial language, the word *Poromboke* represents people and land that are impure and worthless, and it exposes the subalternity of both the commons and the commoners. *Poromboke* is an important source of sustenance and livelihood for the subaltern communities—pottery, reeds, cane and bamboo, fish, water for drinking, irrigation, bleaching and washing, fuelwood and fodder, medicinal plants, and construction materials. By declaring *Poromboke* as useless wasteland, the State is preparing the way for the corporates to colonize the *Poromboke* by commodifying the life-giving commons and uprooting the commoners from their abode and livelihood. This organic womb and source of life and survival for the commoners is being taken over to build the infrastructure of the Empire. A *Poromboke* ecotheology, therefore, is an attempt to engage in ecotheology in India trans-sectionally at the interface of caste, class and gender.

Problematizing the "Metanarrative" of the "Global" Perspective

Ecological consciousness, thanks to the rising ecological degradation of the earth in recent past, has given birth to several global initiatives to develop platforms and covenants of solidarity to affirm and practice creation-care. These initiatives have been successful in "globalizing" ecological awareness, by developing universal metaphors and categories to problematize and address the ecological crisis. Global Ethic is one such initiative pioneered by Hans Küng during the 2003 World Parliament of Religions held in Chicago, USA. In his "Principles of a Global Ethic,"[1] Küng observes that "the world is in agony," caused by social disarray, marginalization, patriarchy, religious strife, and ecological crisis." He further observes that it is the absence of a *grand vision* and the leadership of mediocre political leaders that has worsened the situation. In the midst of this agony, Küng recognizes the presence of a *common ethic* that already exists within the religious teachings of the world and affirms the potential of this global ethic to provide the moral foundation for a vision to lead human communities away from despair, and society away from chaos. For Küng, this Global Ethic is hence a "minimal consensus concerning binding values, irrevocable standards and fundamental moral attitudes,"[2] which can be affirmed by all people with ethical convictions.

The Earth Charter (2000) is yet another example for global solidarity for a just, sustainable, and peaceful global society. It is a covenant that emerged through a decade-long, global, cross-cultural dialogue on common goals and shared values, and that seeks to "inspire in all peoples a sense of global interdependence and shared responsibility for the well-being of the human family, the great community of life, and future generations."[3] The preamble of the Earth Charter articulates the philosophy and ethics of this global covenant:

> We stand at a critical moment in Earth's history, a time when humanity must choose its future. As the world becomes increasingly interdependent and fragile, the future at once holds great peril and great promise. To move forward we must recognize that in the midst of a magnificent diversity of cultures and life forms we are *one human family* and *one Earth community* with a *common destiny*. We must join together to bring forth a sustainable global society founded on respect for nature, universal human rights, economic justice, and a culture of peace. Towards this end, it is imperative that we, the peoples of Earth, declare our responsibility to one another, to the greater community of life, and to future generations.[4]

1. http://www.global-ethic-now.de/index-eng.php.
2. http://www.global-ethic-now.de/index-eng.php.
3. http://www.earthcharterinaction.org/content/pages/What-is-the-Earth-Charter%3F.html.
4. http://www.earthcharterinaction.org/content/pages/Read-the-Charter.html (emphasis added).

What are the problems with these strands of eco-consciousness, eco-activism, and ecotheologies? Why should we interrogate them? The logic behind this approach is the faith in the potential of universal categories and metanarratives to inspire diverse communities to engage in global initiatives to save the earth. However, this logic is inherently problematic. Firstly, the mainstream eco-discourses and actions consider human beings as a homogenous entity—*one human family*, living in the *Oikos: Our common home*, and suggest that we are all affected equally by the ecological crisis. Secondly, they tend to blame anthropocentrism and anthropogenic (human-induced) emissions for the present crisis, so much so that the present geological age is named as Anthropocene. Such a diagnosis against human beings *per se* can lead to misanthropy and absolve the ecological sins of the corporations and the industrialized nations. As Utah Phillips reminds us "the earth is not dying; it is being killed. And the people who are killing it have names and addresses."[5] Thirdly, when we use universal categories and homogenized and standardized perceptions of human beings in our diagnosis of the problem, our solutions are also informed and constructed by the same logic and worldview.

The diagnosis of the grand narratives and the global perspectives is a *symptomatic* diagnosis that reduces the problem into a natural calamity. It is a *simplistic* diagnosis that does not investigate the problem at the interface of systems and practices of oppression, inequality, and marginalization prevalent in the society. It is a *biased* diagnosis to cover up deliberately the real culprits, and to perpetuate their interests by absolving their structural sins. It is a *racist and casteist* diagnosis which valorizes nature without recognizing how nature is embedded in unequal social relations. It is a *reductionist* diagnosis which homogenizes human beings and thereby perpetuates the economic, racist, and patriarchal interests of the dominant.

Dominant strands of eco-consciousness, eco-activism, and ecotheology are contested by theologians from the margins. Felix Wilfred observes that unity and universality "could become a cloak to cover the vested interests of the upper castes [races] and classes. True unity is the result of dialogue, negotiation, mutuality, and not a matter of fitting everything into a ready-made system."[6] Exposing its Eurocentric logic and politics, Wilfred further observes, "The universal is applied to the particular because it is supposed to implicitly and eminently contain the particular . . . What is projected as universal through a *common-denominator approach* is not really what is

---

5. Quoted in Paul Hawken, *Blessed Unrest*.
6. Wilfred, *Margins Site of Asian Theologies*, 76.

common; it is often the *universalization* of one particular that easily becomes the essence of all others; it becomes *absolute* and *normative*."[7]

Oikos: Our common home is a frequent theme and overarching metaphor of unity and universality in the theological reflections and writings on the ecological crisis and ecological restoration. This notion of *Oikos* is also informed and inspired by the logic of the necessity of universal categories and metanarratives to problematize and address global problems. Such problematizations are contested by the subaltern communities because accusing all human beings for the ecological crisis is a political strategy to perpetuate ecological injustice and ecological racism and casteism by absolving the ecological crimes of the dominant and the privileged communities and the corporations. James Cone's contestation of mainstream environmentalism and ecotheology is articulated succinctly in his question, "Whose earth is it, anyway?"[8] Why did Cone raise this rather, disturbing question? For him, "it is important to ask, however, whose problems define the priorities of the environmental movement? Whose suffering claims attention? . . . If it is important to save the habitats of birds and other species, then it is at least equally important to save black lives in the ghettos and prisons of America."[9] To state it differently, our universal categories such as *Oikos* do not represent the everyday life experiences of Indigenous and subaltern communities; rather they universalize the particular experiences of the dominant and impose projects and solutions which will not disrupt the prevailing order as universal solution for the present crisis. Cone further elaborates the rationale for his refusal to accept the mainstream universal categories such as *Oikos, our common home*, and *common ethic*: "My identity with *blackness*, and what it means for millions living in a white world, controls the investigation. It is impossible for me to surrender this basic reality for a 'higher, more universal' reality. Therefore, *if a higher, ultimate reality is to have meaning, it must relate to the very essence of blackness.*"[10]

Womanist ethicist Emilie Townes goes further and exposes the environmental crisis as environmental racism: "The effects of toxic waste on the lives of people of color who are relegated due to their poverty to live on ecologically hazardous lands are akin to a contemporary version of lynching a whole people."[11] The correlation between racism and ecological crisis, exposed by Townes and other theologians of color invites

7. Wilfred, "The Language of Human Rights," 208.
8. Cone, "Whose Earth Is It, Anyway?" 30, 32.
9. Cone, "Whose Earth Is It, Anyway?" 30, 32.
10. Cone, "The Gospel of Jesus, Black People and Black Power," 152.
11. Townes, *In a Blaze of Glory*, 55.

us to critically evaluate the politics of the metanarratives and metaphors of universality that continue to be the methodological standpoint of our dominant ecotheological reflections.

We need to understand and engage with the black and womanist theologians' criticism of the mainstream environmentalism and ecotheology movement in relation to the historic campaigns of the Environmental Justice Movement in the US. The Environmental Justice Movement not only exposes the racism of the mainstream environmental movements, but also offers a trans-sectional approach to engage with the crisis of the earth. The first National People of Color Environmental Leadership Summit held in Washington DC in 1991 resolved:

> To build a national and international movement of all people of color to fight the destruction and taking of our lands and communities, to re-establish our spiritual interdependence to the sacredness of our Mother Earth; to respect and celebrate each of our cultures, languages and beliefs about the natural world and our roles in healing ourselves; to ensure environmental justice; to promote economic alternatives which would contribute to the development of environmentally safe livelihoods; and, to secure our political, economic and cultural liberation that has been denied for over 500 years of colonization and oppression, resulting in the poisoning of our communities and land and the genocide of our peoples.[12]

A trans-sectional approach, therefore, informs us that the distress of the earth and the earth community is essentially a justice issue because those who are least responsible for the crisis are forced to bear its gravest consequences. A trans-sectional approach further establishes the correlation between ecocide and genocide, and exposes how colonialism, neo-liberal globalization, racism, casteism and patriarchy are intrinsically connected with the ecological injustice that we experience today. While the Global North has contributed disproportionately to the destruction of life on earth, the Global South—particularly the Indigenous and subaltern communities in the Global South—continues to suffer the worst environmental catastrophes. Global negotiations and covenants on climate change are always controlled by the wealthiest developed nations, and instead of changing their carbon-intensive economic orders, they use the climate crisis as an opportunity to continue their economic colonization of the Global South through "disaster capitalism." It is the polluters and colonizers of the global commons who decide which communities are worth

---

12. http://www.ejnet.org/ej/principles.html.

protecting and saving. A trans-sectional approach in our environmental activism and ecotheologies, therefore, has the potential to offer an alternative understanding and response to the ecological crisis, privileging the voices of the commons and the commoners.

The trans-sectional approach is succinctly articulated in the writings of the African women: "Earth-healing praxis requires an understanding of the interconnectedness of the different manifestations of violence. The violence of poverty, racism, sexism and classism, of social dislocation, of militarism, of battering and rape are not unrelated to the violence against the environment. They are all rooted in the abuse of power as domination over the exploitation of the other."[13] What we find here is a systematic exposition of the relationship between ecological injustice and structural injustice caused by patriarchy, racism and capitalism. The African women's insistence on a trans-sectional perspective in our earth-healing praxis invites us to critically evaluate our environmental activism and develop alternative perspectives and models of earth-healing. We hear this perspective reverberating in the slogan of the eco-socialist movements: "System Change; not Climate Change."

Commons and Commoning: An Alternative Ecotheological Standpoint

Colonization of the commons is the crisis that we confront today. When it comes to climate change, the excessive emission of green-house gases by the corporations and the industrial nations is nothing but the colonization of the commons as it destroys the integrity of the atmospheric commons. Commons such as forests, water bodies, and land are also colonized by the proponents of neo-liberal capitalism for mining, mega dams, agri-business, and even for the cultivation of biofuel, a solution for climate change developed by those who continue to destroy nature. Hence, this problematization of the ecological crisis as the consequence of the colonization of the commons is crucial for our theological discernment and praxis. Otherwise, devoid of deeper political discernment and engagement, our theological reflections will continue to legitimize the logic and practice of colonization and its conquest of life. A commons perspective, therefore, is profoundly political because of its potential to disrupt and destabilize the prevailing dominant perceptions, diagnosis, and solutions, and to reimagine our theological vocation in solidarity with the subaltern commons and

13. Ackermann and Joyner, "Earth-Healing in South Africa," 125.

subaltern commoners in their creative resilience to challenge the forces that continue to desecrate the commons.

Commons is a paradigm for redeeming life in the context of the ecological crisis. As David Bollier explains:

> Even though commons are often criticized as 'wastelands' or 'tragedies,' the truth is that they are *generative*. Commons quietly meet important household needs—the original goal of economics. They also disproportionately benefit women [and subaltern communities], who rely so much on commons to provide household food, care work and community. Natural systems, too, are more likely to be happily integrated with a culture of commoning than with the culture of global capitalism. For all these reasons, the commons can help us move beyond the problematic history of conventional development because it proffers different theories of value and human aspiration than those of the price system and the state.[14]

For Silke Helfrich, the commons paradigm is alternative because its logic is antithetical to the logic of the market economy. According to her, the commons paradigm proposes and practices the sustainable use and sharing of resources through creating equitable and just social relations. The commons paradigm understands human beings as "cooperative social beings" who are "nested within each other [including commons] and mutually reinforcing."[15] The Zapatista Movement in Chiapas, Mexico, enables us to understand how the commons paradigm is practiced among the subsistence and subaltern communities: "In Zapatista territory, land is not an artificial commodity. Territory is a space of responsibility. Occupation is not equivalent to property or tenure. A Cosmo-centric attitude before nature prevents the possibility of owning it. Within communal territory, land is allocated to the commoners without granting private property, but respecting stable family rights."[16] Based on this practice of commoning in the Zapatista commons, Gustavo Esteva articulates the alternative politics of the commoners: "To enclose the enclosers, as they begin to do, they are allied with those searching for alternative ways of life or attempting to protect the water, the air, the forest, the ecology ... All of them are creating a world in which many worlds can be embraced."[17]

---

14 http://www.countercurrents.org/2016/06/30/beyond-development-the-commons-as-a-newold-paradigm-of-human-flourishing/.

15. Helfrich, "The Logic of the Commons and the Market," 15.

16. Esteva, "Hope from the Margins," 195.

17. Esteva, "Hope from the Margins," 197.

Our search for alternatives should lead us beyond a study of commons to the organic activity of commoning. Commoning is a verb; not a noun. We are surrounded with commoners all over the world who are involved in the everyday practices and experiences of commoning. As Bollier and Helfrich observe, "Commoning is an attitude, an ethic, an impulse, a need and a satisfaction—a way of being that is deeply inscribed within the human species. But it is up to us to make it thrive. We must *choose* to practice commoning and reflect on the impact on our lives and the earth, the more consciously, the better."[18]

Commoning is an organic activity that breathes life into the commons. Commoning happens outside the logic of private property. Commoning is a multi-generational activity. Commoning requires a context of mutuality and relationality. Commoning is not possible where systems and practices of exclusion and domination are prevalent. Since commoning is meant to enable the flourishing of life, a commitment to contest and defeat the colonization of the commons is essential for commoning.

However, what we witness today is not only the colonization of the commons, but also the introduction of new "commons" developed in the mold of neo-liberal capitalism. This calls for the political discernment to reject the neo-colonial commons of the market and to engage in the creative work of "commoning," reclaiming and creating life affirming commons. The struggles of the Standing Rock Sioux Tribe (SRST) against the Dakota Access Pipeline (DAPL) is an example of communing praxis. The original path of the pipeline ran next to Bismarck, the North Dakota capital and predominantly white, but it was rerouted because of concerns over potential contamination of water supplies. The new route instead takes it through the ancestral Native American lands, including their burial grounds, and would cross beneath the Missouri River at the border of the Standing Rock Indian Reservation. The Sioux Native communities object that the current route will threaten their water supply, upset the ecological balance of the region, disrupt tribal traditions, and desecrate their commons: the sacred lands.

Standing Rock is a conflict between two world views. On the one hand, we see the proponents of the doctrine that land is merely a warehouse of lifeless materials that have been given to some of us by God or by conquest, to occupy, consume and exploit. Human vocation, according to this doctrine, is to convert the commons: water, soil, minerals, wild-lives, and the commoners into corporate wealth, and the state is committed to support and protect this plunder. On the other hand, we see people who consider land as commons: a nourishing gift to all living beings. The fertile soil, the fresh water, the clear

---

18. Bollier and Helfrich, "Finale," 393.

air, and the creatures require gratitude and respect. These gifts are not commodities. The land is sacred and a living breathing entity. We see commoning happening in the struggles of the Sioux native communities in their resolve to reclaim their commons from the colonizing forces.

Commons and commoning offer alternative ecotheological standpoints to re-imagine our theologies and praxis of earth-care for the flourishing of life. Commons and commoning affirm the situatedness of our ecotheologies in the particularities of each commons, and thereby reject all attempts to impose dominant perceptions and reflections claiming universal relevance. This paradigm contests all attempts to homogenize human beings, and instead privileges the perspectives and politics of the commoners by exposing the correlation between unjust social relations and ecological injustice. Commons further offers a corrective to our dominant Judeo-Christian anthropocentric cosmology and develops an alternative understanding drawing from the animistic and panentheistic traditions and cosmologies of subsistence and Indigenous communities. Commons and commoning enable us to develop alternative reflections on theological anthropology. Commoning as the vocation of human beings to cause life to flourish provides us alternative models of being and becoming the church in the midst of death and destruction.

Poromboke: Eco-casteism, Polluted Commons, and Impure Commoners

Commons and commoning betray the reigning neo-liberal doctrine; "there is no alternative." When the colonization of the commons is presented as the patriotic mantra for "making our nation great again," and the vocation of commoning is condemned as an anti-national seditious activity, it is our moral imperative to protect and restore the commons through our participation in the vocation of commoning. However, it is also important to critically engage with the commons and the commoning paradigm and prevent the possibility of them becoming universal theories and models without respecting the distinctiveness of particular commons and the practice of commoning in different parts of the world.

Even though the commoning paradigm affirms the importance of trans-sectional approach in our ecological consciousness and activism, mainstream discussions of commons and commoning are limited to the neo-liberal colonization of the commons. Hence, commoning is proposed as a counter-cultural activity against the logic and onslaught of market forces. Of course, there are attempts to reinterpret the paradigm from the perspectives of the Cosmo-visions and the struggles of the Indigenous communities. Similar scholarly attempts are also there to re-read the paradigm through feminist lenses. However, a conscious and consistent attempt to reflect upon the commons and the commoning paradigm from the vantagepoint of the victims of racism and casteism seems to be rather absent. This calls for a deeper engagement with the struggles of the commons and commoners in solidarity with the Dalits and the African American communities. In the context of eco-casteism *Poromboke* becomes paradigmatic of the kind of alternative ecological consciousness and activism needed in our time today. We need to privilege the wisdom and politics of the "polluted" commons and the "impure" commoners of the *Porombokes* to develop alternative ecological consciousness and eco-theological reflections in the context of eco-casteism.

T. M. Krishna, the renowned Indian Carnatic classical musician, begins his classical recital, *Chennai Poromboke Paadal*, with the following lines:

Poramboke (n.) /por-um-bokku/

1. places reserved for shared communal uses
   (water bodies, grazing lands . . .)

2. a pejorative intended to demean and devalue
   a person or place.[19]

Krishna, then poses a question: "How did the meaning change from the first to the second?"[20] The metamorphosis of the commons from one that was formerly a place of thriving for land, water, forests, and humans into an "impure" space inhabited by "polluted people" is the history of *Poromboke* in South India. *Poromboke* is a term that is used by the state to denote land classification. In South India, since the time of the Chola dynasty, the term *Poromboke* has been used to "designate stretches of land reserved for shared communal use which cannot be bought or sold."[21] As Perumal Murugan rightly observes, it is the "land exempt from assessment, either because it is set aside for communal purposes or because it is uncultivable."[22] Ever since, the communal wetlands, grazing land, salt pans, marshlands, lakes, estuaries, mangrove forests and river valleys are known as *Poromboke*. Etymologically, the word *Poromboke* comes from two Tamil

19. Ambedkar, "The Poromboke Song."
20. Ambedkar, "The Poromboke Song."
21. Gopalakrishnan, "No Man's Land."
22. https://thewire.in/culture/t-m-krishna-ennore-creek-permual.

words: *Puram* (outside) and *pokku* (books of account). *Poromboke*, therefore, indicates the community land which could not generate any revenue for the state. The English East India Company and the British Raj named it "wasteland" because, within the logic of colonialism, any resource that could not generate a revenue/profit was considered "waste." Today, *Poromboke* is commonly used as a derogatory word in Tamil and Malayalam to demonize and ostracize both the commons and the commoners who are worthless and untouchable to the market and casteist forces.

From a postcolonial perspective the British attempt to christen *Poromboke* as wasteland needs to be problematized as a colonial construction and for its appropriation of nature. The colonialists could not comprehend and appreciate the organic relationship between the commons and the commoners, and the significance of the commons in the corporate life of the community. They did not even recognize the communal practices of the commoners which in fact sustained them and regenerated the *Poromboke*. The post-independent Indian State, thanks to neo-liberal development and globalization, has unleashed the mission of colonizing the commons, by commodifying the *Poromboke* and uprooting the *Poromboke* people (commoners) from their roots. This is the context in which T.M. Krishan's *Chennai Poromboke Paadal* affirms the importance of the *Poromboke* identity as distinctive for a new politics, ethics and spirituality celebrating the organic relationship between the commons and the commoners:

> For one who sold the waterbodies, the lake is mere *Poramboke*
>
> You and I, then; what are we to him?
>
> We are *Poramboke* too
>
> I certainly am *Poramboke*.[23]

For Harshavardhan Bhat, the metamorphosis in the meaning of the term *Poromboke* signifies the transformation of commons "perceptually and materially to a surface of toxic space, expelled and demonized as waste."[24] He further observes that "modernity, capitalism and the extractive consensus is what caused the transformation of the common land to the wasteland in the politics of the *Poromboke*." Today, *Poromboke* is a symbol of resilience and resistance; contesting the colonization of the commons and the commoners by transnational corporations and the state. *Poromboke* land is now part of the revenue land. Creeks, marshlands, and even lakes are reclaimed for private businesses and infrastructure development to facilitate corporate

23. Ambedkar, "The Poromboke Song."
24. Bhat, "Over Skies of Extraction," 23.

interests. Rivers are dead with toxic wastes. Ancestral lands are converted into mines and coal fields. Estuaries today house thermal power stations. *Chennai Poromboke Paadal* becomes paradigmatic here as it invites us to reclaim the *Poromboke* affirming the agency of the *Poromboke* communities.

Environmental thoughts and activism in India have always been caste-blind. Eco-casteism is a theoretical category which helps us to understand and contest the role that caste has played and continues to play in the colonial and neo-colonial attempts to colonize the commons and commoners through the centralized state apparatuses for corporate and casteist interests. It is a distinctive form of Indian environmentalism, which is often grounded in the justification of the caste system and opposition to modernity and enlightenment. In eco-casteism, caste system is glorified as a kind of conservation from below and a remarkable system of ecological adaptation, where caste groups in a web of mutually supportive relationships purportedly contribute to the wellness of nature. For eco-casteism, the caste system is essentially ecological in its logic.

According to Mukul Sharma, the history of caste has shaped the history of environmentalism in India. Sharma elaborates two distinctive traits of eco-casteism. Firstly, by glorifying the casteist ancient Indian culture, eco-casteism valorizes and legitimizes casteist traditions as organic and natural. The glorification of the ancient casteist ecological ethos and practices constitutes the metanarratives on which the mainstream eco-consciousness, environmentalism, and ecotheologies are based. Secondly, eco-casteism has "created a concept of natural and social order where people, place, occupation, and knowledge are characterized by pollution and ritual cleanliness; where bodies, behaviours, situations, and actions are isolated, 'out of place,' and 'untouched,' because of deep-down hierarchical boundaries."[25] *Porombokes* are therefore polluted lands and *Porombokis* (commoners) are impure people who inhabit such polluted places. The metamorphosis of the meaning of *Poromboke* into places and bodies that are polluted, worthless, untouchable is hence an example of eco-casteism.

Eco-casteism perpetuates casteism by attributing ecological motifs and legitimizations to the ideology and structures of casteism. According to O. P. Dwivedi, "the Hindu caste system can be seen as progenitor of the concept of sustainable development."[26] Kailash Malhothra elaborates it further: "The caste system . . . was actually based on an ancient concept of sustainable development which disciplined the society by partitioning the use of natural resources according to specific occupations (or castes); and

---

25. Sharma, *Caste and Nature*, xix.
26. Dwivedit, "Satyagraha for Conservation," 159.

created the right social milieu in which sustainable patterns of resource use were encouraged to emerge."[27] Eco-casteism thus offers justification for the caste system through naturalistic explanations, and perpetuates the caste system as an ecological model.

The casteist logic of eco-casteism perceives impurity and pollution as the major ecological problem of India. In India, perceptions of the commons are infected with casteism as they are perceived as landscapes of purity and pollution. The identity of a place is determined by caste. Dalits are excluded from the public commons based on the purity maps of identity, exclusion, and domination. Boundaries of villages are identified with caste. Water bodies such as ponds, wells, and rivers are marked by caste. Dalit transgression of the casteist cartography of the commons often leads to violence and the massacre of Dalits. One of the most humiliating occupations of casteism is the work of manual scavengers. According to the caste system, manual disposal of the human excreta is the caste dharma of a particular Dalit community. While Gandhi glorified the work of manual scavengers and proposed to offer them education and practical skills, Ambedkar campaigned for the eradication of manual scavenging. Most of the mainstream environmental movements work around issues of impurity and pollution, with the objective to take back India to the ancient days of purity. Here eco-casteism pathologizes the other—Dalits, indigenous communities, immigrants, and minorities as "impure" and "untouchables" responsible for the ecological degradation of the nation. Prime Minister Narendra Modi's initiative of *Swatch Bharath* (Clean India) originates from the same logic of eco-casteism.

One can identify the role played by eco-casteism in the metamorphism of *Poromboke* from an organic commons to a polluted space with impure people. Corporate occupation of the *Poromboke* is hence justified as a civilizing and ecological action which helps the land to become pure and unpolluted. Cleansed of its accumulated impurity contracted through the "touch" of the impure castes, the *Poromboke* is now being converted into Special Economic Zones for corporate plunder, with the *Porombokis* (impure commoners) being uprooted from these colonial and casteist commons to make them "pure" for the market.

---

27. Cited in Sharma, *Caste and Nature*, 10.

Towards a *Poromboke* Ecotheology: A Tentative Preface

What are the methodological standpoints of a trans-sectional ecotheology? A trans-sectional ecotheology explores how the care of creation is integrally connected with the care of the subaltern and Indigenous communities. It examines how dominant expressions of creation-care are envisioned and practiced at the expense of the communities at the margins. It further investigates why certain communities are unrepresented or silenced in the mainstream ecological discourses and actions. It exposes the correlation between social location (race, caste, gender, ethnicity, class), and access to ecological wellness and well-being. It also evaluates the racial, caste, gender, and ethnic bias of various ecological philosophies, ideologies, theologies, and movements. It uncovers what has been *trans*acted (stolen, commodified, thingified, colonized) through the colonization of the commons. A trans-sectional ecotheology is essentially a *trans*gressive and *trans*formative theology.

A *Poromboke* Ecotheology is a trans-sectional ecotheology which attempts to develop alternative eco-consciousness, ecotheologies, and eco-activism in the context of eco-casteism from the vantagepoint of the *Poromboke* commons and the *Poromboke* commoners. It is the caste-blindness of the dominant ecotheological reflections that necessitates the need for a *Poromboke* ecotheology. The caste-blindness of the mainstream ecotheologies is not an innocent deficiency or omission; rather, it exposes the social location and the caste privilege of the ecotheology movement in India.

Why a tentative preface of a *Poromboke* Ecotheology? Contextual theologies are always critical about the danger of representation. They caution us about the moral limits of allyship. They affirm that the *Porombokes* can speak, and they do speak. Hence the attempt here is to propose a tentative preface to a *Poromboke* Ecotheology. What are the methodological standpoints of the *Poromboke* Ecotheology, and what are its epistemological sources? A *Poromboke* Ecotheology is a trans-sectional theology that emerges from the subaltern resolve to problematize the ecological crisis at the interface of caste, patriarchy, and neo-liberal capitalism. Informed and inspired by Dalit theology, the Poromboke Ecotheology originates from the pathos of the community, and hence *Poromboke*—the living and breathing community at the margins, condemned as polluted, impure, worthless, and waste by the casteist, corporatist forces—is its loci. *Poromboke* is a site of contestation—contestation of different ecological visions, practices, virtues, ethics, projects and policies. These contestations not only expose and challenge the casteist, patriarchal, and neo-liberal politics of the colonization of the *Poromboke*, but also proposes alternative ecological visions, politics and ethics. For *Poromboke* Ecotheology, annihilation of caste and the redemption of the earth are integrally connected.

A *Poromboke* Ecotheology begins with a deeper engagement with the Dalit environmental traditions around the commons. Dalit ecological visions emerge from their constant interaction with the commons. However, there is no valorization of the commons in Dalit environmentalism. Sadly, for them, the commons and their labor are closely connected with caste exploitation. It is caste that mediates the relationship of the Dalits with the commons. The Dalit experience with the animals provides us insights about Dalit environmentalism. Their kinship with the black buffalo is a reason for its lower status in the hierarchy of animals in the casteist India. Their food habit, particularly their liking for non-vegetarian food like beef, has been condemned as the greatest ecological crime by the ecocasteists for whom vegetarianism and cow vigilantism are the purest ecological virtues. In short, a *Poromboke* Ecotheology begins with a deeper knowledge of Dalit environmentalism manifested in their relationship with the commons. Dalit spirituality, rituals, and religiosity are resources that can inform a *Poromboke* Ecotheology.

Another important source for a *Poromboke* Ecotheology is the Dalit struggles for their rights over the commons. Dalits, in general, are the landless people. Land reforms in India have always been caste-biased. Access to common water bodies such as wells, tanks and rivers has been denied to them in the name of purity and pollution. Water is a marker of caste, and it is integrally connected with social hierarchy. The following poem by Challapalli Swaroopa Rani, a Dalit woman writer articulates it concisely:

> For us, water is not simply H_2O
>
> For us, water is a mighty movement
>
> It is the Mahad struggle at the Chadar tank
>
> A single drop of water embodies
>
> Tears shed over generations.[28]

There is a long history of Dalit struggle for water rights. The Mahad Satyagraha under the leadership of Ambedkar to reclaim Dalit water rights is one such struggle. A deeper engagement with the Dalit movements and their struggles for rights over the commons is hence a major epistemological source. A *Poromboke* Ecotheology further draws from the theoretical contributions of Dalit intellectuals such as B. R. Ambedkar. What we find in their

28. Rani, "Water," 702.

writings is a rejection of the eco-casteist environmentalism, and an attempt to look at nature trans-sectionally. For Ambedkar, "environment could not be disentangled from the ugliness of caste injustice, the development of rural landscape could not be disconnected from social relations and structures of power in which it was embedded, and ecology had to confront the transitions to democracy."[29] Such theoretical mediations help us to understand with clarity how Dalits approach the environment and the commons at the interface of caste and other ideologies and practices of exclusion.

The Bible is an important source for a *Poromboke* Ecotheology. For Dalits, the Bible *becomes* the "Word" when read in community in the light of the community's experiences of exclusion and resistance. As Monica Melanchthon rightly observes, "Dalit biblical interpretation and the material force that grips the Dalits are grounded in a materialistic epistemology that is characterized, among other things, by its location of truth not in a world beyond history but indeed within the crucible of historical struggles."[30] Biblical hermeneutics, thus, becomes a political activity of *resistance* and *liberation*. Reformulation of the doctrines and moral axioms informed by the above-mentioned sources and resources of the Dalit and subaltern communities is a major task of a *Poromboke* Ecotheology. *Poromboke* is not only the site of the polluted commons and impure commoners who routinely experience exclusion and exploitation, but now also a site of contestation of the logic of the empire, patriarchy, and casteism—an ecclesia happening in our times. For a *Poromboke* Ecotheology, commoning is more than protecting the commons from colonial conquest; rather commoning is the organic politics of annihilating all forces, systems, cultures, traditions, and ethics that practice and perpetuate hierarchical relations socially, economically, and ecologically.

Bibliography

Ackermann, Denis, and Tahira Joyner, "Earth-Healing in South Africa: Challenges to Church and Mosque." In *Women Healing Earth: Third World Women on Ecology, Feminism, and Religion*, edited by Rosemary Radford Ruether, 121–34. Maryknoll, NY: Orbis, 1996.

Ambedkar, P. G. "The Poromboke Song." https://www.newsclick.in/poromboke-song.

Bhat, Harshavardhan. "Over Skies of Extraction." *Lo Squaderno Explorations in Space and Society* 48 (June 2018) 23–25.

---

29. Cited in Sharma, *Caste and Nature*, 130–31.
30. Melanchthon, "Unleashing the Power Within," 49.

Bollier, David, and Silke Helfrich. "Finale." In *Patterns of Commoning*, edited by David Bollier and Silke Helfrich 393–94. Amherst: The Commons Strategies Group, 2015.

———. *The Wealth of the Commons: A World beyond Market and State*. Amherst: The Common Strategies Group, 2012.

Cone, James H. "The Gospel of Jesus, Black People and Black Power." In *Border Regions of Faith*, edited by Kenneth Aman, 151–60. Maryknoll, NY: Orbis, 1988.

———. "Whose Earth Is It, Anyway?" In *Earth Habitat: Eco-Injustice and the Church's Response*, edited by Dieter Hessel and Larry Rasmussen, 23–32. Minneapolis: Fortress, 2001.

Dwivedit, O. P. "Satyagraha for Conservation: Awakening the Spirit of Hinduism." In *The Sacred Earth: Religion, Nature, Environment*, edited by Roger S. Gottleb, 151–63. London: Routledge, 1996.

Esteva, Gustavo. "Hope from the Margins." In *The Wealth of the Commons: A World beyond Market and State*, edited by David Bollier and Silke Helfrich, 192–98. Amherst: The Commons Strategies Group, 2012.

Gopalakrishnan, Seetha. "No Man's Land." https://www.indiawaterportal.org/articles/no-mans-land.

Hawken, Paul. *Blessed Unrest: How the Largest Social Movement in History Is Restoring Grace, Justice and Beauty to the World*. New York: Penguin, 2007.

Helfrich, Silke. "The Logic of the Commons and the Market: A Shorthand Comparison of Their Core Beliefs." In *The Wealth of the Commons: A World beyond Market and State*, edited by David Bollier and Silke Helfrich, 35–36. Amherst: The Commons Strategies Group, 2012.

Melanchthon, Monica Jyotsna. "Unleashing the Power Within: The Bible and Dalits." In *The Future of the Biblical Past: Envisioning Biblical Studies on a Global Key*, edited by Roland Boer and Fernando F. Segovia, 47–65. Semeia Studies 66. Atlanta: Society of Biblical Literature, 2012.

Rani, Challapalli Swaroopa. "Water." In *Steel Nibs Are Sprouting: New Dalit Writings from South India*, edited by K. Satyanarayana and Susie Tharu, 702. Delhi: HarperCollins, 2013.

Sharma, Mukul. *Caste and Nature: Dalits and Indian Environmental Politics*. Delhi: Oxford University Press, 2017.

Townes, Emilie. *In a Blaze of Glory: Womanist Spirituality as Social Witness*. Nashville: Abingdon, 1995.

Wilfred, Felix. "The Language of Human Rights: An Ethical Esperanto?" In *Frontiers in Asian Christian Theology: Emerging Trends*, edited by R. S. Sugirtharajah, 206–20. Maryknoll, NY: Orbis, 1994.

Wilfred, Felix. *Margins: Site of Asian Theologies*. Delhi: ISPCK, 2008.

12

Land Lovers

*From Agropornography
to Agroecology*[1]

NANCY CARDOSO

We see then, commodities are in love with money, but "the course of true love never did run smooth." . . . At the same time, the prices, wooing glances cast at money by commodities, define the limits of its convertibility, by pointing to its quantity. —KARL MARX[2]

LUST. LOVE. DESIRE. SEDUCTION. Love eyes. They do not seem to be proper words for an economic discussion. But think about soy and its fervent love for the euro, or iron ore and its turbulent love affair in the international dance of prices. Money reads and mirrors all bodies; prices wanting to be consumed in the form of profit cast their seductive looks by trying to

---

1. An earlier shorter version has been published in German under the title, "Landlust und Landliebe: Von der Agropornografie zur Agroökologie" in the Swiss journal, *Neue Wege* Nr 2/2016 110 Jahrgang, Zurich, Februar 2016, 1–4 https://docplayer.org/40535369-Beitraege-zu-religion-und-sozialismus.html

2. Marx, *Capital*, vol. 1, sec. 2, chap. 3: Money, Or the Circulation of Commodities (http://marxengels.public-archive.net/en/Capital1.htm#ch03).

make their commodity attractive. The price of sugar on the international market is sugar cane's pure charm being sweet and at the same time calculating how much should be delivered. Soy—so, so vulgar—agrees to lower 0.5 cents to turn its trick. Young chickens expect their slaughter at the right time for the pimp to hit the right price and obese cows offer their backside to the avid buyer for meat. It is all so exciting in the sexy and pornographic world of merchandise!

Is it only a joke that this semantic field appears in Marx's *Capital*? Or are there unconfessable desires in Marx's theory that need the language of lovers, virtuous or vulgar?

> In fact, commodities appear not only as animated beings, but they also establish relations . . . The exchange relation between commodities is set as a game of seduction in which they flaunt themselves for each other seeking exchange.[3]

More than just a play on words, I believe that economic reflection has approached the field of amorous and erotic phenomena with the need to express an important perspective on modes of ownership and forms of capital accumulation—two vital points for understanding the capitalist model, especially in capitalist agriculture or what we know as agribusiness. What is important here is the process of intuition that brings together scenarios and power relations that can and must be articulated.

> The figurative use of language can, of course, be very important in theoretical work. Not only for didactic reasons or as an author's particular style of ornamentation, although in these two respects the merits of the figurative use of language are positively obvious. The important point philosophically speaking is that figurative expressions may reflect the very process of intuition.[4]

Let me take those "wooing glances" then and map out their tasks. My goal is to "undress" the roles of economy and sexuality (economic and sexual desires) in the construction of culture, in particular, of fetish culture as a sexual reality that can speak to theology and disrupt the fixed symbolic field which supports the ideal heterosexual matrix. Take for example the trope of patriarchy: of bed, table, and bath and their metabolism in industry (oh, how long lasting! How dynamic!), in commerce (oh, how beautiful! Cute! I want them!) and in finance (oh, not all at once . . . Take it all, but only a little at a time . . . Handcuff me and hit me! I know it will hurt . . . but I like it!).

3. Sousa Júnior, "Mercadoria, fetichismo e discurso figurado n' O Capital."
4. Mészáros, "Filosofia, ideologia, e ciência social," 238.

In the words of Marcella Althaus-Reid,

> The paradigm is an indecent paradigm, because it undresses and uncovers sexuality and economy at the same time. Not only do we need an Indecent Theology which can reach the core of theological constructions, insofar as they are rooted in sexual construction . . . we also need it because theological truths are currencies dispensed and acquired in theological economic markets.[5]

With ecofeminism we understand that we organize "nature" (while it also organizes itself!) through complex power relations. Queer ecofeminism adds sexuality as a category of power. Sexuality, as a shaft power (both structural and symbolic), organizes the way we define what counts as "nature," how we understand the term, and how we relate to that which we call "natural." By questioning the social constructions considered as "natural" we approach "nature itself" and visualize the various uses of Christianity—as one of the logics of domination—and the rhetoric of colonialism over what is natural and what is not (i.e., aberration, contamination, dirt).[6]

In order to face these tasks, I insist with the feminists that a system of violence demands the liberation of the erotic, not in some easy liberal scheme but through a true critique of the uses of Western conceptions of the erotic and their belonging to models of domination by patriarchal capitalism. I will approach this reflection by asking about the land-agriculture-food system, and by considering the domestication and subordination of the land in capitalism. Coming out of my location as a theologian in Brazil, my reflections are also informed by my involvement in two vibrant agroecological movements, led primarily by women, one in Bahia, Brazil and the other in Mexico and Central America. I end my discussion with a summary description of their unique dynamic as a way of enfleshing the more theoretical discussion in the first half of the essay.

Colonialism and the Missionary Position

"The earth is our mother"—says propaganda, slogans, the Pope, politicians, and NGOs. Its meaning is this: land and de-eroticized mothers, "naturally" subordinated in a cultural context of sacrifice, self-denial, and over-exploitation. Our task then is to stop reducing our idea of nature to a heterosexual "beautiful mother" and motherhood and women to mere means of

5. Althaus-Reid, *Indecent Theology*, 19.
6. Gaard, "Rumo ao ecofeminismo queer."

production. In a historical perspective that has not yet been overcome completely, for example, there is the naturalization of the "missionary position" as defended by the Spanish theologian Thomas Sanchez in the seventeenth century. He calls it a sacrament, *De Sancto matrimond*, and considers it:

> as the "natural form of sexual intercourse ... Man must be on top and woman underneath, because that form is most suitable for the spilling of the male seed, for its reception in the female vessel." Sanchez compared the phallus to a plow and the woman to the ground; the missionary position would be the most propitious for procreation and therefore more 'natural'. In contrast, the position mulier supra virum (woman over man) was "absolutely contrary to the order of nature."[7]

The imposition of European colonialism and capitalism—and its cultural forms of organizing sexuality—on various native communities was intended to civilize land-based peoples (who were seen as being close to animals and nature) and put them at the service of the colonial project. Thus, the savage—both in the popular imaginary and scholarly thought—had to be distanced from nature and pacified through evangelization. Nature itself was also disciplined by the idea of the "all-giving" land. This letter from a Portuguese expedition describes the land:

> The land itself is of very good airs, so cold and temperate ... Waters are many; endless. And it is gracious in such a way that, wanting to seize it, everything will be in it, for the sake of the waters that it has.[8]

Gracious. Enjoyable. The land gives all of itself! In the case of Brazil, it is seen as the "gentle motherland," its superlatives of production, intensity, extensiveness, and monoculture as qualities of a political and economic project of colonization of nature and human work. The juxtaposition of the feminine with nature in the idea of motherhood de-eroticizes the land and the mother. At the same time, it maintains the political and working modes of masculinity and establishes, naturalizes, and consolidates a compulsory heterosexuality as an intrinsic part of power. A text from a government research institute says this about our (Brazil's) "nature":

> The natural vocation that Brazil has for agriculture is known worldwide. Its territorial vastness combined with an abundant supply of sun and water, fundamental resources for

---

7. Sanchez, *De Sancto matrimond*.

8. Ministério da Cultura, "Fundação Biblioteca Nacional Departamento Nacional do Livro."

agricultural activity, are qualities that put it ahead of other producing countries. Brazil is the fifth largest agricultural producer in the world.[9]

A natural vocation to give and give much: fruits! Profits! Abundant offering of sun and water! Come, take and drink!

In what follows, I propose a counter-narrative reading coming from an ecofeminist and queer approach to Brazilian agribusiness in terms of an old and new predation on the body of the earth and the social body as well.

Agribusiness is Pornographic, Agroecology is Erotic

No, there is absolutely no moralism here. My understanding of pornography relates to the emergence of print technologies (in the sixteenth century) that have put in circulation cheap and abundant reproductions of sexual scenes "creating a thriving market for the obscene"[10] associated with the realistic intention of depicting sexual activity breaking away from forms that are considered virtuous. Pornographic imagery as it relates to market needs cites the available modes of sex and heightens them in order to broaden their market by creating temporary, mass-produced, and easily replaceable products. There is nothing obscene except the interest of making money. In the name of liberating sexual customs and manners, the pornographic industry offers itself as having a pragmatic and true relationship to sex, sensuality, and all its vulgar and easy-to-market temptations. A scene or a word can be reproduced and sold over and over again, going from hand to hand even if you have lost touch with the real scene. It doesn't matter! Pornography wants to make a profit.

But in life we deal with the real desires and relationships of real people and their unrealized selves, orgasmic hunger, and the alienation of pleasure—real needs that pornography seeks to mimic and commodify. In a quote from Slavoj Žižek:

> Pornography is the absence of pornography . . . it is an example of the desexualization of sex, it promises to offer "more and more sex," to show everything, but what it gives us is emptiness and pseudo-satisfaction that are infinitely reproduced and more and more of raw reality.[11]

---

9. Tenório, "Agricultura."
10. Moraes, "O efeito obsceno."
11. Passos, "Prazer, gozo, Slavoj Žižek."

Hunger with the urge to eat. The porn market takes a real desire/need and appropriates its response circuits, offering the desired merchandise, but at the same time, disciplining the desire in the commodification offered. It promises enjoyment, but only offers the likeness of mere simulation, not anything real. It is an imitation and regulation in favor of technocapitalism.[12]

> The pornographic machine could also produce by itself the penis, the vagina, the mouth, the anus, the moans, the "fuck me" and "oh, shit" (in the sense that these organs use) and know what words to use, where to put one's mouth, hands, feet etc. Clearly, pornography is a device and . . . a sexual technology, excluding practices, expressions and bodies that do not fit the "norm."[13]

Beatriz Preciado suggests that "orgasmic force" would be equivalent to "work force" in classical economics. The concept is intended to explain how sexuality and the (excitable) body erupts at the center of political action, becoming the object of a new type of management of the State and the industrial model, a process that began in the nineteenth century.

> The orgasmic force is both the most abstract and the most material of all the labor forces, inextricably fleshly and numerical, thick and digital. Ah, phantasmic and molecular glory that can be transformed into capital![14]

Preciado speaks of a pharmacopornographic capitalist regime—associating media products, pharmacists and sexual service: what matters is the expropriation of the substrate of the work force that is the orgastic force, *potentia gaudendi*. In this sense the merchandise offered does not want to respond fully to the desire: "the promise of satisfying infinite human desires will only remain seductive in this type of society as long as the desire remains unfulfilled and also as long as there is a suspicion that the desires have not been fully satisfied."[15] It does this because it needs to keep the consumer active, that is, always in debt to physical pleasure.

> We are bodies that are docile and produced, our potentia gaudendi [organic strength] is regulated and at the service of the production of capital. In this sense, gender programming is a technology that sets the order: an individual = a body = a sex = a gender = a sexuality (what Judith Butler calls the order of sex

---

12. Passos, "Preciado na cama com Slavoj Žižek."
13. Passos, "Prazer, gozo, Slavoj Žižek."
14. Preciado and Gaydendi, "Orgia Ideológica."
15. Rego, "A modernidade analisada."

/ gender / desire), producing bodies with fixed identities that pass as essence.[16]

Such pharmacopornography also expresses itself in agro-food industry in the form of agropornography. Agribusiness is the dis-inculturation of agriculture. It is agriculture without culture! Out goes culture and in comes business! Millions and millions of tomatoes, chickens and cheeses, juice boxes, crackers and fast food at cheap reproductions along with plentiful food scenes "creating a thriving market for hunger in the obscene world." Agribusiness promises to end hunger, while it uses beautiful images of abundance and packs products in design and science. Here, too, it is necessary to reveal the ways in which communities are alienated, as well as discuss agropornographic workers and consumers and the place of agropornography in the consolidation and reproduction of capitalism. We will refer to desire and need: hunger and the desire to eat, as well as forms of stable relationship with the land.

My understanding of pornography is related to the appearance of printing technologies (in the sixteenth century), which put into circulation cheap reproductions and abundant sex scenes.[17] The pornographic market needed to capture the sex modes available and make them commonplace in order to expand itself, creating obsolete products and making use of both mass production and easy replacement in doing so. There is nothing more obscene than the interest of making money. Pornography wants to make profit out of life and out of the real desires of real people, mediated by the impossible achievements, orgasmic famines, and the sale of pleasure and promises that never fulfill. Orgasmic force is a concept developed by philosopher Beatriz Preciado, and is equivalent to classical economics' "labor force."[18] The concept is meant to explain how sexuality and the (excitable) body erupt in the center of political action, becoming objects of a new state management and the industrial.

Pornography, as Žižek tells us, is an example of the desexualization of sex: "It promises to offer 'more and more sex', show everything, but what it gives us is emptiness and pseudo satisfaction infinitely reproduced." After all, pornography promises us a gift that cannot fulfill. Yet, pornography thrives on its own failure: "the masturbatory hand" at the empty work with the copy that tries to pass for enjoyment.[19]

16. Passos, "Regulações farmacopolíticas."
17. Coopersmith, "Pornography."
18. Preciado, "The Forces of Reproduction."
19. Zizek, "Masturbation."

In the same vein, agribusiness is the deculturation of agriculture. Exit culture . . . enter business! I suggest that the relationship that agribusiness has with the land is no less than rape! It is an indecent assault without consent. The capital surrounds the land, declares it private and sacred property of sacred matrimony, enters with its swollen member—huge Massey Ferguson tractors, John Deere, New Holland, Claas, Caterpillar, Valtra. It makes erection even easier with Viagra's pharmacopornographic products: pesticides from Monsanto (US), Syngenta (Switzerland), Dupont (USA), BASF (Germany), Bayer (Germany), and Dow (USA), and ejaculates in the casino of commodities. One more of capitalism's solitary orgasms.

In agribusiness, not only land, water, and forests and their creatures are exhausted by the uncontrolled power of profit, but communities as well. Attempts to legislate and control its exploitative operations are continually denied and criminalized; It's quick sex without consent, without preliminaries . . . only capital gets any enjoyment out of the process. The raped and depleted land is abandoned, and the business goes to another scenario, another biome, another technology: it has to produce! It has to bear fruit and money! It has to make a profit.

The hegemonic model of development in Brazil and in the world requires the private appropriation of nature and the inexhaustible promotion of consumption, production and waste. Agribusiness mortgages the future, creating serious environmental risks and reinforcing social inequality, both on an interregional and international scale. Agropornography has a "totalitarian" character, it cannot coexist with peasant and agro-extractive agriculture, and even less with the agroecological option. Diverse hunger with monoculture on a global scale with just four grains—rice, corn, wheat and soy—constitutes almost all grain consumption. Agribusiness "imposes" itself on the earth; it intervenes violently in search of the maximum profit in the shortest possible time. Trees are made to grow faster in order to be cut; animals are fattened to be slaughtered more quickly; marketed water has no more time to recover and works super-intensively in irrigation snapshots by eliminating springs, streams, and rivers. Modified seeds are designed to respond more predictably and faster and compelled to die within one planting cycle. Indeed, one of the most frightening scenarios is that of seed control and manipulation by food industry giants: the control of genetic diversity and changing of record logs in line with business interests, eliminating fundamental aspects of biodiversity and over the centuries accumulation of species that are at the same time copies and innovations. The control of seeds by agropornography reduces and interferes with possibilities and makes explicit the anti-cultural character of capitalism. It's all so pornographic! Agropornography turns the fruit of the land into product factoids in rows at large supermarkets; artificial flavors in alluring packaging! It seems to be food, but it is not! A piece of the world can be reproduced for mass consumption, even if it has lost touch with the real thing, with real life. Foods are edited to look better, bigger, and healthier than they really are. The use of preservatives and colorants distances food goods from their trajectory on earth. The monoculture of fast food is the most complete expression of the dramatic reduction in variety, diversity and innovation of the fruits of the earth.

Furthermore, agropornography tells us what to eat, when to eat and why to eat. It reinvents our tastes, our recipes, and even our food memory; it's not even food anymore! Instead, we see in media chemical and gastronomic products that participate in the expropriation of the workforce, severing the relationship of mouth to taste and the orgastic force of eating. In a world of abundance and apparent multiple choices, agropornography leaves us increasingly sub-nourished, obese, and unsatisfied. The food that looks at me wanting to be consumed does not know about biodiversity or agrarian reform and it does not imagine what would be food sovereignty. Agropornography generates billions in the commodification of agriculture and food, leaving in its wake a trail of hunger and shortages.

Agroecology—One Peasant Told Me— Is to Call the Land "My Love"

There is no need to idealize agroecology: the ways and means of agro-ecological relationships are demanding; they are slow, they are patient and full of preliminaries (or foreplay). It is a relationship with the earth that requires scientific knowledge and enchantment, knowing and contemplation; killing the urgency of hunger and the desire to eat with fruit in the mouth without sacrificing the tree. Land as a "body" has desires and erogenous zones; in agroecology, land's vulnerable portions are known, its ability to give and receive pleasure is recognized and stimulated, but with no pretense to know and master all of its processes, all of its possibilities.

Agroecology handles with care; it uses theories and practices that value the cessation of doing, degrowth, growing old, and of waiting patiently as vital ways to exist. Land has rights. Peoples and communities have the right to maintain their own spiritual and material relationships to their land. In Latin America it is called *sumak kawsay*, or "land without evil." The core of our cosmovisions is the necessary equilibrium between nature, the cosmos and human beings. We recognize that as humans we are but a part of nature and the cosmos. We share a spiritual connection with our lands and with the web of life. We love our lands and our peoples, and without that, we can neither defend our practice of agroecology and fight for our rights, nor feed the world.

Agriculture is a part of knowledge established and metabolized by social groups in relation to nature. This body of knowledge consists of forms of work, leisure, value and enchantment that are much more complex than the processes of production, distribution and consumption. Agroecology is the application and living out of ecological principles and concepts in the management and design of sustainable agroecosystems considering the relationships and values of time and place, and integrating scientific and socio-environmental knowledge. This is why it is "culture." The "body" of the place is known, its vulnerable places are respected, its capacity to give and receive pleasure is recognized and stimulated, but with no pretense of knowing and mastering all processes or possibilities.

In agroecology, science does not pretend to know as a process of exhaustion: the earth and its beings remain alive throughout the process of production and reproduction of life. In this sense, the forms of relationship and management do not always have to be in search of production, to make the land "give birth." Agroecology has means of caring, means to stop doing, means to grow old, to wait and to see the ways of existing and happening as vital.

Finally, agroecology is erotic. The erotic is a displacement of the mono-cultivated order of sexuality beyond the objectification of reproduction or the realization of a desire. It is an agriculture that is not aimed at the intensive production of food but at the experience of the land with its possibilities of life, cultivating food, and performing seduction.

Seeing agriculture as a ritual driven by uncertainty, flexibility and the unforeseen does not seem to be serious enough to account for coping with the food crisis and hunger in the world. However, it is these qualities of an eco-erotic project that can enable a relationship between the social body and the body of the world that is not suicidal, as is the current capitalist model, in dealing with land and nature. The challenge is to abandon the mercantile relationship with the land and reestablish the relationship of culture where uncertainty, flexibility and unforeseen values are fundamental to reorganizing the relationship with nature beyond pretentiously controlling the culture of the market and the economy of capital.

The truth is, these forms of coexistence with the earth and its beings are not nostalgia for a remote past or a futuristic utopia. They are present and resistant in various means of relating to and living with nature on the part of the traditional communities.

The native seed is the result of a process of breeding embedded within non-Western cosmologies, between indigenous peoples, the seed, and all other living beings. The concept of the Cultures of the Seed is a tool of analysis that highlights the fact that the seed is neither a simple commodity that the breeders can manipulate in a laboratory, nor something to buy in a seed store, nor does the seed evolve into a cultural or biological vacuum. It implies specific cosmological points of view and cognitive models, diverse technological and ecosystem strategies, as well as very different types of social, religious and productive organizations.[20]

The role of women in agroecology cannot be based on idealizations: no, women are not more sensitive or sexier or more erotic beings. This is a socially constructed role and idea. And no, women are not closer to nature because they are historically associated with the reproduction of family forms and their communities. They deal with and understand places beyond the models of patriarchy. Peasant women and traditional communities have developed a vast knowledge of agro-systems and for this reason they understand biodiversity, plant domestication, seed management and play a fundamental role in the struggle to defend biodiversity and food sovereignty.

For this and other reasons, women peasants are protagonists in the defense and struggle for land and contribute decisively to the transition to an ecologically based agriculture, overcoming violence, patriarchy, and agribusiness. They represent an economy of life. An economy that articulates the backyard, the kitchen, the forest, the animals, celebrations of being alive, the diverse needs of the family and the land. Peasant women have a love affair with the land. And the land can be a mother, but it can also be an eroticized woman, or a friend, a teacher, a brother: eroticized land can be whatever one wants as an expression of a relationship beyond commodity, beyond production and technological bureaucracy. In this sense we recognize Indigenous peoples, small farmers and agro-ecological communities as their most attentive interpreters, and we believe that these communities are already preparing the processes of an agro-ecological transition that can guide us on our way to post-capitalism.

In what follows I give examples of the ways peasant women and communities that I have been involved with are seeking to recover this different relationship to land, food, and cultivation. I speak as a participant in the movement, not an observer.

---

20. Gonsalez, "The Cultures of the Seed in the Peruvian Andes."

Latin American Agroerotisms: Cabruca and Milpa

In Brazil, a group of women comprising the Agroecological Web of the Peoples of Bahia get together regularly to perform ancient dances, torés and persistent drumming. They have not given up on enchanting the territory of southern Bahia and its beings. "Enchanting" here is the embodying of memory and of ancestors not defeated by death and forgetfulness. Their goal is to enchant the land, agriculture, work and food. The rhythm and beauty of the bodies in dance and prayer, games and music are expressions of the agroecological modes of relating to the land, the seed, the water, the sun and the small animals.

> The People's Web was created from the ongoing dialogues of the 1st Agroecology Day in Bahia, held in 2012 and has the role of setting the agenda of annual actions that help in the development, empowerment and emancipation of integrated communities. Segments such as camps, settlements, quilombolas, Indigenous people, masters and leaders of oral tradition, small producers, students, researchers and professionals in Agroecology participate in these dialogues.[21]

The entire south of Bahia is inhabited by plural deities Enchanted Orixás and Caboclas. There, on the coast, between the sea and the forest, the first native communities met the invaders over 515 years ago. So much for taking the land, pulling out the forest, enslaving the people and dis-enchanting the continent! It only made their local gods and goddesses even more beautiful and necessary as the gospel was discreetly mixed with dancing and conversations in a round.

This is a history of the radical permanence of peoples and their modes of beliefs in the struggle for land and territory. Within a circle and going around the roundness, nothing is lost. We are Cabruca: the forest and life system of the traditional peoples of southern Bahia. Cabruca is everything mixed together: large and old trees with recent forms of planting that combine cocoa with the fruits, the vegetable garden and the forests that still remain on the coast of Brazil. From Cabruca and within Cabruca the people of the forest take their livelihood, keep their tastes and flavors, and enjoy life. It is an agriculture that coexists with the landscape, which grows in the fields among the insects, flowers and necessary roots.

---

21. https://m.youtube.com/watch?v=nUYZ-pGpl4o.

> To belong to a place is to be part of it, to be the extension of the landscape, the river, the mountain. It means having its elements of culture, history and tradition in this place. That is, instead of us giving meaning to the place, the place gives meaning to our existence.[22]

What brings the women together at the meeting of the People's Web are the practices and debates on agroecology within a difficult and conflicting political scenario advancing the artificial eucalyptus forests, pasture for cattle, mining and tourism enterprises. Against economic, political and cultural monocultures, the women from the People's Web affirm agroecology: they exchange seeds, share planting methodologies, develop techniques and learn the new mixed with the ancestor. Between conversations about agroecology, we would gather under the shade of the old trees and their pluralities. The erotic is a change in the mono-cultivated order of life and sexuality—a confrontation with the phallocratic rationality of capitalism that is based and focused on the reproduction, or in the exclusive realization, of its own desire in the form of surplus value. Monocultures create equal rows of equal plants. Cabruca, on the other hand, is the planting technology in which cocoa and other species coexist together with the forest, feed on the shade and natural nutrients of a landscape that does not require uniformity or "cleanliness."

It is here that indecency must happen—in the model of interpretation of the culture-nature relationship in the ways of doing agri-culture. Agriculture is queer . . . always has been! The more diverse, the more resistant, the more mixed and coexisting with all beings—from river, sun, forest, climate, rain, mist, animals, wind—the more capacity for life. All this together in order to put pieces of the world in our mouth and taste it, smell the smells and touch the textures of what was rubbed on the floor and made food: queerness! From seed to shit and the remains that fertilize the earth: it's culture.

The Mexican and Central American "Milpa"

Another Latin American way of queer-agroecology is the "milpa": a complex concept of the Mexican Indigenous peoples, since it covers many dimensions, from agriculture, beliefs, art and also nutrition.[23] "Milpa" is a word that comes from Nahuatl: "milli, campo e bread, above; over the place." It consists of the Mesoamerican triad: beans, corn and pumpkin,

22. Krenak, "Sempre estivemos em guerra."
23. La milpa, mujer de tierra, agua y cana (https://www.youtube.com/watch?v=aygCy3NjolI).

three of the essential ancestral products that grow together, mixed together. The use of these elements has been found in excavations dating from 2,000 to 6,000 years.

> Here, an analogy with Milpa's Pedagogy seems opportune in pointing out that the educational dimension of the political struggle in defense of the territory and of an agroecological matrix of production constitutes a process that articulates the pedagogical appropriation of the intersubjectivity and rationality inherent in the Indigenous worldview and linguistic-cultural approach within the communities.[24]

The elements that make up the milpa are not only used as an important base for nutrition, but are essential to medical and ritual compositions, both from old and new knowledges. The Mesoamerican triad is a complex "world" because the way in which they are sown is combined, making each of the elements contribute something different but equally nutritious to each other, forming a rich composition. Furthermore, as a crop, it is much more sustainable than just planting corn: milpa carries food all year round and the land is more fully nourished. The alliance of women claim:

> In our investigations and activities, we employ participatory methodologies that favor the exchange of knowledge as well as processes of emancipation, self-recognition and the visibility of knowledge and the capabilities of women: from the design and management of community properties and family patios; the cultivation, collection and recollection of wild foods, herbs and animals; the creation and coordination of organizations and collective projects that foster awareness and education in sustainable agriculture and environmental care; and all the specialized knowledge in the practices of handling native roots and their commercialization channels . . . So we decided together with the Zapatista women that our profits are for life! And we must say that without women there is no agroecology! But also that without agroecology there is no feminism! Because we cannot take care of our bodies and Mother Earth with pesticides and non-native seeds.[25]

In the milpa chelite, pepper and some vegetables or medicinal plants are also cultivated. On the banks there are also fruit trees, maguey and even nopales / cacti, which offer protection. These vary from region to region, as

24. Barbosa and Rosset, *Educação Do Campo*.
25. Alianza de las Mujeres en Agroecología AMA-AWA (https://www.ecosur.mx/sin-mujeres-no-hay-agroecologia/).

they feed on what exists in each environment. In some places you can even find papaya, chile or jamaica.

> The most unique thing in the history of corn, as an axis of Mexican food, is that it gave rise to a complex cultural system that gave harmony and recirculation of the human relationship with the environment. The milpa in its realization has given destination to agricultural uses, nutrition and the celebration of festivals, ceremonies and rituals; it created techniques, tools and procedures that expanded and facilitated the optimal uses of this cereal and gave it a powerful force for social cohesion. It is the plant of coexistence. With it, other plants grow, which together provide basic food for the life of communities, giving a sense of reciprocity and shared solidarity.[26]

Seeds and plants seem peaceful and domesticated, but anyone who lives from the struggle to defend Creole seeds knows that they are always the same and yet so different: never with a definite identity! This diversity is due to the high dispersion capacity of the Creole varieties, which is due to the constant exchange of seeds between the peasantry and traditional peoples; to the continuous crossings that take place between these varieties and differences that live from this random circle that modifies the characteristics and generates new varieties.

It is necessary to sharpen feminist and cutting-edge queer theory analysis to fight the hegemonic models that exploit nature. Equally important is to review our imaginary and overcome the heteronormative and fixed landscapes that we have of nature in our minds. We need a queer and feminist ecology. An erotic agriculture.

Bibliography

Alianza de las Mujeres en Agroecología AMA-AWA. https://www.ecosur.mx/sin-mujeres-no-hay-agroecologia/.

Althaus-Reid, Marcella. *Indecent Theology: Theological Perversions in Sex, Gender and Politics*. London: Routledge, 2000.

Barbosa, Lia Pinheiro, and Peter Michael Rosset. *Educação do Campo e Pedagogia Camponesa Agroecológica Na América Latina: Aportes da la Via Campesina e da Cloc*. Educ. Soc., Campinas, V. 38, N. 140, P. 705–24, July 2017, http://www.scielo.br/scielo.php?script=sci_arttext&pid=S0101-73302017000300705&lng=en&nrm=iso.

Caporal, Costabeber. "Agroecologia: Enfoque Científico e Estratégico." http://coral.ufsm.br/desenvolvimentorural/textos/31.pdf.

26. Garcia, "La Milpa."

Coopersmith, J. "Pornography, Technology and Progress." http://berlin.robinperrey.com/imgpo/pornography-technology-and-progress.pdf.
Gaard, Greta Claire. "Rumo ao Ecofeminismo Queer." *Revista Estudos Feministas, Florianópolis* 19.1 (2011) 197–223. http://www.scielo.br/scielo.php?script=sci_arttext&pid=S0104-026X2011000100015&lng=en&nrm=iso.
Garcia, Costantio Marcías. "La Milpa." http://web.ecologia.unam.mx/oikos3.0/images/Pdfs/2017-01.pdf.
Gonsalez, Tirso. "The Cultures of the Seed in the Peruvian Andes." http://www.crcnetbase.com/doi/abs/10.1201/9781420049824.ch8.
Krenak, Ailton. "Sempre Estivemos em Guerra." https://www.goethe.de/ins/br/pt/kul/fok/zgh/21806968.html.
La Milpa, Mujer de Tierra, Agua y Cana. https://www.youtube.com/watch?v=aygCy3NjolI.
Mészáros, I. *Filosofia, Ideologia, e Ciência Social: Ensaio de Negação e Afirmação*. São Paulo: Ensaio, 1993.
Ministério da Cultura. "Fundação Biblioteca Nacional Departamento Nacional do Livro. http://objdigital.bn.br/Acervo_Digital/livros_eletronicos/carta.pdf.
Moraes, Eliane Robert. "O Efeito Obsceno, Cad. Pagu no.20 Campinas, 2003." http://www.scielo.br/pdf/cpa/n20/n20a04.pdf.
Passos, Lucas. "Beatriz Preciado na cama com Slavoj Žižek." https://ensaiosdegenero.wordpress.com/tag/beatriz-preciado/.
———. "Prazer, gozo, Slavoj Žižek: leitura abusada n° 2." https://ensaiosdegenero.wordpress.com/2012/12/01/prazer-gozo-slavoj-zizek-leitura-abusada-no-2/.
———. "Regulações farmacopolíticas da potentia gaudendi: uma introdução" (https://ensaiosdegenero.wordpress.com/2012/06/23/regulacoes-farmacopoliticas-da-potentia-gaudendi-uma-introducao/.
Preciado, Beatriz. "The Forces of Reproduction, Public Seminar, 2013." http://www.publicseminar.org/2013/12/testo-junkie-by-beatriz-preciado/#.WICyWtIrLMw.
Preciado, Beatriz, and Potentia Gaudendi. "Orgia Ideológica." http://coletivocaju.blogspot.com.br/2012/06/potentia-gaudendi.html.
Rego, Adna, "A Modernidade Analisada Sob a ótica do Consumo: Algumas Contribuições de Zygmunt Bauman e Anthony Giddens." https://periodicos.unifacex.com.br/Revista/article/download/36/17.
Sanchez, Thomas. *De Sancto Matrimond*. http://www.leituraspdf.com.br/livros/desancto-matrimonii-sacramento-disputationes.
Sousa Júnior, Justino. "Mercadoria, Fetichismo e Discurso Figurado n' O Capital." http://www.unicamp.br/cemarx/ANAIS%20IV%20COLOQUIO/comunica%E7%F5es/GT1/gt1m2c3.pdf.
Tenório, R. "Agricultura—Do Subsídio à Política Agrícola, IPEA, Desafios de Desenvolvimento, 2011." http://www.ipea.gov.br/desafios/index.php?option=com_content&view=article&id=2599:catid=28&Itemid=23.
Žižek, Slavoj. "Masturbation, or Sexuality in the Atonal World." https://zizektimes.wordpress.com/2015/10/20/masturbation-or-sexuality-in-the-atonal-world-by-slavoj-zizek/.

13

"Wise as Serpents, Innocent as Doves"

Recovering an Indigenous Politics of Spirit by Way of Quetzalcóatl, Guadalupe

James W. Perkinson

Behold, I am sending you out as sheep in the midst of wolves, so be wise as serpents and innocent as doves" (Matt 10:16)

I enter without fear the serpent's jaws that formed the entrance to the temple of Quetzalcóatl."[1]

THIS ESSAY EMERGES OUT of the multi-layered emergency of our time. Its animating force answers most immediately, in my particular case, to a "manufactured emergency," generated by legislative policy beginning in 2012, enabling large banks to plunder City of Detroit assets under an Emergency Manager imposed by the Michigan Governor, empowered to hire and fire at will, void contracts (including with unions), sell city resources to whomever at whatever price entirely outside any democratic process or accountability, across an urban landscape already long decimated by white flight and corporate abandonment. The writing here rep-

---

1. Lafaye, *Quetzalcóatl and Guadalupe*, 299.

resents an effort, by a white straight male, being re-made in slow motion over thirty years under tutelage to inner city black struggle and insurgent native memory and irrepressible watershed vitality, to grapple with such an "imposed apocalypse." But that forty-year "baptismal itinerary"—going "back" and "down" into the history of white supremacy's genocidal legacy at this Great Lakes Strait—has also meant more recent congress with another educational challenge. This latest plunge encompasses Latinx experience on Motown's southwest side—a presence and *fuerza* of folk long faced with colonial predations Spanish, US, and globalizing, now forced to immigrate "north" of the imperial border, so violently imposed in 1848, in order to survive. As the writing here first addressed a global gathering of theologians seeking to grapple with world-questions at a forum hosted in Mexico City, it is this southwest Detroit forum that weights the piece with its particular gravitas. And that heaviness was quadrupled in the wake of climate upheaval's latest onslaught, raking the US "territory" of Puerto Rico in the fall of 2017 with storm surge and testing the empire's response in the mix. Abysmal as Trump's "paper towel" response proved to be, on the ground in the Port of Riches, ordinary people, already long wrestling with neo-liberal debt bondage, had already begun reclaiming ancestral savvy in adapting and thriving. The untamable Wind and Water Creature named "Maria" they named "teacher," as She clearly revealed in Her aftermath what worked and didn't work—traditional methods of intercropping fruits and root-crops proving quite durable where export-oriented monocrops were devastated.[2] And it is in honor of such a "wild Marian pedagogy," readily embraced by people living close to the soil that this work goes forth.

    The methodology offered traces an itinerary of crossing over and coming back—re-learning the world through Indigenous encounter. In particular, the approach seeks "schooling" from the creative adaptations of cultures of color under colonial duress on their own terms and in their own codes, in order to return to biblical text and Christian practice with a sensibility heightened for the traces of Indigenous wisdom and wiles still present in that tradition not entirely erased by its imperial formation. The focus keys off of the climate crisis provoked by the last 6,000 years of state plundering of environments and peoples to ask how we might learn to live otherwise and turns especially to Indigenous modes of symbiotic dwelling and ritual telling for inspiration and interdiction. The Cult of Our Lady of Guadalupe/Tonantzin and the myth of Quetzalcoatl/Topiltzin will supply the sites of "crossing over" where Indigenous and *mestiza* peoples in Mexico have continuously re-worked their memories, pain, and beauty into

---

2. Klein, "The Battle for Paradise."

textures and artifacts and ceremonies that encode ancient understandings of native cultures that human beings are not simply "human," but finally a form of trans-species, in origins and daily life, living in the big body of their local ecosystems with kin-species of plants and animals, waters and soils, answering to the Big Mystery of on-going and irrepressible reciprocity and metabolism of loss into grief and creativity. "Coming back" will involve brief constructive re-imagination of this kind of "gift-economy[3] eco-hermeneutics" in relationship to North American struggles with the on-going history of supremacies white, Christian, and anthropocentric.

Lafaye as Tutor

But such an accounting entails a first moment of recognition of an achievement perhaps unique on the planet not so much in its content as its prodigality. And that is the import of a new hybrid collectivity named on its own terms *La Raza*. "The Race"—as Mexicans of various dispositions and locations sometimes designate the larger reality from which they descend and to which they orient—is a *mestizo*-meld of Spanish colonial and ancient Native genetic lines and cultural *traditios* that emerged out of the detritus of modern Euro-conquest with singular durability and genius. That creative conjunction is richly concentrated and densely occulted in the renowned image of Our Lady of Guadalupe. In his *tour de force* exegesis of what he calls Mexican national consciousness titled *Quetzalcóatl and Guadalupe*, Sorbonne scholar Jacques Lafaye (as translated by Benjamin Keen) asserts that this Guadalupe cult of the Tepayac Virgin now centered in a basilica just north of Mexico City's urban core is "the central theme of the history of creole consciousness or Mexican patriotism."[4] What was early described as the "Mexican Mariophany" combines, he insists, a major Christian current expressed in "the cult of Mary the Immaculate" with a fundamental belief of ancient Mexican religion glossed as "the dual principle."[5] And at heart the question he finds compelling in such an epiphany is not whether the image is the result of miraculous intervention or (alternatively) native artistry, but that so many

---

3. The reference here is to an anthropological trope designating Indigenous practices of communally circulating, rather than privately accumulating, goods, foods, tools, clothes, and resources. The values put in play in such practices give greatest honor to those who "give away" the most. Not at all, as sometimes misperceived, a "counsel of poverty," but a wisdom of social bonding, the practice is nearly the exact opposite of modern capitalist focus on private ownership.

4. Lafaye, *Quetzalcóatl and Guadalupe*, 299.

5. Lafaye, *Quetzalcóatl and Guadalupe*, 239, 244, 299; Dussel *The Invention of the Americas*, 74, 173.

people, as he notes Marxist scholar Marc Bloch has intoned, "'believed and still believe' (in a Mexico in which there triumphed a revolution of positivist inspiration, followed by a revolution under Marxist influence) in the miraculous character of the image of Tepeyac."[6]

Our own interest here will not quite drill down on the same focal point but ask after the import of such a vital fetishism for an Anglo-Christian resolve centered in the imperial juggernaut of El Norte to be taught and checked by the baroque prodigality thus exhibited, as already hinted. As this writing is necessarily quite limited, and my own knowledge of the historiography, linguistic complexity, and cultural prolixity so woefully puny, I will take Lafaye's work as the primary interlocutor for the effort, supplemented and/or backed up by his preface writer Octavio Paz and cross-referenced with liberation theologian Enrique Dussel and Azteca historian Burr Cartwright Brundage. Since my own goal is heuristic—the conjuration of a possible wonderment largely dependent on imaginative ferment—and space limited, I will not try to engage other possible voices on the subject.

In nuce, the work here is one of crossing over and coming back. I take for granted that a white Western settler colonial formation such as I have received growing up needs schooling in vision and imagination, as indeed in lifestyle and hands-on skill, in seeking to recover a more symbiotic way of dwelling. The need is not only economic and political, but spiritual. In what follows, I will hunker down at length with Lafaye's work, seek to sketch the *mestizaje* genius it recounts, and then push behind and below that evident five-hundred-year-old effort at re-invention to catch glimpse of Indigenous insight and savvy yet extant in the re-mix, before concluding with a few hints about how such might rebound on a US Protestant approach to Christian resolve and exegesis.

Re-Mixing Origins

There is much to note on the way. In his concluding summary, Lafaye styles the Guadalupe cult the "spiritual aspect of the protest against the colonial regime"—in reference to the elite *criollo* drive to become independent of Spanish *gachupine* control in the independence movement of the eighteenth century.[7] Of course, we would quickly add, it just as certainly perpetuated that regime in its racialized hierarchy and modernist nation-state fascinations. Lafaye continues in asserting within Mexican history the trenchant passion of a "permanent search for identity," naming itself, *Mexicanidad,* or

---

6. Lafaye, *Quetzalcóatl and Guadalupe,* 299.

7. Lafaye, *Quetzalcóatl and Guadalupe,* 299.

in more critical "indigenizing" compass today, *Mexicayotl*.[8] Citing Francisco de la Maza's trope of the "mirror of national consciousness," Lafaye unpacks his earlier Mariophany allusion to the ancient principle of a duality of deity (Ometeotl). This mirror, he notes, has at various times solicited memory of an ancient "Plumed Serpent" wind-deity known as Quetzalcóatl. This deity was re-cast as the Apostle Thomas, in Spanish colonial anxiety to ground their claim to "mission rights" in New Spain, as he supposedly translated himself to Anahuac and preached throughout central "Mexico" in the 1st century.[9] Alternatively, the mirror divulged the present cast of the "national soul" in the bright paints of the Guadalupe face, at once Black Madonna-apparition of a Marian tradition centered in Estremadura, Spain and the re-appearance of the Aztec Earth-Mother-Goddess variously known as Tonantzin Coatlaxopeuh ("serpent crusher") on the Tepeyac hill, site of Her Aztec shrine, destroyed by the conquistadores. Thus, Quetzalcóatl Myth and Guadalupe Cult appear as the double-basin "reflection pool" of Mexican cultural creativity—in whose shimmering depths recurrently flashes a continuing advent of the Indian male-female dual divinity, Ometeotl, re-cast! And already we are deep in the mix.

While this "enigmatic hybridization" in emblematic language denotes a "maximum interiorization" of cultural fusion, Lafaye does not lose sight of the complexity. He reads the Iberian symbiosis with Amerindian hieroglyph as an instance of mythic "originality" licensing the birth of a new culture that yet does not occlude the continuing expression of the "two mother cultures"—each in [her] own language.[10] And here the richness of his elaboration begins to issue in what concerns my interest.

Spanish Improvisation

On the Spanish side of the mixture, Lafaye describes a "resurgence of the call of Abraham in the new form of the *call of Guadalupe*" and emphasizes that this resurgence is a "clear loan from a Hispano-Portuguese Christianity saturated over long centuries with Judaism."[11] Earlier, Lafaye had traced the advent of the Guadalupe cult in New Spain across a convoluted history of transmission—torqued by intervening political concerns and spiritual vortices—to its own origins in the founding Guadalupe "apparition" in Estremadura, Spain. There a 1440 Codex transcribes the legend, rooted in a

---

8. Lafaye, *Quetzalcóatl and Guadalupe*, 300.
9. Lafaye, *Quetzalcóatl and Guadalupe*, 300.
10. Lafaye, *Quetzalcóatl and Guadalupe*, 301.
11. Lafaye, *Quetzalcóatl and Guadalupe*, 302, 287 (my italics).

(supposed) 1322 appearance of the Virgin to a poor shepherd of the region.[12] The historical details of this prior "Old Spain" appearance pile up into a virtual totem of "Indigenous" signification. In the memory of legend, the shimmering apparition directs the herder to a little buried statue whose countenance is "dark"—part of the mysterious "Black Madonna" emblems that begin to populate the European countryside post-crusades whose provenience remains uncertain, but likely Byzantine in origin. The region is montane—an "outback" in the southwest of Spain, offering haven historically to renegades and refugees, fleeing the "sword of the Moor," who supposedly, in the eighth century, transported valued relics into remote sites out of the way of threatened profanation.[13] It is the region that grants this relic its vaunted name, likely Arabic in denotation: *"quad-al-upe"* signifying *rio occulto*, a shadowed river, descending the elevated recesses through high banks.[14] The Lady is thus, in Middle Ages advent, a watershed toponym.

Of particular note, among Her accumulated accoutrements is a golden scorpion, bestowed by regional "homeboy," Hernan Cortés, returned from his Mexican campaign of conquest, in gratitude for healing after being stung by a scorpion.[15] Likewise of note, is the sanctuary's notoriety as safe harbor for cryptojudaic ceremonies, subverting Inquisitorial suppression of Sephardim in the hubris of the Reconquista triumph, as well as sympathy and support for regional resistance against foreign sovereign Charles I in the early years of his rule and the Comunero Revolt of 1521.[16]

All of which is to say, that the Spanish inheritance of the Tepeyac Virgin is itself profoundly hybrid, fusing borrowings "Celtiberian, Arabo-Maghrebian, Visigothic, Latin, and Judaic," and if unwound with care and nuance, offers tendrils thick with regional innovation and Indigenous intuition, not fully eclipsed in the hegemony of state appropriation and colonial imposition.[17]

Mexica Innovation

On the ancient *Meshica*[18] side of the Guadalupe mix, there is likewise regional genius and Indigenous uniqueness not entirely "disappeared" in

12. Lafaye, *Quetzalcóatl and Guadalupe*, 217–24, 294–95.
13. Lafaye, *Quetzalcóatl and Guadalupe*, 220, 222.
14. Lafaye, *Quetzalcóatl and Guadalupe*, 217–18.
15. Lafaye, *Quetzalcóatl and Guadalupe*, 222.
16. Lafaye, *Quetzalcóatl and Guadalupe*, 224.
17. Lafaye, *Quetzalcóatl and Guadalupe*, 309.
18. The spelling here offered hints the older [ʃ] pronunciation of the Nahuatl-

Aztec conquest of other native groups (such as the Toltecas). Emphasizing that "the avatars of the myth of Quetzalcóatl... and the cult of Guadalupe, have been among the most characteristic aspects of this Mexican national 'soul' in the process of formation, from the sixteenth to the twentieth century," Lafaye insists that "other mythical figures, other beliefs, would reveal the same texture."[19] What will be found in each are the "substitutions and reinterpretations of beliefs borrowed from the dominant culture by the dominated culture [that] in the last analysis represent efforts at salvaging the latter."[20] "The cult of Tonantzin," he says, "was prolonged for centuries in the shelter of a sanctuary of the Virgin Mary."[21]

But it is not only traumatized Indians who take refuge there. Paz's Preface succinctly rehearses the potent breadth of this "divine numen" whose depths Lafaye is plumbing. For Paz, Guadalupe is a veritable "constellation of signs come from all skies and all the mythologies."[22] For creoles—"both womb and grave," a "little brown Virgin," "composed of American earth and European theology," allowing New Spain to "strike roots in Anahuac soil."[23] For mestizos—an even deeper service of origins in the face of profound "orphanage" and contradiction: at once the violated mother ravaged by Conquest replicated as *la Chingada,* and the Virgin Mother, intact as Tonantzin-Guadalupe, carrying child within.[24] But it is especially in relationship to native savvy in the midst of apocalyptic savagery that we take note of the salvage strategy Lafaye is underscoring. For Indians also, Paz notes something like the comforts of "an orphanage"— a "compensation" of the imagination, he says, that pushes his own eloquence towards an Indigenous insistence. Tonantzin-Guadalupe is not mere human harbor but comports as "mother of gods and men, of stars and ants, of maize and agave."[25] She is a refuge whose lap is that of "the mother-mountain, the mother-water."[26]

This question of language marks Lafaye's text as well. His own similar exuberance and poesy issues in a methodological challenge crucial to

speaking people (subsequently replaced with an "x" in writing) that contributed to the more recent Chicano movement in the U.S.

19. Lafaye, *Quetzalcóatl and Guadalupe,* 307–8.
20. Lafaye, *Quetzalcóatl and Guadalupe,* 308, 61, 217, 229, 242, 285.
21. Lafaye, *Quetzalcóatl and Guadalupe,* 308.
22. Lafaye, *Quetzalcóatl and Guadalupe,* xix.
23. Lafaye, *Quetzalcóatl and Guadalupe,* xix.
24. Lafaye, *Quetzalcóatl and Guadalupe,* xix–xx; Dussel, *The Invention of the Americas,* 125–26.
25. Lafaye, *Quetzalcóatl and Guadalupe,* xix.
26. Lafaye, *Quetzalcóatl and Guadalupe,* xix.

Euro-theology and modern hubris alike, as noted above. Appreciation of the role of the "myth of the Indian Past" that nurtured and nurtures Mexican struggle, requires a turn to what he calls "emblematic expressions"— a "baroque exuberance" of preaching, complemented with a mingling of image and heraldry of plastic expression and danced and sung sentiment "whose semantic content remains to be discovered."[27] Inside the "euhemeristic optimism" of such "baroque luxuriance," he insists, we will find antique heroes side-by-side with polytheistic gods.[28]

He concludes with a prognostication. While the star of Guadalupe may well be "setting" in a de-christianized urbanizing Mexico, the mythic image of Quetzalcóatl—"more closely linked to Mexican polytheism" and detached from his appropriating twin, St. Thomas—may well undergo a sacred "re-charge."[29] The Plumed Serpent has indeed been Phoenix-like in history, "reborn with each new 'sun' from the ashes of the previous one."[30] Paz helps us follow the track back.

Whence the Wind?

In his Preface, Paz paraphrases Quetzalcóatl as "the winged eternity of the wind."[31] Noting his name as Nahuatl, he yet asserts that this Deity of the Air is very ancient, showing up first as a "coastal divinity, associated with the sea and wind," before gravitating in-land to the central plateau and "establish[ing] himself at Teotihuacan as a great god."[32] After the destruction of the city, he re-appears centuries later at Tula, gains his current name, "duplicates" himself as simultaneously "creator and culture god Quetzalcóatl," inherited or stolen from Teotihuacan, and as a human "priest-king" presiding ritually as Topiltzin-Quetzalcóatl."[33] In the religious war subsequently devastating Tula, which Paz denotes as "also a mythic combat between the warlike divinities of the nomads [from north of Anahuac] and the culture god from Teotihuacan," Quetzalcóatl gains his figurement as "messianic."[34] Fleeing according to prophecy, he disappears "to the place 'where water joins sky': the marine horizon on which Evening

---

27. Lafaye, *Quetzalcóatl and Guadalupe*, 309, 200, 240, 247.
28. Lafaye, *Quetzalcóatl and Guadalupe*, 240.
29. Lafaye, *Quetzalcóatl and Guadalupe*, 310–11.
30. Lafaye, *Quetzalcóatl and Guadalupe*, 310–11.
31. Lafaye, *Quetzalcóatl and Guadalupe*, xx.
32. Lafaye, *Quetzalcóatl and Guadalupe*, xx, 140, 143, 153.
33. Lafaye, *Quetzalcóatl and Guadalupe*, xx.
34. Lafaye, *Quetzalcóatl and Guadalupe*, xx, 14–15.

Star and Morning Star alternately appear."[35] But the mythic memory is that he also promises to return and reclaim his power in the same year (*ce acatl* or "one reed") that he accomplished his disappearance (in 987 CE) and transfiguration into the morning star.[36]

And thus, the stage is set for a continuing series of transmutations and epiphanies. Tula's fall introduces, according to Paz, an interregnum on the Anahuac plateau. The rise of the Aztec state—like Tula before it, created by "newly civilized barbarians"—recapitulated honored origins. Mexico-Tenochtitlan was founded "in the image of Tula, which had been founded in the image of Teotihuacan."[37] Cortés' arrival in a "one reed" year on the calendar suggests his presence as Quetzalcóatl-returned, seemingly closing the interregnum—until too late the Aztec elite realize the conquistadores are mere men, not Tulans *redivivus*.[38]

But the Spanish themselves eventually recapitulate Aztec strategies. Seeking to locate New Spain "origins" elsewhere than in the horrific Apocalypse of Conquest, all manner of missionary invention threads the Quetzalcóatl myth back into a convoluted theology.[39] The major ruse was the "discernment" that Quetzalcóatl was actually the Apostle Thomas, evangelizing the Indians in the first century and setting up the current moment of Spanish New World arrival as the penultimate development issuing immediately in the eschaton.[40]

Post-independence in the nineteenth century, Quetzalcóatl disappears as god or apostle only to reappear as national hero.[41] Now he is called Hidalgo; Juarez; Carranza. Each defining event in the historical concatenation—independence in 1821, the liberal revolution of 1857, the popular revolution of 1910—births new hope that the interregnum, opened by the Plumed Serpent's 987 CE flight, has finally been closed and legitimacy re-established.[42]

---

35. Lafaye, *Quetzalcóatl and Guadalupe*, xx; Brundage, *The Fifth Sun*, 112, 119–20, 127.

36. The Aztec calendar "round" making up the equivalent of a century, was fifty-two years, composed of four sets of thirteen years each and named for the initial year of that set, respectively, 1 Rabbit, 1 Reed, 1 Knife, and 1 House. Brundage, *The Fifth Sun*, 22; Lafaye, *Quetzalcóatl and Guadalupe*, xx, 151, 163.

37. Lafaye, *Quetzalcóatl and Guadalupe*, xx, 143.

38. Lafaye, *Quetzalcóatl and Guadalupe*, 273, 285; Dussel, *The Invention of the Americas*, 40, 99–102; Brundage, *The Fifth Sun*, 61, 125.

39. Lafaye, *Quetzalcóatl and Guadalupe*, 192–93.

40. Lafaye, *Quetzalcóatl and Guadalupe*, xx–xxi, 134, 180–86.

41. Lafaye, *Quetzalcóatl and Guadalupe*, xxi.

42. Lafaye, *Quetzalcóatl and Guadalupe*, xxi, xxv, 126.

But Paz divines otherwise. The search is not resolved; the Evening Star and Morning Star continue to haunt the horizon.

Seeds of the Past

In his discussion of the precipitating cause of the eighteenth-century Independence Movement, Lafaye explores the "explosive power"—in the deep layers of the "collective consciousness"—of the Virgin of Guadalupe emblem, showing up as a messianic avatar of the *Iglesia Indiana* of the sixteenth century, "after long subterranean journeys."[43] The language is suggestive. The image is perhaps of a seed, recurrently sprouting into new life, under pressure of adversity and season, buried again and again, blossoming into life irrepressibly, dizzying in color, before returning to dark soil and the invisible way of roots and kernels. It is exactly such a premonition I want to liberate now from its supposed banality to reimagine in relationship to both Earth-Mother cult and Quetzal-Bird myth. The presumption in our own apocalyptic hour is that there remains a "soul-memory," at some inchoate species level, of our having lived differently, not destined to doom, not innately "wired" to violate the planet, though marinated in a multi-thousand year nightmare of imperial state domination and elite predation, to be sure: a DNA-orientation steeped in a multi-million year history of hunter-gatherer symbiosis and savvy, bound in symbiotic reciprocity with plants and animals, weather and water, seasons and soils, that remains the taproot for all of our now desperate fumbling for the rules and roles of a sustainable future. There is not space here to justify the presumption by way of review of our species' history as I have elsewhere written,[44] but I can only say, simply, that I take such for granted for this argument and am concerned rather to call up and high-light the images and sounds, smells and tastes such an indigenously oriented seed-memory might find inviting if it is to re-awaken and re-sprout with creative fervor in our own stark hour.

In this vein, it is the very history itself of missionary conundrum—trying to gerrymander horrific Conquest into livable narrative—that gives pause. The sixteenth century frenzy of theory on the origin of the heretofore unrecognized "Fourth World" of the Americas—comprehending native peoples under a vast array of extant ideas as Amazons, Cyclops, Sirens, etc.—by the seventeenth century even offered in the thought of Isaac La Peyrère that native folk were "'preadamites,' *exempt from original sin.*"[45]

---

43. Lafaye, *Quetzalcóatl and Guadalupe*, 105–6, 72.
44. Perkinson, *Messianism*.
45. Lafaye, *Quetzalcóatl and Guadalupe*, 39–43.

By the late seventeenth century, renowned poetess of the Mexican Golden Age, Sor Juana Ines de La Cruz, has given the idea terse brilliance.[46] This "Phoenix of Mexico" as her country called her, offered the following among the fifty quatrains she dedicated to *Doña María de Guadalupe Alencastre, la única maravilla de nuestros siglos*:

> Señora, I was born
>
> in America, land of plenty,
>
> Gold is my compatriot,
>
> and precious metals my comrades.
>
> Here's a land where sustenance
>
> is almost freely given,
>
> to no other on earth
>
> is Mother Earth so generous.
>
> From the common curse of man
>
> its sons appear to be born free
>
> For here their daily bread
>
> costs but little sweat of labor.
>
> Europe knows this best of all
>
> for these many years, insatiable,
>
> She has bled the abundant veins
>
> of America's rich mines.[47]

Lafaye's brief exegesis is telling. The earth mother here, as both land and country, is "generous and sustaining," a telluric and mythic realization of a "Western Paradise" whose people are deemed Eden-ically free from the original curse—which is to say as "Immaculate" as the Virgin herself![48] And this in virtue of a "freedom" where sustenance does not require hard labor! A hint exactly of the point underlying this entire writing that when we lived in concert with Earth's own generosity, we had no need of state or force, and could even embrace metal as a "comrade" rather than a feared weapon!

---

46. Lafaye, *Quetzalcóatl and Guadalupe*, 68, 71.
47. Quoted in Lafaye, *Quetzalcóatl and Guadalupe*, 70–71.
48. Lafaye, *Quetzalcóatl and Guadalupe*, 71, 227.

The history of our species' creative mimicry of the biosphere's own intricacies of reciprocity is exactly what contemporary movements like permaculture design are trying to recover and what the planet in effect "demands" as a sustainable posture of our species with respect to (and "for") all else. Except what is missing in modern scientifically-informed efforts at re-inventing such is the dimension of "Spirit"—mythologizing the food-web and watershed in story and ritual, opening the community to a web of kinship and ancestry that embraces non-human others as in some mysterious manner, also "Persons" and Spirit-Creatures, in dreams and vision, gifting us with adaptation-wisdom and warning us of overreach and hubris. The exact form of such human/non-human "gift-economies" depends on exigencies local and historical. For most of our species' history on the planet, they were expressed in the *longue durée* of hunter-gatherer savvy and subsistence. But they were also maintained for more than four thousand years after we first began to settle and supplement such foraging with low-tech agriculture and animal husbandry in the Fertile Crescent area.[49] And often enough, partially re-invented in creative resistance once bands of oppressed laborers in early state formation go "feral" and return to the land with their herd animals (like Abraham and family or later Moses and early Israel).

The work here is that of adopting a posture of learning from what our deep ancestry knew about "living well and long-term in place" and stimulating re-imagination and re-appreciation of such a lifeway by attending to the memory-fragments and practice-traces kept alive even inside colonial ritual and story, like so many winter seeds awaiting the rains and sun of a Spirit coming back from the dead. Sor Juana did not live such. But her poesy does remember and ventriloquize the possibility. It also laments the "fall," figured, in her fourth quatrain, as "Europe insatiable"—incarnating in modern form the ancient emergence of states and empires—"hell-bent" on "bleeding" the land and her peoples, mining the metals for currency and weapon. And in more recent modalities, we might add, converting—in the name of capital—all of the Mother's abundance as rapidly as possible into market-commodities destined to garbage bins and a half-life of toxicity and pollution, now poisoning a planet.

The hint in Sor Juana's conceit that *Mexica* of old was free from the "malediction of origin sin," as already noted, effectively claims, as says Lafaye, the *Immaculada's* condition for the indigenes of the land. The issue, as just argued, is not some supposedly pristine "virginal" purity, but a way of living respectfully inside the natural world's own gift-economy and abundance. Certainly, such was not the dominant early missionary sense of

---

49. Scott, *Against the Grain*, 7, 58.

Mary's "immaculate-ness," but the evaluation of native culture and economy as archaic and even "innocent" (to the point of ante-dating the Fall) apparently re-currently troubled the thinking—else there would have been no speculation that these original inhabitants were "pre-Adamite." Here my interest is in the irony of the predication.

Seeds in the Mix

Part of the fame of the Guadalupe image in New Spain was founded in her first large-scale "miracle" after appearing.[50] In 1629 her image carried in procession from Tepeyac to Mexico City was credited with halting a catastrophic flood threatening the city.[51] September flooding was an old and recurrent scourge for the Valley, product of the autumnal rains that Aztec emperors had sought to wrestle into a standoff by means of irrigation works and drainage systems.[52] Subsequent Indian insistence on keeping the Guadalupe feast day in September (when it was first celebrated) rather than follow the official switch of the date to December 12, kept Her potency locked into an Indian sensorium attuned to natural cycles.[53] And such is a theme Lafaye notes throughout. Guadalupe (as indeed Quetzalcoatl) anchors a baroque space of nurture: inside Christian mission and creole politician manipulation, Indigenous rootedness in the priority of natural rhythm and cyclical provision remains alive and succulent.[54] Seasonal rains and autumnal floods associated with geographic contours (the Tepeyac hill and the Mexican Valley) continue to "inform" the image in Indian usage.

Small details here hide large realities, like oaks inside acorns. Here I can only hint (and guess) at the Indigenous depth-perception. The blue of the Virgin's mantle cannot be distinguished, says Lafaye, "from the jade blue of Quetzalcóatl," reinforcing the "accumulated sacred power" of the effigy by invoking a primal color of Indigenous religion.[55] The mantle likewise hosts an array of stars, investing the doubly azure cloth with another

---

50. Lafaye, *Quetzalcóatl and Guadalupe*, 243.

51. Lafaye, *Quetzalcóatl and Guadalupe*, 254, 269–70; Taylor, "Mexico's Virgin," 277–98.

52. Lafaye, *Quetzalcóatl and Guadalupe*, 254.

53. Lafaye, *Quetzalcóatl and Guadalupe*, 233, 266, 291–92.

54. Lafaye, *Quetzalcóatl and Guadalupe*, 104, 134, 146, 150, 187, 257, 266, 292.

55. Lafaye, *Quetzalcóatl and Guadalupe*, 258. Michael Taussig's book, *What Color is the Sacred?* details in depth the profound vertigo and incapacity when Euro-colonizers began to be immersed in and seduced by a native sense of color.

hint of the Quetzal Serpent in his avatar as Morning Star.[56] The cloth itself on which the image appears is a "coarse tissue of agave fiber (*ayatl*)," from which Indians made cloaks (*tilmatli*).[57] The maguey plant source, all by itself, is the equivalent of a divine mediation—at once building material for houses, fiber for clothes and rope, a meal and a drink—as central to the culture as cattle to Maasi in Africa or sheep and goats to an Abraham exiting Harran.[58] Native ken would recognize such.

Nor should the role of flowers here be forgotten.[59] It may well be as a 1556 sermon by Fray Bustamante hinted: the image on Juan Diego's agave cloak was likely the work of one of the Indian painters, whose reputation for flourish and artistry had gained fame by the sixteenth century.[60] Lafaye notes the New Spain custom of hanging images painted by Indians on cloth and wood on church walls, along with "images made of flowers" and "the ancient art of featherwork."[61] Indeed, in the story of the original appearance to Juan Diego, as well as subsequent veneration of the event in poesy like that of Balbuena and Sor Juana, what is invoked is the virtual Edenic quality of the flowering Mexican Valley in April, the subsequent "miracle" of roses in December on the Tepeyac hill (that the Indian peasant will gather up in his *tilma* to take to the bishop as a sign), and a native propensity, found throughout much of the Americas (the Guarani of Brazil come to mind alongside the Azteca *tlamatinime* philosophers), to tell their own origins stories in terms of a flowering of divinity that is not mere symbolism, but metaphysical claim and personal aspiration.[62] Lafaye will resort to the language of transubstantiation to assert the native belief baldly: "the Virgin of Guadalupe is a marvel composed of flowers."[63]

Perhaps informed by the Estremadura Guadalupe myth, the Tepeyac Mother is also at one point described as "found among the rocks."[64] Here we have a hint of the convoluted history of the Virgin's move from Spain to Mexico. To the degree modeled initially on the "Dark Virgin" Guadalupe of Estremadura, the Tepeyac Mother may have arrived initially as a wood

---

56. Lafaye, *Quetzalcóatl and Guadalupe*, 259.
57. Lafaye, *Quetzalcóatl and Guadalupe*, 301; cf also 244, 261, 266.
58. Brundage, *The Fifth Sun*, 36.
59. Dussel, *The Invention of the Americas*, 97–99, 112, 204.
60. Lafaye, *Quetzalcóatl and Guadalupe*, 232.
61. Lafaye, *Quetzalcóatl and Guadalupe*, 232, 75.
62. Lafaye, *Quetzalcóatl and Guadalupe*, 58–59, 74–75, 232, 292; Dussel, *The Invention of the Americas*, 85–86, 97–99, 112.
63. Lafaye, *Quetzalcóatl and Guadalupe*, 75.
64. Lafaye, *Quetzalcóatl and Guadalupe*, 243–44, 294.

statue (later copied in paint), bringing with Her the murky traditions of Her discovery by a shepherd in a rock-guarded cave in the Sierra de las Villuercas of Spain.[65] Whatever the actual truth of its origin as a cult figure (Indian painted image on an agave-fiber *tilma* or cedar-wood statue transported earlier on from Spain), the myth of Guadalupe of Tepeyac "emerges" as a Marian version of an earth-enwombed, rock-protected apparition of the Mother Goddess. Near the end of his work, in asserting the "popular character" of the Virgin traditions common to both Villuercas and Tepeyac, Lafaye notes their topographic constants. The prodigy takes place at a distance from the city, in rocky heights, near a fountain or river.[66] Said otherwise Guadalupe is a haunt of the wild.

And of course, central to the image is the sun-moon encounter. At least one interpretation had it that Guadalupe in the representation interposed Herself as "Immaculate Moon," conquering the Divine Sun in creole heraldic celebration over the Spanish monarchy (as supposedly "the empire over which the sun never set").[67] A 1742 sermon went further: the Tepeyac image, channeling Woman of Revelation inference as well as the Greco-Roman lunar tradition and hints of Qumran and Old Testament elaboration, "eclipsed the divine sun" understood "as no less than "God himself.""[68] And this at a time deeply churned up by "supernatural signs" such as the solar eclipses of 1752.[69] Looming in the background are the ancient holy city of Teotihuacan's double pyramids, the Pyramid of the Sun (Tonatiuh) and the Pyramid of the Moon (Teteoinnan)—the latter of which, during Azetc rule, "doubled" herself in the goddess Toci, whose sanctuary crested Mount Tepeyac.[70] Thus: Guadalupe as Mother Moon, in front of and displacing the sun! On the other hand, Lafaye underscores the way Sánchez delineates the Mexican Virgins of *Remedios* and *Guadalupe* as, respectively, Moon Mother of the Rains, giving remedy for drought and Woman Clothed in the Sun, drying up floods as She had done in 1629, enabling the Mexicans 'to rediscover . . . their solar emblem, obscured by Conquest.""[71] Thus: Guadalupe as dawn of the sixth sun, rising out of the ashes of apocalypse! But these two complimentary Virgins—ultimately

65. Lafaye, Quetzalcóatl and Guadalupe, 233–37, 219–21.
66. Lafaye, Quetzalcóatl and Guadalupe, 297.
67. Lafaye, Quetzalcóatl and Guadalupe, 259, 249.
68. Lafaye, Quetzalcóatl and Guadalupe, 87.
69. Lafaye, Quetzalcóatl and Guadalupe, 97.
70. Lafaye, Quetzalcóatl and Guadalupe, 87.
71. Lafaye, Quetzalcóatl and Guadalupe, 261; Dussel, *The Invention of the Americas*, 126, 205.

made to compete in *criollo*-Spanish political machinations—harbor *Indigenous* intimations of what Lafaye calls "'a reciprocal imbrication' or overlap of the different aspects of the mother-goddess."[72]

There is (obviously!) not space to recount an equally rich genealogy of the Feathered Serpent. Suffice it here to list and note import. Early on, the Franciscans stereotyped Mexicans by means of their denigration of Jews as idolators: the projected Indian version of the idol-worship was supposed serpent-adoration, especially in the forms of Xiuhcoatl[73] and Quetzalcóatl.[74] The latter appears in Lafaye's litany as just as "imbricated" and densely layered in significance as Guadalupe Herself. Titled "Phoenix Bird" by the author for his recurrent returns from the cinders of the "burned up suns" of previous epochs, the Quetzal-God hosts on-going predication. He is called Camaxtli at Tlaxcala and Serpent of Plumes at Cholula.[75] As Tlauizcalpantecuhtli, he is known as the Deity of Dawn.[76] Now named God of Air[77] and the Sea;[78] now Venus Star of Morning (for the Spanish, Hesper/Lucifer)[79] and Lord of Night,[80] Quetzalcóatl is famed as Possessor of all riches, gold, silver, and green stones. He is also Ehécatl-God of the Four Winds and Cross-Wearing-Presider over the four cardinal points of space;[81] and Scarification Initiator in championing a life of mortification.[82] As Priest-King Topiltzin of Tula, he proves "Prophet of the Conquest."[83] He is also Self-Immolator or Self-Exiler, depending upon the tradition;[84] Embodiment of Tolteca migration history in his toponymic and lengthy circumambulation into exile;[85] Sailor over the eastern hori-

72. Lafaye, *Quetzalcóatl and Guadalupe*, 213.

73. A serpent-headed boomerang "warrior-weapon" that, in battle, came to life as a "fire-breathing sky dragon," acting like a thunderbolt blast; Brundage, *The Fifth Sun*, 150.

74. Lafaye, *Quetzalcóatl and Guadalupe*, 43, 147, 197.

75. Lafaye, *Quetzalcóatl and Guadalupe*, 140.

76. Lafaye, *Quetzalcóatl and Guadalupe*, 141, 151, 167.

77. Lafaye, *Quetzalcóatl and Guadalupe*, 140.

78. Lafaye, *Quetzalcóatl and Guadalupe*, 143.

79. Lafaye, *Quetzalcóatl and Guadalupe*, 141.

80. Lafaye, *Quetzalcóatl and Guadalupe*, 141.

81. Lafaye, *Quetzalcóatl and Guadalupe*, 205.
Lafaye, *Quetzalcóatl and Guadalupe*, 143, 153; Brundage, *The Fifth Sun*, 108.

82. Lafaye, *Quetzalcóatl and Guadalupe*, 140; Brundage, *The Fifth Sun*, 114–15.

83. Lafaye, *Quetzalcóatl and Guadalupe*, 163, 172; Dussel, *The Invention of the Americas*, 193.

84. Lafaye, *Quetzalcóatl and Guadalupe*, 141, 147.

85. Lafaye, *Quetzalcóatl and Guadalupe*, 146, 104, 204.

zon on his singularly constructed "raft of coiled serpents," according to Sahagun;[86] and "[B]ridge over the gulf of metahistory and the juridical fault of Conquest"[87]—the figure is at once Man, Hero, God, Necromancer-Shaman.[88] For colonial Christian consternation, this Wind Serpent is a Moses or Jesus, virgin-born of a down ball as light and airy as holy spirit,[89] perhaps even one saved from the Great Deluge and destined to become Creator of the World.[90] Re-cast as the first *papa*/high priest, renowned ascetic critic of human sacrifice, as Thomas, he is called "Twin."[91] But for all that, he is also vilified as a Balaam-revived or Demon-incarnate.[92]

Seeds for the Future

So what to make of this great prolixity—author Lafaye reflecting in his own language the voluptuous mix of origins and traditions that *La Raza* secrets and celebrates inside Quetzalcóatl-Tonantzin? I have been concerned in this slow tracery across such a baroque landscape of words to hint the nexuses and nodes where an Indigenous resolve to survive hid out under a modernist uptake hankering for revolution and independence. Lafaye's work aimed at an outline and augury of "national consciousness," centered in eighteenth-century creole commitments to break with Spain. My own has sought to crawl further down the root of conservation to the place where the image and practice "disappear" under soils Indigenous and oral, where the mode of life and visage of Spirit can only be guessed and sketched, imaginatively. In seeking to discern, from such a rich mix, a vector of direction and an influence for our own conundrum of apocalypse—likely planet-wide and as intricate as the climate itself—I can only suggest. In concluding, I revert back to beginning.

As outlined above, for my own journey, the way forward as white male Christian has been back and down, through layers "black," "red," yellow, and "brown." The dense drama of *Mexica* creativity imbricated in

---

86. Lafaye, *Quetzalcóatl and Guadalupe*, 143, 147; Pike, "Latin America," 438; Brundage, *The Fifth Sun*, 116.

87. Lafaye, *Quetzalcóatl and Guadalupe*, 151.

88. Lafaye, *Quetzalcóatl and Guadalupe*, 151; Dussel, *The Invention of the Americas*, 188.

89. Lafaye, *Quetzalcóatl and Guadalupe*, 155, 166; Dussel, *The Invention of the Americas*, 192.

90. Lafaye, *Quetzalcóatl and Guadalupe*, 166–67, 172.

91. Lafaye, *Quetzalcóatl and Guadalupe*, 156.

92. Lafaye, *Quetzalcóatl and Guadalupe*, 170–74, 152.

the Guadalupe cult and Quetzalcóatl myth has no correlate in north-of-the-border US Protestant memorialization of Euro-colonial conquest. Certainly, Native traditions have their own remarkable syntheses of survival innovations underneath the great national ignorance comporting itself as "Manifest Destiny" and "White Man's Burden." But the Northern European Protestant exorcism of Catholic excess back in the Euro-homeland of the sixteenth century, ramified in settler colonial hubris and (later) rationalist Enlightenment arrogance, promulgating Great Chain of Being celebrations of Euro-ascendancy as Lords of Genocide and Enslavers of Indigenous and Executioners of Witches, has been ruthless in suppressing fertile symbol and sensual practice, and ultimately re-inventing the human in the image of the corporation and the machine. The US Constitution indeed enshrines deep Native wisdom in the form of Haudenosaunee (Iroquois League) comity[93]—but the influence is commonly denied and the document nothing like the cult or myth in its popular culture potency.

In consequence, the task as I conceive it, in letting this *Mexican* bombast and poesy have its political say and spiritual effect, pushes toward what *can* be re-deciphered culturally in north-of-the-border formation. And that is the biblical corpus, so venerated in Protestant *sola scriptura* fulminations. It is just such a re-reading of the Bible that has engaged my own attention and work in the last two decades, seeking to cross over to Indigenous ken to learn and then return to the Christian "side" of things, with "nose wide open" (as inner city Detroit used to say when one falls in love) for the scent of ancient practice and close-to-the-soil wisdom. The biblical tradition, I am discovering, is full of it! For instance, the brief mention above of Cortés' post-conquest "gift" of a golden scorpion to the Estremadura Guadalupe back in his Spanish homeland—as thank-offering for healing from a New Spain sting—begs reading alongside Moses' bronze serpent fetish. The latter is sculpted at divine direction to fashion the (in literal Hebrew) *seraph*-snake image as healing for the bites of the *seraph*-snake "border guards," interdicting (like Edom) an ungrateful "Israel," recently escaped, but not yet disabused of imperial Egyptian values, who are complaining about having to eat "manna" (Num 21:4–9; likely the aphid defecation widely extant in that desert environment that Arab Bedouin collect and eat today, called, in their language, "man").[94] From an Indigenous point of view, such snake-scorpion aggressions may not be merely adventitiously painful encounters, but omen-messages from the Spirit-World. Certainly, the geopolitical positioning of Cortés and Moses is quite different. But the role of wild animals

---

93. Lowen, *Lies My Teacher Told Me*, 108–11.
94. Eisenberg, *The Ecology of Eden*, 15–16.

and frankly also, "wild metals" (gold and copper), must no longer be comprehended from a merely anthropocentric mindset—if we would halt our lockstep march into the Sixth Great Extinction or our Defense Department-mining corporation lust to "mineralize" the entire planetary surface as an inescapable AI-Fortress of weapons-slaves.

Would that there were space to call to the surface older Indian embrace of the maguey plant as much more than mere surface for a prodigious image, but prodigious in its own right as a plant and recognized as such, in traditions identifying such a remarkable creature as agave as Progenitor of Culture and Divine Mediator of the entire possibility of living as humans in Mexican deserts.[95] Mexican *criollo* and *mestizo* Christians focus on the Guadalupe image; natives may well have been communing with an ancient friend in the fiber itself, where the Real Presence of consequence is not the Virgin per se, but the *plant body* woven into the form of "cloak"—the Great Goddess who sustains life through the regular giving up and "transubstantiation" of her flesh in being eaten, drunk, made into shelter and clothes.[96] "This," indeed, "is my body given for you!" What might similar attention to Elijah's mantle or John the Baptist's leather turn up? And what of the role that rocks and even color hint and suggest? In Indigenous savvy these are not objects and phenomena, but "bodies" of divinity and auguries of Spirit.

In a more general sense, probing the Guadalupe-Quetzalcóatl complex for intimations of older Indigenous practices—politico-economic and spiritual-cultural alike—rebounds upon biblical studies with nuance and provocation. In particular in this writing, I have been foregrounding questions of origins. Whether speaking of the Estremadura version of fourteenth-century Spain or the Tepeyac tradition in the Valley of Mexico, the Guadalupe cult embeds its origins narrative in high country. The original apparition is to a marginal denizen of the land in an out-of-the-way place—shepherd in the mountains in the former case, Indian peasant on a hill in the latter. The entire discussion to this point has focused largely on ferreting out subtleties of Mexican practice that might harbor Indigenous proclivity and strategy in making an imposed regime carry traces of a lifeway and cosmology antithetical to colonial monoculture. But the shepherd of the Spanish sierra is also a sign of such. What appears in Christian histories of the advent and sweep of Jewish messianism out of its Middle Eastern "manger" to its routinization in Roman imperial and European aristocratic orders, typically comprehends the fourth-through-the-eleventh century waves of steppe nomads, moving west under pressure from imperial forces

---

95. Brundage, *The Fifth Sun*, 58, 178; Gentry, *Agaves*.
96. Prechtel, *Disobedience*.

further east, as "barbarians." Though obviously a profoundly complex succession of incursions contributing to the implosion of city life in Europe and the development of feudalism, on the whole, the nomad peoples thus encompassed—Scythian, Sarmatian, Alani, Hun, Goth, Visigoth, etc.—were more "Indigenous" in their lifeways, more sustainable in their land practices, more egalitarian in social concourse, and more broadly skilled and capable than their counterparts in the cities they raided and often enough settled. Again, there is not space here to sustain the argument. But a text like *Parzival* (among many others), and the entire development of the European tradition of knighthood and chivalry, enshrines an equestrian gift and summons inside of and to a decrepit and imploding culture of imperial arrogance and self-absorption.[97]

Indeed, pastoral nomadism represents the first sustained social resistance movement our species ever organized in its time on the planet—the early impulse of captive and coerced labor to escape the drudgery, disease, and debt of the first states by "going feral" with herd animals, and living independently in the semi-arid steppe.[98] And such is the origins of the biblical tradition and witness. Through a convoluted and multifaceted history virtually untraceable in its vast tributaries and windings, but nonetheless imaginable in its broadest outlines, the shepherd of Estremadura points back across the ages to the herder that Abraham became in leaving Harran of the Euphrates, to "found" a line of feral-going innovators (Jacob, Moses, Elijah, etc.) seeking greater justice and more sustainable concourse with the land in the highlands south of Mt. Hermon and west of the Jordan. Shepherd calls to shepherd across the heights in hint of a tradition of witness immensely rich and practical, but not well known because denigrated and feared among the scribal classes penning party lines for the kings who fed them. Learning from Guadalupe, by reading "deep down and far back," could readily enjoin a similar task *vis a vis* the Bible, for a Protestant-enculturated nation, hell-bent on re-making an entire world in its image and subservient to its demands.

With the Quetzal-myth, the work goes even deeper. Here we encounter a living set of representations, ever morphing into new combinations, whose root and power is first natural and wild before they are human and political. A Wind-Serpent, Stellar Denizen of the Sky after his advent as Priest-Shaman and Human-King, Dweller on and as the Horizon where Night meets Ocean and births Dawn, Bird-Apparition in His Feathered

---

97. Corbett, *Goatwalking*, 4, 14–15, 75–76, 84; *A Sanctuary for All Life*, 220–221, 228.

98. Scott, *Against the Grain*, 211; Perkinson, *Messianism*, 11–12.

Dress and Dance, irreducible to any singular incarnation across his multiplying appearances, an instantiation of multiplicity. It is Quetzalcóatl who most seems to lend himself to messianic expectation among the ancient *Mexican* Powers of a world at once concrete and mysterious. His coming is looked for in New Spain in the form of whatever political leader seems to emerge with promise.

But the power he marks out is not limited merely to a human aspect for an Indigenous mindset. Certainly, messianism for Euro-culture has typically been a matter of human expectation. But even a cursory glance through the Hebrew text makes apparent how often the "intervening grace" celebrated or feared is wild nature in the theophanic form of sirocco wind from the south or thunderstorm deluge from the west and north that does divine work of deliverance or rebuke.[99] Jesus himself is baptized into the central water-conduit of his bioregional habitat, a Riverine Creature, imaged in Orthodox icons as tiny Dragon-Serpent, but for all that, understood in ancient Jewish savvy as "Living" and worthy of being kept free from human tampering and piping (both John the Baptist and Jesus can be read as sharply challenging the Roman-Hasmonean commitment to incarcerate the "wild offering" of rains and springs in aqueduct systems).[100] And he is adopted by the Dove of Noah in his initiation—a Holy-Spirit-Incarnating "Bird-Shaman" who (we could say) becomes his Animal-Familiar in subsequent healing encounters, according to the gospel writers (Lk 3:22; Mt 12:28). He is driven by that migratory Wind Creature to the wild side of the Jordan to face the settler colonial wounds ("trials") of his own people's advent into Canaan from the eastern desert, wrestling there, like ancestral herder Jacob long before him, with the Angel-Demon Powers of the Water Fords and Wadis—before he is ready to don a prophet's mantle and lead a movement.

Learning from Quetzalcóatl would push biblical exegesis toward a much more robust embrace of divine agency—human *and* natural, economic *and* meteorological, political *and* stellar. A priest-king, incarnating ancient Wind God of the Sea Coast, who sacrifices himself in a given historical exigency, promises return, sails east on a coiled serpent raft and disappears at horizon's edge to become Morning Star and Night Guardian, among other challenges, raises a huge question of language. Pueblo-Indian-raised, Tzutujil-Mayan-adopted, musician-scholar Martín Prechtel precisely identifies the issue:[101] Many Indigenous languages do not have a

---

99. Fitzgerald, *East Wind*, 25–27, 33–37, 47, 74–75.

100. Sawicki, *Crossing Galilee*, 24, 100, 121–23, 140, 171; Perkinson 2016.

101. Prechtel, "Saving the Indigenous Soul," 2011.

"verb-to-be" and do not then pretend to lock reality into separate boxes of meaning and agency, discretely engaged and neatly hierarchized, where a star is not a serpent and a woman not a mountain. There has perhaps been no more damaging determination operative in the history of "civilized" domination than the continuous attempt coercively to quarantine "good" from "evil"—by means of "race," of "gender," of " class," of "sex," for sure, but also of "human," of "resource," of "commodity" and "machinery" and "technology"—typically in the name of some fantasized notion of "purity." Not so among most Indigenous narratives codifying eco-system and human alike in terms of multistoried myth. (Even Paz will insist on replacing "to be" with "between.") Humans are not merely themselves in such a ken, but rather unique and only briefly cohering realizations of entire eco-community-symbioses, whose "other" bodies they consume and whose "other" bodies they will become, in subsequent dispositions. And likewise—"other-than-human-creatures" are not simply "non-human," but can be understood and embraced as the "non-human part" of humans, or what humans once were in their own ancestry and will become again after death.

The Hurricane to Come

And it is on this huge note of difference—only barely hinted here—that I will conclude. The door opened on such a question of representation and disposition of our species on the planet has profound ramifications for the planet itself. The gauntlet thrown down is challenge *to* our entire modern Western (now globalized) conceit that virtually everything non-human is mere object to be used and used up at will by our species and even within our own species-being, where "membership," "economics," and "politics" are primarily a matter of "individuality," "private property," and "human rights." Over such a destructive heritage of civilizational hubris and settler colonial fatuity Guadalupe floats in rose-blossom resplendence, a little brown *Morenita*, offering refuge to the poor, to *mestizos* and *inditas* alike, but even more (as Paz offers): a Mother of gods and [humans], of stars and ants, of maize and agave, the Mother-Mountain, the Mother-Water.[102] And the Quetzal-Bird flits and lights, dances and rushes, summons to new mixes and old trances,[103] storms like the sea and sits in serenity like the Morning Star of Venus. The Serpent and the Eagle embodying these deities of Water and Wind as the Azteca well knew before these two were embossed on the national coat of arms, are not primarily interrelated by predation and

---

102. Lafaye, *Quetzalcóatl and Guadalupe*, xix.
103. Lafaye, *Quetzalcóatl and Guadalupe*, 199–200.

destruction—as if one were good and the other evil—but can soar and hiss together, each in magnificence, within the same Valley. And each teaches of Spirit and possibility. If we persist in destroying them as of secondary import to the priority of human survival at all costs . . . well, there was a hurricane named Maria . . .

Bibliography

Brundage, Burr Cartwright. *The Fifth Sun: Aztec Gods, Aztec World*. Austin: University of Texas Press, 1979.
Corbett, Jim. *Goatwalking*. New York: Viking, 1991.
Corbett, Jim. *A Sanctuary for All Life: The Cowbalah of Jim Corbett*. Englewood, CO: Howling Dog, 2005.
Dussel, Enrique. *The Invention of the Americas: Eclipse of the Other and the Myth of America*. Translated by Michael D. Barber. New York: Continuum, 1995.
Eisenberg, Evan. *The Ecology of Eden: An Inquiry into the Dream of Paradise and a New Vision of Our Role in Nature* New York: Vintage, 1999.
Fitzgerald, Aloysius. *The Lord of the East Wind*. Catholic Biblical Quarterly Monograph Series 34. Washington, DC: Catholic Biblical Association of America, 2002.
Gentry, Howard. *Agaves of Continental North America*. Tucson: University of Arizona Press, 1982.
Klein, Naomi. "The Battle for Paradise: Naomi Klein on Disaster Capitalism and the Fight for Puerto Rico's Future." Interview by Juan González. *Democracy Now*, March 21, 2018. https://www.democracynow.org/2018/3/21/the_battle_for_paradise_naomi_klein.
Lafaye, Jacques. *Quetzalcóatl and Guadalupe: The Formation of Mexican National Consciousness, 1531–1813*. With a foreword by Octavio Paz. Translated by Benjamin Keen. Chicago: University of Chicago Press, 1987.
Lowen, James W. *Lies My Teacher Told Me: Everything Your American History Textbook Got Wrong*. New York: New Press, 1995.
Perkinson, James W. *Messianism against Christology: Resistance Movements, Folk Arts, and Empire*. New York: Palgrave Macmillan, 2013.
———. "Protecting Water in the Anthropocene: River Spirits and Political Struggle in Detroit, Standing Rock, and the Bible," *CrossCurrents* 66 (2017) 460–84.
Pike, Frederick. "Latin America." In *The Oxford Illustrated History of Christianity*, edited by John McManners, 420–54. Oxford: Oxford University Press, 1990.
Prechtel, Martin. *The Disobedience of the Daughter of the Sun*. Berkeley: North Atlantic Books, 2001, 2005.
———. *The Unlikely Peace at Cuchumaquic: The Parallel Lives of People as Plants: Keeping the Seeds Alive*. Berkeley: North Atlantic, 2012.
———. "Saving the Indigenous Soul: An Interview with Martín Prechtel." Interview by Derrick Jensen. *The Sun Magazine*, April 2001. http://www.thesunmagazine.org/issues/304/saving_the_indigenous_soul.
Scott, James C. *Against the Grain: A Deep History of the Earliest States*. New Haven: Yale University Press, 2017.

Sawicki, Marianne. *Crossing Galilee: Architectures of Contact in the Occupied Land of Jesus.* Harrisburg, PA: Trinity, 2000.

Taussig, Michael. *What Color Is the Sacred?* Chicago: University of Chicago Press, 2009.

Taylor, William B. "Mexico's Virgin of Guadalupe in the Seventeenth Century: Hagiography and Beyond." In *Colonial Saints: Discovering the Holy in the Americas, 1500–1800,* edited by Allan Greer and Jodi Bilinkoff, 277–98. New York: Routledge, 2003.

14

Transdiasporic Indigeneity and Decolonizing Faith

Recovering Earth Spirituality in a Settler Colonial Context

S. Lily Mendoza

THIS STUDY GRAPPLES WITH the thorny issue of what it means to recover a sense of indigeneity—an issue rife among decolonizing diasporic Filipinos in North America who find themselves living on other peoples' native lands, disconnected from homeland ancestral traditions (largely through prejudice arising from their mostly Christian socialization and modern subject formation), enveloped in technological urban infrastructure, and bereft of intact place-based communities where initiation and elder mentorship remain as living practice. Framed inextricably within the author's own life history, the significance of this problematic is tracked specifically within the context of a movement that she is part of, spearheaded by a non-profit organization called the Center for Babaylan Studies ("babaylan" being one of the terms used to refer to the healing/shamanic/spiritual tradition still extant among Philippine Indigenous communities). The uniqueness of this decade-old movement,[1] as compared to other progres-

---

1. Composed of academics, artists, social justice advocates, cultural workers, healing practitioners, and community members.

sive activist organizations among North American diasporic Filipinos that are mainly political (and anthropocentric) in orientation, is in its turn to the more-than-human world as grounding for its decolonization work and justice vocation in the world. Its overarching vision is a resolute pursuit of a different mode of relation with living Earth, both as spiritual practice and as the primary way out of colonial subjection.

"Earth spirituality," as understood in this writing, is a way of being in the world that holds sacred all beings in the natural world—plants, animals, insects, marine and riparian beings, mountains, minerals, storm clouds, etc.—who are embraced as relatives rather than "dead objects" or "resources." It is what fundamentally divides the Indigenous worldview from that of modernity.[2] To speak of "earth spirituality" is to invoke rootedness in place, i.e., a cultivation of relationship with a particular ecology and the diverse beings in that ecology, in contrast to the "everywhere but nowhere" mobility that tends to characterize urban postmodern existence, romping about, as British mythologist Martin Shaw says, as "scatterlings," rather than genuine nomads.[3]

For decolonizing diasporic Filipinos, recovery of such earth-based awareness and spirituality emerges as a two-pronged demand for tutelage to living Indigenous elders in the homeland (and other bearers of ancestral wisdom in the diaspora), on the one hand, and for continuous "unlearning" of settler colonial subject formation through relationship-building with local Native peoples in their respective land bases, on the other. To the extent that settler colonialism, as historically enacted in the projects of European colonial conquest, operates through a "logic of elimination,"[4] it requires sharp interrogation of its power. Its dynamic of supplanting long-standing Indigenous cultures with the culture of the colonizing power while simultaneously occupying Indigenous lands as supposedly sovereign titleholder, enjoins unrelenting counter-vigilance. How halt the ever-proliferating onslaught of dispossession, domination, and land theft and work toward repair and justice in the here and now?

2. Contrast this with the view from Francis Bacon, the father of modern science, who would encourage boldly the torture and enslavement of Nature, urging that she be put on a rack (similar to the one used in the Middle Ages to torture so-called "witches") to make her yield her secrets. See quote from Francis Bacon in *The Great Instauration and New Atlantis* as cited in: http://sentientpotential.com/acceptance-vs-questioning-kurzweil-jobs-and-francis-bacon/.

3. According to Martin Shaw, "Scatterling is someone that wanders the world without a fixed abode; they are everywhere and nowhere. They are thirty miles wide and two inches deep. That's a scatterling." "Storytelling from the Edge" (https://www.youtube.com/watch?v=7aCOuWxEm6Q). See also Shaw, *Scatterlings*.

4. Wolfe, *Settler Colonialism and the Transformation of Anthropology*.

The conundrums of doing this kind of work in a context where the ideological underpinning of the culture militates against everything signified by the term "Indigenous" are both challenging and instructive. The lessons offered here take the form of critical interrogations into the complexities posed by shapeshifting spiritual practices and traditions as these travel across the global diaspora—a space always already compromised not only by historic, but ongoing settler colonialism. The unpacking will begin with the author's own life itinerary as a decolonizing post-evangelical Filipina subject, followed by her learnings and journey as part of a Filipino transdiasporic movement committed to recovering Indigenous spirituality and unlearning settler colonial formation and praxis on Turtle Island. I conclude with noting both the challenges and opportunities inherent in such work.

Hailed by (Another Kind of) Spirit

The subject of this study has provenance in a moment of personal epiphany—one that served as catalyst for this author's deep cultural and spiritual transformation. I had been raised a pastor's kid, my father being one of the early converts to Methodist Protestantism in the Philippines at the turn of the twentieth century (when the US, in its first formal imperialist venture, took over the Philippines and claimed it for its own colonial possession[5]). Our family lived in a town in the Philippines called San Fernando in the province of Pampanga, located not too far from the former Clark Air Base, then the largest US military installation outside the continental US.[6] I, along with my five siblings, grew up under the long cast of the shadow of the US colonial regime, albeit not thinking of it as anything anomalous then; it was just our normal everyday reality. School meant learning English, the mandated medium of instruction. Without knowing the word for it, my body understood keenly the meaning of "linguistic terrorism" when we were fined five centavos-a-piece for getting caught speaking in our native tongue and I felt my tongue cut off unceremoniously by the punishment. When two of my older sisters began teaching Philippine Music and Culture at the Wurtsmith Elementary School inside the base where children of US military personnel went to study, our family got an even greater dose of white American culture. We learned Army and Navy songs and acquired

---

5. With the US invasion leaving in its wake half a million to a million Filipinos massacred in a country with only 7.5 million population at the time.

6. The century-long treaty (the Military Bases Agreement of 1947) was finally terminated in 1991 after a vigorous grassroots protest of its renewal (and aided by the massive eruption of Mount Pinatubo close to the area).

all manner of "civility" and etiquette that made us feel like we were "a cut above the rest," notwithstanding our family's modest means. That whole other world of the US base, with its manicured lawns, fancy vending machines (that you had to learn to operate), and the fabulously-supplied commissary that served all kinds of foods you would normally not find outside captured our imagination. Once a year, on the fourth of July, it opened its gates and we "locals" were then "allowed" to come in and take a peek at a magical other world. One give-away "crumb" that we were offered from such a lavish and otherwise forbidden table (I'll never forget!) is the bag of apple, imported chocolate bar, and hamburger sandwich wrapped in stars and stripes that we got to take home.

Being Protestants in a predominantly Catholic country, our family was further marked off as "different" in that our church, not the immediate neighborhood, served as our community. I remember us being the only ones without our doors open with a huge spread to share with neighbors during the barrio fiesta of the town's patron saint. Sadly, the feeling of being excluded from all the festivities was barely assuaged by the smug conviction that, at least, we were no idolaters, unlike our ignorant Catholic neighbors who worshipped saints, devoutly parading them in the streets in gaudy robes and gilded carriages. But one thing we did share with the Roman Catholics was a deeply inculcated sense of sin, guilt, and shame, first drilled into us by Spain (US's colonial predecessor), then doubled down on by the American Protestant missionaries. The only caveat was the consolation that Jesus had already paid for our transgressions and all we needed was to believe in him to be delivered from hell and our inherited "depravity."

In time, I graduated from Sunday school to become part of a born-again, intellectually more sophisticated, student Christian movement once I got to the university. Thus, began a new phase in my ideological formation. Trained by brilliant mentors in Christian apologetics and "contextualized" incarnational theology, I ended up becoming an undercover missionary to the intelligentsia while finishing my college and master's degrees and, later on, joining the faculty in the country's premier state university.

But unbeknownst to many, underneath the avid (and outwardly successful) missionizing, I harbored a secret shadow, a "thorn in the flesh," as I called it—a mysterious soul affliction marked by the constant feeling of being "weighed and found wanting" that no amount of preaching of God's unconditional love could assuage. Although the university I attended offered anti-colonial nationalist politics as an alternative grounding for identity and self-valuing (something I gave mental assent to as a "progressive" Christian activist), a part of me remained ambivalent, suspecting the anti-colonial stance in my case as, perhaps, at some level, merely compensatory—a form of "sour-graping" for those who, like myself, were unable to "make it" (i.e., unable to enter and successfully navigate the supposedly superior, more civilized, white world of the West). Lacking the conceptual tools with which to understand the psychic dimensions of the colonized condition, I took the malaise as simply my own failing, one that showed up in obsessive self-recrimination and morbid self-introspection, the outward success (both academically and in the missionizing endeavor) merely deepening the contradiction. Many times, driven close to despair, I nonetheless kept my hand to the plow in a courageous effort to "surrender to the mystery."

It was not until a graduate seminar in the Humanities titled, "The Image of the Filipino in the Arts," taught by an ethnomusicology professor who conducted first-hand research on the arts of our various Indigenous communities least penetrated by the forces of modernization and Christianization that I finally found a clue to my mysterious affliction. This is the moment of epiphany that I spoke about in the opening of this essay—one that came as a bodily jolt, to borrow the words of the esteemed Christian writer, C.S. Lewis, an experience of being "surprised by joy," although for quite different reasons than his. It is a story that has now unfolded (and continues to unfold) in my life and that has required thoroughgoing theorization (among others, in the dynamics of colonial subject-formation, the politics of representation, and the historical contingency of what I now understand as the "civilizing process"). In that class, I learned and encountered for the first time the world of our Indigenous peoples—through their rhythmic dances, mellifluous songs, the wild and vibrant colors of their textiles and complex weaving designs, their epic chants, basketry, sculptures, etc. and what they expressed in terms of a different way of being in the world.[7] As I wrote in my journal:

> For the first time, I was introduced to the supple world of non-individualistic interconnectedness, the delicate sensitivity of *kapwa* (shared being), the generosity of community, the lack of divide between the material and the spirit world, the openness of *loob* (interiority of being), the gracious receiving of gifts of beauty and creativity from the other world through dreams, visions, and the power of ritual.

7. Renowned anthropologist Michael Taussig, in his book *What Color Is the Sacred?*, intimates that there is something deep in such an aesthetic in that bright, "wild" colors are characteristic of people in "a state of nature" and that "people of refinement" (i.e., civilized folk) tend to "banish vivid colors from their presence altogether" (3). I can only surmise that with nature being their primary "other," the mirroring of the dizzying array of diverse ways and forms of being in their specific ecologies cannot but show up in such peoples' unique cultural forms and ecologically-inflected aesthetics, cosmologies, and ritual practices.

I would walk out of every class session bawling my heart out on my way back to my dorm room, overcome with emotion and a deep sense of awe, longing, and newly awakened desire, not knowing what it was that hit me from all the innocent, "matter-of-fact" descriptions of the ways of being of that other world. To speak of it as falling in love or being swept off one's feet is perhaps no exaggeration. Although my mind at that time could not (yet) make sense of the significance of what was happening, my body apparently knew and registered immediate recognition. Only much later would I come to understand the meaning of those tears—that, indeed, they were tears of recognition. Here at last is a people I could belong to and identify with—our Indigenous peoples who, in their radical alterity, embodied a way of being that I knew I had always shared but had not been allowed to assume or embrace, much less embody. The Brazilian educator Paolo Freire once remarked in an interview[8] that when all the authoritative representations around you have nothing to do with your reality, it is like looking into a mirror and finding no one. And in that class, in the beautiful works of art and the way of being of the people who authored them—the exuberance and respect with which they related to land, ancestors, and to all living beings—I finally saw myself. A new mirror was held up to me that for the first time reflected myself back to me—the self that has been imprisoned and disallowed from coming into being by the disapproving, surveilling, and judging, eye of Empire. I would journey forward from that point on, unpacking and diving ever deeper into the healing significance of such a paradigm-shifting encounter. Trained heavily in left-brain Western modes of cognition, the task required, among others, recovering those parts of myself that I have had to repress, if not reject outright, in both my academic training and my Christian socialization. These included the sense of *kapwa* or shared being (vs. individualism), *pakikiramdam* or tacit or intuitive knowing (vs. rationalism), *kagandahang loob*, literally, "beautiful heart" or generosity (vs. acquisitiveness or the drive to accumulation), *paggalang* or respect (vs. entitlement), *pakikiisa* or cooperation (vs. unbridled competition/getting ahead) and *dangal* or honor (vs. duplicity).

An Intellectual Turn(ing)

Interestingly, up until my moment of epiphany in the classroom, my Christian journey had been my life's one big adventure. That it accorded me less than the wholeness and well-being (*ginhawa*) it had promised was

---

8. The interview is one I remember viewing on YouTube, but is now no longer available.

puzzling, but the unrelieved pain and dis-ease did provide a counter-point for this eventual irruption in my life of an alternative, far more redeeming, story that proved in every way compelling and irresistible. Ironically, it was a story and reality that in my Christian formation could only be seen as, at best, a faint precursor to a much larger, universal divine revelation meant to find its fullness and eventual supersession in Christ, or, at worst, as nothing more than a pagan rendering of life's meaning by an ignorant, backward, and superstition-ridden people[9] needing deliverance from the influence of demons and evil spirits, if not of Satan himself. All of which is to say, from within my Christian formation, there was almost no room for rapprochement in what appeared to be a zero-sum game where the totalizing Christian claim to being the only "way, the truth, and the life" trumped every other story in the end.

But, in the end, joy would have its way with me. Having been hailed powerfully by the winsome beauty of that other world (of the Indigenous), I prepared to dive fully into its exploration. Not long after that fateful classroom encounter, I began learning about a budding movement in the academy that was beginning to be critical of the type of knowledge produced in the Western-originated disciplines and the need to re-root knowledge-making within the context of "Filipino" socio-cultural realities. Among the first disciplines to attempt such a break with their colonialist histories were psychology, history, anthropology, and the humanities. I would have pursued a doctoral degree in Filipino Liberation Psychology or *Sikolohiyang Pilipino*, as the indigenizing strand in psychology was called, had not a confluence of personal crises compelled me to leave the country and instead pursue graduate studies in the US.[10] Auspiciously, I learned that the *Sikolohiyang Pilipino* movement had by now reached the US with its pioneer, Virgilio Enriquez, being invited to teach at UC Berkeley as a Visiting Faculty in the early 1990s. As I watched the movement spread like wildfire among Filipino American communities across the US, I would end up studying the wider movement for indigenization both in its articulation in the Philippine academy and in the US diaspora for my dissertation project. Faced at the time with the dominance of the "post-theory discourses" (such as postmodernism,

---

9. Later, I would learn that what are often called "superstitious beliefs" are ancient beliefs that have lost their mooring in larger narrative structures rooting them in an ethic of relation with all beings, characterized by the kinds of ritual honoring and courtesy that effectively limited our species' proclivity towards greed, selfishness, and disregard of others (e.g., the practice of saying, *"Tabi, tabi po"* ["May we pass, please"] when entering a forest or nature habitation).

10. On the invitation of a professor that I had gotten to know during a short visiting scholar stint I did at a US university a few years earlier.

poststructuralism, and postcolonialism) that regarded with suspicion all identitarian politics,[11] I wrote in defense of the movement, arguing against its easy dismissal (as simply another "nativist" movement) and calling for a more nuanced distinction between any emergent discourse's (early) liberatory phase and its (later) accession to dominance.[12] By now equipped with the conceptual tools I needed to critique Western cultural hegemony and the historical contingency of all disciplinary discourses, I threw myself into creating space in the marketplace of ideas in the academy for an alternative report from the margins. My theoretical work—now a book publication[13] and considered the first programmatic mapping of indigenization efforts to systematically transform knowledge production in the Philippine academy—also began recursively lending support to both indigenization movements (in the homeland and the diaspora) in their respective struggles to gain legitimation within a still heavily Western-dominated academy.

Yet Another Turn(ing)

The emergence and spread of this theoretical tradition in both the homeland and the US diaspora was initially energizing and immensely productive. In the US, inspired by the decolonization imperative, many Filipino American (FilAm) youth, identifying as "born-again Filipinos," began taking interest in pursuing advanced studies for the first time, having now found a sense of

11. Movements purporting to reclaim an originary/essential identity for the purpose of self-empowerment.

12. I speak of the principle of needing to distinguish a discourse's or a movement's insurgent phase vs. its dominant formation in my book, *Between the Homeland and the Diaspora*:

> Such moments of theoretical, ideological, and paradigmatic triumph when power condenses into monopolistic centers in the realm of the symbolic, I submit, constitute dangerous moments in the life of a scholarly community. And this is true even where success is originally fought for and won in the name of democratic or liberatory imperatives. Indeed history is replete with examples of how the articulation of any social or discursive order to dominant power results invariably not only in smug arrogance and the self-congratulatory poses on the part of its architects, but in a stance that makes self-reflexivity and interrogation extremely difficult, if not altogether impossible. Such may be said of almost any system of thought, be it that of liberalism, modernism, nationalism, Christianity, or, for that matter, any other social or political doctrine no matter its concededly radical beginnings. One can note the very different spirit, politics, and material effects of such systems of thought in their insurgent forms versus their dominant expressions. (4)

13. Mendoza, *Between the Homeland and the Diaspora*; cf. Strobel, "Born-Again Filipino."

purpose and direction for their lives. At the same time, FilAm professionals, i.e., social workers and mental health practitioners, found in *Sikolohiyang Filipino* a way to name and counter the pathologizing oeuvre of the "cultural deficit" models (rooted in Western epistemologies) that they had been using up to that point, adopting instead more "culturally-appropriate" frameworks that pushed back on assimilationism as the only model for "success" for diasporic Filipinos. Meanwhile, in the homeland, Filipino scholars began working in earnest for disciplinary transformation by engaging boldly in original research and conducting their scholarly exchange exclusively in Tagalog/Filipino. This was in a deliberate bid to move away from the idiom of Empire and to begin taking seriously "native" categories of thought and Filipinos' own ways of "doing" knowledge.

The flourishing of the indigenization movement would last decades, but to the extent that indigenization tended to be understood primarily as "nationalization," it was not long before the momentum began to flag as it reached a kind of theoretical exhaustion (I speak extensively about this impasse particularly within the *Sikolohiyang Pilipino* movement in the US diaspora in my book [Mendoza, 2002/2006]).[14] After all, what more is there to be had after having awakened to our sense of self as "Filipinos," after mounting countless "Pilipino Cultural Nights" across campuses on Turtle Island and getting tattoos and donning native garb in celebration of "our unique identity and culture as Filipinos"? In the Philippines, ironically, despite the theoretically articulated commitment to go beyond the stance of anti-colonialism (disavowed earlier as merely reactive to Empire) towards the construction of a discourse on knowledge that is finally "by us, of us, and for us," the prioritization of national unification appeared to have hitched the movement almost exclusively to a modernizing imperative. Uncritical of the colonial dynamic within the process of nation-state formation itself, it fell short of seeing the implications of such a push for nationalization for the fate of the country's 14-17 million Indigenous peoples who now serve as unwitting targets for Filipino-controlled assimilationist integration into the "Philippine" nation-state.[15]

Within the FilAm diaspora, awareness of such a theoretical lacuna would happen serendipitously in two separate but related developments:

14. The impasse in the homeland case I have yet to document in writing.

15. As I wrote elsewhere (Mendoza, "The Philippine Nation-State," 97): "[T]he prevailing discourse governing the nation-state's relation with the country's Indigenous communities appears to remain one of assimilation and incorporation into the national polity and market economy, with the allowance of "otherness" only within the realm of cultural expression (and for purposes of tourism) that precludes acts of resistance and/or demands for autonomy or the right to their ancestral territories."

one in a meeting of three FilAm women (a feminist cyberactivist, concerned with countering the degrading images of the Filipina in cyberspace [either as "mail order brides" or as nannies and domestic workers], a poet/publisher committed to showcasing the literary talent of Filipino American writers, and a multiculturalism professor who had been at the forefront of the *Sikolohiyang Pilipino* movement in the US diaspora). It was in the caucus of these three women that the figure of the Philippine *babaylan* (Indigenous woman priestess, healer, ritualist, mediator between realms, and fierce warrior in the resistance movement against colonial oppression) would emerge as a rallying symbol for what would later become the successor movement to *Sikolohiyang Pilipino*. The historic *babaylan*, typically female and known ethnolinguistically by many names,[16] embodies in her calling a form of spirituality wholly embedded in a local ecology, her appropriation signaling a return to such spirituality as a necessary touchstone for freeing oneself from colonial oppression.

The other development was the participation of a number of FilAms in a unique week-long forum in the Philippines called the *Kapwa Conference* that brought together academics, cultural workers, and Indigenous elders from the various tribes across the archipelago in a gathering centered on the relevance of Indigenous cultures in an age of globalization. This latter event became serial and gave its FilAm participants (such as myself) an experience of being "hailed by beauty" similar to the epiphany I had enjoyed in that earlier class in the humanities, except, this time, even more powerful, given the actual face-to-face meeting with the Indigenous culture-bearers in real place and time. At the close of that (first) conference, the FilAm participants gathered together and, with newly awakened desire as their main compass, resolved to replicate as best they could something of that transformational experience of encounter with the country's remaining Indigenous culture bearers back in the US.

The new movement to be ignited by these two developments came to adopt for its name the Center for Babaylan Studies (CfBS). Movement pioneer Leny Mendoza Strobel[17] writes in an online conversation: "When we named our organization as a Center for Babaylan Studies, it's because that's how we began: as an inquiry" (i.e., an inquiry into this new/old spiritual tradition that is still practiced today by our Indigenous peoples). It is this turn to the country's precolonial spiritual tradition—rooted in sacred Earth as the primary relationship—that came to be understood as key to deepening

---

16. E.g., *balian, bailan, mumbaki, patutunong, mambunong, manganito, mandadawak*, etc.

17. Who happens to be this author's older sister.

the task of decolonization. It was not enough merely to unlearn Empire. It was equally important to enter into tutelage to an alternative ethos if one were not simply to end up stuck in a phase of reaction (and thus "always revolting against the parameters of the colonizing world" without ever attaining true freedom as articulated in Dion-Buffalo & Mohawk's "bad subject" formulation[18]). That alternative ethos was to find exemplary and instructive embodiment in the subjectivity of Indigenous peoples, and, in particular, in the tradition of the *babaylan*. Its rough summation amounts to a profound interconnectedness rooted in the sacredness of living Nature. As one anthropology student, summoned by what might be called the magnificent "ordinariness" of such a spirituality (that she found among the Indigenous of her own town of Negros in the Visayas, Philippines) notes,

> There is no real separation between the physical world and the spiritual world, and most natural spaces are to be respected as belonging to the People Who Can't be Seen (at least, that's a translation of what some tribal leaders I've spoken to call them). So . . . I guess as far as the local practices I've observed [are] concerned, it mostly involves acknowledgement and a general respect for natural spaces.[19]

I, for my part, was slow to embrace the turn to the *babaylan*, wary of a "too easy appropriation" and dabbling in a tradition I hardly knew anything about (in addition to having been raised Christian and taught that such was largely "the work of the devil and of evil spirits"). While I was comfortable theorizing *Sikolohiyang Pilipino* as a socio-cultural-political project, I was less certain about the ethics and political trajectory of this newly-forged discursive focus on the homeland's precolonial spiritual tradition—a concern that I thought was warranted; after all, despite historic persecution from the Spanish friars (who ordered many *babaylans* executed), the demonization by the American missionaries, and the ongoing attempts by church-planting missionaries to snuff out the practice (not to mention the regular assaults by "development aggressors" or agents of modernization), the *babaylans* are still around, keeping the old ways alive even under the surface of a partially embraced dominant religious practice (such as Catholic, Protestant, or Islam) and the unrelenting press of modern schooling and development. Hounded daily by such assimilationist forces, their fate grows ever more precarious; many of the communities they are embedded in are beleaguered, if not perishing, as we speak. But my own diffidence would be challenged by what I also saw as a powerful

18. Esteva and Prakash, *Grassroots Post-modernism*, 45.
19. Says Chris, Facebook post (May 24, 2019).

response from the Fil-Am community to the invocation of the figure of the *babaylan*. The very first CfBS conference held at Sonoma State University in 2010, for example, drew 250 participants from all over the country. Subsequent CfBS-hosted events likewise burst at the seams. Ten years later in 2019, the momentum shows no sign of waning; on the contrary, interest seems only to intensify. CfBS conferences now attract participants from Canada, Hawaii, Singapore, the Netherlands, Italy, Germany, and the Philippines, making them truly international and transdiasporic.

Interestingly, quite apart from the *babaylan* movement, Filipino Americans have not been lacking in activist advocacies around issues of human, women, immigrant, worker, and other minority, rights. Postcolonial FilAm intellectuals, working in diverse disciplines, have also made laudable efforts in countering the popular culture erasure of the Philippine-American War at the turn of the twentieth century and the role the US takeover of the Philippines played in its catapult to superpowerdom. On the cultural front, *Balik-Aral* Study Abroad programs for US-born Filipino youth wishing to (re-)connect with their homeland roots also became popular, as well as FilAm activist groups partnering with NGOs in the homeland advocating for the rights of Indigenous peoples. Yet, in all these endeavors, what has never been foregrounded is the spiritual aspect of doing cultural (and political) empowerment work.

Meanwhile, in the homeland, while there has been much study of the *babaylan* tradition, the approach has been typically Western, adopting a "distancing stance," and treating the phenomenon as an object of study, rather than a practice that implicates those doing the study (indeed, would-be academic "converts" and "initiates" risk the likely ridicule and suspicion of colleagues who would deem them as "having gone off the deep end").[20] In other words, there remains within the academic tradition of indigenization—whether speaking of the academy in the homeland or its counterpart in the US diaspora—the Western norm of "objectivism" that proscribes breaching the intellectual/praxis divide. Not so in the CfBS. As I wrote elsewhere:

> The turn to the *babaylan* tradition among Filipino scholars in the U.S. disapora brought the challenge of doing intellectual work differently. Whereas most scholarly writings on the *babaylan* in the homeland were in the tradition of social scientific writing that was careful not to breach the norm of objective study, the personal journeys of those involved in the budding

---

20. For a similar example vis-à-vis the study of Voudou, see the witness of Karen McCarthy Brown of *Mama Lola* fame.

CfBS movement began embarking on scholarly work that became its own hybrid genre, committed to modeling an ethic of "embodied knowing." Strobel's writing, in particular, was both literary and deeply personal, effectively translating theory into the idiom of the popular (cf. Strobel 2001, 2005, 2010). It was as if this whole other world of spirit demanded its own language and forms of honoring.[21]

The conferences themselves were nothing like the academic conferences that one is used to. As I wrote of my first attendance at a CfBS-hosted conference:

But the conference space itself, with the plenary hall adorned richly with exquisite Indigenous fabrics, baskets, wooden sculptures, rice gods, colorful mats, and other materials of prehistoric significance, immediately invited one into a different kind of awareness, hailing one into the fullness of embodied presence, not simply cognitive engagement. At the entrance, one was greeted by a visually stunning Talaandig altar set up in the Indigenous tradition of ritual offering to the spirits and ancestors. Then, once participants had quietly settled in, an Ilokano healer-researcher, dressed in traditional garb and speaking in his native tongue, opened the conference with a ceremonial incantation calling on the ancestors to bless the gathering. This was followed by an honoring of the *babaylan* ancestors through a ritual invocation of their names, as these were culled from history books written by the Spanish chroniclers. Clearly, this was no place for bystanders and aloof observers.[22]

It took time for me to become aware of my own distrust of emotion and "non-rational" modes of cognition as simply part of my socialization in Western rationalism (my own scholarly comfort being in the heady register of theoretical language that brooked neither feeling nor subjective expression—this, before the eruption of the affective turn[23] in social theorizing). But my bodily "hailing" in that first time encounter with Indigenously-authored beauty in the Humanities classroom, my face-to-face encounter with our country's Indigenous culture bearers in the Kapwa Conferences in the Philippines, and now my witnessing of the impact of the embodied

21. Mendoza, "Babaylan Healing," 96.
22. Mendoza, "Babaylan Healing," 96–97.
23. That takes subjective experience, emotive desire, bodily responses, and unconscious habituations as powerful sites of agency and productive reflection (cf. Brennan, *The transmission of affect*; Clough and Halley, *The Affective Turn*; and Gregg and Seigworth, *The Affect Theory Reader*; Negri, "Dossier," among others.

enactment of ritual and ceremony within the context of a CfBS-sponsored conference in the diaspora has upended my hesitancy. I now understand for the first time what Freud's nephew, propagandist, and public relations pioneer, Edward Bernays, has long insisted upon and ecophilosopher Derrick Jensen has likewise echoed: the impossibility of either decisive action or radical transformation without first engaging cultural desire.[24]

Over time, CfBS has become known for its clear articulation of embodied spiritual practice grounded in both study and observance of Indigenous ritual protocol. Unlike its precursor movement *Sikolohiyang Pilipino*, CfBS has now made a full turn away from a strictly nationalist cultural advocacy toward referencing the country's land-based Indigenous communities for orientation in envisioning an alternative ethos and subjectivity for its constituency. As articulated in one of its documents informally christened as its "Manifesto:"

> While "the" nationalist "Filipino" culture (in the singular) is a portal for many, there is need to go beyond this mainstreamed, nationalized cultural tradition (as well as beyond the still mainstreamed, if smaller, regional cultural traditions like Kapampangan, Bicol, Tagalog, Ilokano, Visayan, etc.) to the older ancestral peoples we ultimately all come from (e.g., Itneg, T'boli, Manobo, Ayta, Ifugaw, Hanunoo, etc. and for some, from particular older ancestries behind Chinese, Spanish, European, lineages), before these older traditions became forcibly assimilated by colonial, political, economic, and religious processes.[25]

The mandate then is recovery of Indigenous memory not just in abstraction (e.g., in the generality of "how precolonial Filipinos lived") but in the historical specificities of one's particular ancestral lineage(s). My own work in this regard, for example, brought me to the realization that I, myself, despite my heretofore singular identification as a "colonized subject" vis-à-vis the US, may have also actually come from settler ancestors, as I shared in a talk:

> We [Kapampangans] are told that we are mostly descended from the Chinese who came from Taiwan, but oral traditions passed down through generations say we actually descend from a much older people—from the Malays migrating from the Malay Peninsula and Singarak Lake in what is now West Sumatra who settled by the riverbanks as early as the 300 to 400 AD with many more arriving in the 11th to the 12th century.

24. Jensen, *A Language Older than Words*, 264–65.
25. Drafted by this author herself.

Interestingly, what is not mentioned in this story of my people's origins is that prior to our Malay ancestors' arrival, there was a much older people, called the Ayta tribes, dark-skinned, kinky-haired, skilled hunters and gatherers, who were already in the area 20 to 30 thousand years ago, having migrated from Borneo using land bridges that began to be submerged only around 10–15,000 years later—aboriginal peoples that my Malay farming ancestors [likely] subsequently displaced.[26]

For diasporic Filipinos, there is the added work of understanding whose lands they are on, what histories of genocide and displacement occurred in the places where they reside, and what sort of relationship-building and repair they are committed to engaging in with regard to the lands and the original keepers of their respective places (without any prompting, for example, a typical round-robin introduction of many CfBS conference participants now would most likely result in a litany of the Native names for the peoples and places where they currently dwell such as Lenape, Ohlone, Ojibwa, Potawatami, Ottawa, Wendet Huron, etc., followed by their more commonly-recognized Euro-colonial monikers such as New York, California, Detroit, etc.). What invariably surfaces in this kind of exploration are the wounds of a history deeply implicated in the progressivist trajectory of civilizational discourse, i.e., the purported "destiny" of more "advanced" (i.e., "civilized") peoples displacing "primitive" ones, with settlement and surplus production eclipsing hunting and gathering, as well as other subsistence modes of production as the more viable way to live. Alas, this notion of civilizational "progress" is a saturating assumption in modernist (and Christian) discourse that invariably underpins and legitimizes both the historic and ongoing racialization and decimation of Indigenous cultures not only in the Philippines but all over the globe—an assumption codified in the Doctrine of Discovery[27] and inscribed in the unreformed epistemologies of academic disciplines and nation-state media. Only with climate change and the growing endangerment of planetary life is there a chance now to finally peel back the layers of mystification and begin to expose the catastrophic end-logic of

26. "Healing from Colonial Trauma: The Power and Gift of Shadow Work. Invited Presentation at the Catholic Call to Action Conference, Milwaukee, Wisconsin (October 2015).

27. Comprising a series of papal bulls issued in the 1400s legitimizing European nations' takeover of non-Christian lands provided no other Christian nation had yet laid claim to such. Cf. Newcomb, *Pagans in the Promised Land*; Miller et al., *Discovering Indigenous Lands*.

such progressivist ideology and make room for alternative ways of "worlding the world," in the words of postcolonial scholar, Gayatri Spivak.[28]

But It's not All Romance

But along with opportunity comes danger. Within a culture of unbridled commodification and marketization, Indigenous spirituality quickly becomes one more commodity to mine, market, and manipulate. For CfBS, this challenge had to be faced head-on from the get-go. From the initial inspiration of the historic *babaylan*[29] came the call to refrain from merely using the "figure" of the *babaylan* for self-edification and instead engage the more demanding work of actually getting to know the living *babaylans* who are still around—their plight, their material conditions, and their ongoing struggle to survive.[30] It is with this challenge in mind that tutelage to living elders and *babaylan* practitioners in the homeland was conceived in partnership with a grassroots organization that shared a similar vision of responsible mentorship and beneficial exchange with Indigenous elders. For without even the semblance of place-based intact communities to facilitate the relearning of the wisdom traditions, many earnest seekers often proceed in their search rudderless, often ending up with partial knowledge that then gets temptingly packaged into protocol prescriptions for "becoming a modern-day bruha (witch) or *babaylan*" as a new career-path (with eager clients a-plenty!).

But, alas, no such ideal spaces of encounter are to be had. Whether in attempted 10-day PAMATI gatherings in the homeland (of an equal number of acculturated/urbanized Filipinos, on the one hand, and Indigenous elders from differing tribal communities, on the other, co-hosted in the homeland with Tao Foundation founder and president, Grace Nono.), or in organized gatherings in the diaspora with invited guest elders from the homeland, potential landmines abound. For one, as we quickly learned, the opened-up world of spirits (not just of human derivation but of natural potency and being) is something not to be trifled with. As we've experienced in a number of these ritual gatherings, we call, and the spirits come (!)—an entirely new schooling for us Westernized, urbanized, Christianized, albeit decolonizing

---

28. Spivak, *The Postcolonial Critic*, 1.

29. Some of whom were so feared in their power by the Spanish friars that they not only executed them; but fed their impaled bodies to the crocodiles (cf. Brewer, *Holy Confrontations*).

30. The call as issued by one homeland scholar, Grace Nono, who has been doing immersive work among the *babaylan* for years.

and indigenizing, modern subjects. As CfBS pioneer Leny Strobel recently articulated for this pivotal moment in the life of the movement:

> I think if we are honest, we can all admit to the seduction of romance. It's the first feeling of falling in love, of attraction to something or someone's Beauty. The Beauty that is also ours within.
>
> CFBS, I assume, has been one of the portals where this romance blossomed as FilAms were looking to find a way to connect with their Filipinoness beyond the usual cultural discourse of lumpia [spring rolls] and hiya [shame]. I have watched as folks saw the beauty of our *baybayin* [Indigenous scripts], our tattoos/ batok, our weaving traditions, our carvings, our chants, our myths, our stories. We felt enlivened. We felt that finally we have a taste of the wholeness and beauty of Filipino identity.
>
> So, we created events, retreats, workshops, and attended festivals—where we donned our ethnic attire, created altars as tutored and permitted by Indigenous elders. We got tattooed, we learned to sing our songs again. We re-created ceremonies. We wrote and published our personal stories. People read the books and responded that they have found narratives they have been yearning to hear for so long.
>
> Over the years, many started returning to their places of [ancestral] origin in the homeland, connecting with IPs [Indigenous Peoples] we met at Kapwa conferences, visiting IP communities, starting personal projects, writing research papers, supporting IP projects, many of us doing individual work of reconnecting with our Indigenous roots and ancestors.
>
> The romance has begun to give way to deeper questions...[31]

Beyond that first blush of romance—so necessary to the journey of love, but inadequate to its continuity and long-term navigation—I can only, in the remaining space, list as questions some of the conundrums that we have faced in doing this kind of Indigenous spiritual reclamation work.

1. Given the fraught economic relations between those of us coming from the diaspora and the participating Indigenous Peoples, what happens when enterprising *babaylan* practitioners, who are otherwise amazingly gifted and generous in sharing their gifts, see an opportunity to enlist their spirit guides in "targeting" those of us they perceive to be "with means" to enter into transactions, with the corresponding subtle threat of something calamitous befalling us if the wrangled financial

---

31. Facebook Post, October 18, 2016.

contribution (e.g., for a designated ritual) is not delivered in a timely manner? How embrace, recognize, and wrestle with the very real challenge of unequal economic, material, and spiritual authority power-positioning without fleeing or bailing and without reductively placing sole responsibility (or blame) on the "erring" *babaylan* practitioner/ elder? How might such situations be made to serve as schoolhouses for creating awareness and praxis that take into account the larger historic, economic, and material structures that constrain our relations notwithstanding our mutually good intentions?

2. Relatedly, can genuine relationships of parity be cultivated in the encounter between non-Indigenous and Indigenous groups? If so, what would true reciprocity look like? How not replicate, one more time, the extractive operations of the "civilized" in mining the territories and resources of the "uncivilized"—this time, for intangible spiritual and cultural knowledge or "capital"? How create sustainable relationships beyond the limited physical encounter in space and time?

3. What happens when Indigenous practitioners from differing regions with varying ritual protocols, *babaylan* traditions, and histories of relations with outsiders, brought together for the first time through our organizing initiative, report receiving differing guidance or directives from their spirit guides? Or when some aspiring apprentices automatically attribute authority to those they regard as having power to transact with spirits, thereby abdicating their own responsibility to exercise discernment or work on a very human plane to resolve misunderstandings without immediately transposing such to the realm of spirit demand?

4. Or when in the cross-cultural setting of, say, a conference, spirits show up through the well-meaning but naïve calling of ancestors in ritual space by uninitiated participants who don't know enough of the protocols involved to establish boundaries and close the circle in the end? How do we gain perspective and wisdom in the face of deep colonial trauma that so many of us carry that gets intermixed with spirit expression in possession in the form of rage?

5. How do we, in the absence of place-based communities, care for earnest seekers who are opened up to the spectacle of spirit manifestation but who are otherwise unable to ground such experience in a holistic and deep understanding of decolonized practice and responsible communal relations? What sorts of training and nurturance are necessary and adequate to build cultures capable of hosting *babaylan* spiritual

practice? And how do we develop spiritual muscle adequate for wrestling with the complexities of doing such work in our severely fractured world, wherein the spirit world itself might mirror some of the trauma and chaos of our living world?

This is where the movement is right now, the wrestling becoming even more urgent in the face of ongoing ecological collapse. But what this Indigenous reclamation movement provides is a tinge of hope, as in a quote from Indigenous teacher Martín Prechtel (2012) with which I ended a recent keynote address:[32]

> I'll tell you . . . the seeds we seek are here already, but *we* are not here. When we are here, the seeds will begin to appear, for we first must make fertile cultural ground for them to want to appear . . .[33]

As one who has been unabashedly hailed by the depth of beauty of this way of being in the world, I remain undaunted by the challenges. As such, I end not with an ending per se, but an ode and invocation to the very beings—ancestral and other—whose witness and counsel and very life continues to provoke and summon and demand—not least as only very inadequately "penned" in a journal reflection at the close of one our homeland PAMATI ("deep listening") gatherings with such elders and ancient ones:

> PAMATI 2017 gave us but a tiny taste of that earth-based life that we all used to know, (and perhaps, to a degree, still know in our bones) before a part of our species had the "brilliant" idea of breaking away and building a culture (purportedly) "more advanced" and unconstrained by the collective necessities of village- and land-based living . . .
>
> I imagine this is how it must have been when we still lived embedded in the generosity of the natural world and in the face-to-face sociality of our Indigenous villages: waking up to the first rays of Grandfather Sun whose westward trek is aided by the cacophonous voices and toothless laughter of elders (and the running about of happy children's feet); ordinary conversations spontaneously breaking into song or poetry at a moment's inspiration . . . ; work life spared of tedium by the rhythmic accompaniment of song to motion and/or the trading of *tsismis* (village gossip); young people's bodies naturally

---

32. Keynote Address, Third International Babaylan Conference, Unceded Coast Salish Territories, Vancouver, Canada (September 21–24, 2016), now a published essay in Mendoza, "Composting Civilization's Grief."

33. Prechtel, *The Unlikely Peace at Cuchumaquic*, 314.

synched up to the rhythms of nature's circadian clock, to the beat of gongs, drums, and other native instruments—the energy of dance and movement climbing up their spine and out their nimble limbs without so much as effort or trying. And when death, sickness, or conflict occurs, the gathering of the whole village to grieve, deliberate together, and perform rites of healing and/or reconciliation.

There have been many learnings for me. Despite the limitations of the framework of PAMATI, there is something powerful even in so brief of an encounter. For the younger urbanized participants, the copious tears and heartfelt expressions of gratitude to the elders for their unstinting generosity in sharing their gifts and stories is testament to the need for such initiatory opportunities for mutual encounter. For the elders, to find such openness of hearts and eagerness among the urbanized participants for a taste of what they had to offer served as a deep affirmation of their sense of self (in contrast to the racialization and devaluing of their ways of being that is just their default experience living cheek-by-jowl with mainstream culture). The mirroring back to them by the younger participants of what they still have—the memory of how to live in a good way on the land—that the young ones have lost (and are only now seeking to recover in a world of amnesia) creates a fertile ground for mutual love and transformation. "I see you," they seem to say to each other—and in that deep seeing and affirmation of generations is the seed of wholeness, healing, and recovery of well-being.

Bibliography

Brennan, Teresa. *The Transmission of Affect*. Ithaca, NY: Cornell University Press, 2004.

Brewer, Carolyn. *Holy Confrontations: Religion, Gender, and Xexuality in the Philippines, 1521–1685*. Manila, Philippines: Institute of Women's Studies, 2001.

Brown, Karen McCarthy. *Mama Lola: A Vodou Priestess in Brooklyn*. Oakland, CA: University of California Press, 2001.

Clough, Patricia Ticineto, with Jean Halley, eds. *The Affective Turn: Theorizing the Social*. Durham: Duke University Press, 2007.

Esteva, Gustavo, and Madhu Suri Prakash. *Grassroots Post-modernism: Remaking the Soil of Cultures*. London: Zed, 1998.

Gregg, Melissa, and Gregory J. Seigworth, eds. *The Affect Theory Reader*. Durham: Duke University Press, 2010.

Jensen, Derrick. *A Language Older Than Words*. White River Junction, VT: Chelsea Green, 2000/2004.

Lewis, C. S. *Surprised by Joy*. New York: HarperCollins, 1955.

Mendoza, S. Lily. "Babaylan Healing and Indigenous 'Religion' at the Crossroads: Learning from Our Deep History as the Planet Grows Apocalyptic." In *Just Faith: Glocal Responses to Planetary Urbanization*, 75–102. Capetown: AOSIS, 2018

———. *Between the Homeland and the Diaspora: The Politics of Theorizing Filipino and Filipino American Identities*. New York: Routledge, 2002 (Revised Philippine edition, Manila: University of Santo Tomas Publishing House, 2006).

———. "Composting Civilization's Grief: Life, Love, and Learning in a Time of Eco-Apocalypse." In *Humanity: An Anthology*, edited by Eileen R. Tabios, 1:118–36. San Mateo, CA: Paloma, 2018.

———. "The Philippine Nation-State and the Killing of Indigenous Peoples: Christianity and Modernity as Walls of Legitimation and Conquest." In *Mission and Context*, edited by Jione Havea, 95–110. Lanham, MD: Lexington, 2020.

Miller, Robert J., et. al. *Discovering Indigenous Lands: The Doctrine of Discovery in the English Colonies*. Oxford: Oxford University Press, 2010.

Negri, Antonio. "Dossier: Scattered Speculations on Value: Value and Affect." *Boundary 2* 26.2 (1999) 77–100.

Newcomb, Steven. *Pagans in the Promised Land: Decoding the Doctrine of Discovery*. Golden, CO: Fulcrum, 2008.

Prechtel, Martin. *The Unlikely Peace of Cuchumaquic: The Parallel Lives of People as Plants: Keeping the Seeds Alive*. Berkeley: North Atlantic, 2012.

Shaw, Martin. *Scatterlings: Getting Claimed in an Age of Amnesia*. Ashland, OR: Whiteland, 2016.

Spivak, Gayatri Chakravorty. *The Postcolonial Critic: Interviews, Strategies, Dialogues*. Edited by S. Harasym. New York: Routledge, 1987.

Strobel, Elenita Mendoza. "Born-Again Filipino: Filipino American Identity and Asian Panethnicity." *Amerasia Journal* 22.2 (1996) 31–53.

Strobel, Leny Mendoza. "Born-Again Filipino": Filipino American Identity and Asian Panethnicity." In *Postcolonial theory and the United States: Race, ethnicity, and literature*, edited by A. Singh and P. Schmidt, 349–69. Jackson: University Press of Mississippi, 2000.

Taussig, Michael. *What Color Is the Sacred?* Chicago: University of Chicago Press, 2009.

Wolfe, Patrick. *Settler Colonialism and the Transformation of Anthropology: The Politics and Poetics of an Ethnographic Event*. London: Cassel, 1999.

Index

abyssal thinking, 110
Adam and Eve, 93–106
African American communities, 22, 211
African Indigenous communities, 144–58
African women and earth-healing, 207
agency, 123–24, 137, 156–57, 183, 255–56
agents of change, 195–96
agribusiness, 225–26
agriculture, 151, 194, 228
Agroecological Web of the Peoples of Bahia, 230–31
agroecology, 227–29, 231
agropornography, 225–27
Ahn, Ilsup, 167
Al-Jazzera report, 164
alternative ethos, 98, 157, 185, 207–10, 269, 272–74
Althaus-Reid, Marcella, 221
Ambedkar, B. R., 216–17
Amburayan Kankanaeys, 87
Anat, 29–35
ancestral graves and spirits. *See* sacred groves
ancestral land, 5–6, 149–53
ancestral spirits and *podong* sticks, 83
Andes, 111

androcentric Indigenous theologies, 89
angels, 43–50, 53
Angelus Novus (Klee), 19, 20
animals, 64–65, 69–72, 154–55, 163, 216
Anthropocene, 21, 26, 204
anthropocentrism, 253
antiphonal liturgy, 46, 54–55
Anti-Terrorism Clarification Act of 2018, 52
anti-Vietnamese sentiment, 113–14
Apartheid, 133–34
apocalypses/apocalyptic texts, 24–26, 43–50, 54
Applied Research Institute in Jerusalem (ARIJ), 163
Areyksat, 108–9, 115, 118, 121–23
ARIJ (Applied Research Institute in Jerusalem), 163
art for social change, 193
ASEAN conference, 121
Asian theologies, 77–91
Assembly (Hardt and Negri), 179
assimilationism, 267
atmospheric commons, 176n3, 207
Atrash, Imad, 163
Australia, 42
Aztec state, 243

INDEX

Ba'al-Anat myth, 29–35
babaylan tradition, 268–71, 274–78
Bacon, Francis, 260n2
Bago-Igorots, 87
Bahia, Brazil, 230–31
Bakare, Sebastian, 151–52
Bale, John, 166
Balfour Declaration, 166
Balik-Aral Study Abroad programs, 270
baptism, 33n39
Barkan, Elazar, 142
Bauckhman, Richard, 168
Beelzebul, 30–31
Bellinger, William H., 59
belonging, 23
Benguet Corporation, 82–84, 89
Benjamin, Walter, 31
Bernays, Edward, 272
Between the Homeland and the Diaspora (Mendoza), 266n12
Betz, Hans Dieter, 46–47
Bhat, Harshavardhan, 212
biased diagnosis, 204
biblical eschatology of creation care, 168–72
biblical exegesis, 24–26, 41, 97–106, 111, 255–56
biblical hermeneutics, 55, 98–99, 194–95, 217
big dreams, 111–12
biodiversity, 27–28, 61, 226–27, 229
Black Madonna, 239–40
Blackstone, William, 166
Bloch, Marc, 238
Blount, Brian, 45
Bollier, David, 208–9
Bookchin, Murray, 104–5
Book of the Watchers, 49–50
booth-building, 32
Bourdillon, Michael, 148
bowl plagues, of Revelation, 45–46, 48
Brazil, 222–23, 226, 230–31
Britain, 58–59, 166
Brueggemann, Walter, 59, 194n42
Brundage, Burr Cartwright, 238
B'Tselem, 162–63

Burma War, 58
Bustamante, Fray, 248

Cabruca, 230–31
Cambodia, 108–24
Canaanite memory and practice, 24, 29–34
Canada, 132
capitalism, 6, 177n7, 219–20, 225–26, 228, 231
Carson, Rachel, 2
casteism, 201–17
Catholic statues, 108–24
Catholic Vietnamese settlers, 108–24
CBDR (Common but Differentiated Responsibilities), 136
Center for Babaylan Studies (CfBS), 259–60, 268–75
Cham (ethnic Malay Muslims), 113, 118–20, 118n44
Champa, 109, 115–16
change, 183–86
Chapman, Colin, 165
Chellaney, Brahma, 53
Chennai Poromboke Paadal (Krishna), 211–13
Chenoweth, Erica, 180n13
Chiapas, Mexico, 208
Chico River Basin, 80, 89
Chikandigwa village, 146
Chirongoma, Sophia, 146
Chisase, 148–52
Chisumbanje, Zimbabwe, 153–54
Choul Chnam Thmey (Khmer New Year), 118
Christ-Centered Biblical theology, 170
Christianity, 1–3, 44, 79, 91, 93–106, 132, 140–41, 181, 236–57
Christianization, 78–79
Christian socialization, 221, 261–65
Christian Zionism, 161–66n17
Church, 155, 165, 167, 168–72
Church, Philip A. E., 166
Churches for Middle East Peace (CMEP), 52
Church Fathers, 167

civilization, 36, 36n46
classism, 178
Clean India (*Swatch Bharath*), 214
climate change, 20–21, 24–26, 35–36, 40–41, 131–43, 176, 181, 206–7
climate debt, 131–43
CMEP (Churches for Middle East Peace), 52
Coastal Aquifer, 51–52
cognitive justice, 110
collective moral accountability, 191
Collins, Adela Yarbro, 46
colonialism, 1–6, 58–59, 66–73, 98, 132, 135–36, 160–72, 176, 180, 212, 221–23
coloniality, 4–5, 78–79, 110
colonial oppression. See babaylan tradition
colonization of consciousness, 178, 184–85, 186–88, 190–95
colonization of Palestine, 160–72
colonization of the commons, 202–17
commitment to act, 183
commodification, 224, 227
commodities, 21, 219–20
Common but Differentiated Responsibilities (CBDR), 136
Common Dreams, 36n47
commons paradigm, 201–17
communal societies. See Karanga communities
communities, 85–86, 184–85, 194
compensation, 136, 146, 158
Cone, James H., 205
confession and truth-telling, 141–42
conquest. See colonialism
constructive trespass, 109, 123
contextual theologies, 201
Cordillera Peoples' Alliance (CPA), 80, 89
Cordillera Region, 78–91
corporate occupation. See commons paradigm
corporations as people, 42–43
Cortés, Hernan, 240, 243, 252
cosmogonies, 97

cosmopolitics, 110–11, 123
cosmos, 102, 106, 110, 167–70, 227–28
cosmo-visions, 91, 211
Council for World Mission, 94
COVID-19, 41, 51
CPA (Cordillera Peoples' Alliance), 80, 89
creation, 2–3, 59, 64–69
creation care, 2, 161, 168–72, 202–3, 215
creoles, 241
Creole seeds, 233
"The Crisis of the Ecological Movement" (Bookchin), 104–5
cross-border interaction, 114–23
Cruz, Sor Juana Ines de la, 245–46
cry of Water for justice, 39–55
culpability, 136, 140
Cult of Our Lady of Guadalupe/Tonantzin, 236–57
culture, 261
Cultures of the Seed concept, 229
cultus (mutual care), 84, 86–87

Dakota Access Pipeline (DAPL), 50–51, 209
Dalits, 211, 214, 216–17
Daniel, 49
DAPL (Dakota Access Pipeline), 50–51, 209
Darby, John Nelson, 166
Darwish, Mahmoud, 160
decolonization, 5–6, 24–26, 31, 66–69, 98, 110, 259–78. See also Center for Babaylan Studies (CfBS); colonialism
decreation, 49
deep ecology, 104–5
de-eroticized mothers, 221–22
De Gruchy, Steve, 146
De la Cadena, Marisole, 110–11
Democratic Kampuchea, 115
Deprez, Miriam, 163
De Sancto matrimond (Sanchez), 222
desexualization, 225
Destombes, Emile, 117

Detroit, Michigan, 21–24, 235–36
development. *See* neo-liberal developmentalism
diasporic Filipinos, 266–73
Diego, Juan, 248
Dion-Buffalo & Mohawk, 269
disaster capitalism, 206–7
discernment, 94, 97–106
discipleship, 181
dispensationalism, 166–67
displacement, 144–58, 162–64
divinity, 87
Doctrine of Discovery, 21–23, 273, 273n27
domestication, 27, 153–55
dominion theologies, 3, 66, 79, 169
dorean, 54–55
Douglas, Marjory Stoneman, 2
Douglas, William O., 42
dreams, 109, 111–12, 123–24
dualistic eschatology, 167–68
Dussel, Enrique, 238
Dwivedi, O. P., 213

early Christianity, 167–68
Earth, 25–26, 28
Earth Bible Project, 41, 41n7
Earth Charter, 203
earth spirituality, 260
eco-casteism, 4, 210–17
eco-fascism, 3
ecofeminism, 221
ecological consciousness, 1–2, 202–4, 210–11. See also *Poromboke Ecotheology*
ecological crisis, 68, 70–71, 201–17
ecological debt. *See* climate debt
ecological eschatology, 168–72
ecological injustice, 2, 5–6, 161, 162, 178, 202, 205–7. *See also* Israeli colonization of Palestine; water justice and rights
ecological racism, 202, 205–6, 211
ecological regenerativity, 177–78
ecological threats for Palestinians, 161–62
ecology from a Pacific Indigenous perspective, 104–5

economy
  climate debts, 135–36
  economic advocacy, 192
  economic democracy, 177–78
  economic equity, 54–55, 177–78
  economic justice lens, 190
  economic privilege, 182, 191
  exploitation, 70–71, 84–85, 174–75, 182, 184
  norms, 177–78n8
  restructuring, 179, 182, 191
  right relations, 181
  and sexuality, 220–21
EcoPeace Middle East, 51–52
ecotheologies, 1–6, 43–44, 110, 156–57, 201–17
eco-wisdom, 60–73
Ecuador, 42
ecumene, 110
ecumenical movement, 131, 140. *See also* climate debt
Ecumenical Water Network, 53–54
education, consciousness-raising, and desire-shifting, 193
education, decolonization of, 98
Egyptian Sufis, 112
elders, 260, 274–78
electoral advocacy, 193
Eleele myth skit, 93–106
embodied spiritual practice, 271–72
Empire, 44, 47–48, 54
Enriquez, Virgilio, 265
ensouled statues, 112–13, 122, 123
environmental equity, 177–78
environmental ethics, 58–73
environmental impact of Israeli colonization of Palestine, 161–62
environmentalism, 3–4, 206, 213, 216–17
Environmental Justice Movement, 206
epiphany dreams, 109, 111–12, 114–23
epistemologies, 1, 110, 140–42, 180
eroticism, 228, 231
escape eschatology, 167, 170
eschatology of Christian Zionism, 166–72
Esteva, Gustavo, 208

INDEX

Estremadura Guadalupe myth, 239–40, 248–49, 252–54
ethical methodology in Truth and Reconciliation Commissions (TRCs), 140–42
ethics, environmental, 58–73
ethnic Vietnamese, 113–14
Eucharist, 85, 141–42
European colonial theology, 3, 21–23
evangelicals, 164, 167, 222
Evans, Michael David, 165
exclusion, 2, 209, 217
exploitative and extractive economies, 70–71, 84–85, 174–75, 182, 184
extra-textual hermeneutics, 77

family and communal ties, 146–48
Fertile Crescent agriculture, 35
Fiji's Indigenous cosmogonies, 95–106
Filipino American (FilAm) youth, 266–70
Filipino Liberation Psychology. See *Sikolohiyang Pilipino* movement
Filipino transdiasporic movement, 259–78
Fiorenza, Elisabeth Schüssler, 44, 48
First Enoch, 46, 46n24, 49–50
floods, 154–56
food sovereignty, 227, 229
foreign Catholic clergy, 119
forms of action, 184, 191–95
Fort Laramie Treaty of 1868, 51
fracking industry, 43
Franciscans, 250
Francis (pope), 136
Francis Xavier, 115–16
Freire, Paolo, 264
From Land to Lands, from Eden to the Renewed Earth (Isaac), 170
Frontiers of Asian Theology (Sugirtharajah), 77–78

Gafney, Wilda C., 99
Garcia-Johnson, Oscar, 4–5
Gaza Strip, 51–53, 161–62n1, 164
Gelfand, Michael, 148
gender justice lens, 190
Genesis, 3, 26, 27, 66, 94–106, 168

Germany, 132–33
Gerstenberger, Erhard S., 59
gift-economies, 27, 237, 246
global economy, 176–82
Global Ethic, 203
globalization, 70, 135
Global North, 135–41, 176, 206
global social justice, 110
Global South, 135–40, 176, 191, 206
Gnostic beliefs, 167–68, 171
God, 45–46, 54, 59–72, 83n15, 168–70. See also Psalm 104
God-grappling, 99
Good Samaritan parable, 103
Gran Cordillera, 87
Grant Township, Pennsylvania, 43
grassroots or local level action, 184
graves and burial places, 148–51
Great Extinctions, 26
Great Lakes, 21–22, 42–43
Greendeer, Jon, 43
Grim, John, 2–3
Guadalupe cult, 236–57

Haaretz (news agency), 164
Habel, Norman, 95, 95n4, 99–100
Hammer, Reuven, 95n3
Hardt, Michael, 179
Hauofa, Epeli, 98
Havrelock, Rachel, 52
Hebraic Mosaic and prophetic language, 88
Helfrich, Silke, 208–9
Helu-Thaman, Konai, 98
herd-intimacy, 27
heterosexuality, 222
high consuming classes, 178
Hindu religious environmentalism, 3–4
Hindutva ideology, 3, 3n3
Hispano-Portuguese Christianity, 239
"The Historical Roots of Our Ecological Crisis" (White), 2
The History of Christian Zionism (Evans), 165
Holocaust, 132–33
Horsley, Richard, 48, 49–50
Hosea, 34

human rights abuses. *See* Truth and Reconciliation Commissions (TRCs)
hybridization, 77, 77n3

ideal heterosexual matrix, 220
identitarian politics, 266, 266n11
identity, 151–56, 212, 214
IDF (Israeli Defense Forces), 164
idol-worship, 250
Igorots, 78–91, 78n6
Igorot Sabbath, 70, 87–88
illegal settlements on Palestinian land, 162–64
imaginative discernment, 97–99, 98n12, 100, 106
immersion in place, 23
imperial regimes, 48–50
Ina-Daga, 79
India, 58–73, 202–17
Indian Residential Schools, 132, 135
Indians, 241
indigeneity, 89, 259
indigenization movement, 266–74
Indigenous and subaltern communities
 and agroecology, 229
 and Asian theologies, 77–91
 atmospheric commons, 176n3, 207
 colonization of, 1–6
 colonization of the commons, 201–17
 community practices of, 2
 cosmopolitics, 111
 and creation stories, 93–106
 dwelling, 23–24
 and eco-wisdom, 60–73
 and elders, 260, 274–78
 and encounter, 236–37
 Fiji's Indigenous cosmogonies, 121–23
 Guadalupe cult, 236–57
 industrialization, 22
 Karanga communities, 144–58
 Khasi society of Northeast India, 58–73, 58n1
 knowledge systems, 58–59, 98, 228–29
 living in ways that kill, 181
 and memory, 24–26, 272–73
 and milpa, 231–33
 Quetzalcóatl/Topiltzin myth, 236–37, 239, 241–44, 250–56
 and recognition, 263–64
 rituals, 27, 83–91, 142, 147, 149–51, 155, 156–57
 settler colonialism, 260–61
 spirituality, 268–69, 272–78
 Standing Rock, North Dakota, 50
 Terra Nullius doctrine, 78n5
 Truth and Reconciliation Commissions (TRCs), 132, 135
 and water justice, 39–54
 worldviews and modernity, 260
Indigenous Environmental Justice Network, 179, 192
individualism, 137, 191
industrialization, 22
injustices, 2, 132–35, 137, 140, 162–64, 178
internal critique, 89
Irenaeus, 167
Isaac, Munther, 170–71
Isaiah, 34, 46, 54, 169
Israel, 29–30, 52–53, 59, 70
Israeli colonization of Palestine, 160–72
Israeli Defense Forces (IDF), 164
Israeli Information Center for Human Rights in the Occupied Territories, 162
Itogon, Benguet, Philippines, 80, 89

Jensen, Derrick, 272
Jerusalem, 166
Jesus, 30–35, 54, 169
Jewish apocalyptic literature, 48–50
Jews, 44, 61–62, 165–66, 250
John, 32–35, 170
Jordan River, 53
Judaeo-Christianity, 79
Judaism, 167, 239
judgment doxology, 46
just transitions, 179, 190n34, 193

Kabunian, 83–85
Kalinga *pangats* (chieftains), 80, 90–91
Ka Mei Ramew (Mother Earth), 62–73

Kandal province, Cambodia, 108–9
Kappen, Mercy, 180
Kapwa Conference, 268
Karanga communities, 144–58, 151n19
Karn, Alexander, 142
Keller, Catherine, 168, 171
Kendall, Laurel, 112
Keystone XL pipeline, 51
Khasi society of Northeast India, 58–73, 58n1
Khmer Rouge, 109–24
Khoury, Hind, 53
Kim Yong Bok, 88, 88n23
King, M. L. Jr., 191
King Solomon, 98
Klee, Paul, 19, 20
knighthood and chivalry, 254
knowledge, 58–59, 64–73, 98, 110, 182, 228–29, 265, 267
Konyana, Elias G., 153
Kore Kosmou, 47
kosmos-legein, 106
Krishna, T. M., 211–13
Küng, Hans, 203
kurova guva (bringing back the spirit of the dead), 151

Lafaye, Jacques, 237–51
Lake Erie, 42
Lake Erie Bill of Rights (LEBOR), 42
land, 3–6, 60–61, 70, 72, 86–87, 88–89, 151–54, 169, 171, 221–23, 227–29. *See also* displacement
landfills, 163
language, 241–42
Latin Americans, 136
Latour, Bruno, 110
Laudato Si (Pope Francis), 135
LEBOR (Lake Erie Bill of Rights), 42
legal personhood, 42–43
Leopold, Aldo, 2
Levitical Law, 169
Lewis, C. S., 263
liberation, 77–78, 88, 195n44, 217, 221
lifestyle changes, 184n20, 192
Lin, Wei-Ping, 112
linguistic terrorism, 261–62
liturgical theologies, 87–88, 91, 141–42

livestock loss, 154–55
living in ways that kill, 181
living water, 33–35, 39, 54–55
logic of elimination, 260
Logos hymn, 34–35
Lon Nol, 113
Lourdes statues, 116–24

Maccabees, 49
Macli-ing Dulag, Ama, 80, 82, 91
macro level change, 183–84, 191
maguey plant, 248, 253
Malhotra, Kailash, 213–14
manual scavenging, 214
Maori people, 42
Māori people, 5–6
March of Return, 52
Mark, 30–33
market economy, 68, 208
Mary statues, 116–24
masculinity, 222
Mass for Our Lady of the Mekong, 108–9
Masvingo province, 144
material change, 186–90
Mawrie, H. O., 64–65
Maza, Francisco de la, 239
Melanchthon, Monica, 217
Mendoza, S. Lily, 266n12
Mesopotamian statelets, 27
messenger of the waters, 43–48
messianism, 255
mestizos, 241
Mexican Indigenous peoples, 231–33
Mexico, 236–57
Mickelson, Karin, 136
Military Bases Agreement of 1947, 261n6
military siege, 50–51, 53
Miller, Bruce Granville, 135
milpa, 231–33
mining, 82–84, 89
Mining Act of 1995, 87
miracles, 247
Mishnah, 30
missional eschatology of creation care, 170–72
missionary position, 222

Mittermaier, Amira, 112
modernity, 260
Modi, Narendra, 214
Moe-Lobeda, Cynthia, 135
monocultures, 27–28, 226–27, 231
monotheism, 26–29, 28n22, 79
monster symbolism, in apocalypses, 49–50
Montana, 51
moral accountability and agency, 178–81, 183, 190–91
moral epistemology, 140–42
Moses, 28, 32
Mother Earth *(Ka Mei Ramew)*, 62–73
motherhood, 98n9, 221–22
Mother of Providence statue, 120–21
Muir, John, 2
Murugan, Perumal, 211
Mutangi, G., 158
Mutari, W., 158
mutual care *(cultus)*, 84, 86–87
Mwandayi, Canisius, 147
Myers, Ched, 41
myths
    Ba'al-Anat myth, 29–35
    Eleele skit, 93–106
    Estremadura Guadalupe myth, 239–40, 248–49, 252–54
    Quetzalcóatl/Topiltzin myth, 236–37, 239, 241–44, 250–56
    Tepeyac Guadalupe myth, 237–40, 247–50

national consciousness, 237–39, 251
Nationality Law, 113
nationalization, 267
National People of Color Environmental Leadership Summi, 206
National Power Corporation (NPC), 80, 90
nations, 137
nation-state, 267, 267n15
nature, 4, 44–45, 59–73, 221–23, 228
Negri, Antonio, 179
neoliberal capitalism, 5, 81–82, 84, 175, 186, 189–90, 207, 209
neo-liberal developmentalism, 59, 68–72, 87–88, 90, 156

new economy, 174, 179, 184–85, 191–96
New Jerusalem, 54–55, 170
New Spain, 239, 241, 243, 248, 255
New Testament, 44
New Zealand, 42–43
NGOs, 138, 270
Nicene Creed, 168
Nigeria, 188–89
Ninh, Thien-Huong, 119
nomad peoples, 253–54
non-geographical south, 110
non-humans, 66, 72, 110, 138, 141
Nono, Grace, 274n30
North and South divide, 110–11
Northeast India, 58–73, 58n2
NPC (National Power Corporation), 80, 90
nyikadzimu (the spirit world), 148

O'Brien, Brandon, 97
occupation, 51–54, 208, 214
Oceania, 4
oikos (our common home), 201–17
Old Testament, 165–66, 169
Ometeotl, 239
oneiric ecumene, 109, 111–12
Opoku, Kofi Asare, 147
orgasmic force, 224–25
our common home *(oikos)*, 201–17
Our Lady of the Mekong statue, 117–20

Pacific Indigenous perspective, 93–106
Pacific Theological College, 95
Palestine, 51–53, 160–72
PAMATI ("deep listening") gatherings, 274, 277–78
Panikkar, Raimon, 105–6
papattayans (sacrificial altars), 87
partition plan, 166
passive profiteers, 174–75
pastoral nomadism, 253–54
patriarchy, 220–21, 229
patronage politics, 86
Paul (apostle), 170
Paul (Wright), 167
Paz, Octavio, 238, 241–44
peasantry, 229–33

Pennsylvania Department of
    Environmental Protection, 43
people of color, 22, 176, 190, 205–6, 211
People's Web, 230–31
Perkinson, James, 41
personhood, 27, 42–43
personified imagery, 47–48. *See also* cry
    of Water for justice
perspectival lens, 186. *See also*
    worldview
Peter, 32
petroleum industry, 187–89
Pew Research Center, 164
Peyrère, Isaac La, 244
Phang Vaing Hou, 121–23
pharmacopornograpy, 224–25
Philippine-American War, 270
Philippines, 78–91, 259–74
Phillips, Utah, 204
Phnom Penh, Cambodia, 108–9, 121
physical pleasure, 224–25
place-based communities, 274–78
pochong rite, 83
podong sticks (reed sticks), 79–91
Poitier-Young, Anathea, 48–50
politics of environments, 85–86,
    110–11. *See also* colonialism;
    ecotheologies
pornography, 223–25
Poromboke Ecotheology, 201–17
post-human commune, 79
post-theory discourses, 265–66
praxis theologies, 77n2
prayer, 50, 60, 66–67, 194
Prechtel, Martín, 24–26, 255–56, 277
Preciado, Beatriz, 224–25
precolonial spiritual tradition, 268–69
Pre-Millennial Dispensationalism,
    166–67
"Principles of a Global Ethic" (Küng),
    203
printing technologies, 225
print technologies, 223
privacy, 138
privilege, 6, 135–36, 141, 176, 182, 191,
    195
Promised Land, 165n15, 170
prophecies, 41, 166

Proverbs, 65
Providence of Portieux, 120–21
Psalm 104, 59–73
public accessibility, 138
public policy advocacy, 192–93
public protest, 50–51, 194
Puerto Rico, 236

Queen of Peace church, 108–9, 116–20
queer-agroecology, 231–33
queer ecofeminism, 221
Quetzalcóatl and Guadalupe (Lafaye),
    237–38
Quetzalcóatl/Topiltzin myth, 236–37,
    239, 241–44, 250–56

rabbinic literature, 30
The Race *(La Raza)*, 237
racial justice lens, 190
racism, 178, 202, 204–6, 211
radical change, 94–106, 183, 186
radical monotheism, 79
Raheb, Mitri, 4, 164, 164n12
Rani, Challapalli Swaroopa, 216
reader-response theory, 59–60
rebuilding, 184–85
reciprocity, 45–46, 246
recognition, 263–64
reconciliation. *See* Truth and
    Reconciliation Commissions
    (TRCs)
reconstruction, 2–3
reductionist diagnosis, 204
Reed, Melissa, 40, 40n2
Reformation, 165
relationship with the divine, 61–63
religious environmentalism, 2–3, 181.
    See also ecotheologies
religious iconography. *See* statues
relocations, 144–58
renewal and restoration, 170
reparations, 137–38, 140, 142
repentance, 141–42
residential longevity, 23
resistance, 23–24, 48–50, 81–86, 88–91,
    184–85, 192–95
Resseguie, James, 60
restitution, 134–35

restoration of the Jews, 165–66
resurrection of Jesus, 169–70
Revelation, 39, 43–48, 53–55
Richard, Pablo, 46, 48
Rights of Nature movement, 42–43
right-wing Christian environmentalism, 3
rituals, 27, 83–91, 142, 147, 149–51, 155, 156–57
Rolling Stone Magazine, 43
Roman Empire, 46, 50
Rosenblatt, Louise Michelle, 60
Rotberg, Robert I., 133
Rymbai, R. T., 69–70

sacraments, 141–42
sacred groves, 60–61, 68, 73, 148–51, 156–57
sacredness of nature, 60–73
sacred places, 149–50
sacrificial altars (*papattayans*), 87
salidummay (folk song), 80–81, 80n10
Samoan creation story, 93–106, 101nn19–20, 101nn22–101nn23
Sanchez, Thomas, 222
Santos, Boaventura de Sousa, 110
savage, 222
Scofield, C. I., 166
Scott, James C., 27
Scott, W. Henry, 84
scripture, 27
second creation account, 93–106
seed control and manipulation, 226–27, 229, 233
Seed-Teaching, 33
Seleucid Empire, 49
self-determination, 80–91
Sen, Rinku, 190
Sepulchre Dance Drama, 100
Sermon on the Mount, 169
settler colonialism, 4–5, 21, 201, 260–61
sexuality, 221–25, 228
Sharma, Mukul, 213
Shaw, Martin, 260
Shoko, Tabona, 148, 150–52
Sikolohiyang Pilipino movement, 265–66, 267–69
simplistic diagnosis, 204

Sioux Nation, 50–51, 209–10
Sipeyiye, Macloud, 153
Six-Day War, 53
Sizer, Stephen, 164
Smith, Sherry L., 132, 134
social ecology, 104
social location/organization, 184–86, 215
socio-ecological lens, 190
soil-talk, 78
Sonoma State University, 270
the South, 110–11
South Africa, 133–34
Spanish friars, 269, 274n29
spheres of social organization, 184–86
spirituality, Indigenous, 268–69, 272–78
Spivak, Gayatri, 274
SRST (Standing Rock Sioux Tribe), 209–10
Standing Rock, North Dakota, 50–51
Standing Rock Sioux Tribe (SRST), 209–10
"Standing with Standing Rock Takes All of Us" (Straw), 50–51
statue recovery, 108–24
Stengers, Isabelle, 110
stories of beginnings, 81–82, 88
story-telling, 142
"The Strait" (*wawiiatonong*), 21–23
Straw, Gordon, 50–51
Strobel, Leny Mendoza, 268, 275
subaltern communities. *See* Indigenous and subaltern communities
subject formation, 260
subsistence communities, 4–5, 208–10
Succoth pilgrimage, 32–35
Sugirtharajah, Rasiah S., 77–78, 100
sumak kawsay (land without evil), 227–28
sun-moon encounter image, 249–50
superstitious beliefs, 265n9
Swatch Bharath (Clean India), 214
symptomatic diagnosis, 204
systemic change, 141, 184, 186, 190–91
systemic/structural injustice, 50–51, 137, 178, 207

Tabernacles Fest, 33

Tagaloa, 101
Tamil culture, 100
Taringa, Nisbert Taisekwa, 151, 154
Tarisayi, Kudzayi S., 157
Taussig, Michael, 263n7
Taylor, Charles, 111
Te Awa Tapua River, 42
technocapitalism, 224
technology, 138–39
Temple-State, 32–34
tengao (day of rest), 86–88
Teotihuacan's double pyramids, 249
Tepeyac Guadalupe myth, 237–40, 247–50
Terra Nullius doctrine, 78n5
testimonies, 138–39, 141
Tham, Soso, 62–63, 62n15, 67
theological anthropology, 141, 141n23
Thomas (apostle), 239, 243
Tofaeono, Ama'amalele, 101
tokenism, 6
Tokwe-Mukosi dam, 144–58
Toledo, Ohio, 42
totem animals, 154–55
Townes, Emilie, 205–6
traditional leadership, 149–50, 157–58
transdiasporic movement, 259–78
transformance, 91, 91n32
transnational mining, 111
trans-sectional ecotheology, 202–17
trans-species, 237
transubstantiation, 248
TRCC (Truth and Reconciliation Commission of Canada), 132
TRCs (Truth and Reconciliation Commissions), 131–43
trees, 68, 163
Truth and Reconciliation Commission of Canada (TRCC), 132
Truth and Reconciliation Commissions (TRCs), 131–43
Tucker, Mary Evelyn, 2–3
Tuwere, Ilaitia S., 97

ubuntu concept, 133–34
Ucab, Itogon, Benguet, 82–84
umbilical cord, 150–51
UNICEF, 52

United Nations, 166
unjust systems. *See* injustices
Unmasking the Powers (Wink), 44
UN's Framework on Climate Change, 136
uprooted from land, 151–54
US diaspora, 270–72

Vaai, Upolu Luma, 4, 105
vari pasi (those who inhabit the underworld), 148
Verstraelen, Frans, 152
victimhood, 146, 156
Vietnamese Catholic settlers, 108–24
Vietnamese in Cambodia, 113–14, 119
vindication doxology, 46
Virgin of Guadalupe. *See* Guadalupe cult
voice of the waters, 39–41

wall separating Palestinian Territories from Israel, 162–63
water, living, 33–35, 39, 54–55
water justice and rights, 39–55, 41n5, 71–72, 163–64, 216–17
waters, messenger of the, 43–48
waters, voice of, 39–41
Watershed Discipleship, 40–41
watershed protections, 40–43
wawiiatonong ("The Strait"), 21–23
western colonialism, 164
Whanganui River Claims Settlement, 42
What Color Is the Sacred? (Taussig), 263n7
White, Kyle, 24
White, Lynn, Jr., 2
White, Rob, 71
White Earth Band of Ojibwe in Minnesota, 42
white European metropole colonialism, 22
white flight, 21–22, 235
white supremacy, 3, 5, 21–22, 176, 190, 236
Whose Promised Land? (Chapman), 165
Why Civil Resistance Works (Chenoweth), 180n13
Wilfred, Felix, 204–5

Windt, Jennifer, 111
Wink, Walter, 44, 48
women, 89–90, 103–4, 229–33
World Bank Study, 41
World Council of Churches, 136
World Health Organization, 52
world of vision, 44–45
World Parliament of Religions, 203
worldview, 102, 156, 186, 191
Wright, N. T., 167, 169–71

Xiuhcoatl, 250, 250n73

Zachariah, George, 54, 180
Zapatista Movement, 208
Zechariah, 32–33
Zifunzi, 152–53
Zimbabwe, 144–58
Zionist environmentalism, 3. *See also* Christian Zionism
Žižek, Slavoj, 223, 225
Zunga, 149–51

www.ingramcontent.com/pod-product-compliance
Lightning Source LLC
Chambersburg PA
CBHW061430300426
44114CB00014B/1614